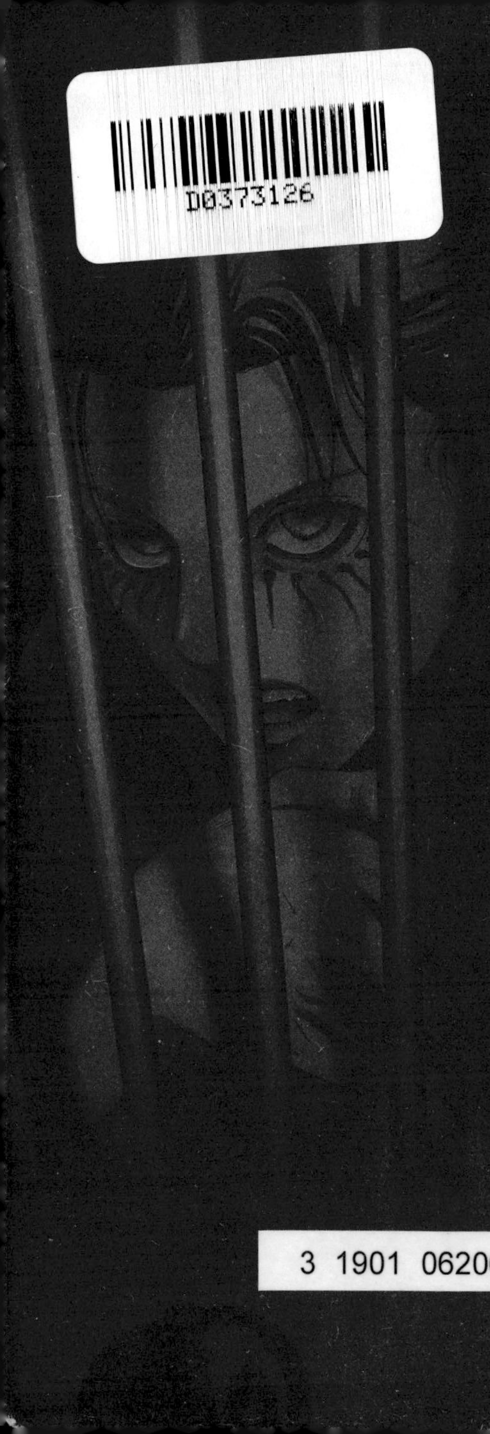

ATTACK ON TITAN 27

HAJIME ISAYAMA

THE CHARACTERS OF ATTACK ON TITAN

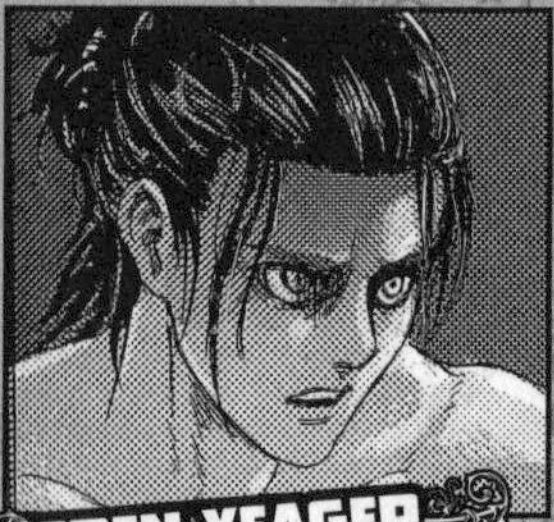

EREN YEAGER

ORIGINALLY A MEMBER OF THE 104TH TRAINING CORPS. CURRENTLY A MEMBER OF THE SURVEY CORPS. HOLDS THE POWER OF THE ATTACK TITAN AND THE FOUNDING TITAN. BOLDLY INFILTRATED MARLEY ON HIS OWN.

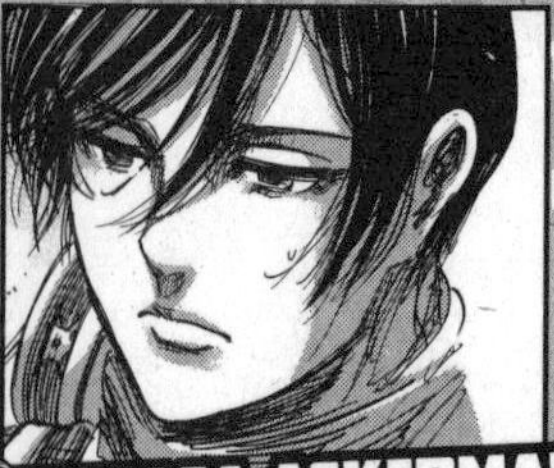

MIKASA ACKERMAN

ORIGINALLY A MEMBER OF THE 104TH TRAINING CORPS. CURRENTLY A MEMBER OF THE SURVEY CORPS. SHE HAS SHOWN OVERWHELMING ABILITY IN COMBAT FROM THE TIME SHE WAS A RECRUIT. SHE SEES PROTECTING EREN AS HER MISSION.

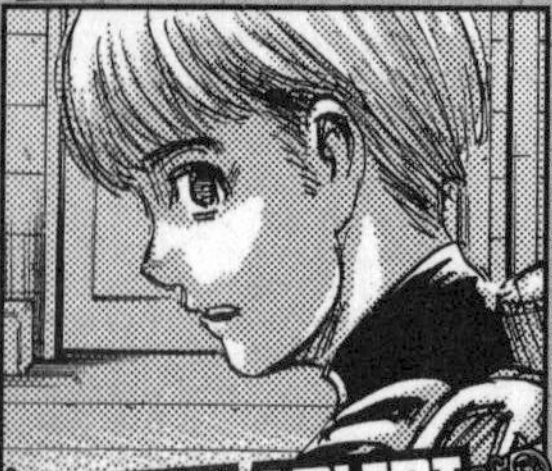

ARMIN ARLERT

ORIGINALLY A MEMBER OF THE 104TH TRAINING CORPS. CURRENTLY A MEMBER OF THE SURVEY CORPS. WITHIN ARMIN DWELLS THE POWER OF THE COLOSSUS TITAN. HE HAS SAVED HIS COMRADES COUNTLESS TIMES WITH HIS SHARP INTELLECT AND BRAVERY.

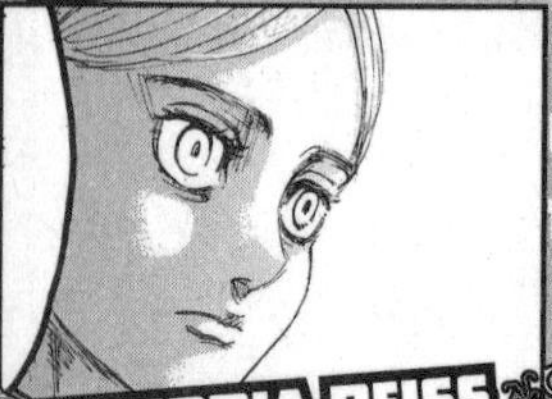

HISTORIA REISS

A DESCENDANT OF THE REISS FAMILY, THE TRUE ROYAL BLOODLINE, HISTORIA HAS NOW ASCENDED TO THE THRONE AS QUEEN. SHE ONCE BELONGED TO THE SURVEY CORPS UNDER THE NAME KRISTA LENZ.

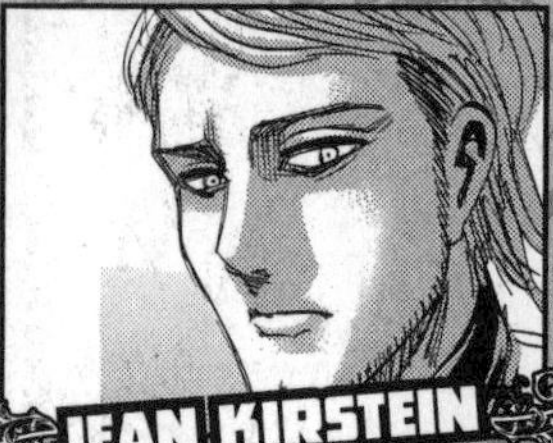

JEAN KIRSTEIN

ORIGINALLY A MEMBER OF THE 104TH TRAINING CORPS. CURRENTLY A MEMBER OF THE SURVEY CORPS. ONCE KNOWN FOR HIS SARCASTIC PERSONALITY, HE HAS NOW GROWN INTO A LEADER FIGURE.

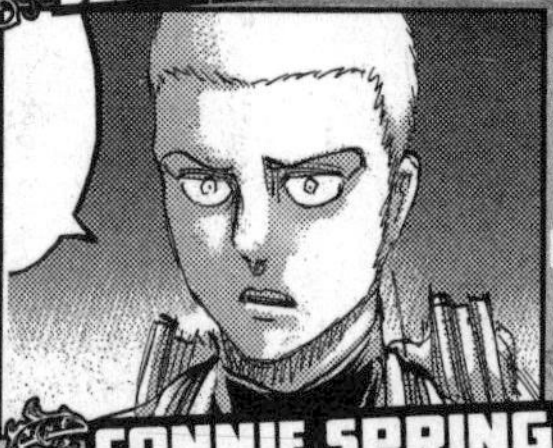

CONNIE SPRINGER

FROM THE 104TH TRAINING CORPS; NOW IN THE SURVEY CORPS. THOUGH HE HAS A CHEERFUL PERSONALITY, HE FINDS HIMSELF LOSING EVERYONE IMPORTANT TO HIM. BORN IN THE VILLAGE OF RAGAKO.

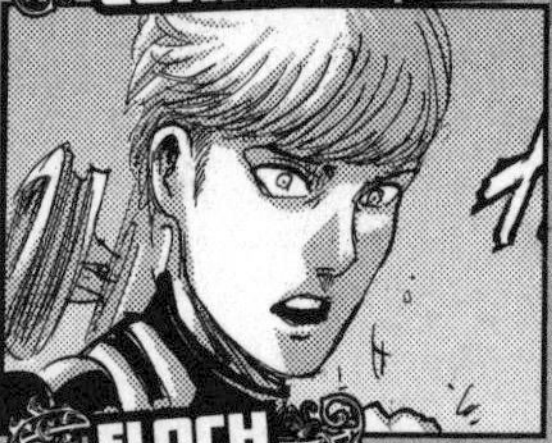

FLOCH

A MEMBER OF THE SURVEY CORPS. A SURVIVOR OF THE DECISIVE BATTLE FOR SHIGANSHINA DISTRICT, WHICH CLAIMED MANY LIVES, INCLUDING ERWIN'S.

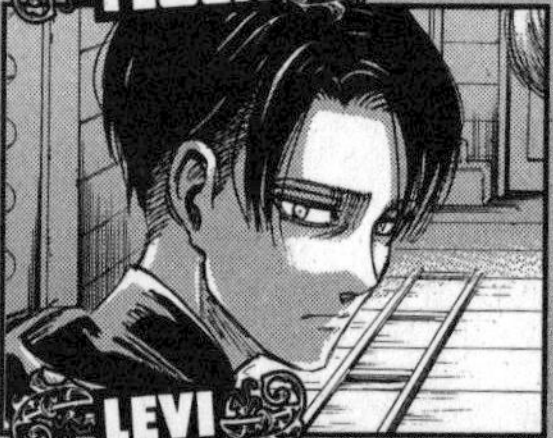

LEVI

A CAPTAIN IN THE SURVEY CORPS. KNOWN AS "HUMANITY'S STRONGEST SOLDIER." HE FIGHTS THROUGH HIS STRUGGLES IN ORDER TO CARRY ON HIS GOOD FRIEND ERWIN'S DYING WISHES.

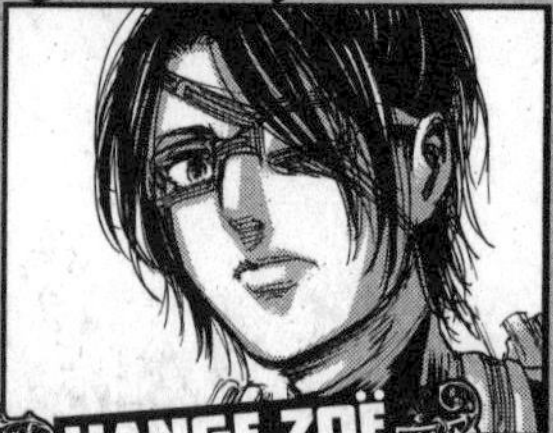

HANGE ZOË

COMMANDER OF THE SURVEY CORPS. DESPITE THE STRANGE WAY HANGE MAY ACT, THEIR KEEN POWERS OF OBSERVATION LED ERWIN TO NAME HANGE HIS SUCCESSOR.

THE NATION OF ELDIA [THE ISLAND OF PARADIS]

THE ELDIAN WARRIORS OF THE MARLEYAN ARMY

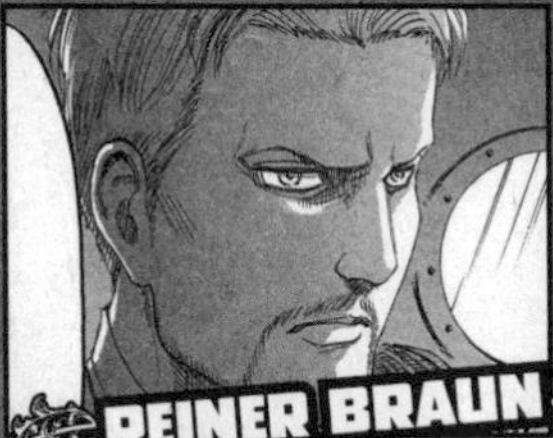

REINER BRAUN

REINER HOLDS THE ARMORED TITAN WITHIN HIM. SINCE HE WAS THE ONLY ONE TO MAKE IT BACK FROM THE MISSION ON PARADIS, HE SUFFERS FROM A GUILTY CONSCIENCE.

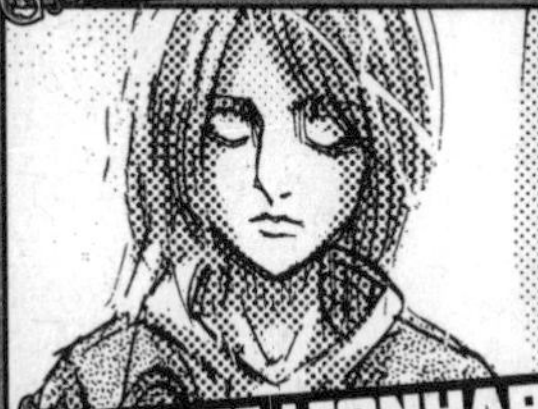

ANNIE LEONHART

ANNIE HOLDS THE FEMALE TITAN WITHIN HER. A MEMBER OF THE 104TH. SHE HAS BEEN SLEEPING WITHIN A HARDENED CRYSTAL EVER SINCE HER TRUE IDENTITY WAS DISCOVERED.

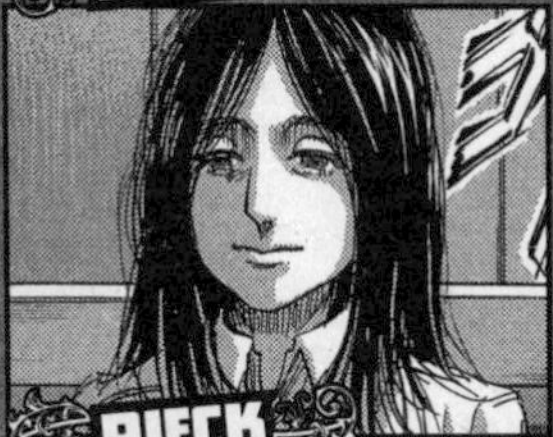

PIECK

PIECK HOLDS THE CART TITAN WITHIN HER, CARRYING THE PANZER UNIT ON THE BACK OF THE "CARTMAN" TO FIGHT. HIGHLY PERCEPTIVE.

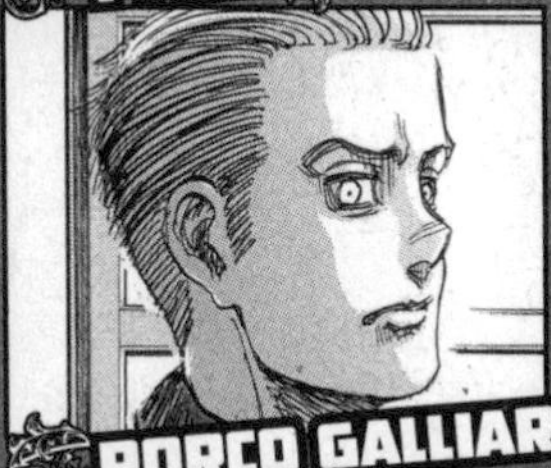

PORCO GALLIARD

PORCO HOLDS THE JAW TITAN WITHIN HIM. THERE IS STRIFE BETWEEN HIM AND REINER OVER BOTH THE INHERITANCE OF THE ARMORED TITAN AND THE DEATH OF HIS OLDER BROTHER MARCEL.

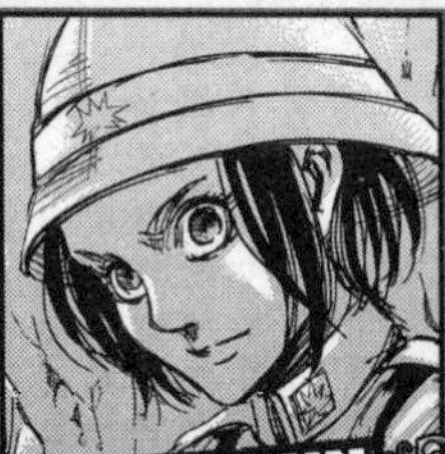

GABI BRAUN

BOLD DESPITE HER SMALL SIZE, GABI IS A DYNAMIC WARRIOR CANDIDATE. HER GOAL IS TO EVENTUALLY INHERIT THE ARMORED TITAN. REINER'S COUSIN.

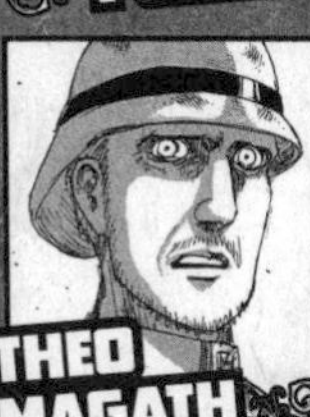

THEO MAGATH

LEADER OF THE WARRIOR UNIT. A MARLEYAN WHO LEADS A UNIT OF ELDIANS.

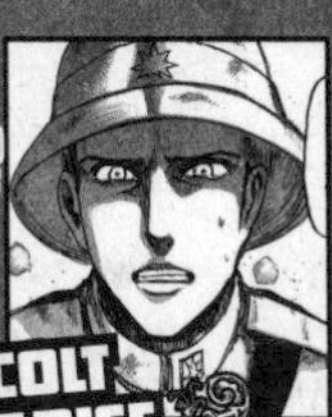

COLT GRICE

FALCO'S OLDER BROTHER. THE OLDEST OF THE WARRIOR CANDIDATES, AND, IN EFFECT, THEIR LEADER.

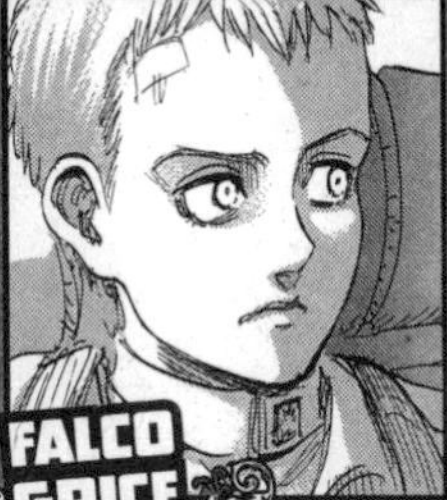

FALCO GRICE

A WARRIOR CANDIDATE. HE HAS AFFECTION FOR GABI AND WANTS TO PROTECT HER. DURING EREN'S TIME INFILTRATING MARLEY, FALCO COMES IN CONTACT WITH EREN WITHOUT REALIZING HIS TRUE IDENTITY.

THE ANTI-MARLEYAN VOLUNTEERS

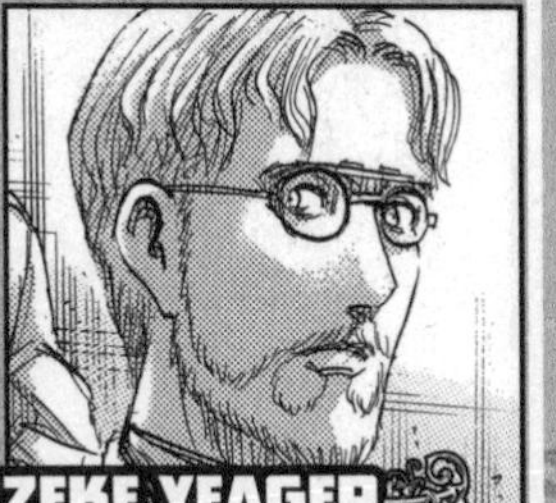

ZEKE YEAGER

ZEKE HOLDS THE POWER OF THE BEAST TITAN WITHIN HIM. A LEADER OF THE WARRIORS ONCE KNOWN AS THE "WONDER CHILD." HIS MOTHER IS A DESCENDANT OF THE ROYAL BLOODLINE, AND HE IS ALSO EREN'S HALF-BROTHER.

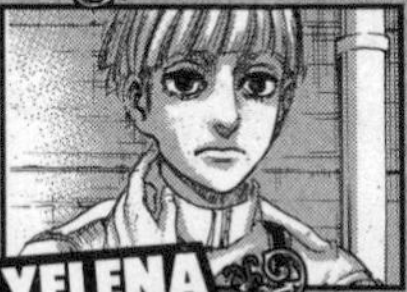

YELENA

YELENA COMMANDS THE VOLUNTEERS AND FOLLOWS ZEKE. SHE DRESSED AS A MAN DURING THE EXPEDITION TO MARLEY IN ORDER TO WORK IN SECRET.

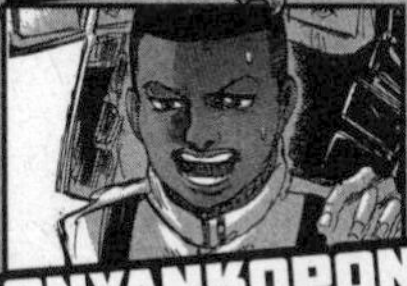

ONYANKOPON

AFTER TRAVELING TO PARADIS WITH YELENA, HE TELLS ITS INHABITANTS OF MARLEY'S ADVANCED CULTURE.

ATTACK on TITAN

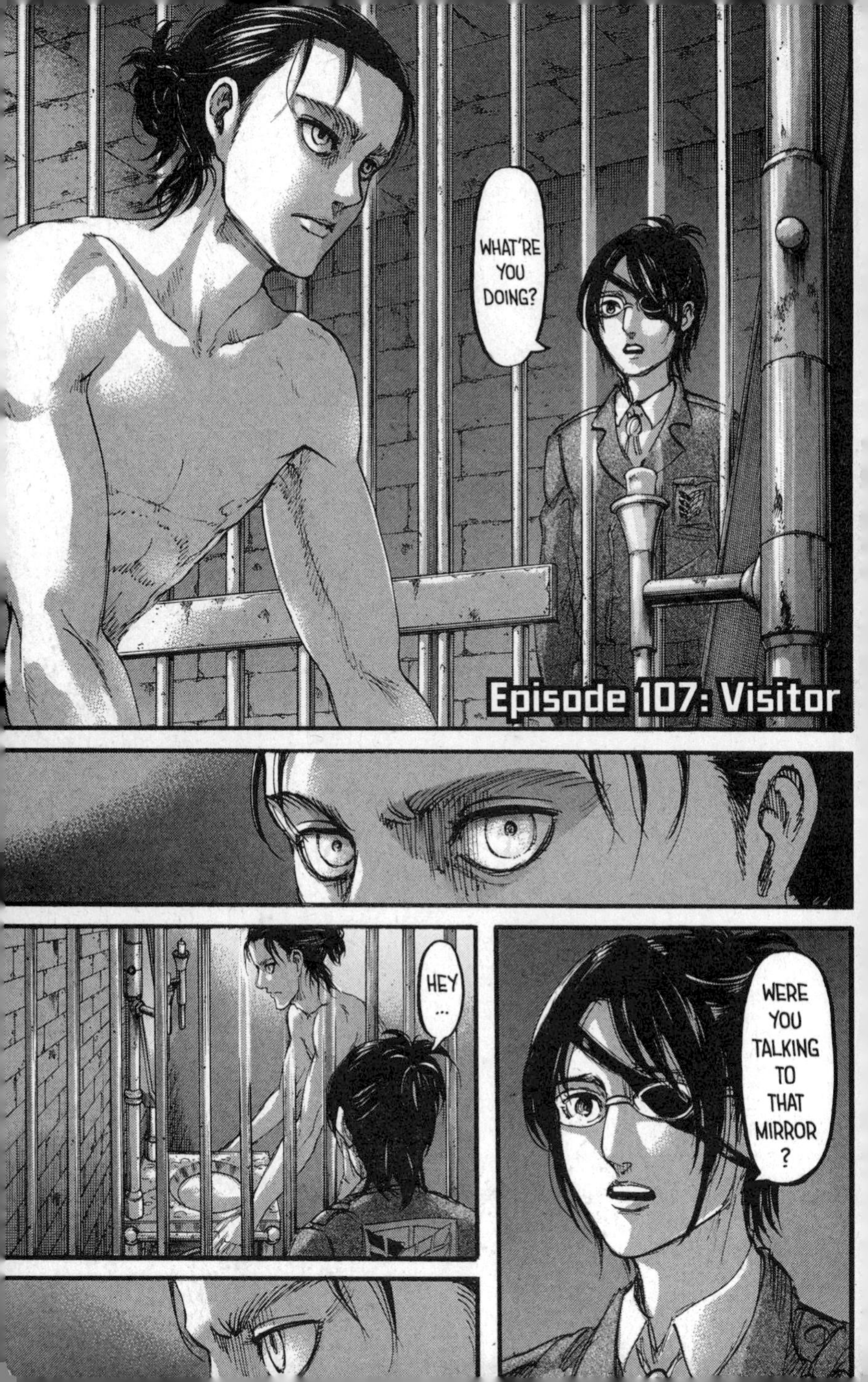
WHAT'RE YOU DOING?
Episode 107: Visitor
HEY ...
WERE YOU TALKING TO THAT MIRROR ?

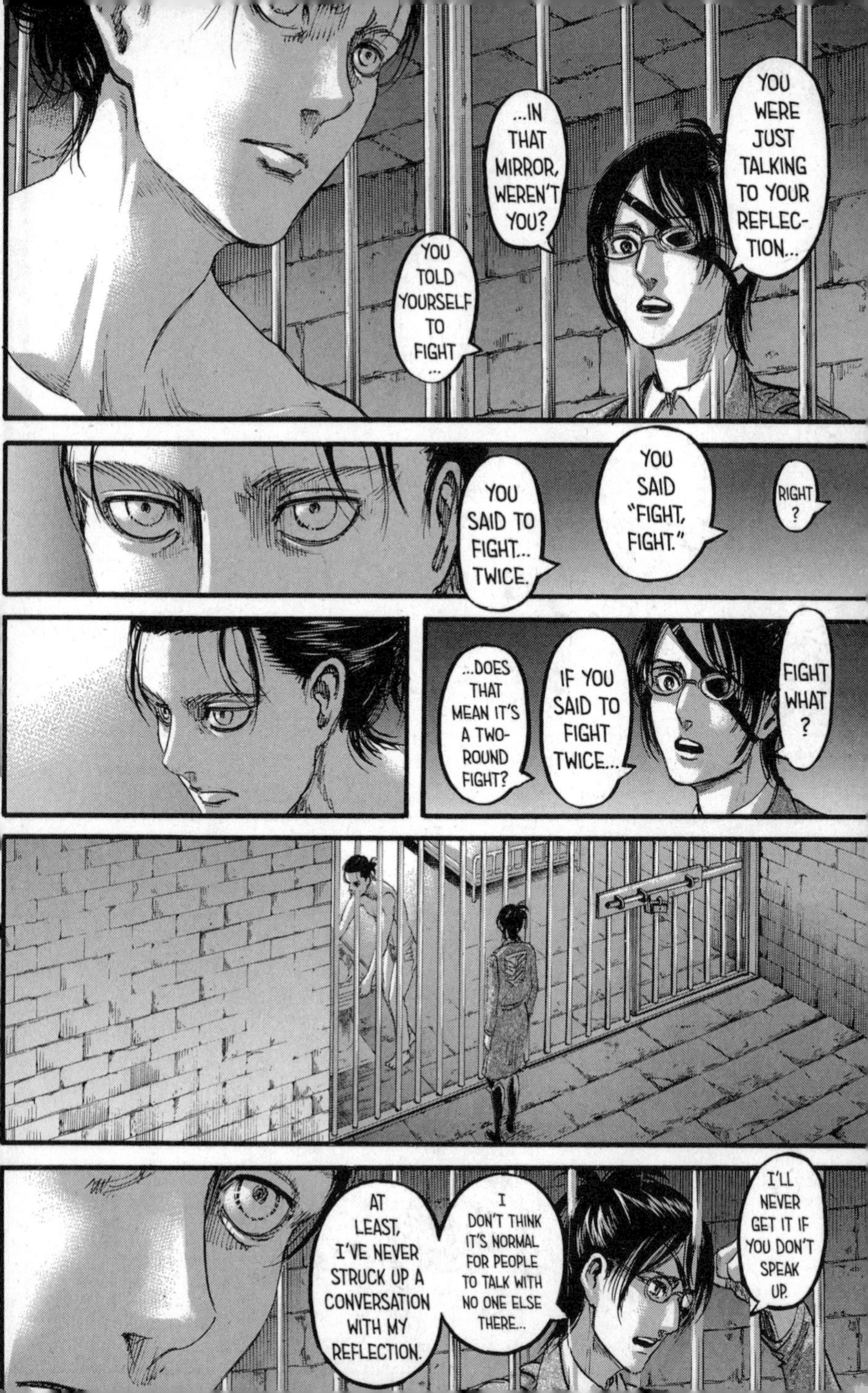
YOU WERE JUST TALKING TO YOUR REFLECTION...
...IN THAT MIRROR, WEREN'T YOU?
YOU TOLD YOURSELF TO FIGHT...
RIGHT?
YOU SAID "FIGHT, FIGHT."
YOU SAID TO FIGHT... TWICE.
FIGHT WHAT?
IF YOU SAID TO FIGHT TWICE...
...DOES THAT MEAN IT'S A TWO-ROUND FIGHT?
I'LL NEVER GET IT IF YOU DON'T SPEAK UP.
I DON'T THINK IT'S NORMAL FOR PEOPLE TO TALK WITH NO ONE ELSE THERE...
AT LEAST, I'VE NEVER STRUCK UP A CONVERSATION WITH MY REFLECTION.

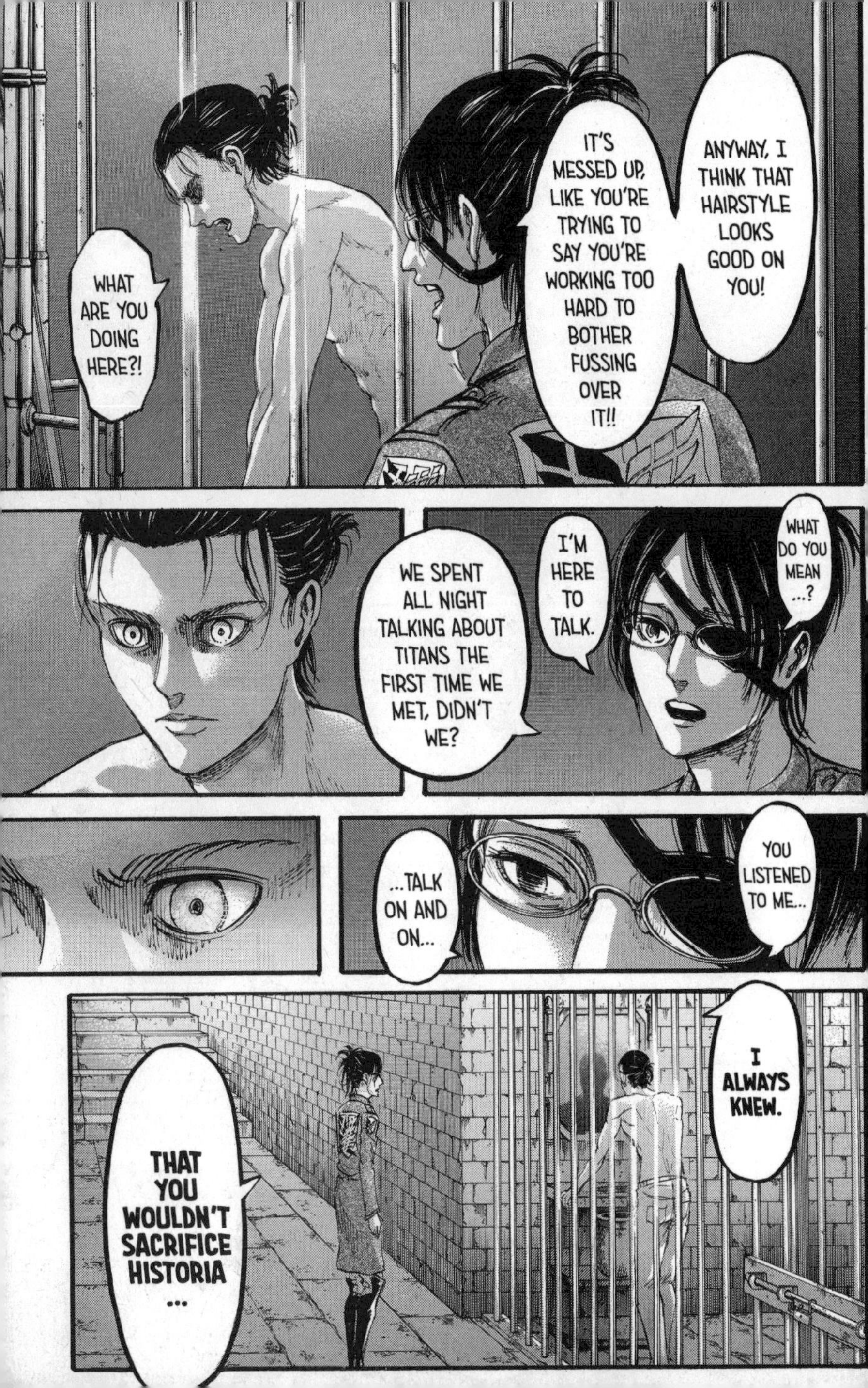
ANYWAY, I THINK THAT HAIRSTYLE LOOKS GOOD ON YOU!
IT'S MESSED UP, LIKE YOU'RE TRYING TO SAY YOU'RE WORKING TOO HARD TO BOTHER FUSSING OVER IT!!
WHAT ARE YOU DOING HERE?!
WHAT DO YOU MEAN ...?
I'M HERE TO TALK.
WE SPENT ALL NIGHT TALKING ABOUT TITANS THE FIRST TIME WE MET, DIDN'T WE?
YOU LISTENED TO ME...
...TALK ON AND ON...
I ALWAYS KNEW.
THAT YOU WOULDN'T SACRIFICE HISTORIA ...

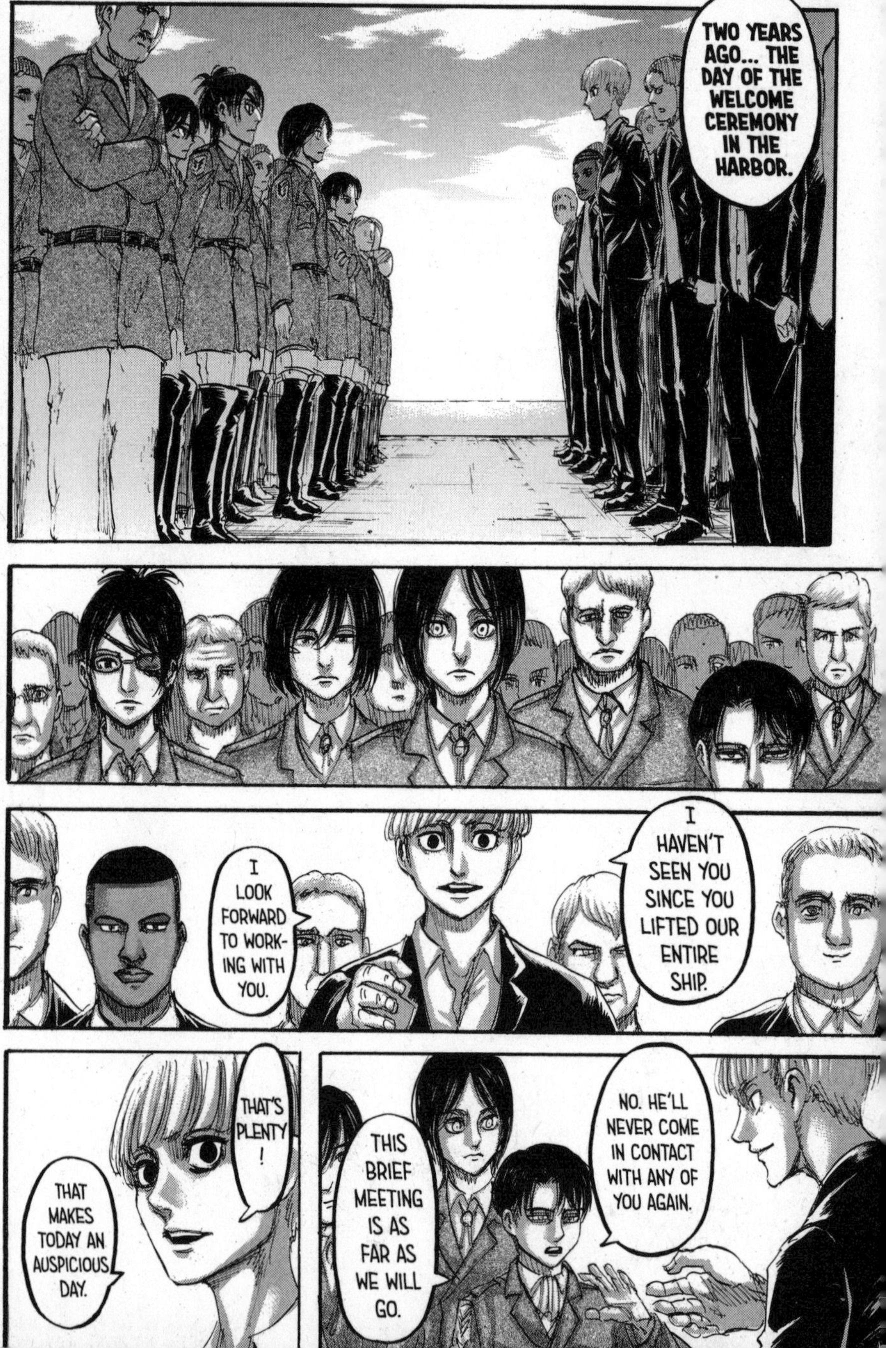
TWO YEARS AGO... THE DAY OF THE WELCOME CEREMONY IN THE HARBOR.
I HAVEN'T SEEN YOU SINCE YOU LIFTED OUR ENTIRE SHIP.
I LOOK FORWARD TO WORKING WITH YOU.
NO. HE'LL NEVER COME IN CONTACT WITH ANY OF YOU AGAIN.
THIS BRIEF MEETING IS AS FAR AS WE WILL GO.
THAT'S PLENTY!
THAT MAKES TODAY AN AUSPICIOUS DAY.

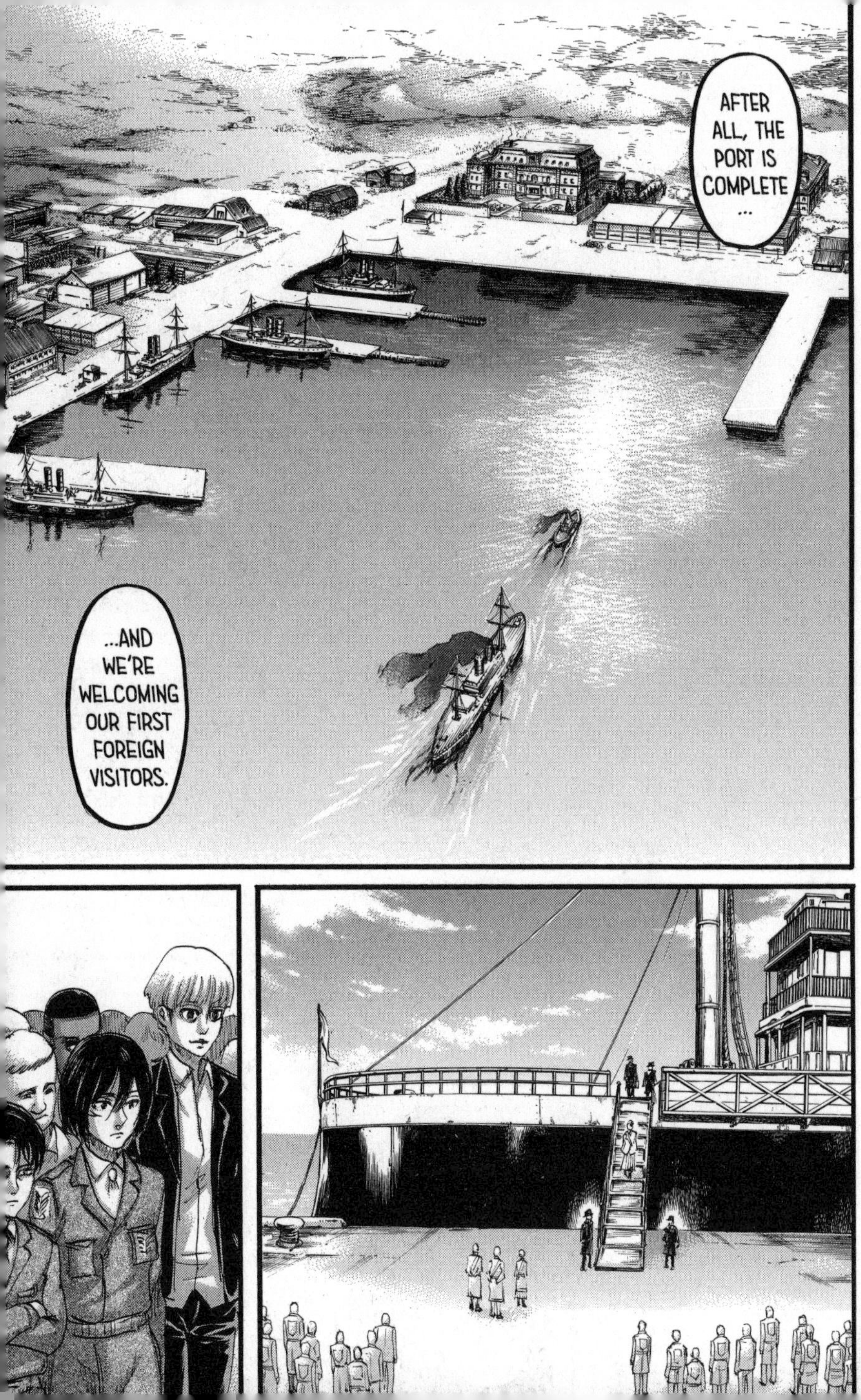
AFTER ALL, THE PORT IS COMPLETE ...
...AND WE'RE WELCOMING OUR FIRST FOREIGN VISITORS.

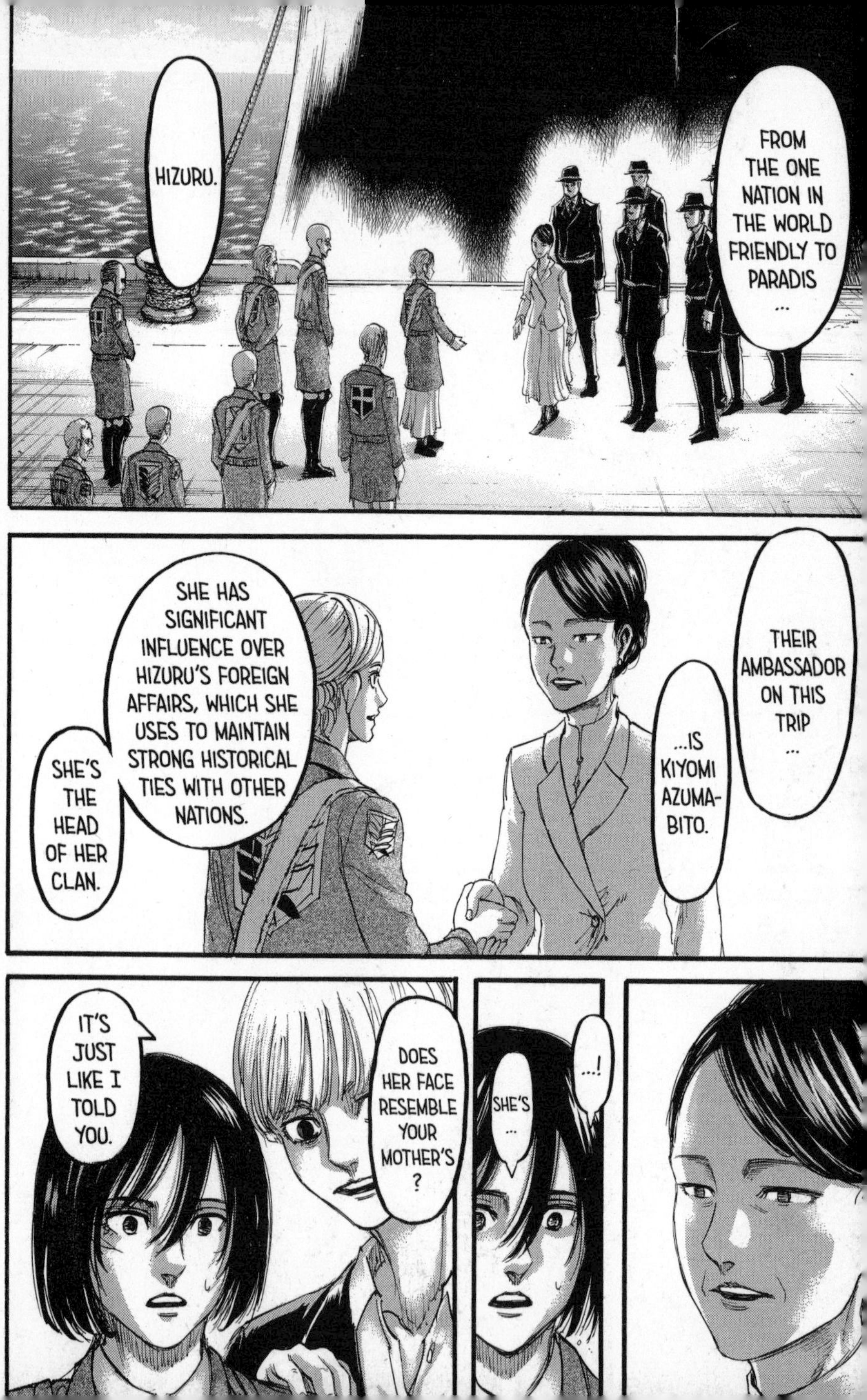
FROM THE ONE NATION IN THE WORLD FRIENDLY TO PARADIS ...
HIZURU.
THEIR AMBASSADOR ON THIS TRIP ...
...IS KIYOMI AZUMA-BITO.
SHE HAS SIGNIFICANT INFLUENCE OVER HIZURU'S FOREIGN AFFAIRS, WHICH SHE USES TO MAINTAIN STRONG HISTORICAL TIES WITH OTHER NATIONS.
SHE'S THE HEAD OF HER CLAN.
...!
SHE'S ...
DOES HER FACE RESEMBLE YOUR MOTHER'S ?
IT'S JUST LIKE I TOLD YOU.

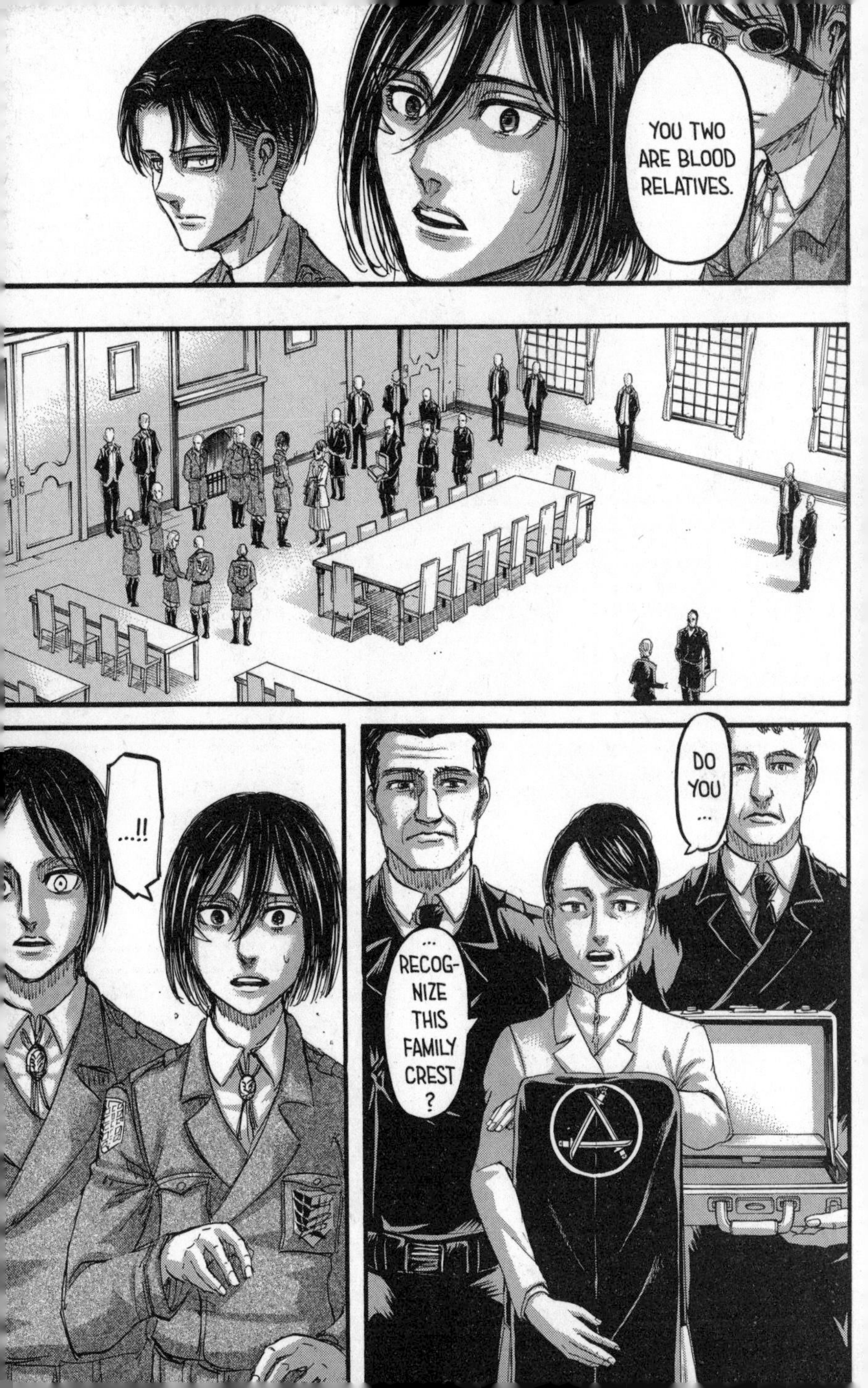
YOU TWO ARE BLOOD RELATIVES.
...!!
DO YOU ...
... RECOG-NIZE THIS FAMILY CREST ?

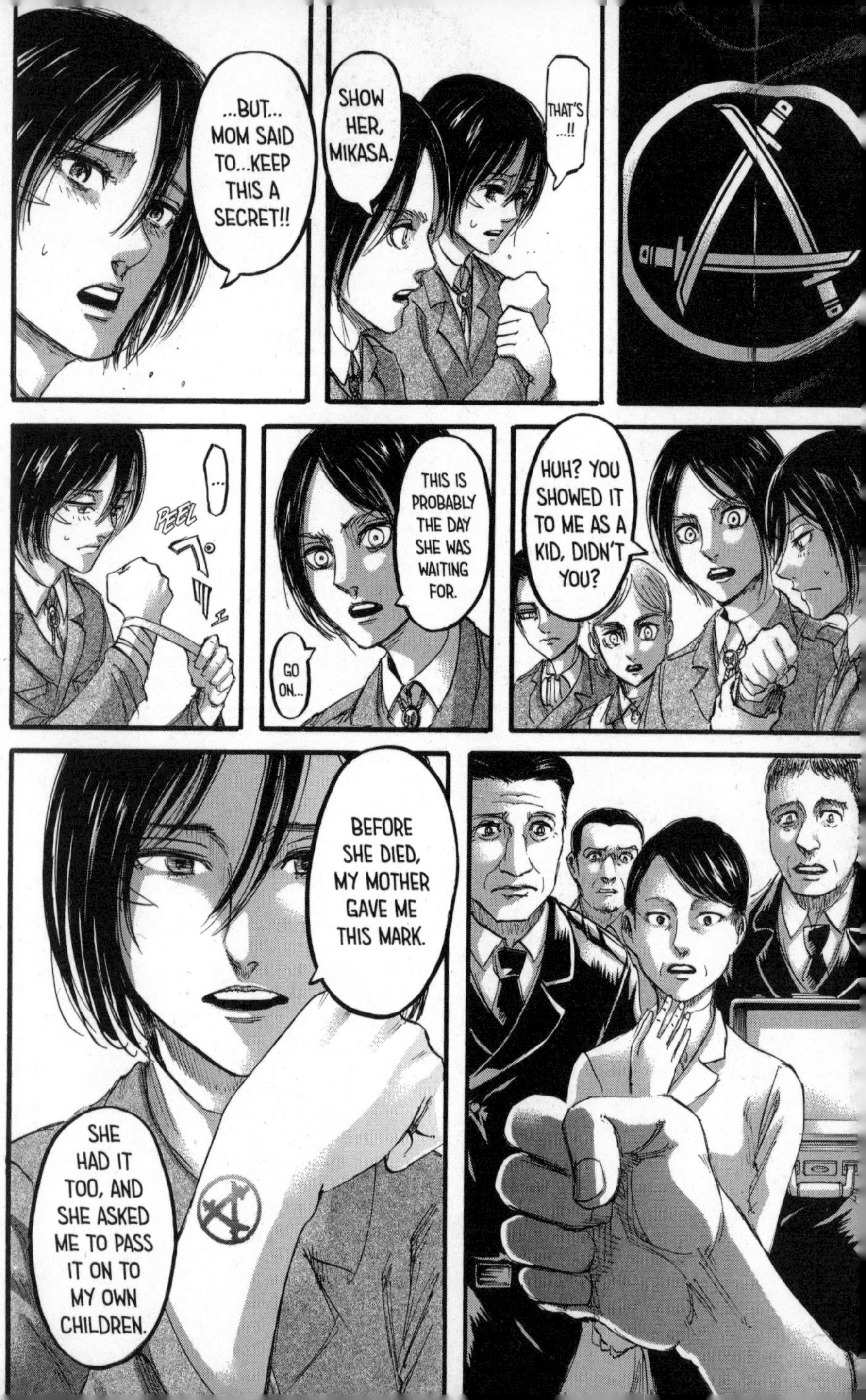
...BUT... MOM SAID TO...KEEP THIS A SECRET!!
SHOW HER, MIKASA.
THAT'S ...!!
...
PEEL
THIS IS PROBABLY THE DAY SHE WAS WAITING FOR.
GO ON...
HUH? YOU SHOWED IT TO ME AS A KID, DIDN'T YOU?
BEFORE SHE DIED, MY MOTHER GAVE ME THIS MARK.
SHE HAD IT TOO, AND SHE ASKED ME TO PASS IT ON TO MY OWN CHILDREN.

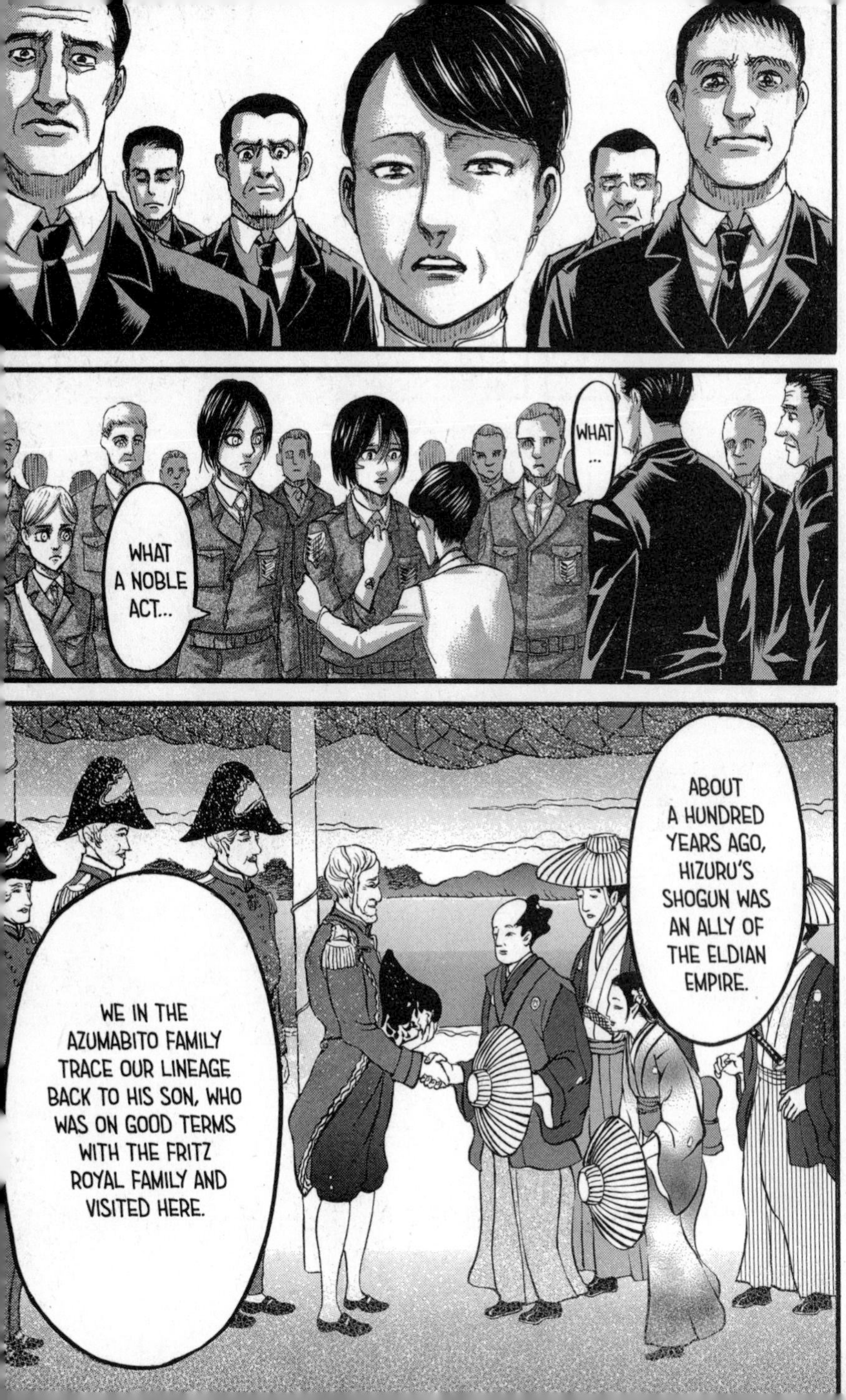
WHAT ...
WHAT A NOBLE ACT...
ABOUT A HUNDRED YEARS AGO, HIZURU'S SHOGUN WAS AN ALLY OF THE ELDIAN EMPIRE.
WE IN THE AZUMABITO FAMILY TRACE OUR LINEAGE BACK TO HIS SON, WHO WAS ON GOOD TERMS WITH THE FRITZ ROYAL FAMILY AND VISITED HERE.

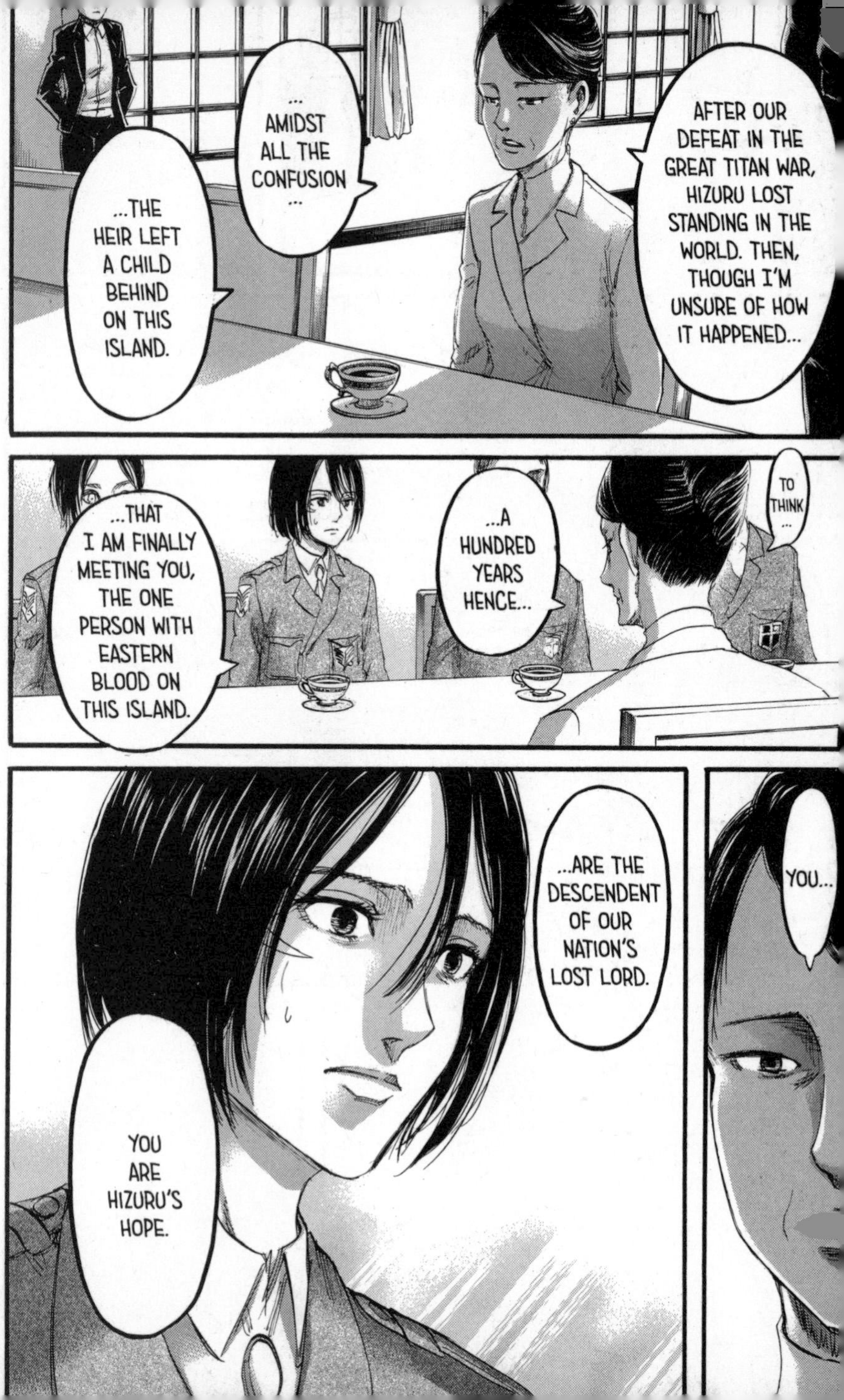

AFTER OUR DEFEAT IN THE GREAT TITAN WAR, HIZURU LOST STANDING IN THE WORLD. THEN, THOUGH I'M UNSURE OF HOW IT HAPPENED...
... AMIDST ALL THE CONFUSION ...
...THE HEIR LEFT A CHILD BEHIND ON THIS ISLAND.
TO THINK ...
...A HUNDRED YEARS HENCE...
...THAT I AM FINALLY MEETING YOU, THE ONE PERSON WITH EASTERN BLOOD ON THIS ISLAND.
YOU...
...ARE THE DESCENDENT OF OUR NATION'S LOST LORD.
YOU ARE HIZURU'S HOPE.

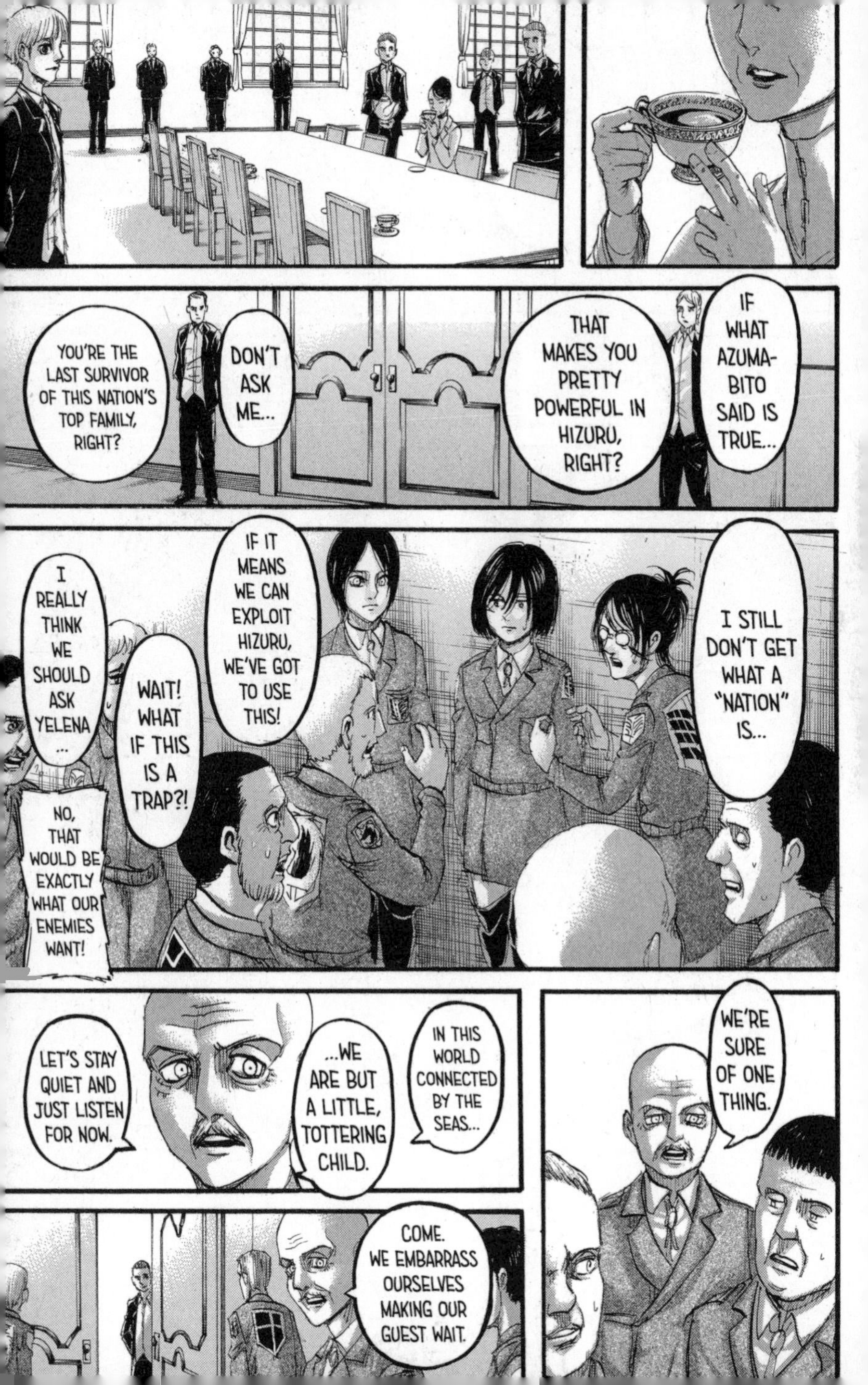
IF WHAT AZUMABITO SAID IS TRUE...
THAT MAKES YOU PRETTY POWERFUL IN HIZURU, RIGHT?
DON'T ASK ME...
YOU'RE THE LAST SURVIVOR OF THIS NATION'S TOP FAMILY, RIGHT?
I STILL DON'T GET WHAT A "NATION" IS...
IF IT MEANS WE CAN EXPLOIT HIZURU, WE'VE GOT TO USE THIS!
WAIT! WHAT IF THIS IS A TRAP?!
I REALLY THINK WE SHOULD ASK YELENA...
NO, THAT WOULD BE EXACTLY WHAT OUR ENEMIES WANT!
WE'RE SURE OF ONE THING.
IN THIS WORLD CONNECTED BY THE SEAS...
...WE ARE BUT A LITTLE, TOTTERING CHILD.
LET'S STAY QUIET AND JUST LISTEN FOR NOW.
COME. WE EMBARRASS OURSELVES MAKING OUR GUEST WAIT.

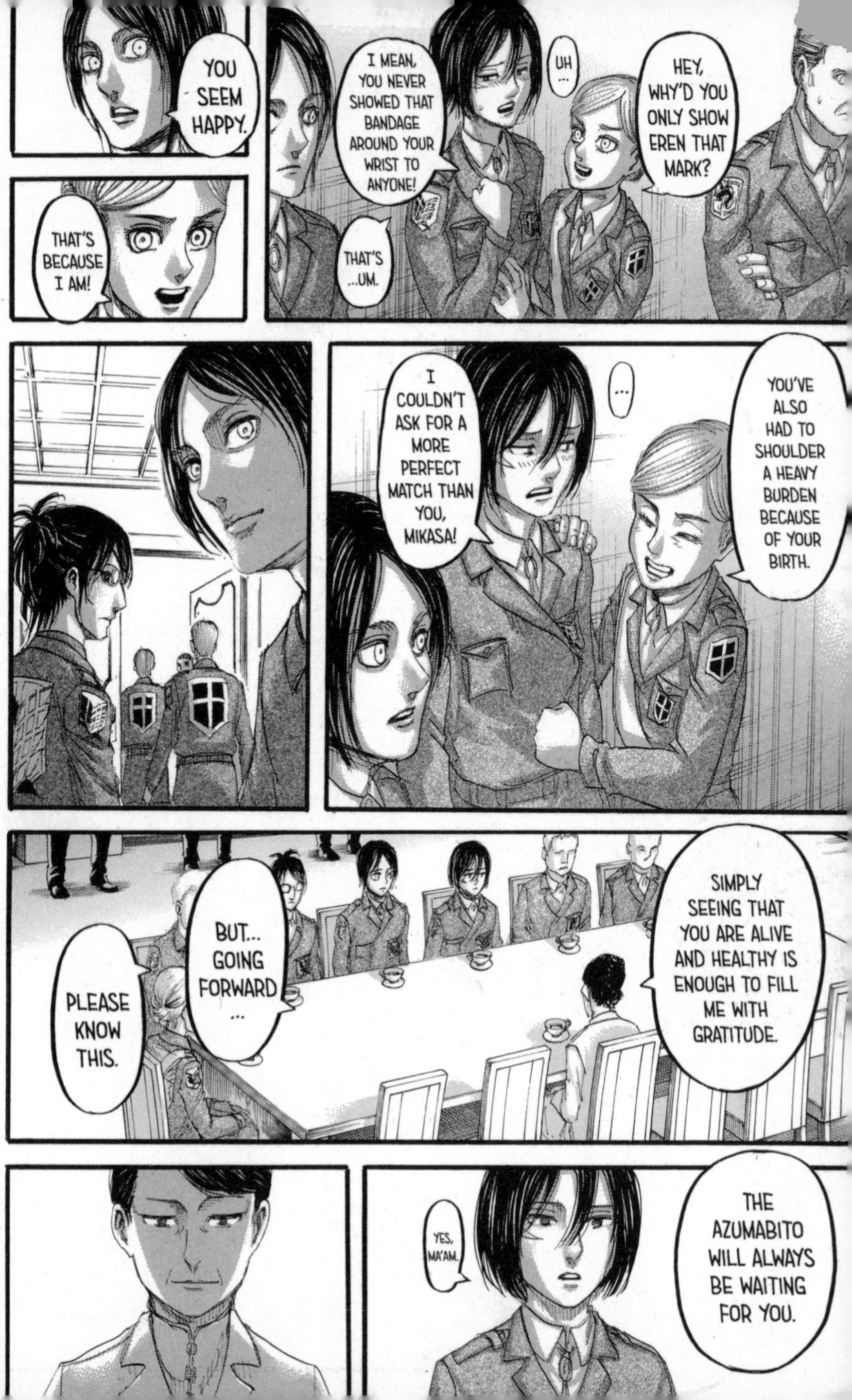
HEY, WHY'D YOU ONLY SHOW EREN THAT MARK?
UH ...
I MEAN, YOU NEVER SHOWED THAT BANDAGE AROUND YOUR WRIST TO ANYONE!
THAT'S ...UM.
YOU SEEM HAPPY.
THAT'S BECAUSE I AM!
YOU'VE ALSO HAD TO SHOULDER A HEAVY BURDEN BECAUSE OF YOUR BIRTH.
...
I COULDN'T ASK FOR A MORE PERFECT MATCH THAN YOU, MIKASA!
SIMPLY SEEING THAT YOU ARE ALIVE AND HEALTHY IS ENOUGH TO FILL ME WITH GRATITUDE.
BUT... GOING FORWARD ...
PLEASE KNOW THIS.
THE AZUMABITO WILL ALWAYS BE WAITING FOR YOU.
YES, MA'AM.

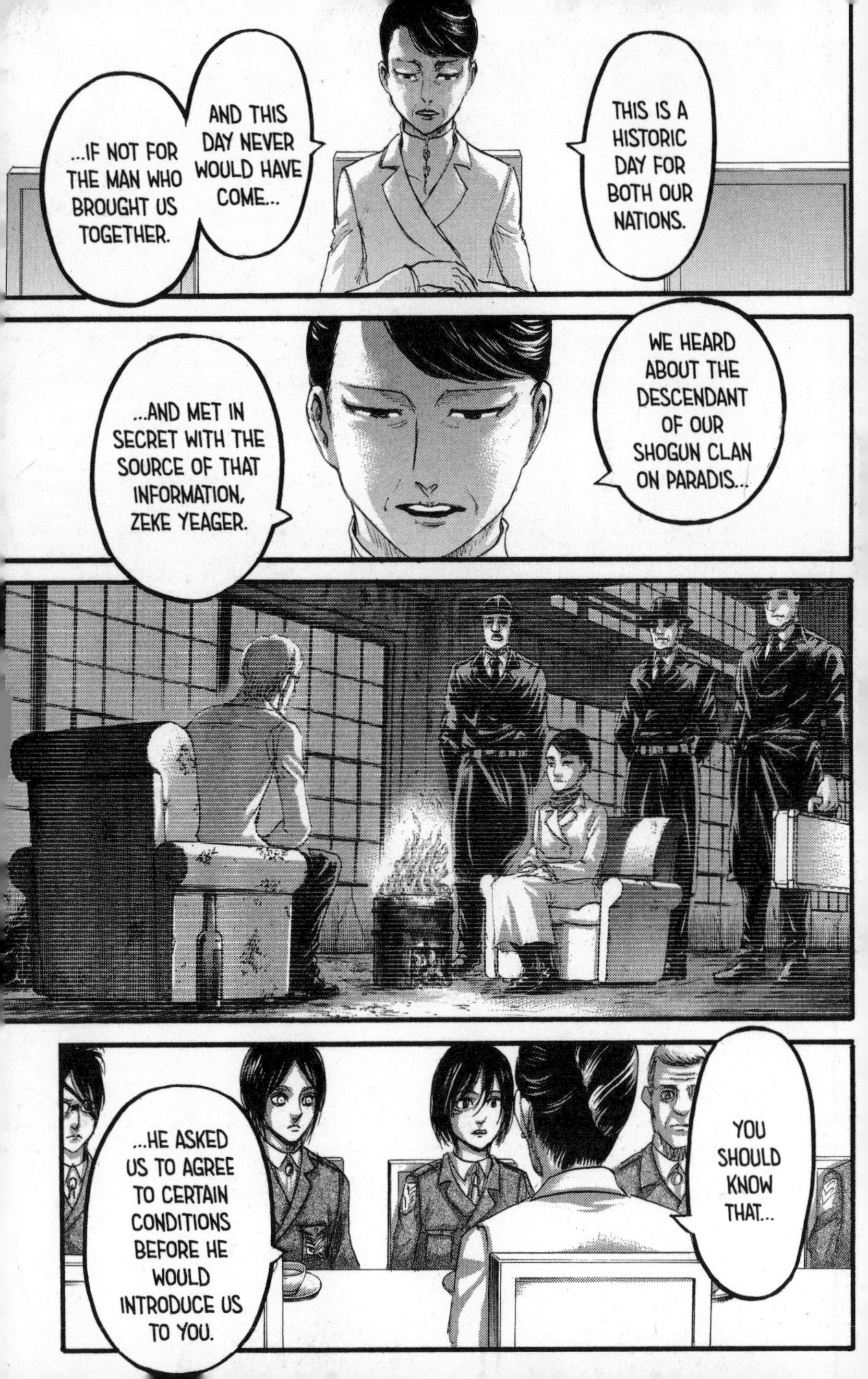
THIS IS A HISTORIC DAY FOR BOTH OUR NATIONS.
AND THIS DAY NEVER WOULD HAVE COME...
...IF NOT FOR THE MAN WHO BROUGHT US TOGETHER.
WE HEARD ABOUT THE DESCENDANT OF OUR SHOGUN CLAN ON PARADIS...
...AND MET IN SECRET WITH THE SOURCE OF THAT INFORMATION, ZEKE YEAGER.
YOU SHOULD KNOW THAT...
...HE ASKED US TO AGREE TO CERTAIN CONDITIONS BEFORE HE WOULD INTRODUCE US TO YOU.

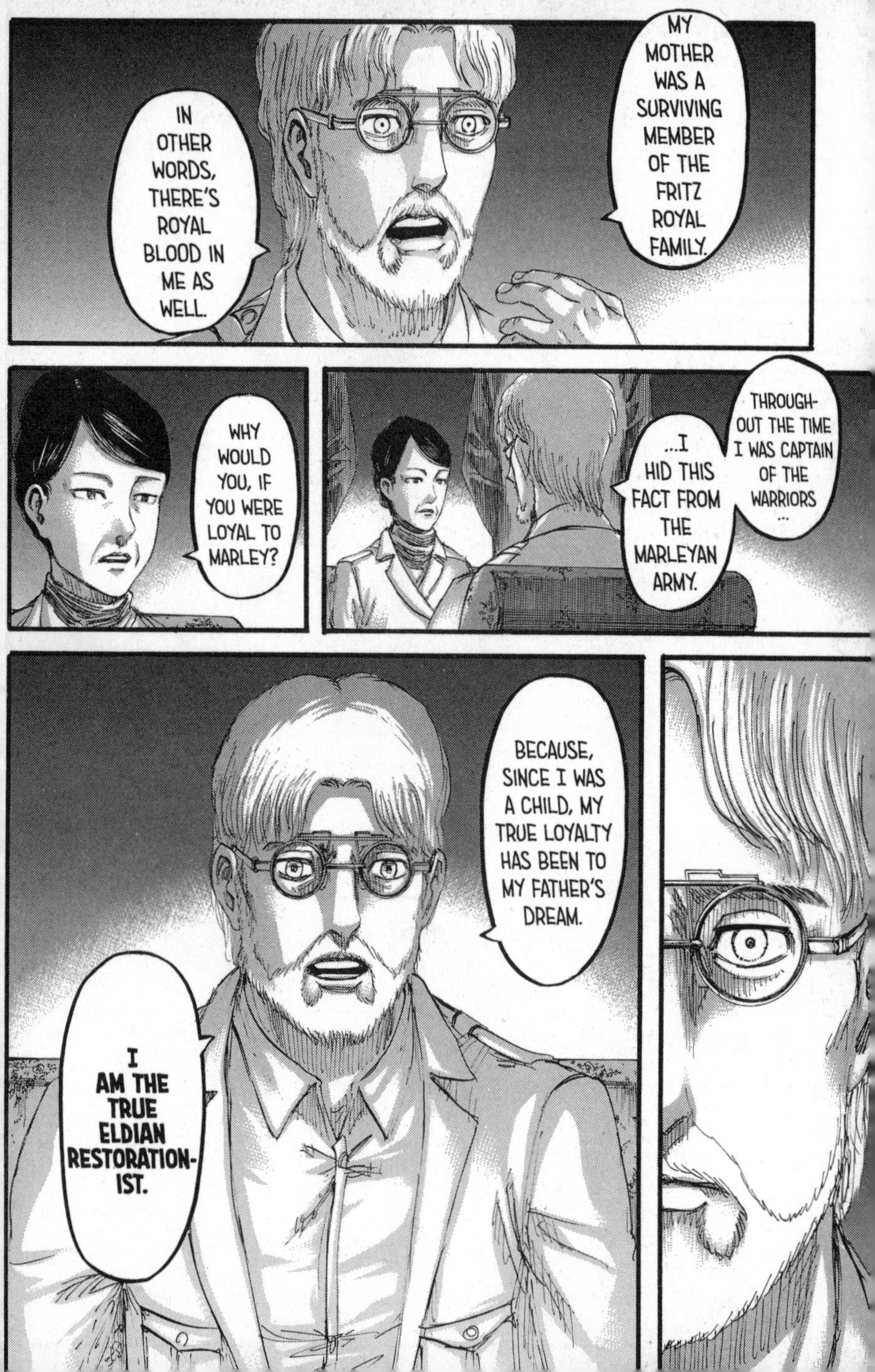
MY MOTHER WAS A SURVIVING MEMBER OF THE FRITZ ROYAL FAMILY.
IN OTHER WORDS, THERE'S ROYAL BLOOD IN ME AS WELL.
THROUGH-OUT THE TIME I WAS CAPTAIN OF THE WARRIORS ...
...I HID THIS FACT FROM THE MARLEYAN ARMY.
WHY WOULD YOU, IF YOU WERE LOYAL TO MARLEY?
BECAUSE, SINCE I WAS A CHILD, MY TRUE LOYALTY HAS BEEN TO MY FATHER'S DREAM.
I AM THE TRUE ELDIAN RESTORATION-IST.

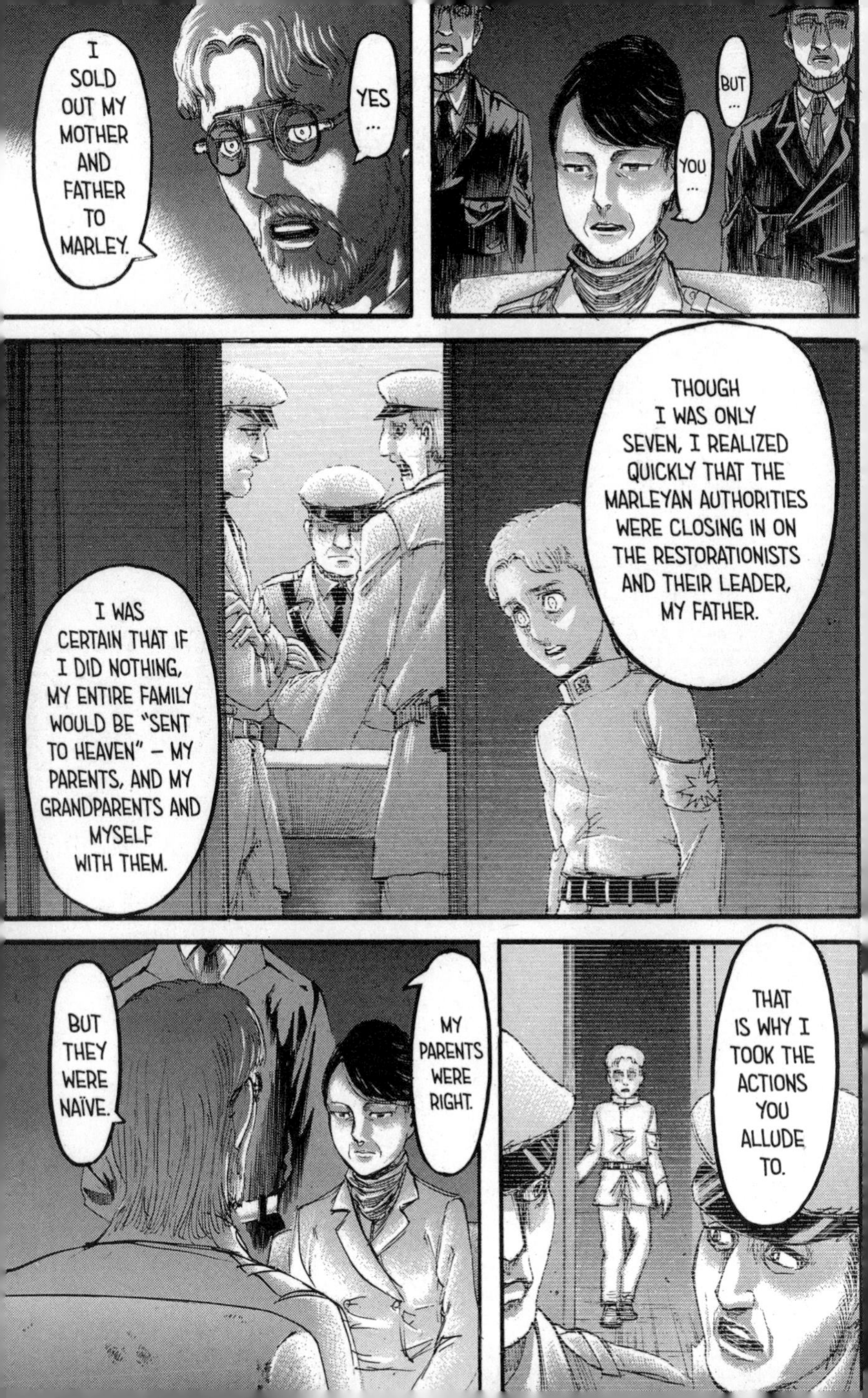
BUT ...
YOU ...
YES ...
I SOLD OUT MY MOTHER AND FATHER TO MARLEY.
THOUGH I WAS ONLY SEVEN, I REALIZED QUICKLY THAT THE MARLEYAN AUTHORITIES WERE CLOSING IN ON THE RESTORATIONISTS AND THEIR LEADER, MY FATHER.
I WAS CERTAIN THAT IF I DID NOTHING, MY ENTIRE FAMILY WOULD BE "SENT TO HEAVEN" — MY PARENTS, AND MY GRANDPARENTS AND MYSELF WITH THEM.
THAT IS WHY I TOOK THE ACTIONS YOU ALLUDE TO.
MY PARENTS WERE RIGHT.
BUT THEY WERE NAÏVE.

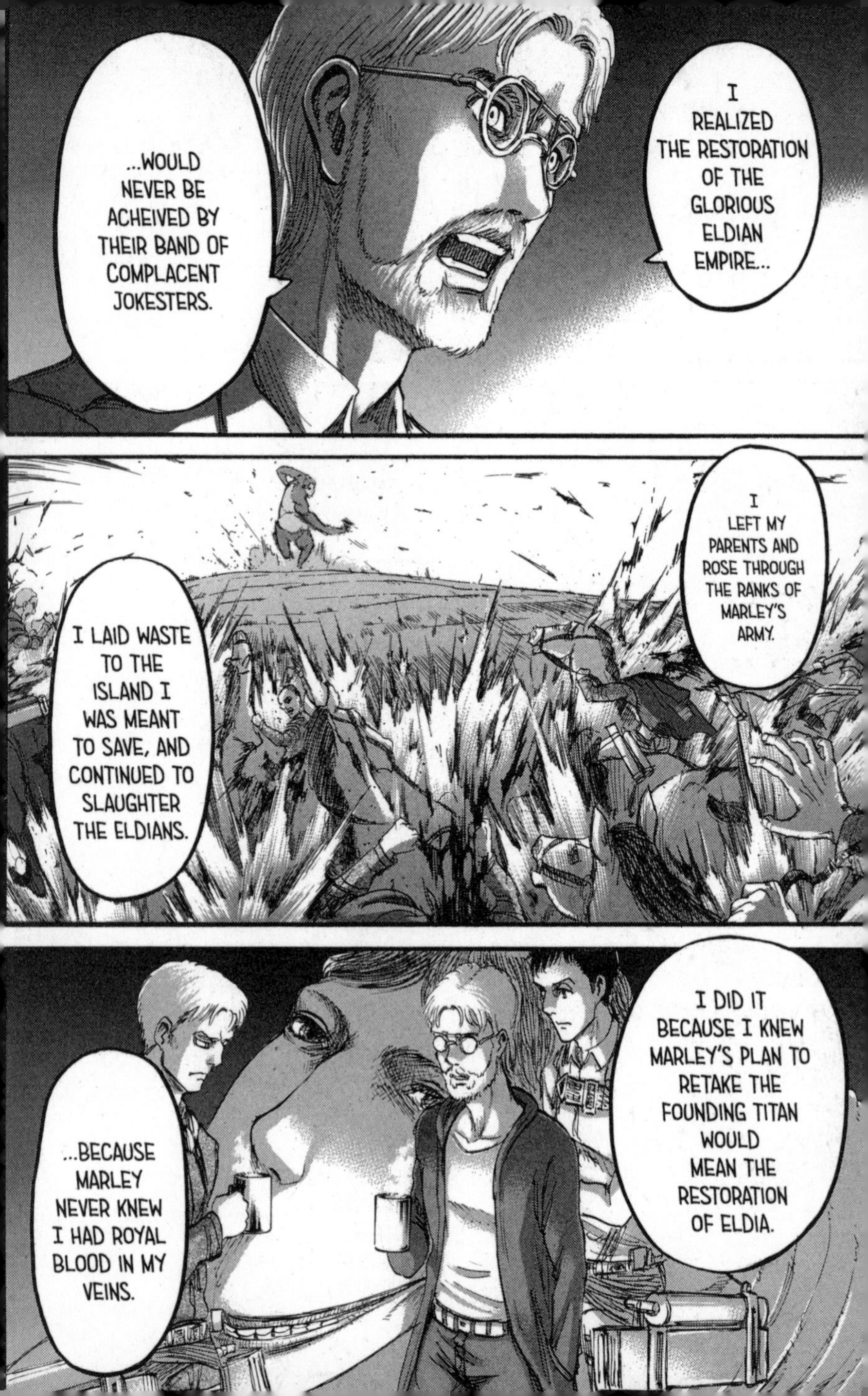

I REALIZED THE RESTORATION OF THE GLORIOUS ELDIAN EMPIRE...
...WOULD NEVER BE ACHEIVED BY THEIR BAND OF COMPLACENT JOKESTERS.
I LEFT MY PARENTS AND ROSE THROUGH THE RANKS OF MARLEY'S ARMY.
I LAID WASTE TO THE ISLAND I WAS MEANT TO SAVE, AND CONTINUED TO SLAUGHTER THE ELDIANS.
I DID IT BECAUSE I KNEW MARLEY'S PLAN TO RETAKE THE FOUNDING TITAN WOULD MEAN THE RESTORATION OF ELDIA.
...BECAUSE MARLEY NEVER KNEW I HAD ROYAL BLOOD IN MY VEINS.

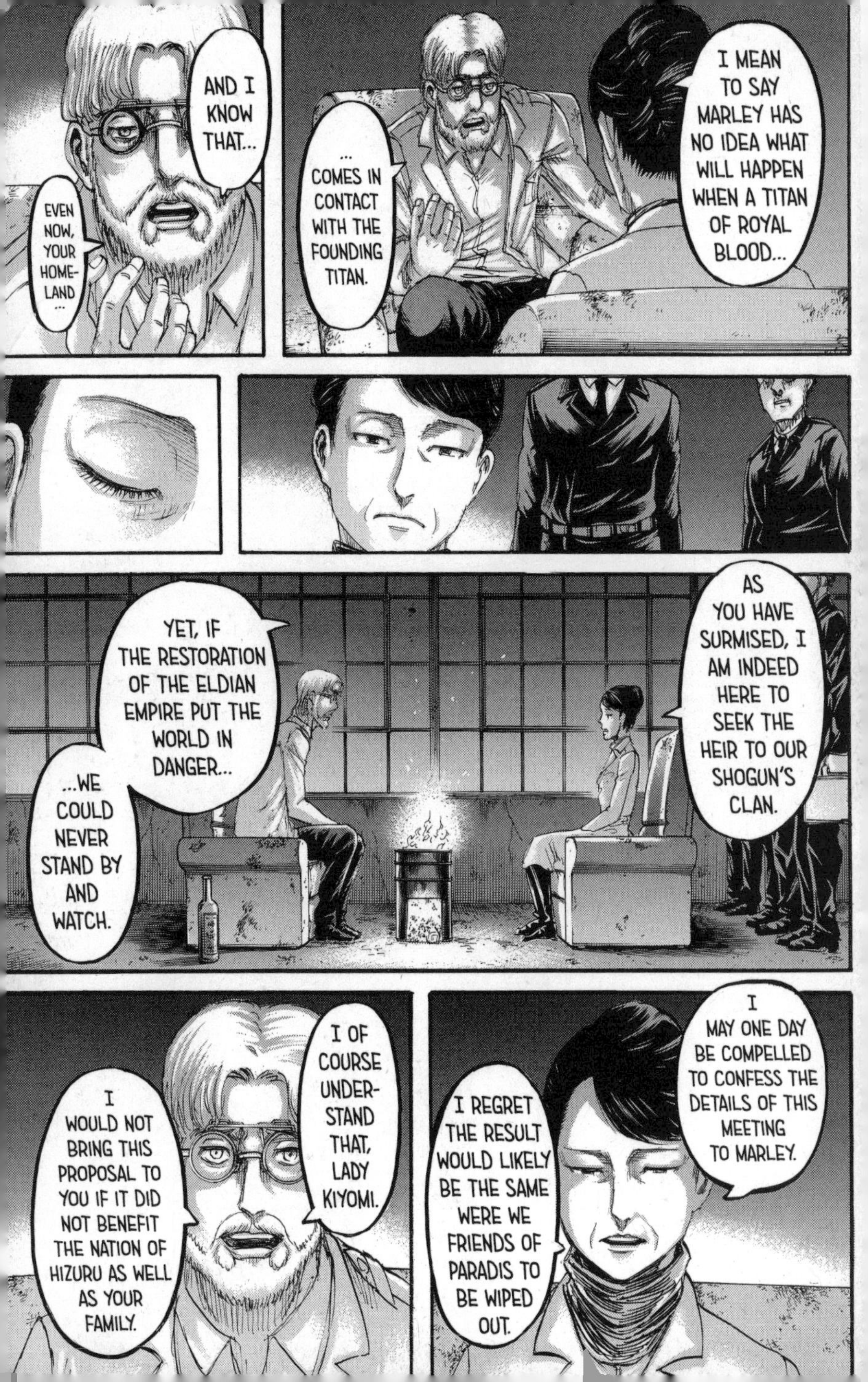
I MEAN TO SAY MARLEY HAS NO IDEA WHAT WILL HAPPEN WHEN A TITAN OF ROYAL BLOOD...
... COMES IN CONTACT WITH THE FOUNDING TITAN.
AND I KNOW THAT...
EVEN NOW, YOUR HOMELAND ...
AS YOU HAVE SURMISED, I AM INDEED HERE TO SEEK THE HEIR TO OUR SHOGUN'S CLAN.
YET, IF THE RESTORATION OF THE ELDIAN EMPIRE PUT THE WORLD IN DANGER...
...WE COULD NEVER STAND BY AND WATCH.
I MAY ONE DAY BE COMPELLED TO CONFESS THE DETAILS OF THIS MEETING TO MARLEY.
I REGRET THE RESULT WOULD LIKELY BE THE SAME WERE WE FRIENDS OF PARADIS TO BE WIPED OUT.
I OF COURSE UNDERSTAND THAT, LADY KIYOMI.
I WOULD NOT BRING THIS PROPOSAL TO YOU IF IT DID NOT BENEFIT THE NATION OF HIZURU AS WELL AS YOUR FAMILY.

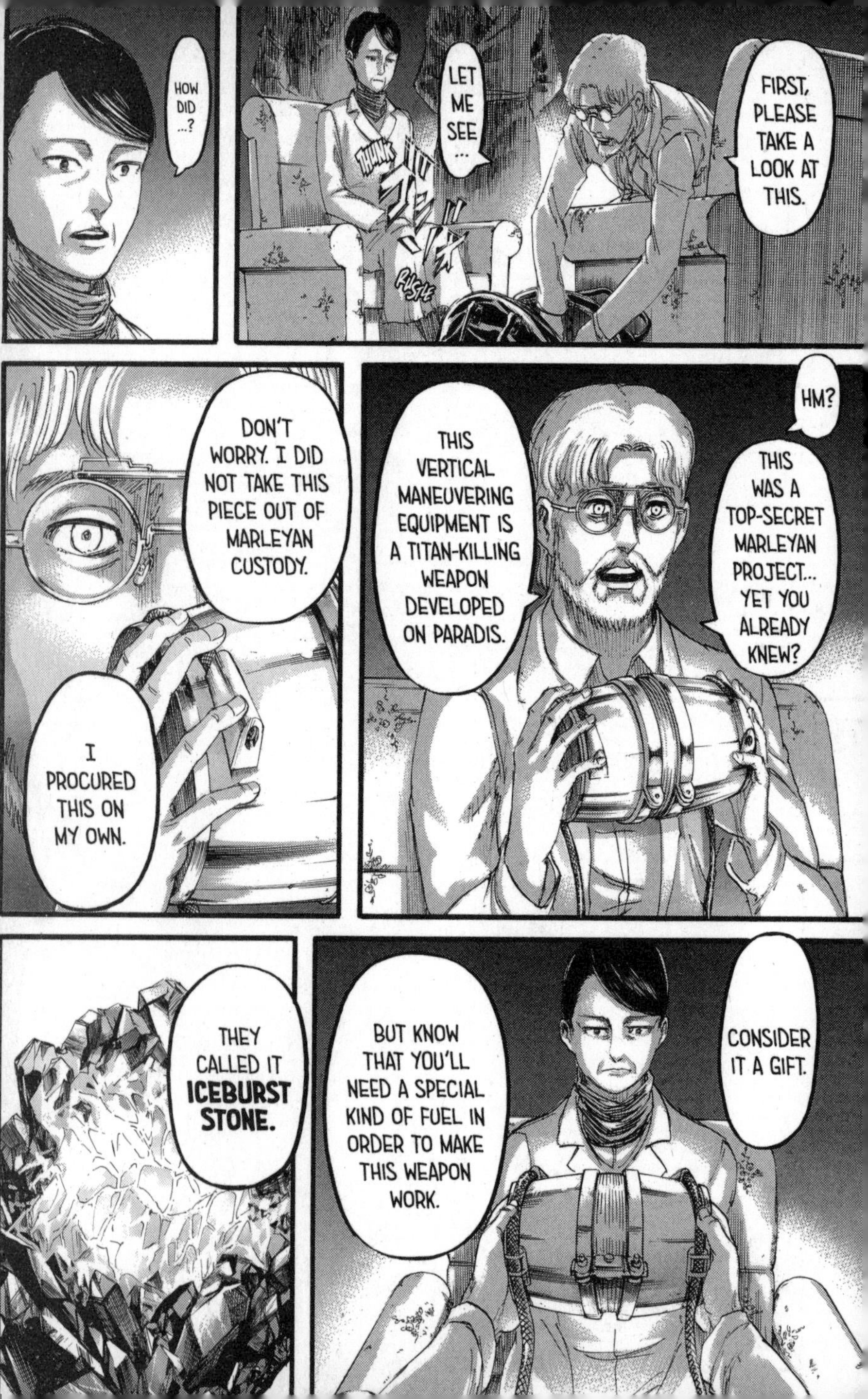

FIRST, PLEASE TAKE A LOOK AT THIS.
LET ME SEE...
THUNK
RUSTLE
HOW DID ...?
HM?
THIS WAS A TOP-SECRET MARLEYAN PROJECT... YET YOU ALREADY KNEW?
THIS VERTICAL MANEUVERING EQUIPMENT IS A TITAN-KILLING WEAPON DEVELOPED ON PARADIS.
DON'T WORRY. I DID NOT TAKE THIS PIECE OUT OF MARLEYAN CUSTODY.
I PROCURED THIS ON MY OWN.
CONSIDER IT A GIFT.
BUT KNOW THAT YOU'LL NEED A SPECIAL KIND OF FUEL IN ORDER TO MAKE THIS WEAPON WORK.
THEY CALLED IT **ICEBURST STONE.**

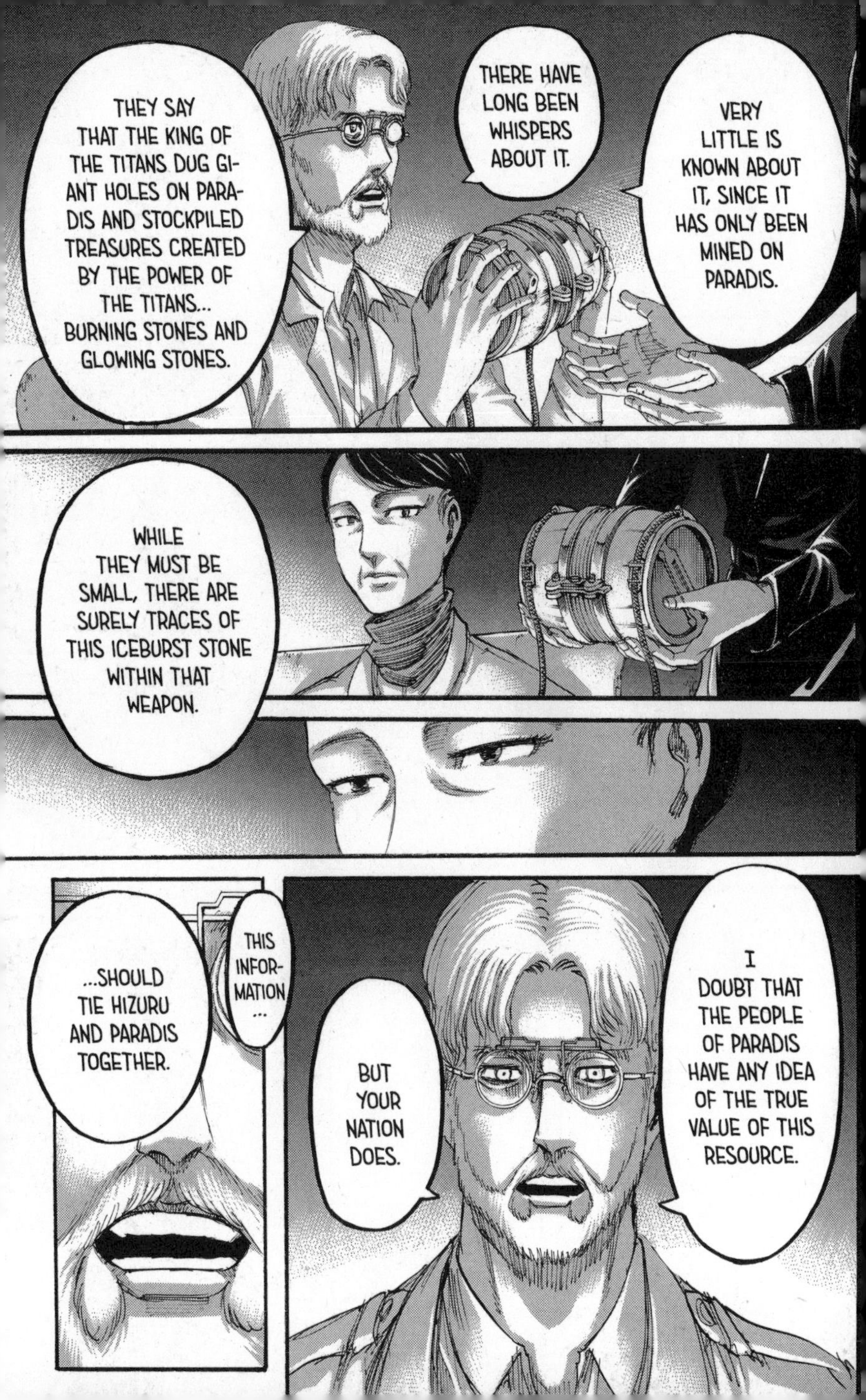
VERY LITTLE IS KNOWN ABOUT IT, SINCE IT HAS ONLY BEEN MINED ON PARADIS.
THERE HAVE LONG BEEN WHISPERS ABOUT IT.
THEY SAY THAT THE KING OF THE TITANS DUG GIANT HOLES ON PARADIS AND STOCKPILED TREASURES CREATED BY THE POWER OF THE TITANS... BURNING STONES AND GLOWING STONES.
WHILE THEY MUST BE SMALL, THERE ARE SURELY TRACES OF THIS ICEBURST STONE WITHIN THAT WEAPON.
I DOUBT THAT THE PEOPLE OF PARADIS HAVE ANY IDEA OF THE TRUE VALUE OF THIS RESOURCE.
BUT YOUR NATION DOES.
THIS INFORMATION...
...SHOULD TIE HIZURU AND PARADIS TOGETHER.

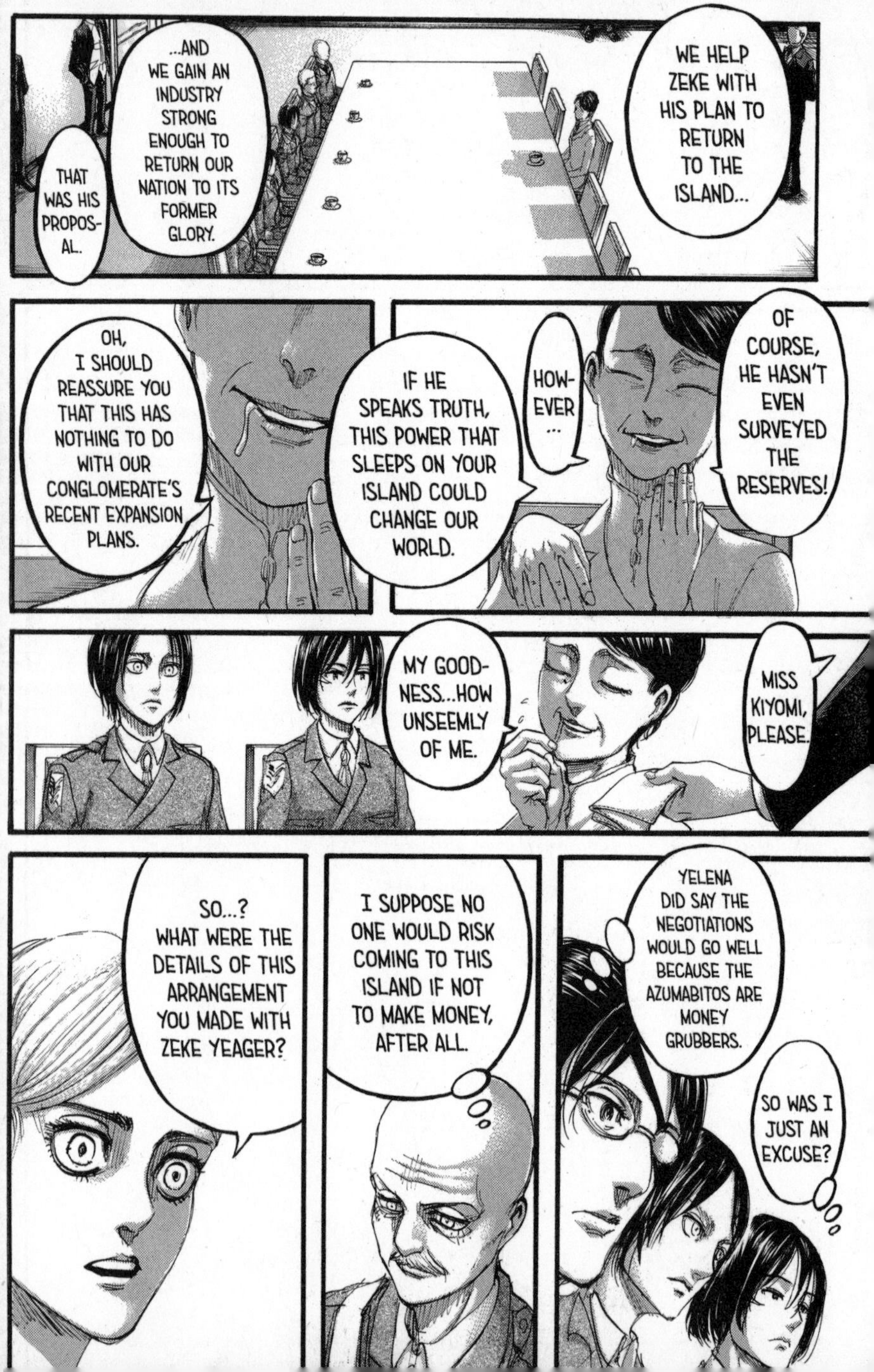
WE HELP ZEKE WITH HIS PLAN TO RETURN TO THE ISLAND...
...AND WE GAIN AN INDUSTRY STRONG ENOUGH TO RETURN OUR NATION TO ITS FORMER GLORY.
THAT WAS HIS PROPOSAL.
OF COURSE, HE HASN'T EVEN SURVEYED THE RESERVES!
HOWEVER...
IF HE SPEAKS TRUTH, THIS POWER THAT SLEEPS ON YOUR ISLAND COULD CHANGE OUR WORLD.
OH, I SHOULD REASSURE YOU THAT THIS HAS NOTHING TO DO WITH OUR CONGLOMERATE'S RECENT EXPANSION PLANS.
MISS KIYOMI, PLEASE.
MY GOODNESS...HOW UNSEEMLY OF ME.
YELENA DID SAY THE NEGOTIATIONS WOULD GO WELL BECAUSE THE AZUMABITOS ARE MONEY GRUBBERS.
SO WAS I JUST AN EXCUSE?
I SUPPOSE NO ONE WOULD RISK COMING TO THIS ISLAND IF NOT TO MAKE MONEY, AFTER ALL.
SO...? WHAT WERE THE DETAILS OF THIS ARRANGEMENT YOU MADE WITH ZEKE YEAGER?

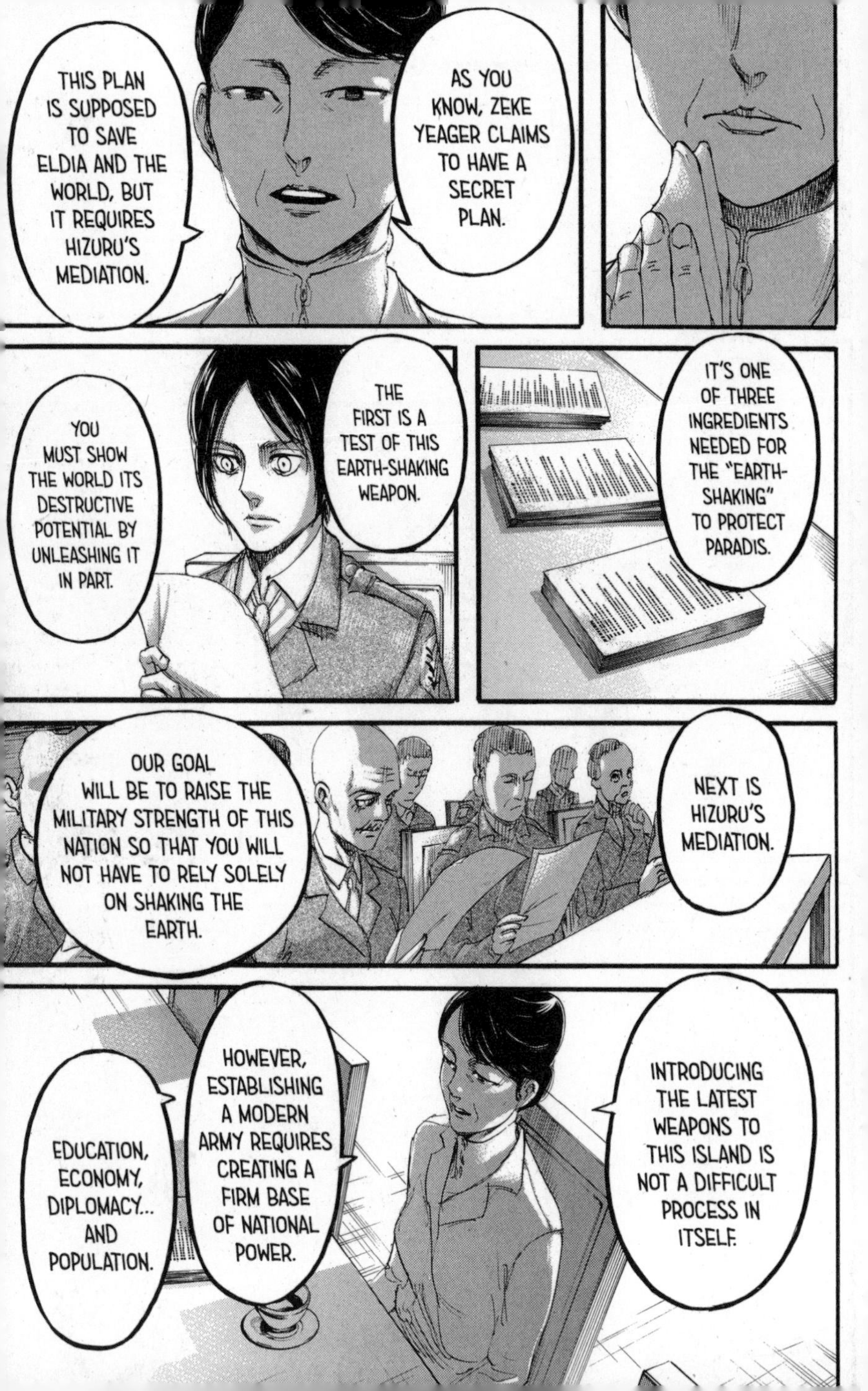
AS YOU KNOW, ZEKE YEAGER CLAIMS TO HAVE A SECRET PLAN.
THIS PLAN IS SUPPOSED TO SAVE ELDIA AND THE WORLD, BUT IT REQUIRES HIZURU'S MEDIATION.
IT'S ONE OF THREE INGREDIENTS NEEDED FOR THE "EARTH-SHAKING" TO PROTECT PARADIS.
THE FIRST IS A TEST OF THIS EARTH-SHAKING WEAPON.
YOU MUST SHOW THE WORLD ITS DESTRUCTIVE POTENTIAL BY UNLEASHING IT IN PART.
NEXT IS HIZURU'S MEDIATION.
OUR GOAL WILL BE TO RAISE THE MILITARY STRENGTH OF THIS NATION SO THAT YOU WILL NOT HAVE TO RELY SOLELY ON SHAKING THE EARTH.
INTRODUCING THE LATEST WEAPONS TO THIS ISLAND IS NOT A DIFFICULT PROCESS IN ITSELF.
HOWEVER, ESTABLISHING A MODERN ARMY REQUIRES CREATING A FIRM BASE OF NATIONAL POWER.
EDUCATION, ECONOMY, DIPLOMACY... AND POPULATION.

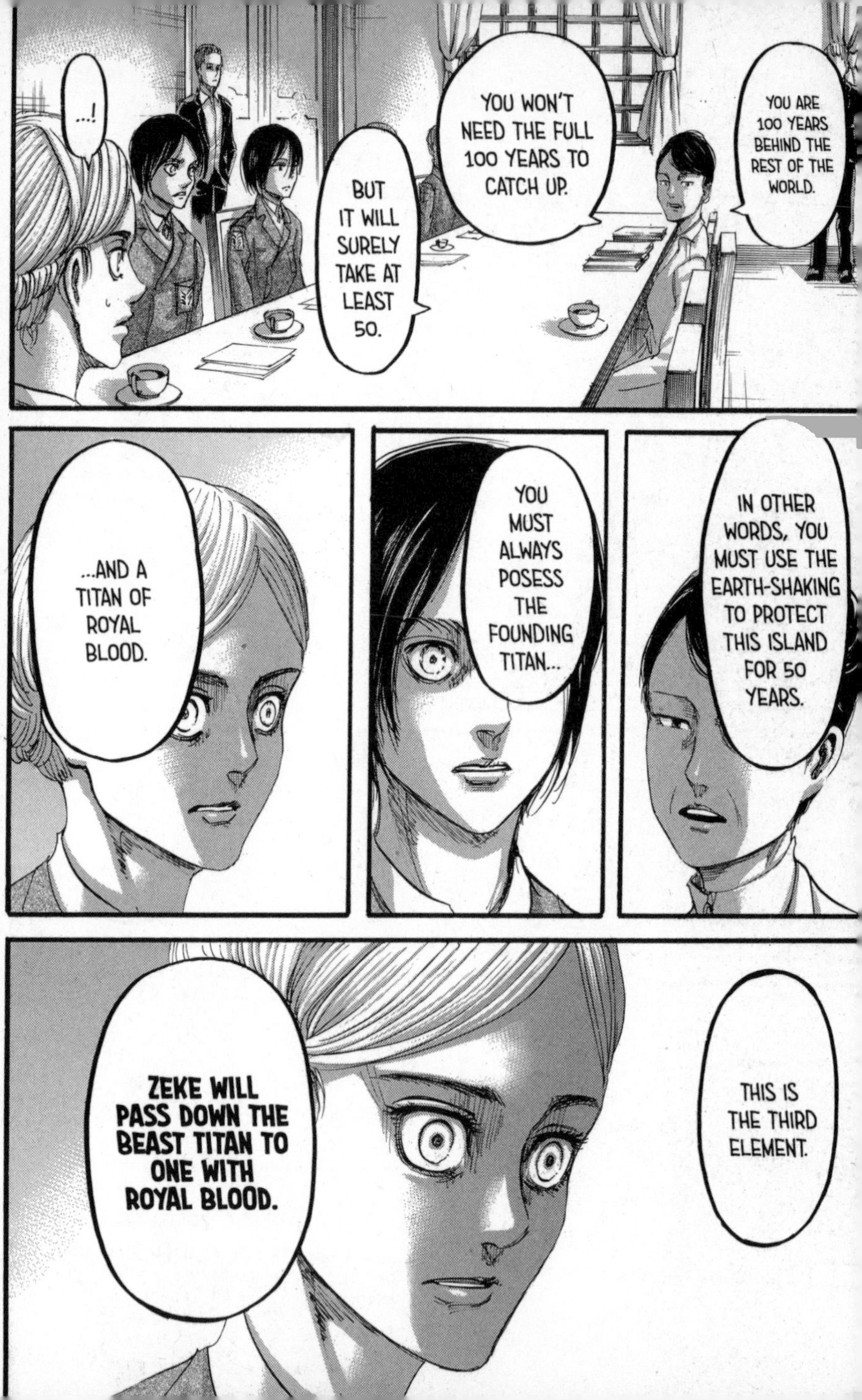
YOU ARE 100 YEARS BEHIND THE REST OF THE WORLD.
YOU WON'T NEED THE FULL 100 YEARS TO CATCH UP.
BUT IT WILL SURELY TAKE AT LEAST 50.
...!
IN OTHER WORDS, YOU MUST USE THE EARTH-SHAKING TO PROTECT THIS ISLAND FOR 50 YEARS.
YOU MUST ALWAYS POSESS THE FOUNDING TITAN...
...AND A TITAN OF ROYAL BLOOD.
THIS IS THE THIRD ELEMENT.
ZEKE WILL PASS DOWN THE BEAST TITAN TO ONE WITH ROYAL BLOOD.

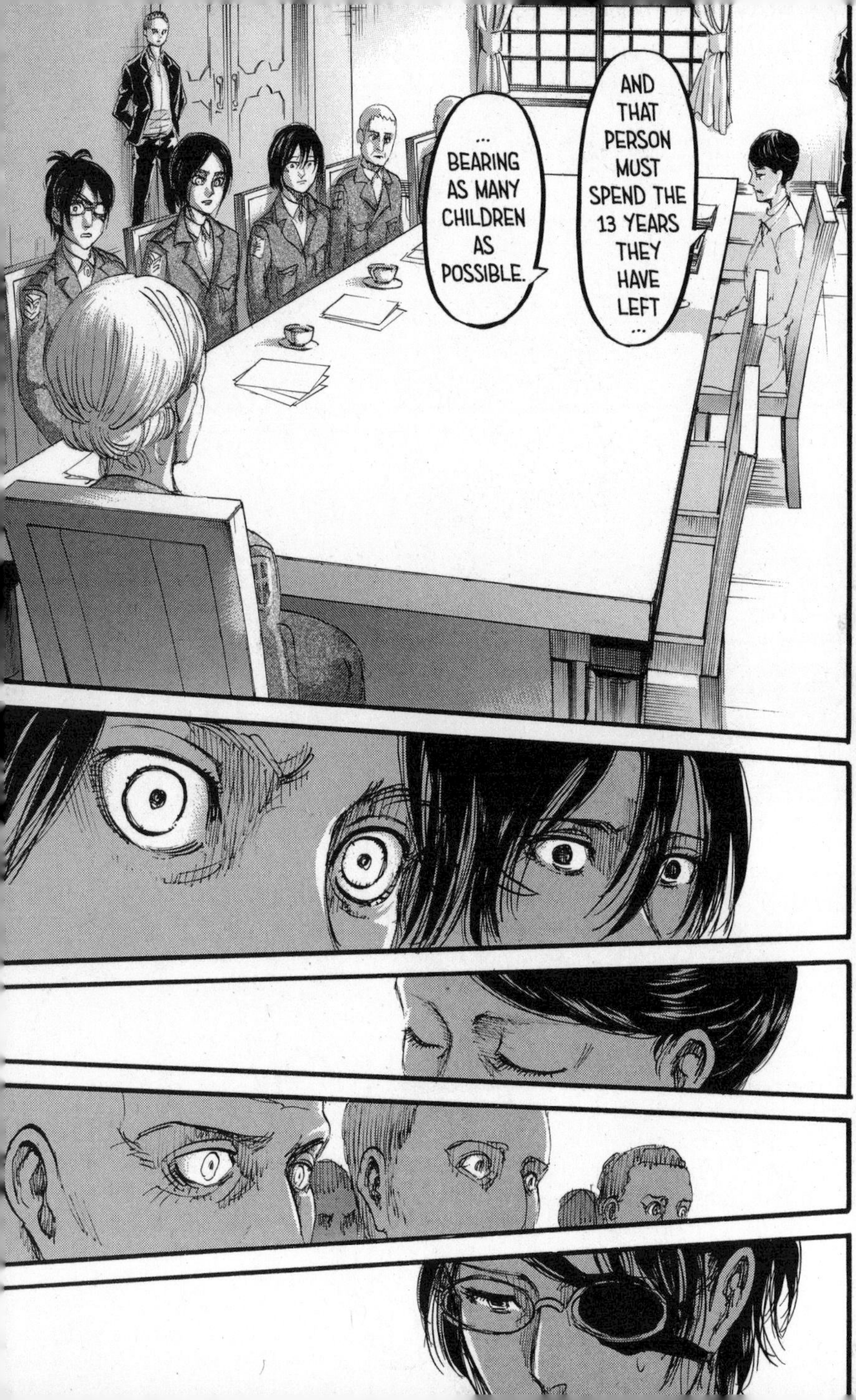
AND THAT PERSON MUST SPEND THE 13 YEARS THEY HAVE LEFT ...
... BEARING AS MANY CHILDREN AS POSSIBLE.

IF WE MUST DEPEND ON IT, THE DANGER OF ASSASSINATION WOULD FOLLOW THESE HEIRS TO THE ROYAL FAMILY DOWN THROUGH THE GENERATIONS...

NO MATTER WHAT ELSE MIGHT BE DEVELOPED, THE EARTH-SHAKING IS AN IMMENSELY POWERFUL WEAPON...

WILL IT REALLY END IN 50 YEARS...?

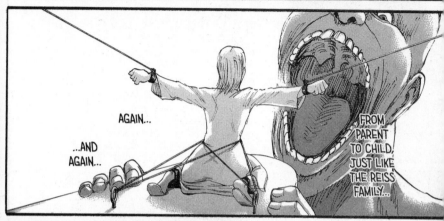

AGAIN...

...AND AGAIN...

FROM PARENT TO CHILD, JUST LIKE THE REISS FAMILY...

JUST BECAUSE IT SAVES US NOW...

...DOES THAT MEAN WE SHOULD LEAVE OUR CHILDREN IN A LOSE-LOSE SITUATION?

THERE'S NO WAY THIS COULD BE ALLOWED...

OF COURSE NOT.

...AND YET.

VERY WELL.

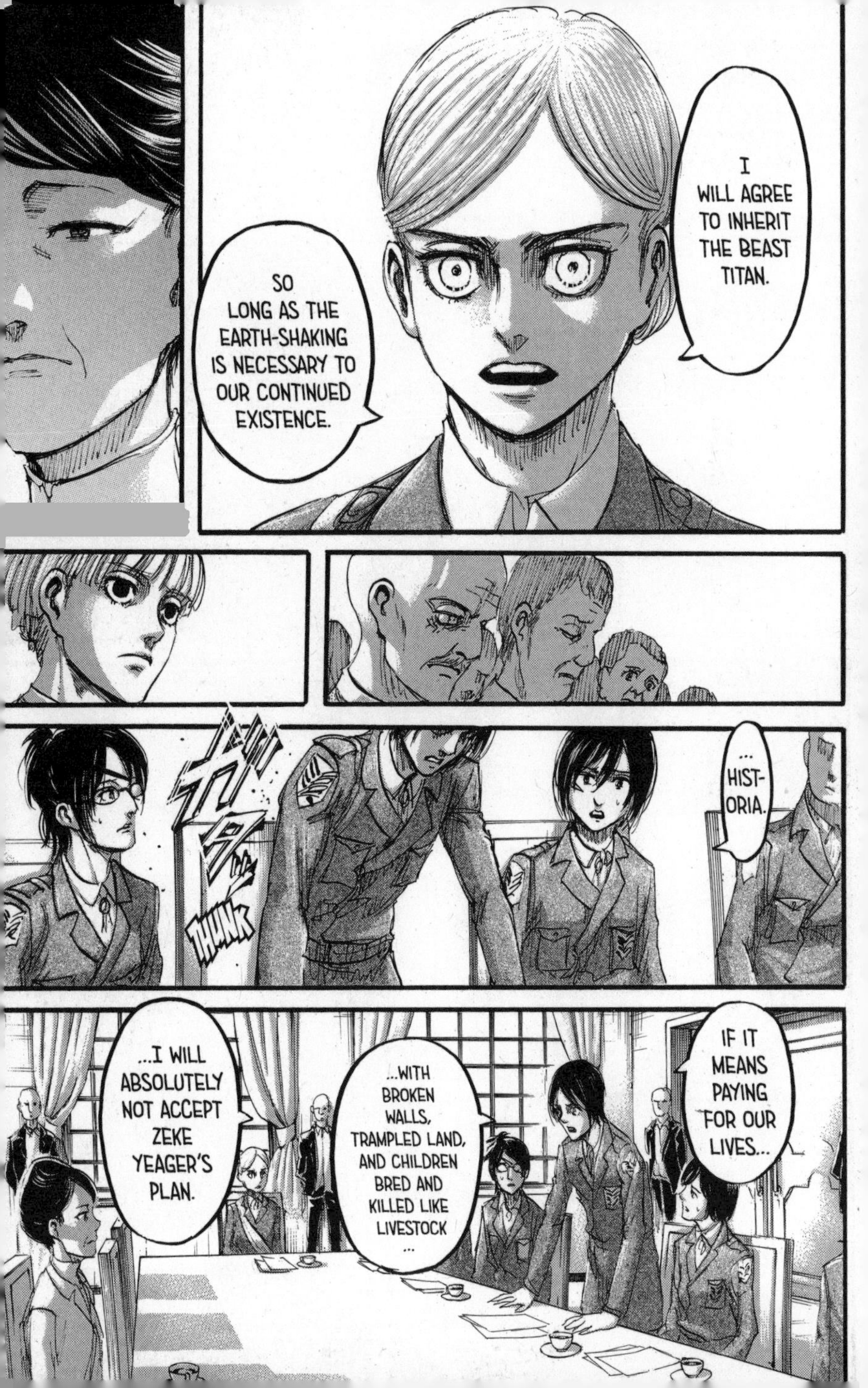
I WILL AGREE TO INHERIT THE BEAST TITAN.
SO LONG AS THE EARTH-SHAKING IS NECESSARY TO OUR CONTINUED EXISTENCE.
... HISTORIA.
THUNK
IF IT MEANS PAYING FOR OUR LIVES...
...WITH BROKEN WALLS, TRAMPLED LAND, AND CHILDREN BRED AND KILLED LIKE LIVESTOCK ...
...I WILL ABSOLUTELY NOT ACCEPT ZEKE YEAGER'S PLAN.

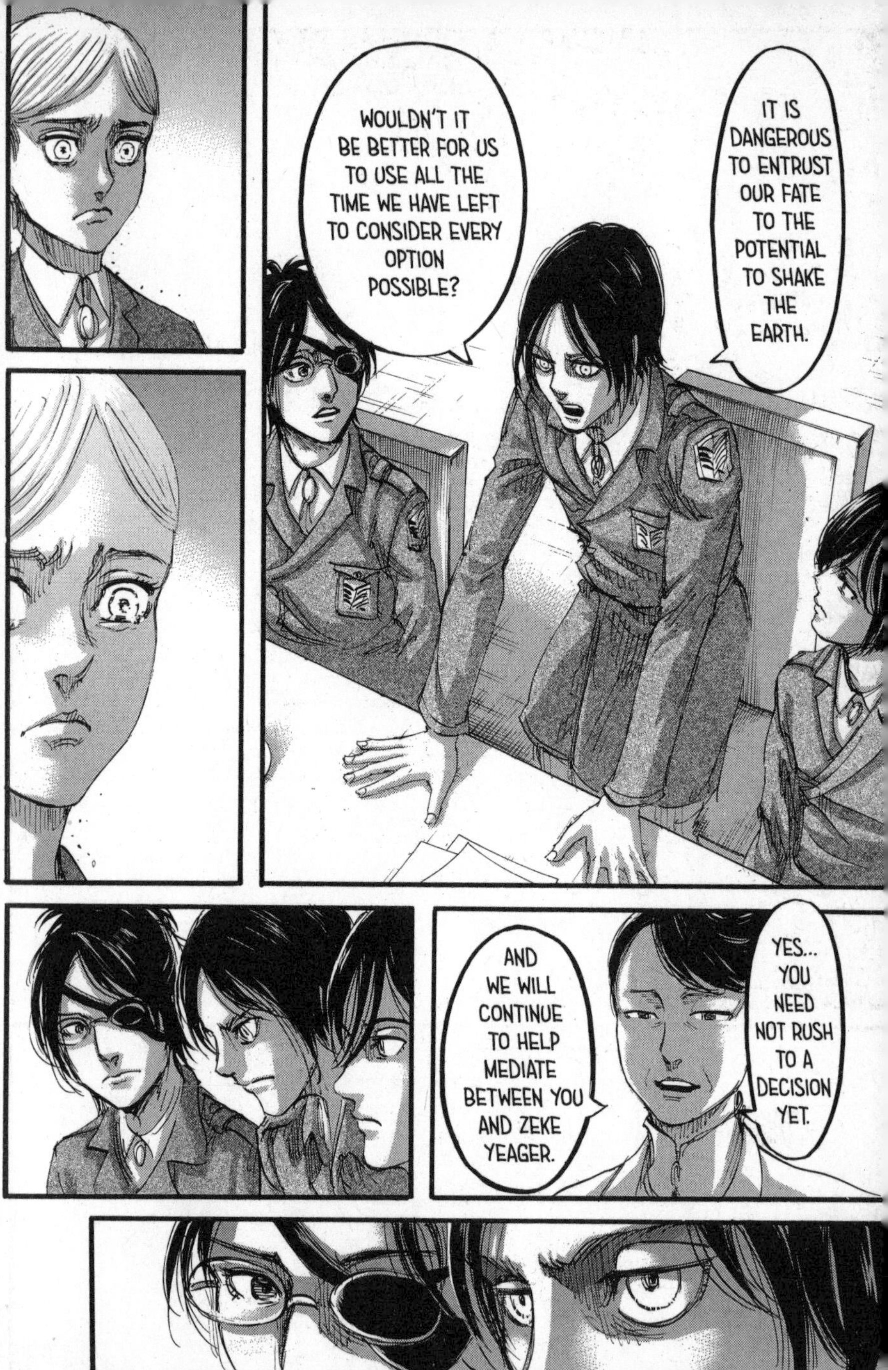
IT IS DANGEROUS TO ENTRUST OUR FATE TO THE POTENTIAL TO SHAKE THE EARTH.
WOULDN'T IT BE BETTER FOR US TO USE ALL THE TIME WE HAVE LEFT TO CONSIDER EVERY OPTION POSSIBLE?
YES... YOU NEED NOT RUSH TO A DECISION YET.
AND WE WILL CONTINUE TO HELP MEDIATE BETWEEN YOU AND ZEKE YEAGER.

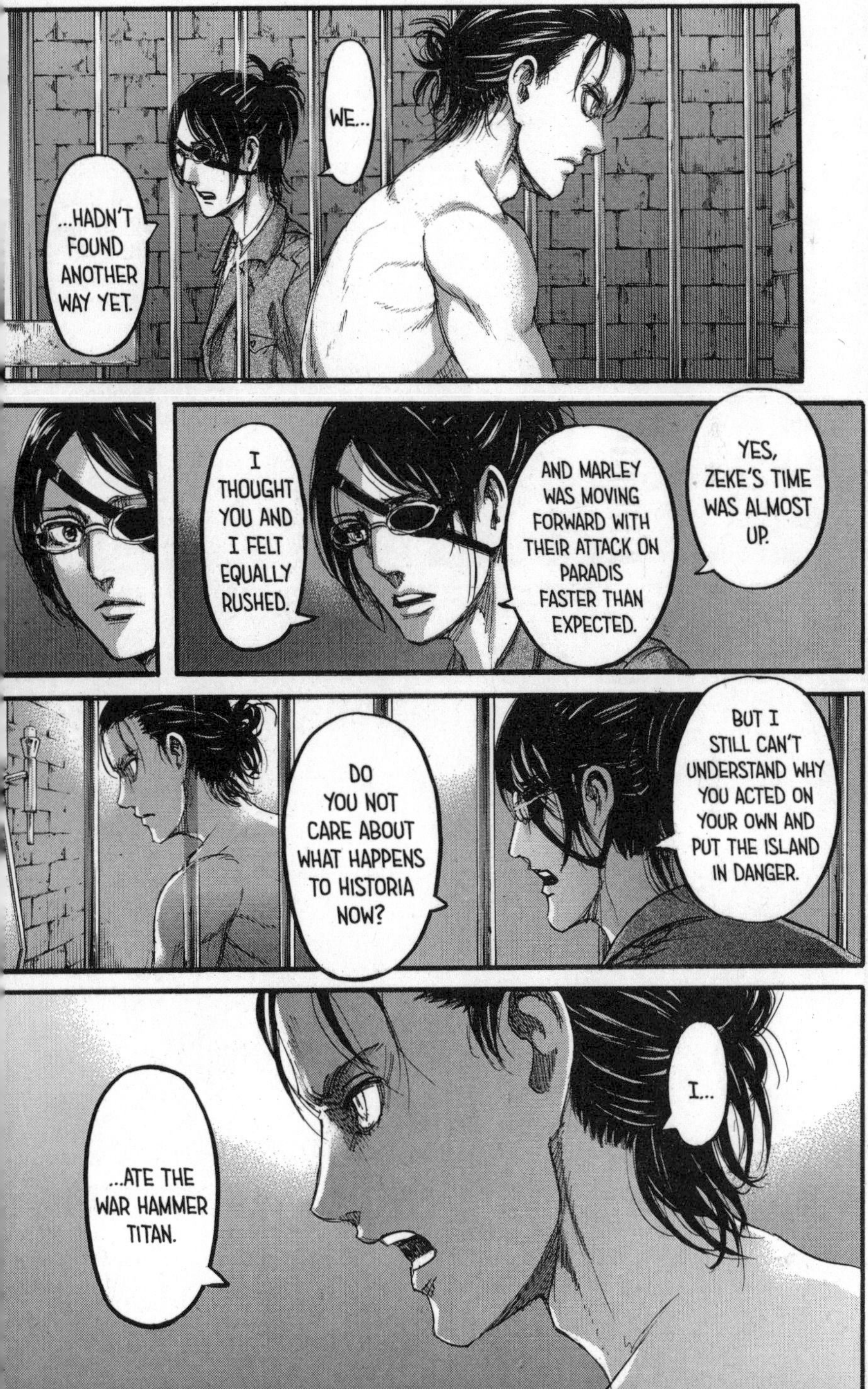
WE...
...HADN'T FOUND ANOTHER WAY YET.
YES, ZEKE'S TIME WAS ALMOST UP.
AND MARLEY WAS MOVING FORWARD WITH THEIR ATTACK ON PARADIS FASTER THAN EXPECTED.
I THOUGHT YOU AND I FELT EQUALLY RUSHED.
BUT I STILL CAN'T UNDERSTAND WHY YOU ACTED ON YOUR OWN AND PUT THE ISLAND IN DANGER.
DO YOU NOT CARE ABOUT WHAT HAPPENS TO HISTORIA NOW?
I...
...ATE THE WAR HAMMER TITAN.

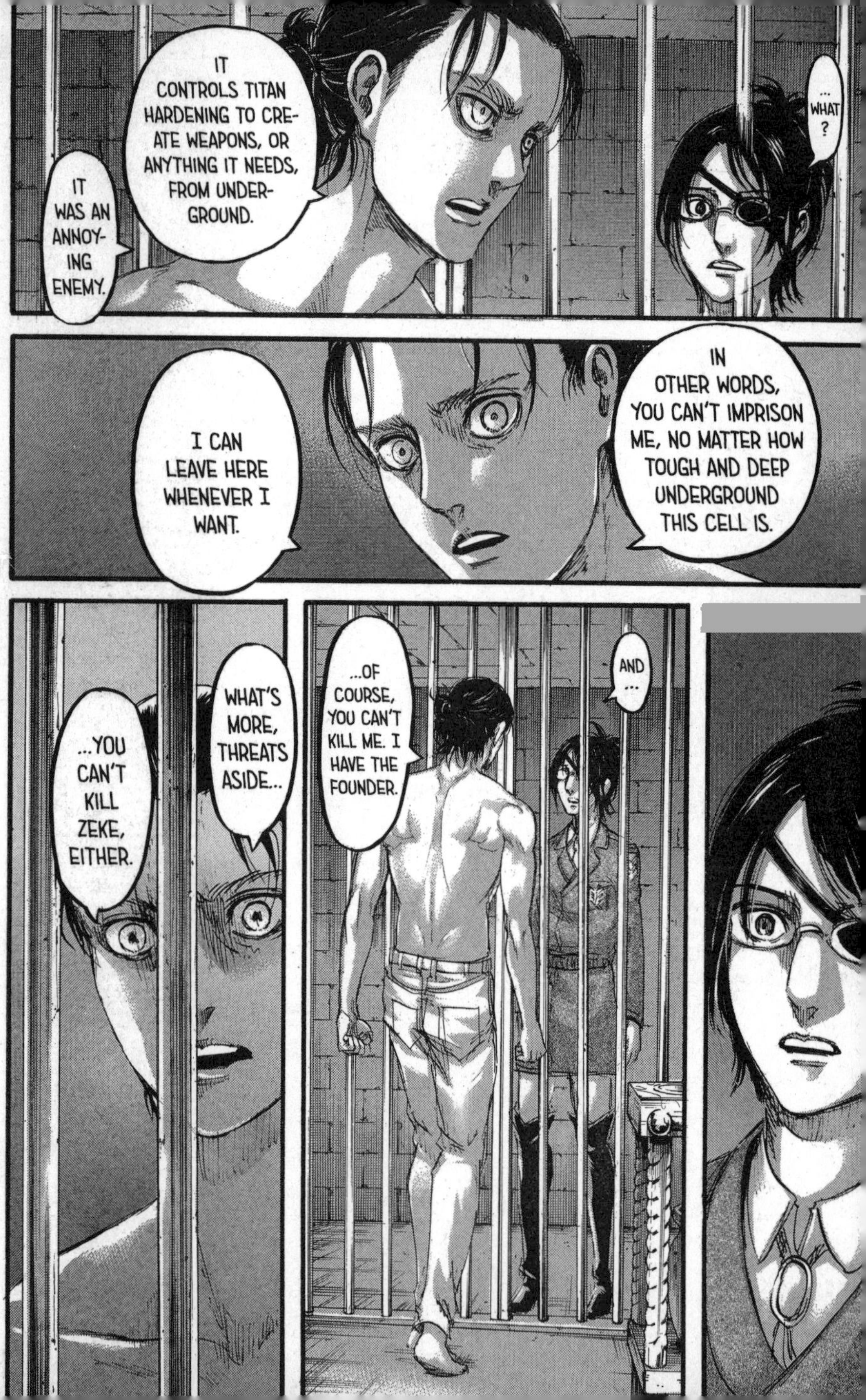
...WHAT?
IT CONTROLS TITAN HARDENING TO CREATE WEAPONS, OR ANYTHING IT NEEDS, FROM UNDERGROUND.
IT WAS AN ANNOYING ENEMY.
IN OTHER WORDS, YOU CAN'T IMPRISON ME, NO MATTER HOW TOUGH AND DEEP UNDERGROUND THIS CELL IS.
I CAN LEAVE HERE WHENEVER I WANT.
AND ...
...OF COURSE, YOU CAN'T KILL ME. I HAVE THE FOUNDER.
WHAT'S MORE, THREATS ASIDE...
...YOU CAN'T KILL ZEKE, EITHER.

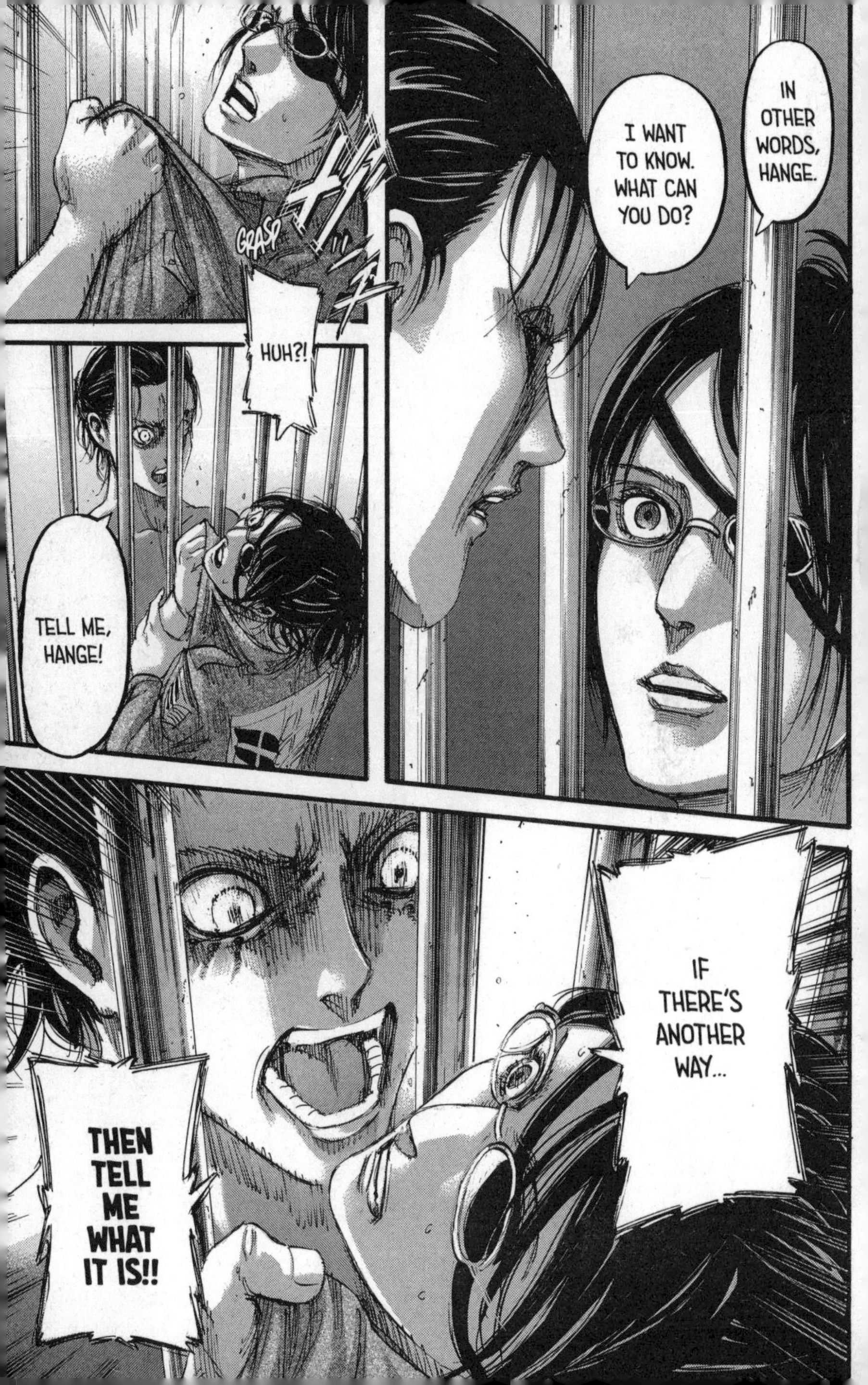
IN OTHER WORDS, HANGE.
I WANT TO KNOW. WHAT CAN YOU DO?
GRASP
HUH?!
TELL ME, HANGE!
IF THERE'S ANOTHER WAY...
THEN TELL ME WHAT IT IS!!

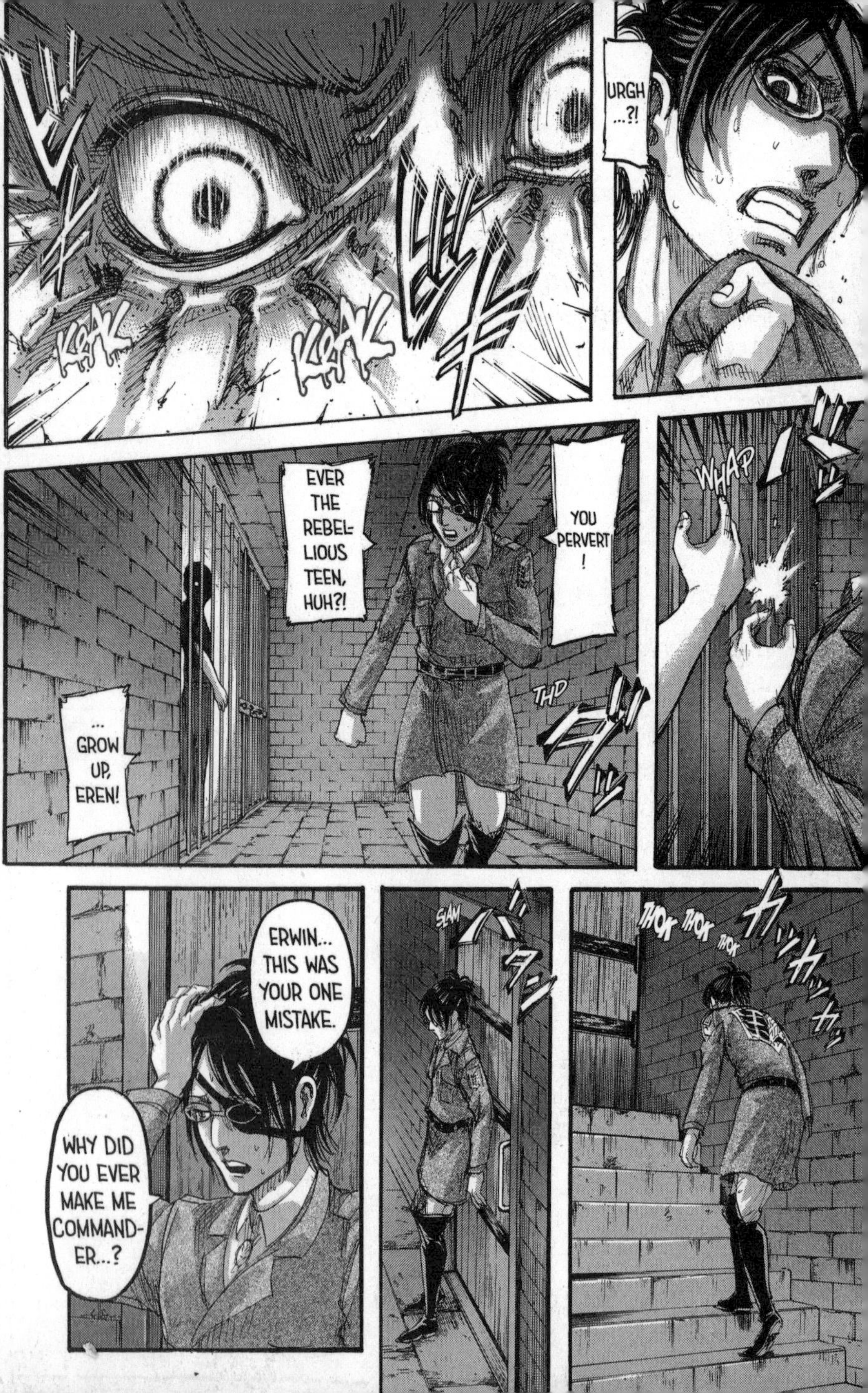
URGH ...?!
KRAK
KRAK
WHAP
YOU PERVERT!
EVER THE REBELLIOUS TEEN, HUH?!
THD
... GROW UP, EREN!
THOK THOK THOK
SLAM
ERWIN... THIS WAS YOUR ONE MISTAKE.
WHY DID YOU EVER MAKE ME COMMANDER...?

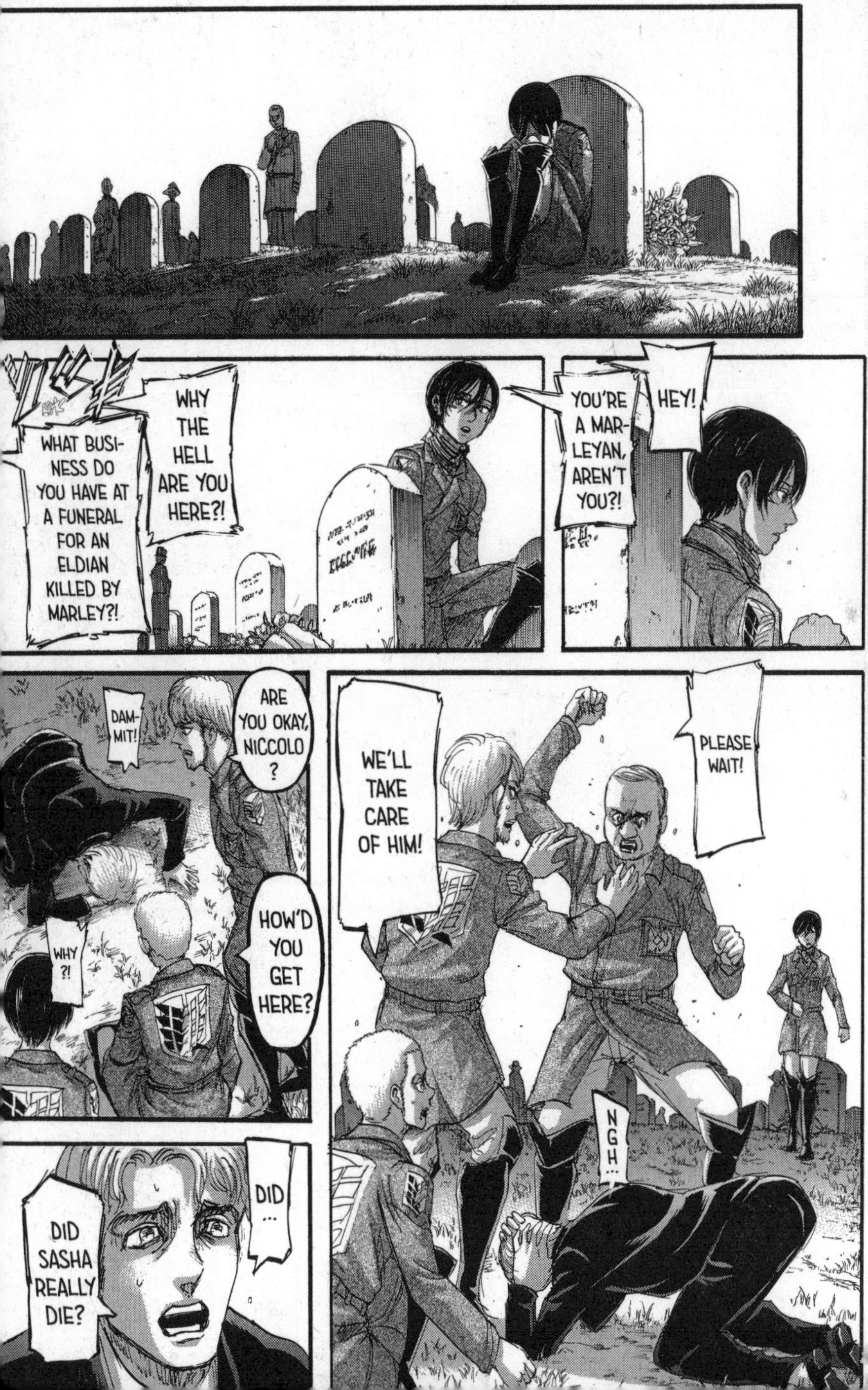
HEY!
YOU'RE A MAR-LEYAN, AREN'T YOU?!
WHY THE HELL ARE YOU HERE?!
WHAT BUSI-NESS DO YOU HAVE AT A FUNERAL FOR AN ELDIAN KILLED BY MARLEY?!
PLEASE WAIT!
WE'LL TAKE CARE OF HIM!
NGH...
ARE YOU OKAY, NICCOLO?
DAM-MIT!
HOW'D YOU GET HERE?
WHY?!
DID...
DID SASHA REALLY DIE?

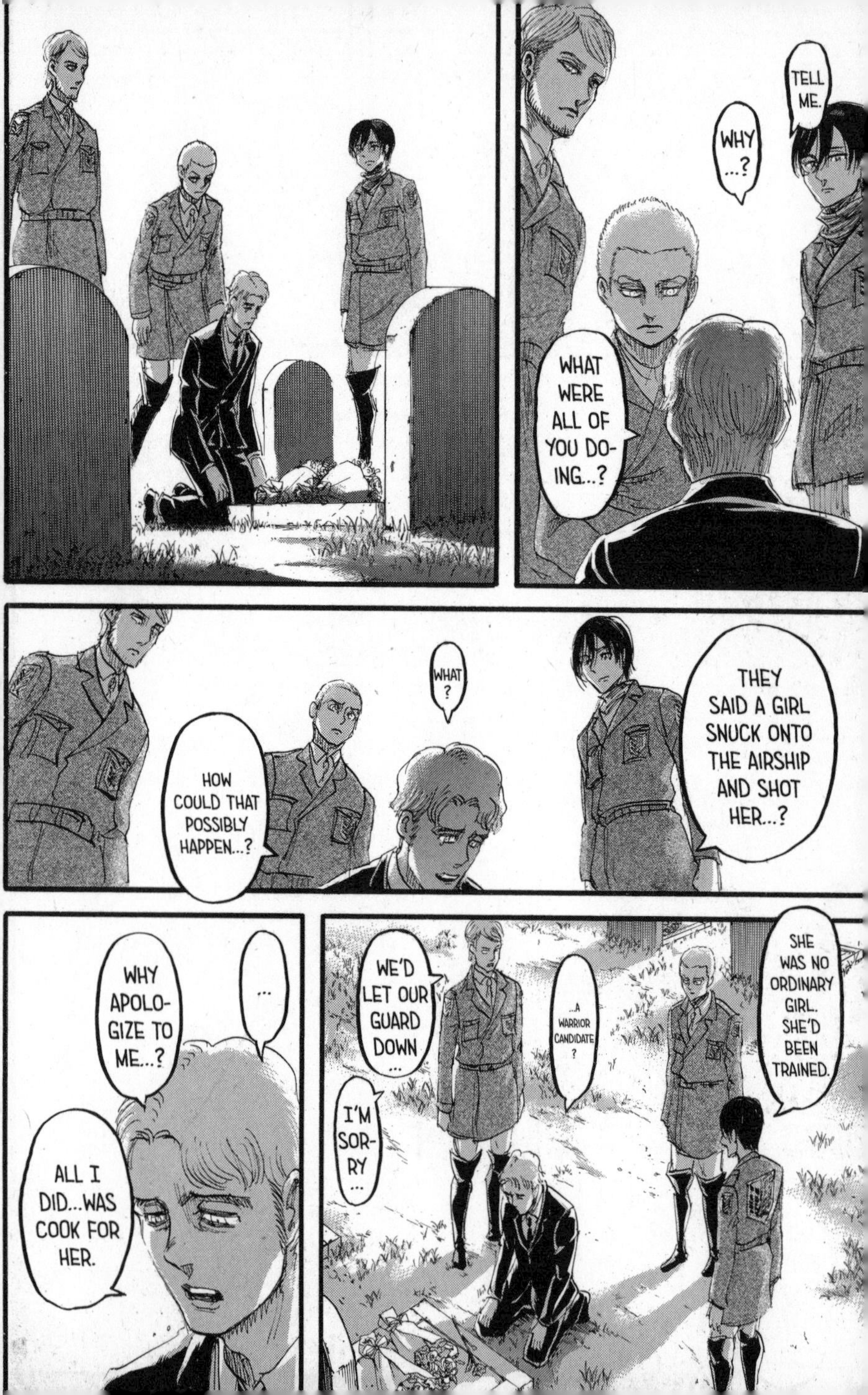
TELL ME.
WHY...?
WHAT WERE ALL OF YOU DOING...?
THEY SAID A GIRL SNUCK ONTO THE AIRSHIP AND SHOT HER...?
WHAT?
HOW COULD THAT POSSIBLY HAPPEN...?
SHE WAS NO ORDINARY GIRL. SHE'D BEEN TRAINED.
...A WARRIOR CANDIDATE?
WE'D LET OUR GUARD DOWN...
I'M SORRY...
...
WHY APOLOGIZE TO ME...?
ALL I DID...WAS COOK FOR HER.

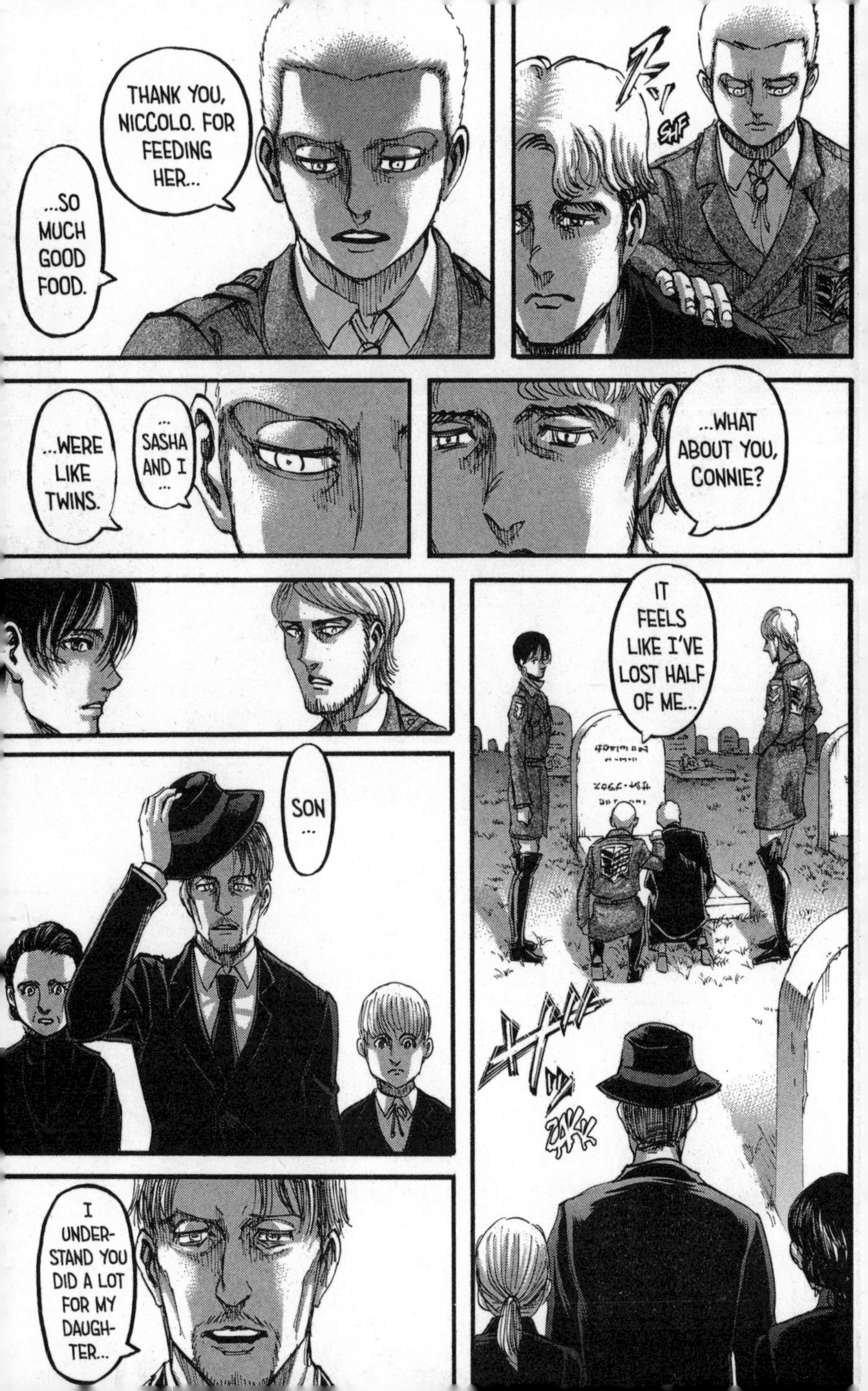
SHF
THANK YOU, NICCOLO. FOR FEEDING HER...
...SO MUCH GOOD FOOD.
...WHAT ABOUT YOU, CONNIE?
...SASHA AND I...
...WERE LIKE TWINS.
IT FEELS LIKE I'VE LOST HALF OF ME...
ZAK
SON...
I UNDER-STAND YOU DID A LOT FOR MY DAUGH-TER...

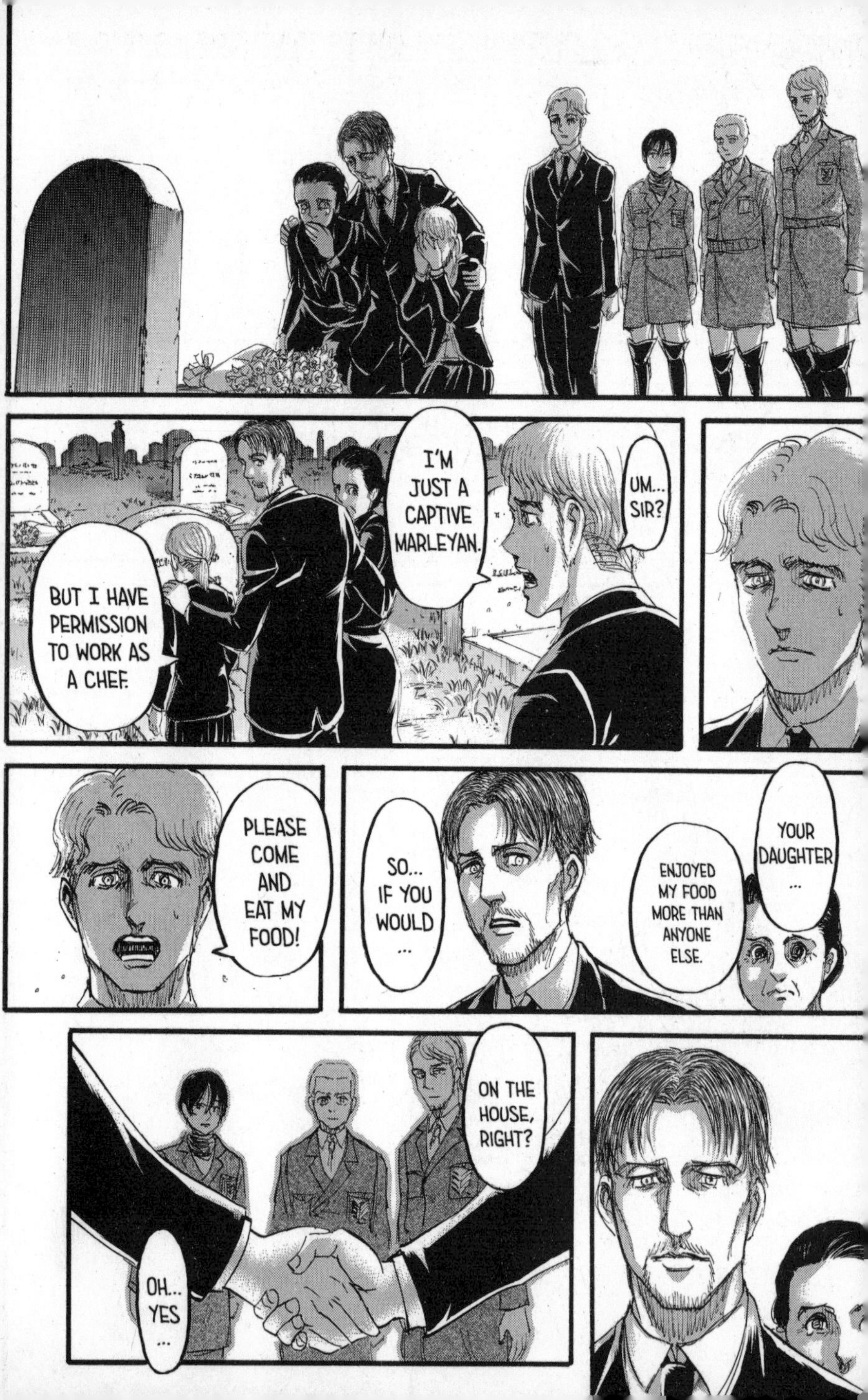
UM... SIR?
I'M JUST A CAPTIVE MARLEYAN.
BUT I HAVE PERMISSION TO WORK AS A CHEF.
YOUR DAUGHTER...
ENJOYED MY FOOD MORE THAN ANYONE ELSE.
SO... IF YOU WOULD...
PLEASE COME AND EAT MY FOOD!
ON THE HOUSE, RIGHT?
OH... YES...

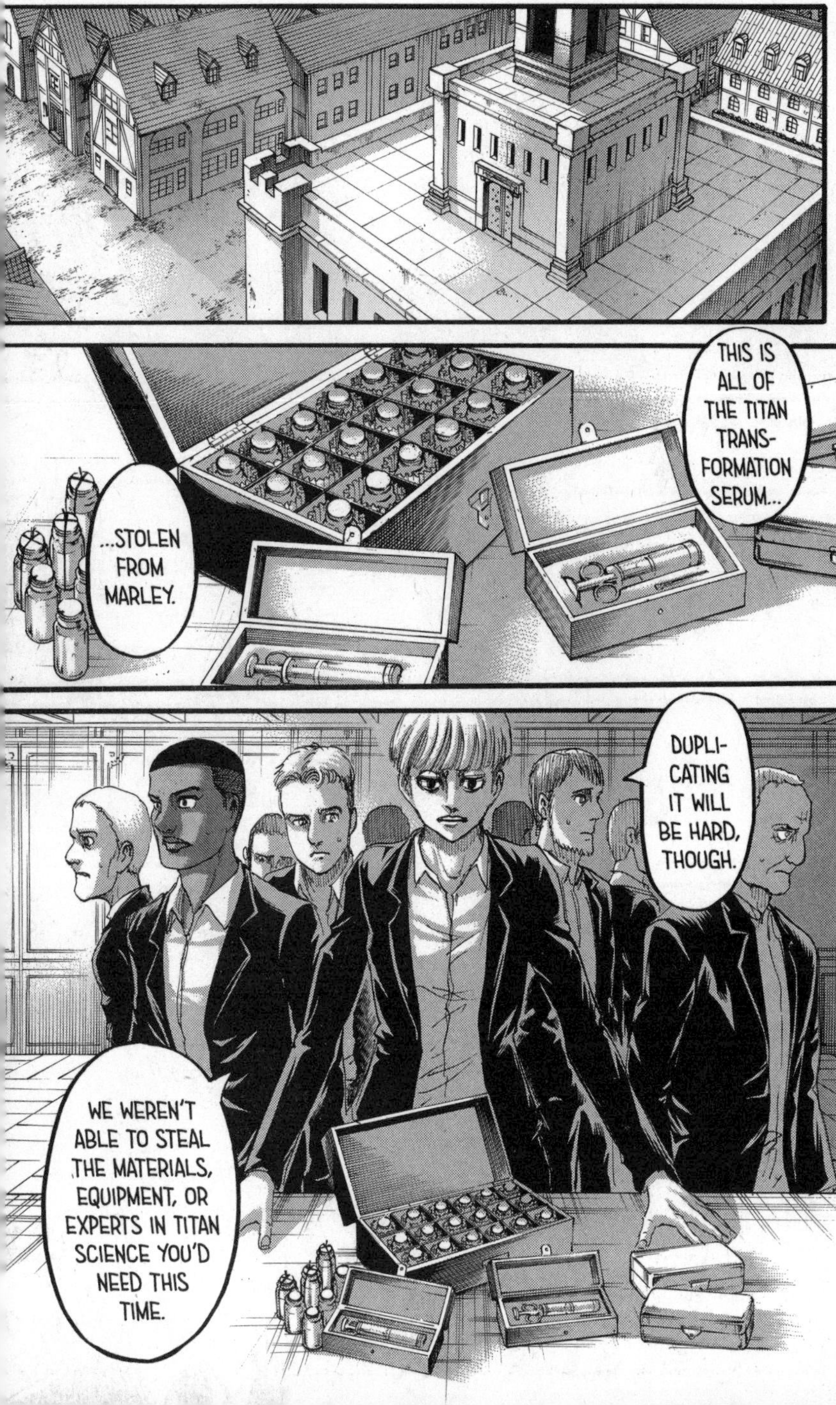
THIS IS ALL OF THE TITAN TRANS-FORMATION SERUM...
...STOLEN FROM MARLEY.
DUPLI-CATING IT WILL BE HARD, THOUGH.
WE WEREN'T ABLE TO STEAL THE MATERIALS, EQUIPMENT, OR EXPERTS IN TITAN SCIENCE YOU'D NEED THIS TIME.

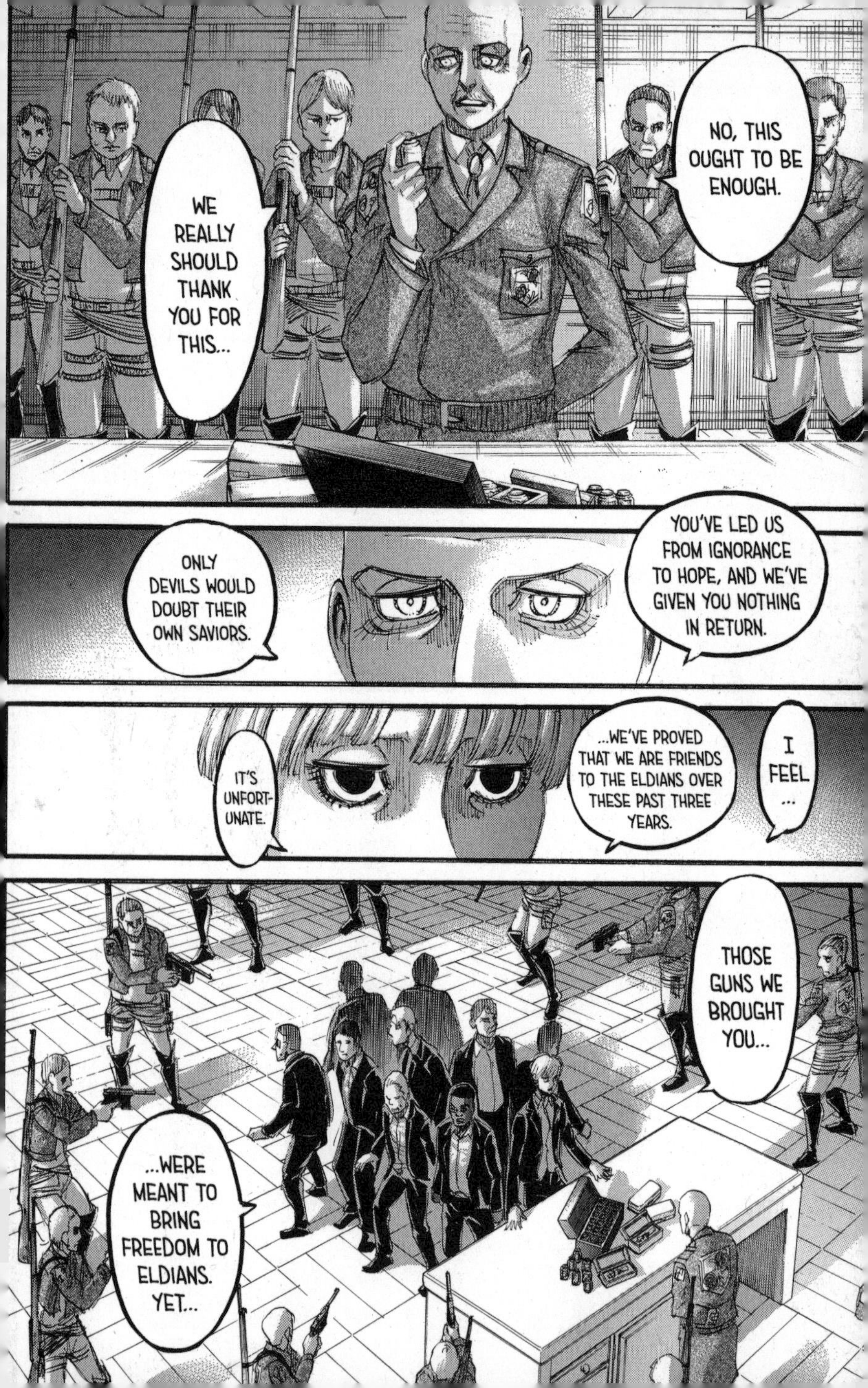

NO, THIS OUGHT TO BE ENOUGH.
WE REALLY SHOULD THANK YOU FOR THIS...
YOU'VE LED US FROM IGNORANCE TO HOPE, AND WE'VE GIVEN YOU NOTHING IN RETURN.
ONLY DEVILS WOULD DOUBT THEIR OWN SAVIORS.
I FEEL...
...WE'VE PROVED THAT WE ARE FRIENDS TO THE ELDIANS OVER THESE PAST THREE YEARS.
IT'S UNFORT-UNATE.
THOSE GUNS WE BROUGHT YOU...
...WERE MEANT TO BRING FREEDOM TO ELDIANS. YET...

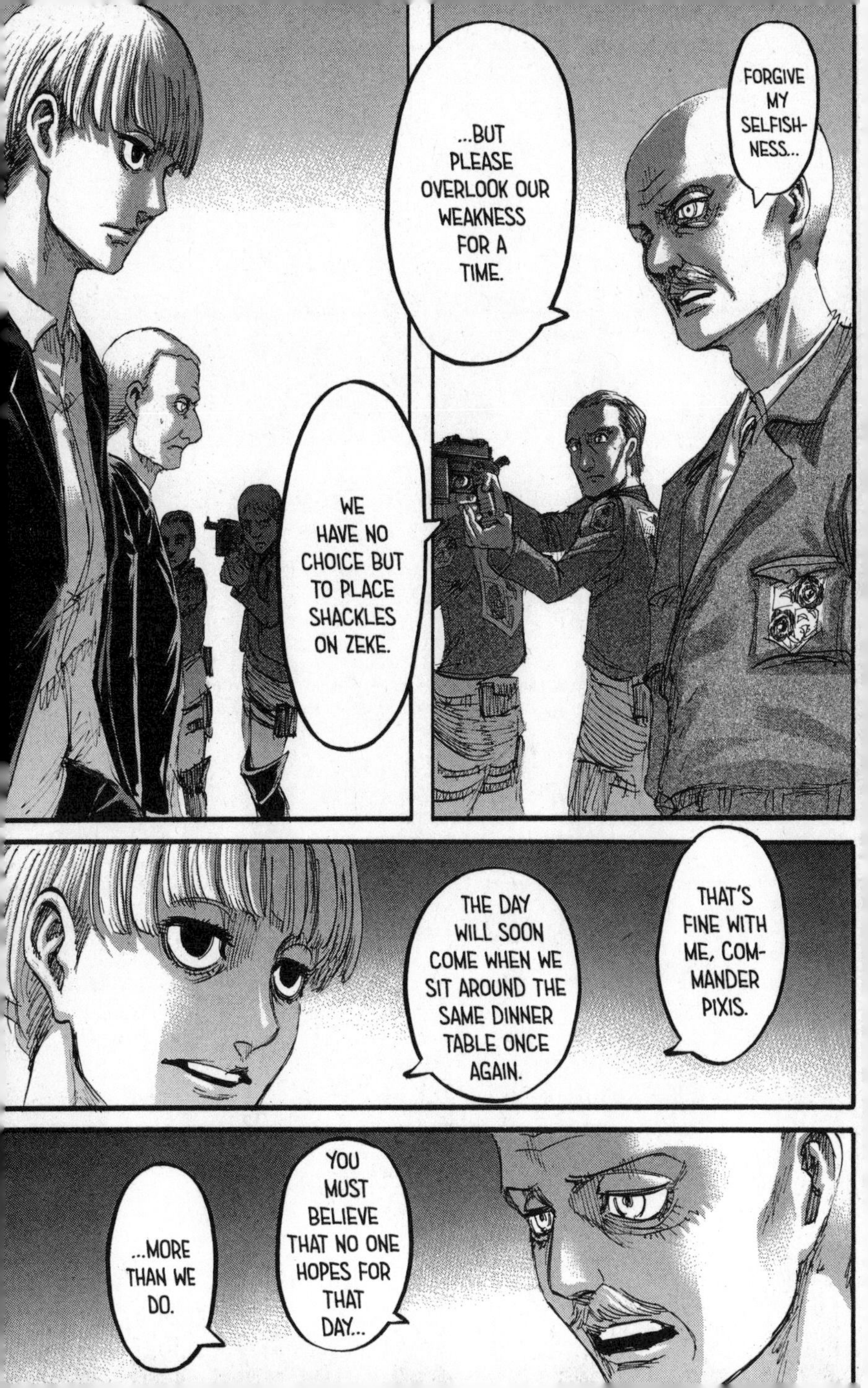
FORGIVE MY SELFISH-NESS...
...BUT PLEASE OVERLOOK OUR WEAKNESS FOR A TIME.
WE HAVE NO CHOICE BUT TO PLACE SHACKLES ON ZEKE.
THAT'S FINE WITH ME, COM-MANDER PIXIS.
THE DAY WILL SOON COME WHEN WE SIT AROUND THE SAME DINNER TABLE ONCE AGAIN.
YOU MUST BELIEVE THAT NO ONE HOPES FOR THAT DAY...
...MORE THAN WE DO.

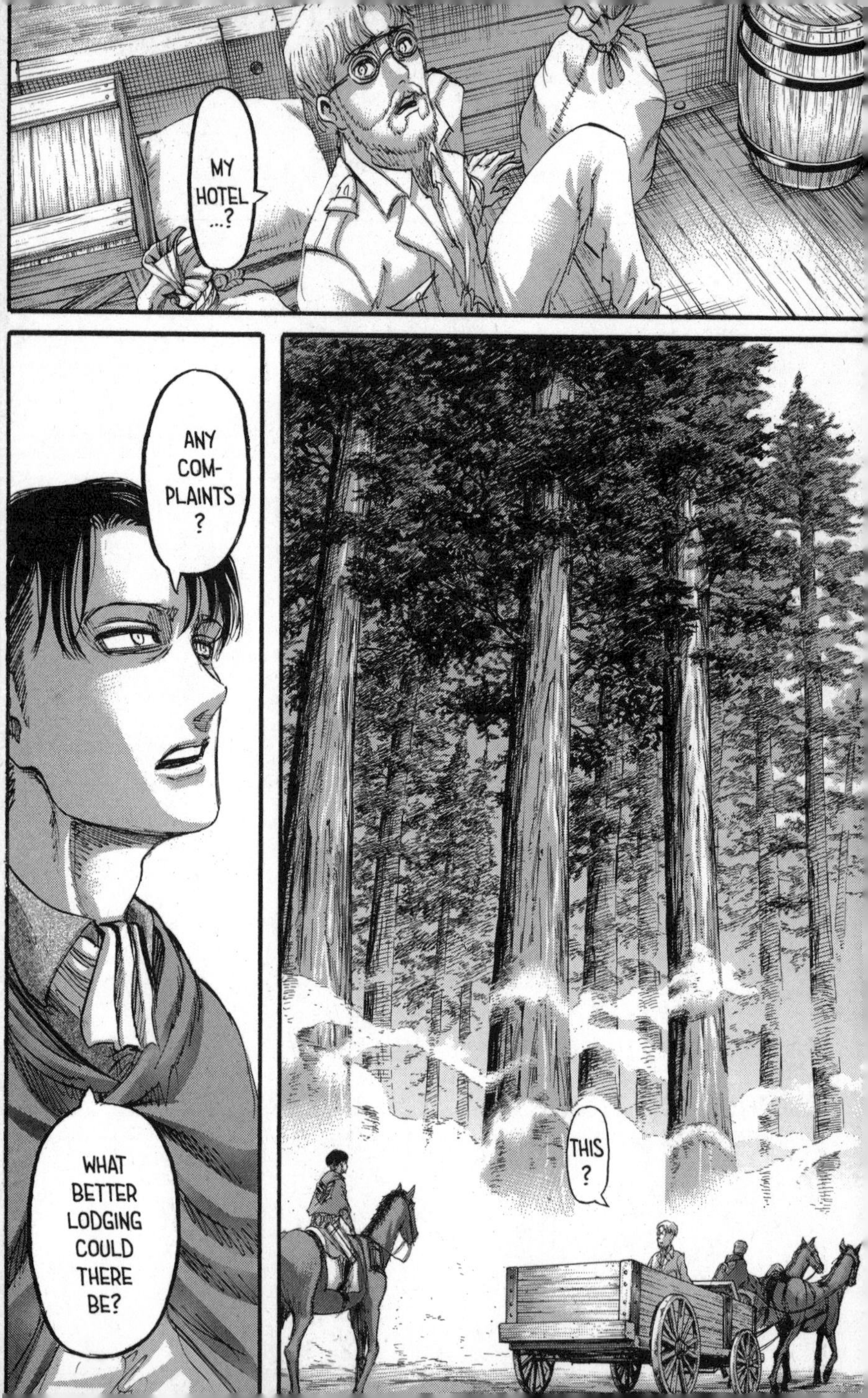
MY HOTEL ...?
THIS ?
ANY COM-PLAINTS ?
WHAT BETTER LODGING COULD THERE BE?

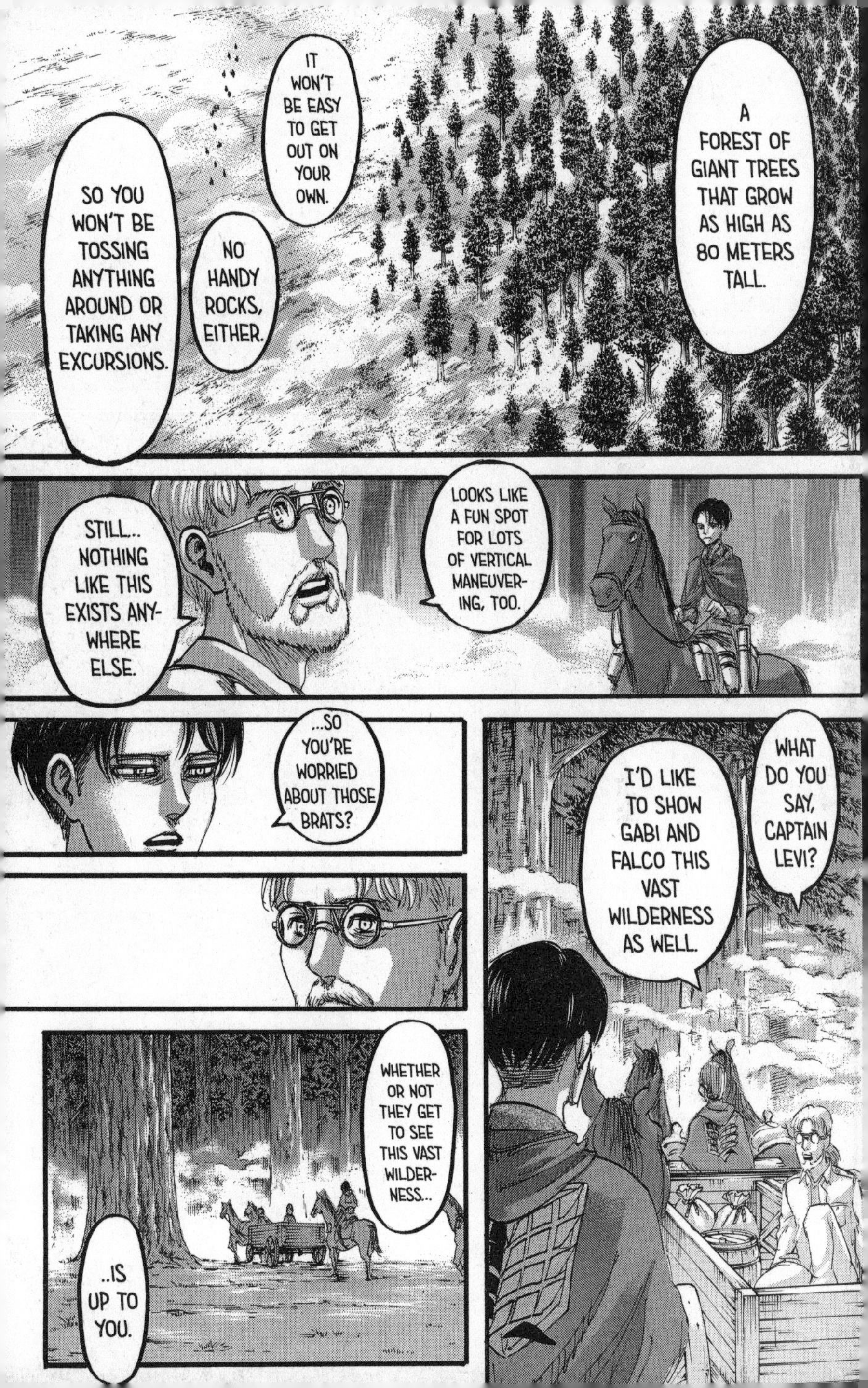
A FOREST OF GIANT TREES THAT GROW AS HIGH AS 80 METERS TALL.
IT WON'T BE EASY TO GET OUT ON YOUR OWN.
NO HANDY ROCKS, EITHER.
SO YOU WON'T BE TOSSING ANYTHING AROUND OR TAKING ANY EXCURSIONS.
LOOKS LIKE A FUN SPOT FOR LOTS OF VERTICAL MANEUVERING, TOO.
STILL... NOTHING LIKE THIS EXISTS ANYWHERE ELSE.
I'D LIKE TO SHOW GABI AND FALCO THIS VAST WILDERNESS AS WELL.
WHAT DO YOU SAY, CAPTAIN LEVI?
...SO YOU'RE WORRIED ABOUT THOSE BRATS?
WHETHER OR NOT THEY GET TO SEE THIS VAST WILDERNESS...
..IS UP TO YOU.

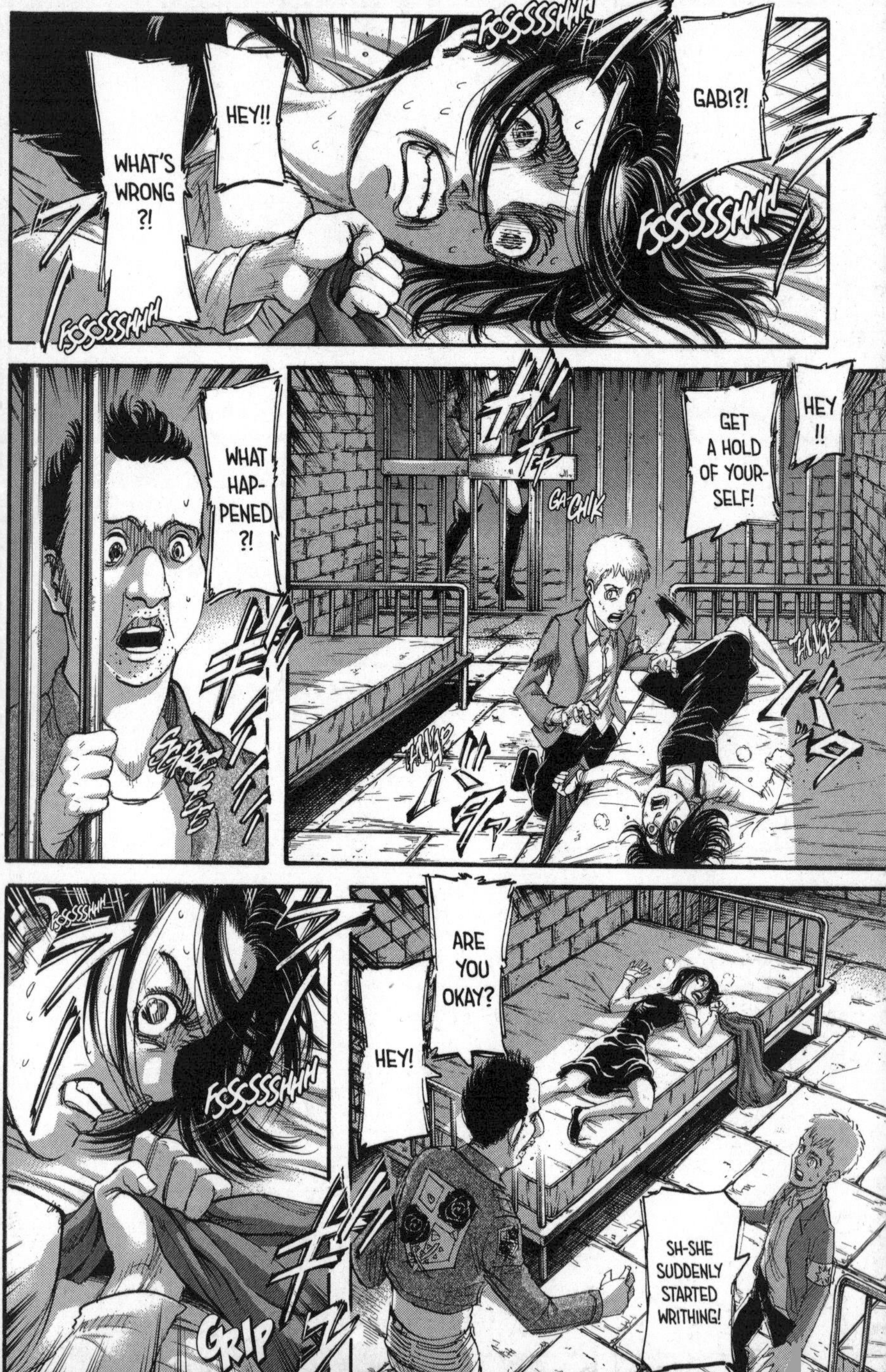
FSSSSSHHH
GABI?!
HEY!!
WHAT'S WRONG?!
FSSSSSHHH
FSSSSSHHH
HEY!!
GET A HOLD OF YOURSELF!
GA-CHIK
WHAT HAPPENED?!
SH-SHE SUDDENLY STARTED WRITHING!
ARE YOU OKAY?
HEY!
FSSSSSHHH
FSSSSSHHH
GRIP

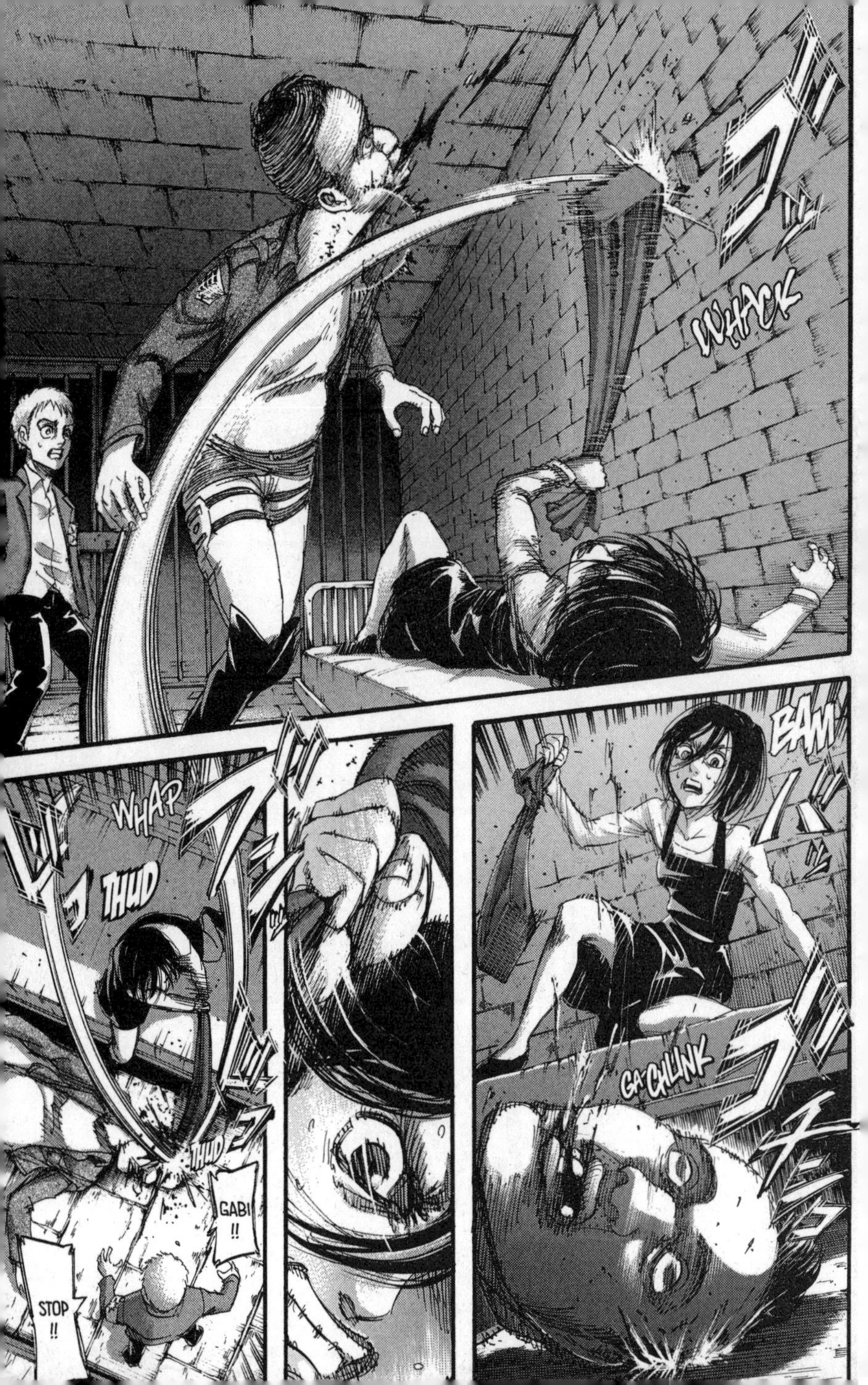
WHACK
BAM
GA-CHUNK
WHAP
THUD
THUD
GABI!!
STOP!!

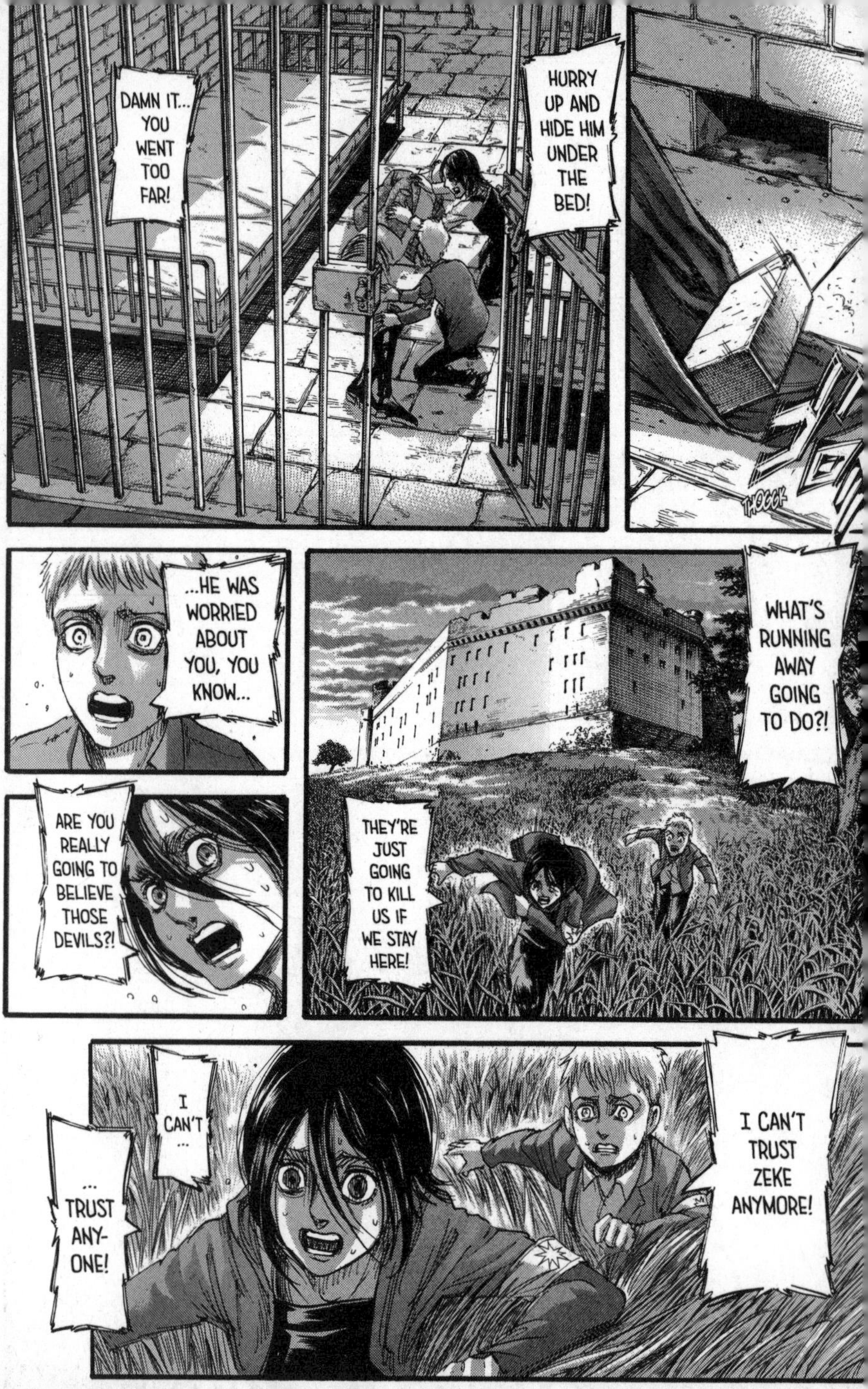
DAMN IT... YOU WENT TOO FAR!
HURRY UP AND HIDE HIM UNDER THE BED!
THOCCK
...HE WAS WORRIED ABOUT YOU, YOU KNOW...
WHAT'S RUNNING AWAY GOING TO DO?!
ARE YOU REALLY GOING TO BELIEVE THOSE DEVILS?!
THEY'RE JUST GOING TO KILL US IF WE STAY HERE!
I CAN'T TRUST ZEKE ANYMORE!
I CAN'T ...
... TRUST ANY-ONE!

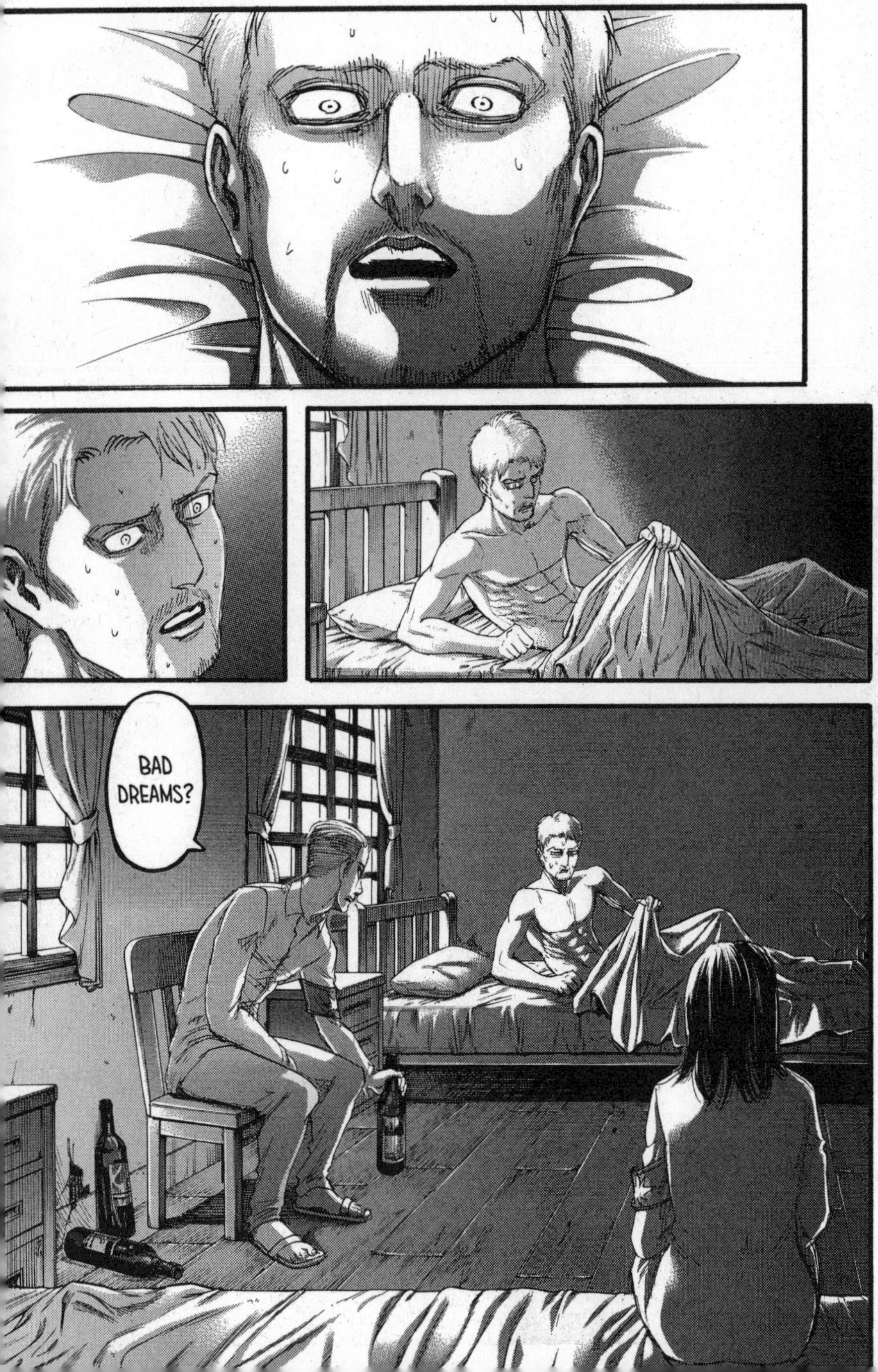
BAD DREAMS?

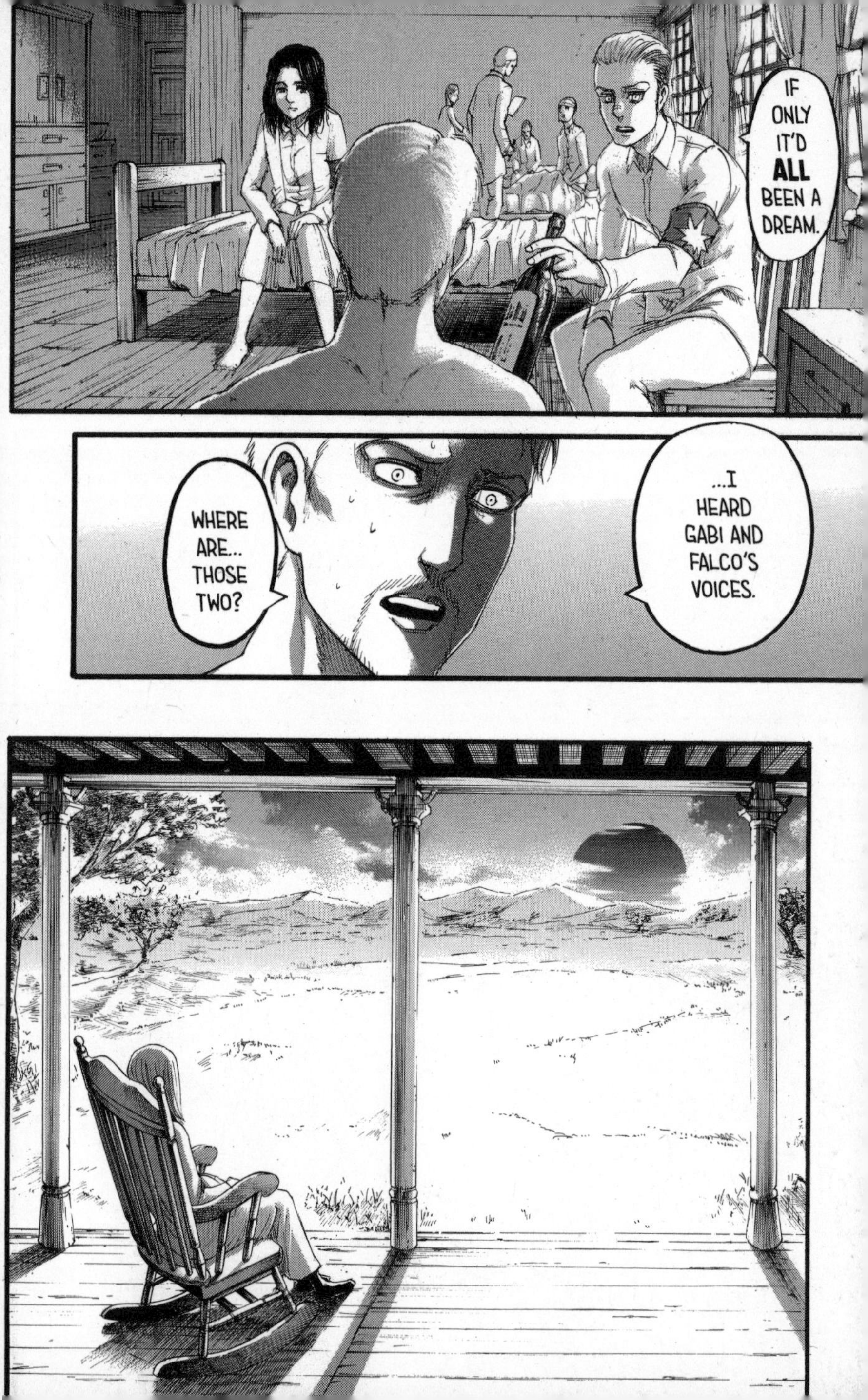

IF ONLY IT'D **ALL** BEEN A DREAM.
...I HEARD GABI AND FALCO'S VOICES.
WHERE ARE... THOSE TWO?

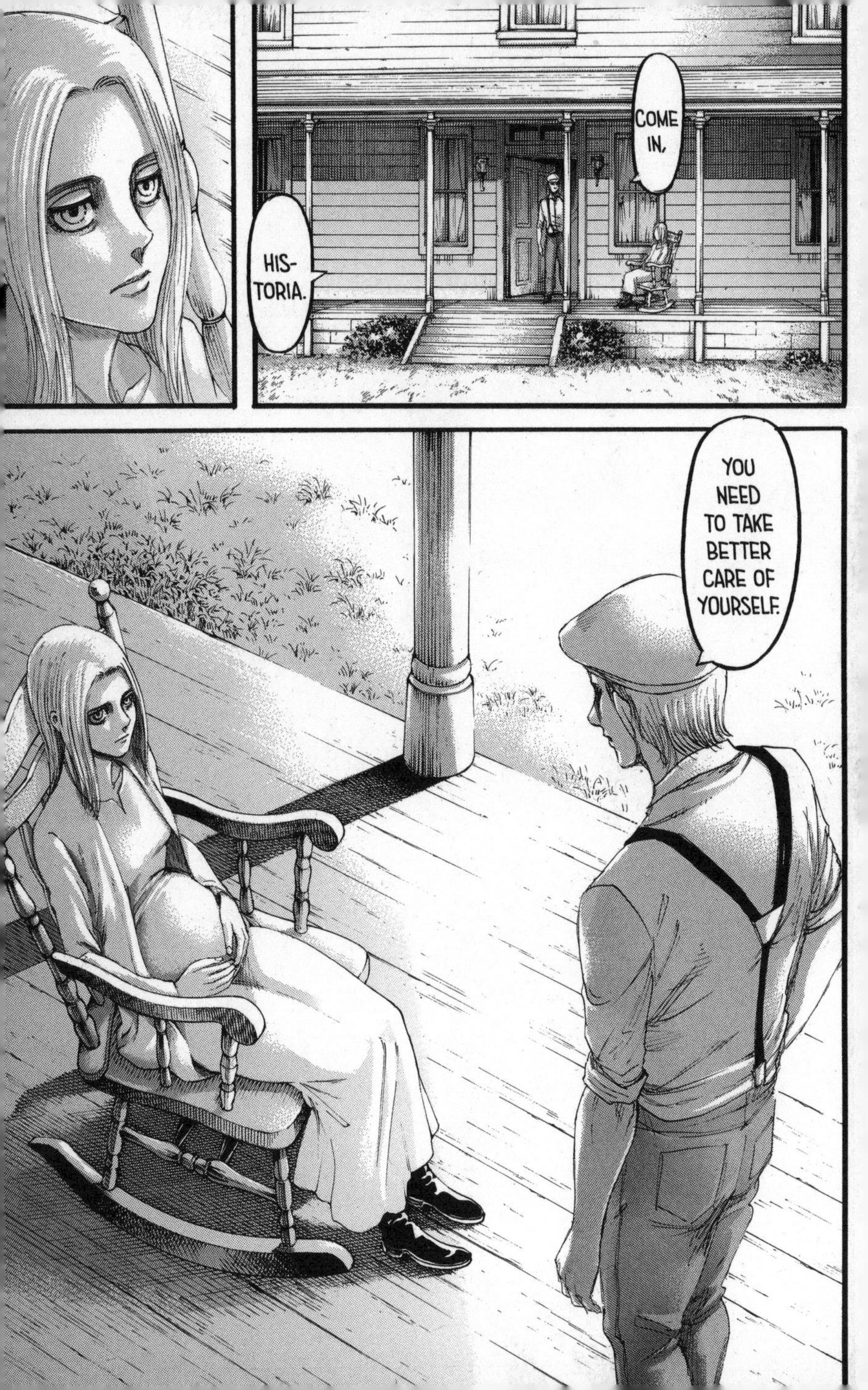
COME IN,
HIS-TORIA.
YOU NEED TO TAKE BETTER CARE OF YOURSELF.

ATTACK on TITAN

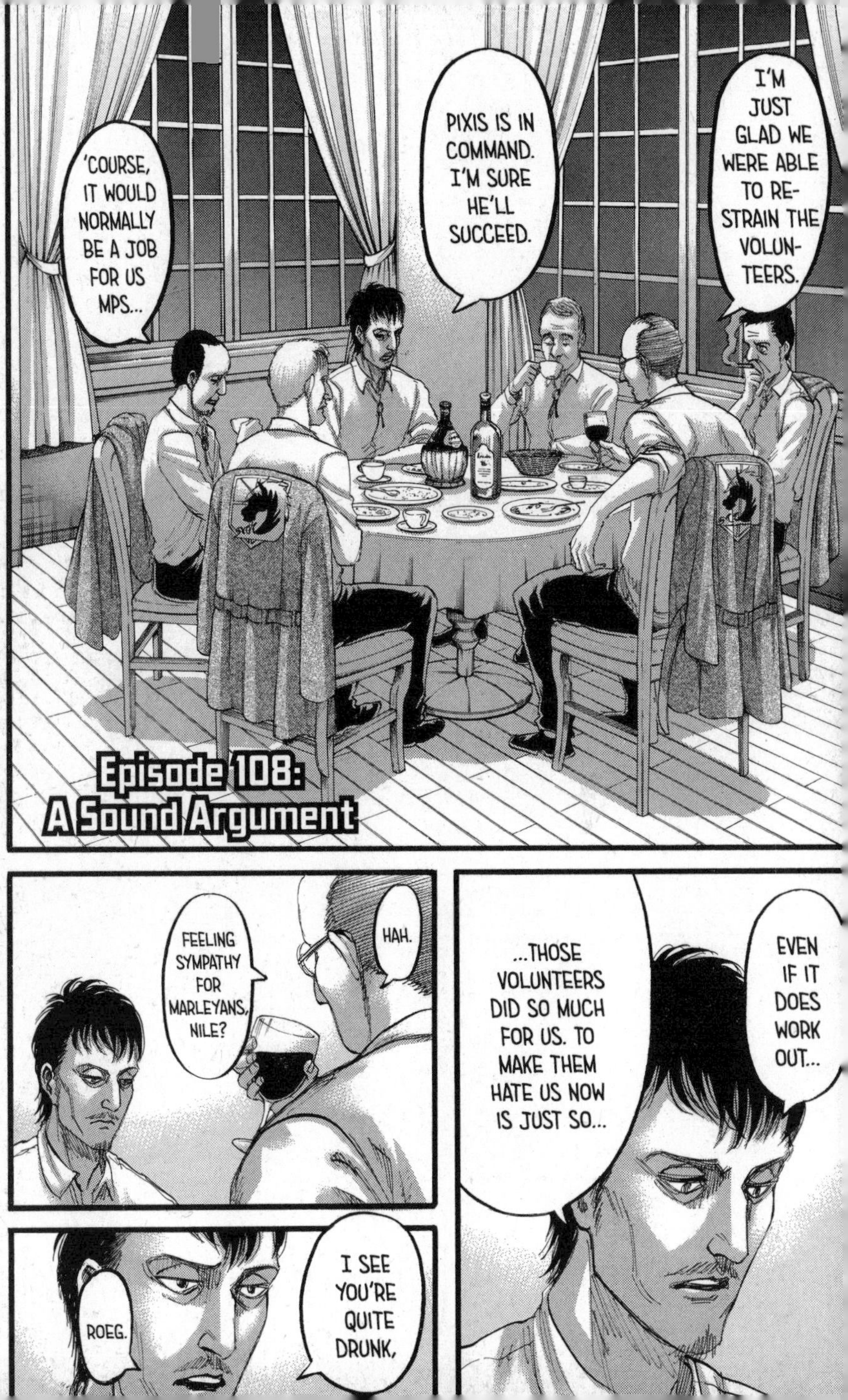
I'M JUST GLAD WE WERE ABLE TO RE-STRAIN THE VOLUN-TEERS.
PIXIS IS IN COMMAND. I'M SURE HE'LL SUCCEED.
'COURSE, IT WOULD NORMALLY BE A JOB FOR US MPS...
Episode 108: A Sound Argument
EVEN IF IT DOES WORK OUT...
...THOSE VOLUNTEERS DID SO MUCH FOR US. TO MAKE THEM HATE US NOW IS JUST SO...
HAH.
FEELING SYMPATHY FOR MARLEYANS, NILE?
I SEE YOU'RE QUITE DRUNK,
ROEG.

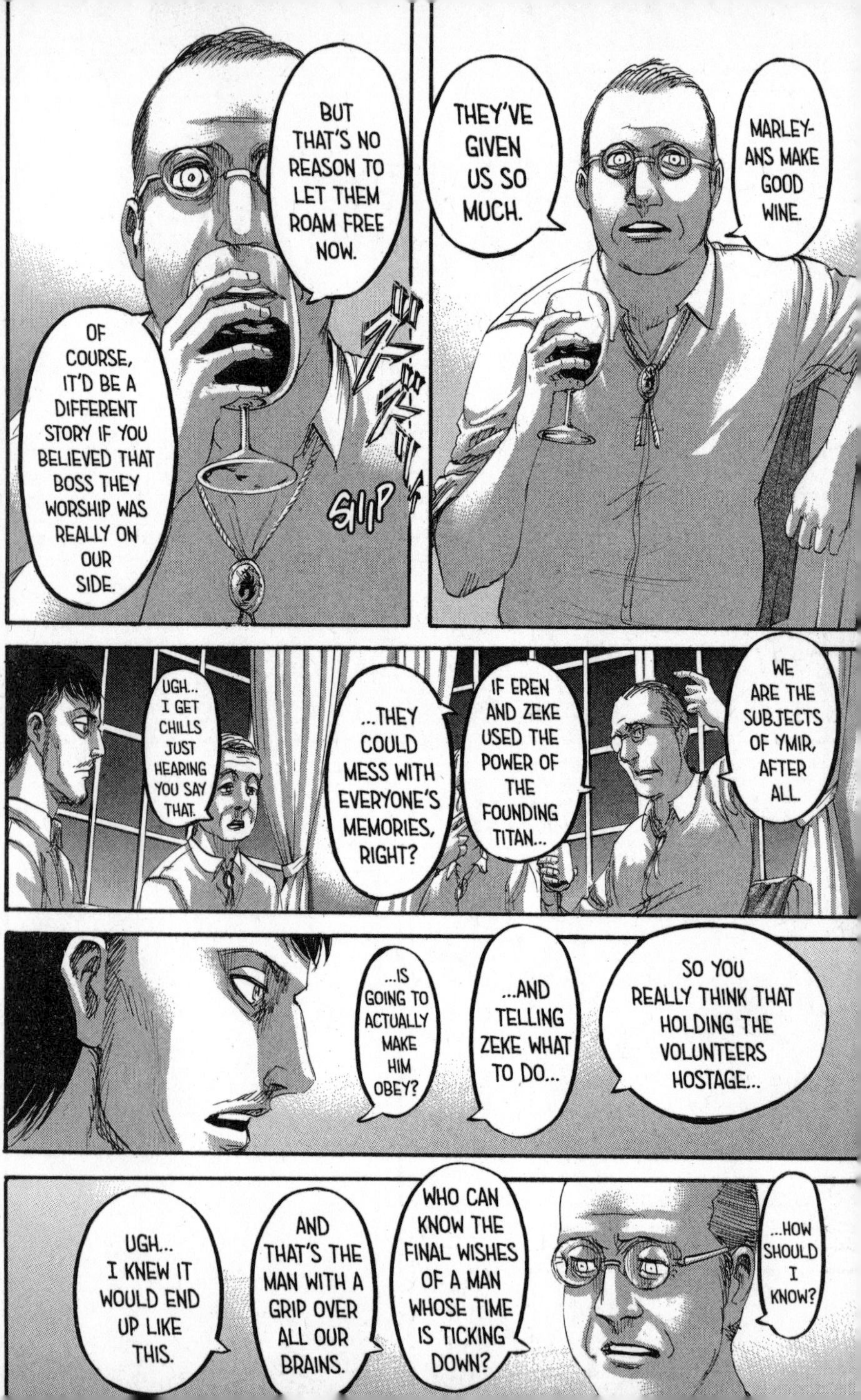
MARLEY-ANS MAKE GOOD WINE.
THEY'VE GIVEN US SO MUCH.
BUT THAT'S NO REASON TO LET THEM ROAM FREE NOW.
SLIP
OF COURSE, IT'D BE A DIFFERENT STORY IF YOU BELIEVED THAT BOSS THEY WORSHIP WAS REALLY ON OUR SIDE.
WE ARE THE SUBJECTS OF YMIR, AFTER ALL.
IF EREN AND ZEKE USED THE POWER OF THE FOUNDING TITAN...
...THEY COULD MESS WITH EVERYONE'S MEMORIES, RIGHT?
UGH... I GET CHILLS JUST HEARING YOU SAY THAT.
SO YOU REALLY THINK THAT HOLDING THE VOLUNTEERS HOSTAGE...
...AND TELLING ZEKE WHAT TO DO...
...IS GOING TO ACTUALLY MAKE HIM OBEY?
...HOW SHOULD I KNOW?
WHO CAN KNOW THE FINAL WISHES OF A MAN WHOSE TIME IS TICKING DOWN?
AND THAT'S THE MAN WITH A GRIP OVER ALL OUR BRAINS.
UGH... I KNEW IT WOULD END UP LIKE THIS.

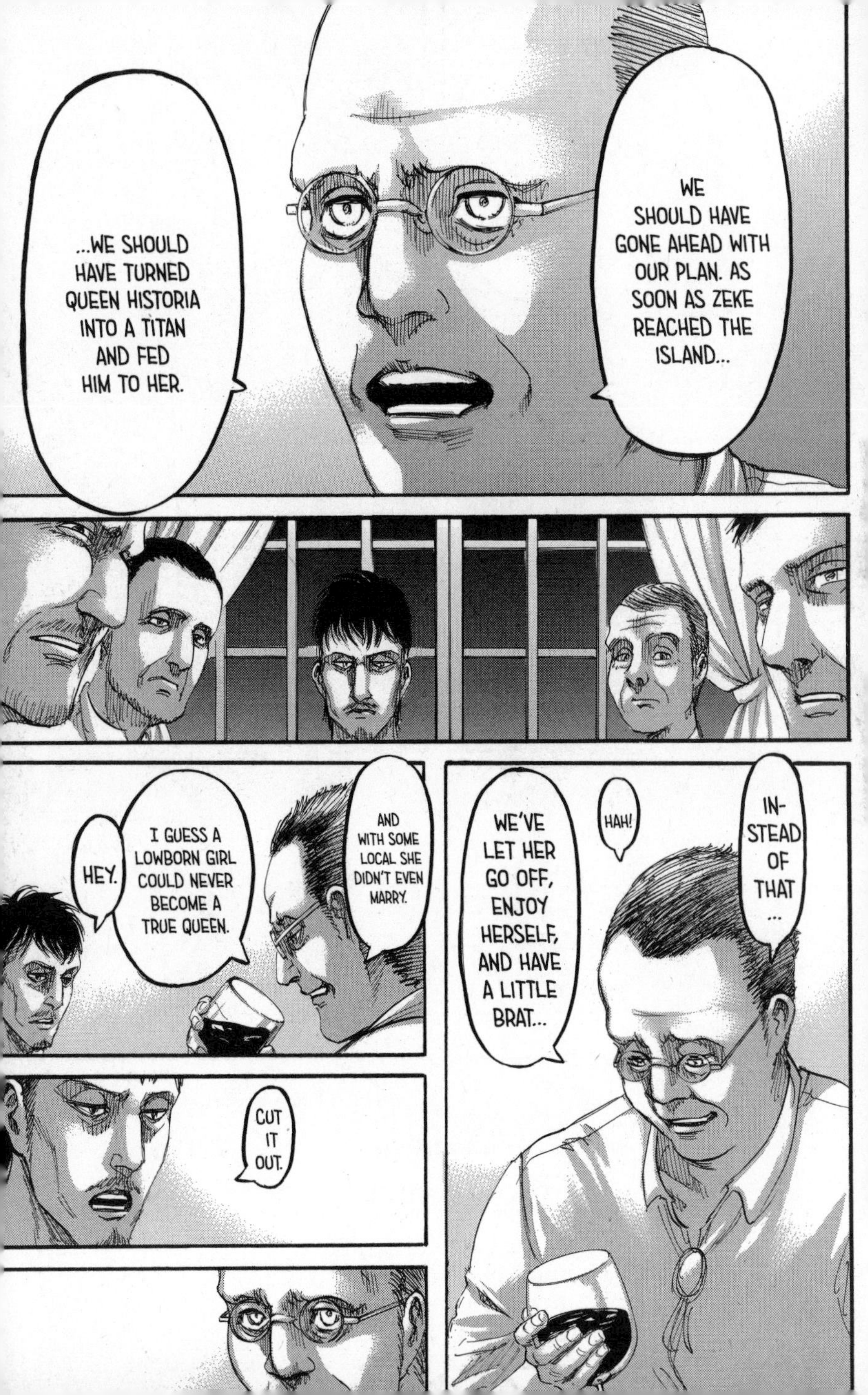
WE SHOULD HAVE GONE AHEAD WITH OUR PLAN. AS SOON AS ZEKE REACHED THE ISLAND...
...WE SHOULD HAVE TURNED QUEEN HISTORIA INTO A TITAN AND FED HIM TO HER.
IN-STEAD OF THAT ...
HAH!
WE'VE LET HER GO OFF, ENJOY HERSELF, AND HAVE A LITTLE BRAT...
AND WITH SOME LOCAL SHE DIDN'T EVEN MARRY.
I GUESS A LOWBORN GIRL COULD NEVER BECOME A TRUE QUEEN.
HEY.
CUT IT OUT.

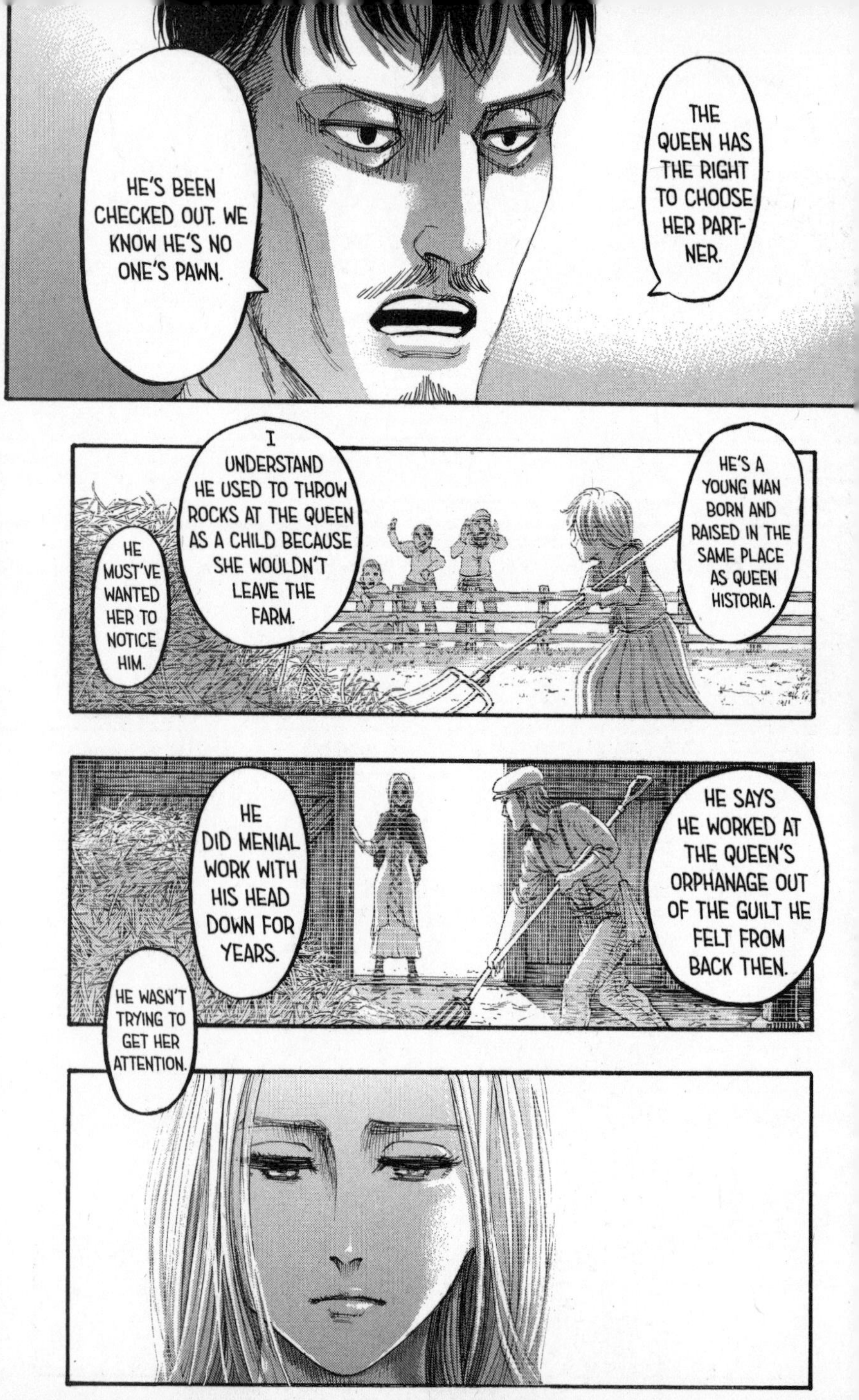
THE QUEEN HAS THE RIGHT TO CHOOSE HER PARTNER.
HE'S BEEN CHECKED OUT. WE KNOW HE'S NO ONE'S PAWN.
HE'S A YOUNG MAN BORN AND RAISED IN THE SAME PLACE AS QUEEN HISTORIA.
I UNDERSTAND HE USED TO THROW ROCKS AT THE QUEEN AS A CHILD BECAUSE SHE WOULDN'T LEAVE THE FARM.
HE MUST'VE WANTED HER TO NOTICE HIM.
HE SAYS HE WORKED AT THE QUEEN'S ORPHANAGE OUT OF THE GUILT HE FELT FROM BACK THEN.
HE DID MENIAL WORK WITH HIS HEAD DOWN FOR YEARS.
HE WASN'T TRYING TO GET HER ATTENTION.

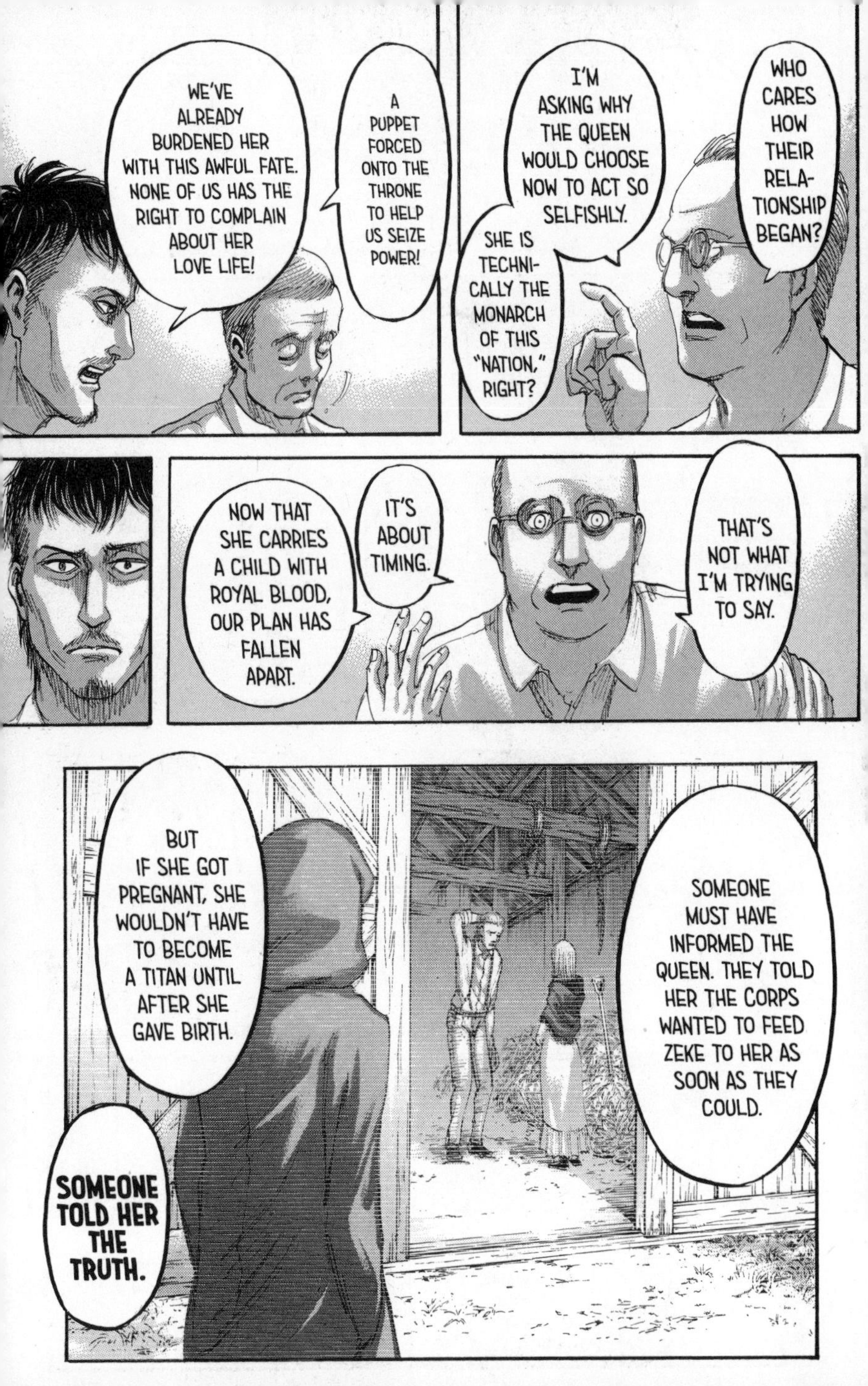
WHO CARES HOW THEIR RELATIONSHIP BEGAN?
I'M ASKING WHY THE QUEEN WOULD CHOOSE NOW TO ACT SO SELFISHLY.
SHE IS TECHNICALLY THE MONARCH OF THIS "NATION," RIGHT?
A PUPPET FORCED ONTO THE THRONE TO HELP US SEIZE POWER!
WE'VE ALREADY BURDENED HER WITH THIS AWFUL FATE. NONE OF US HAS THE RIGHT TO COMPLAIN ABOUT HER LOVE LIFE!
THAT'S NOT WHAT I'M TRYING TO SAY.
IT'S ABOUT TIMING.
NOW THAT SHE CARRIES A CHILD WITH ROYAL BLOOD, OUR PLAN HAS FALLEN APART.
SOMEONE MUST HAVE INFORMED THE QUEEN. THEY TOLD HER THE CORPS WANTED TO FEED ZEKE TO HER AS SOON AS THEY COULD.
BUT IF SHE GOT PREGNANT, SHE WOULDN'T HAVE TO BECOME A TITAN UNTIL AFTER SHE GAVE BIRTH.
SOMEONE TOLD HER THE TRUTH.

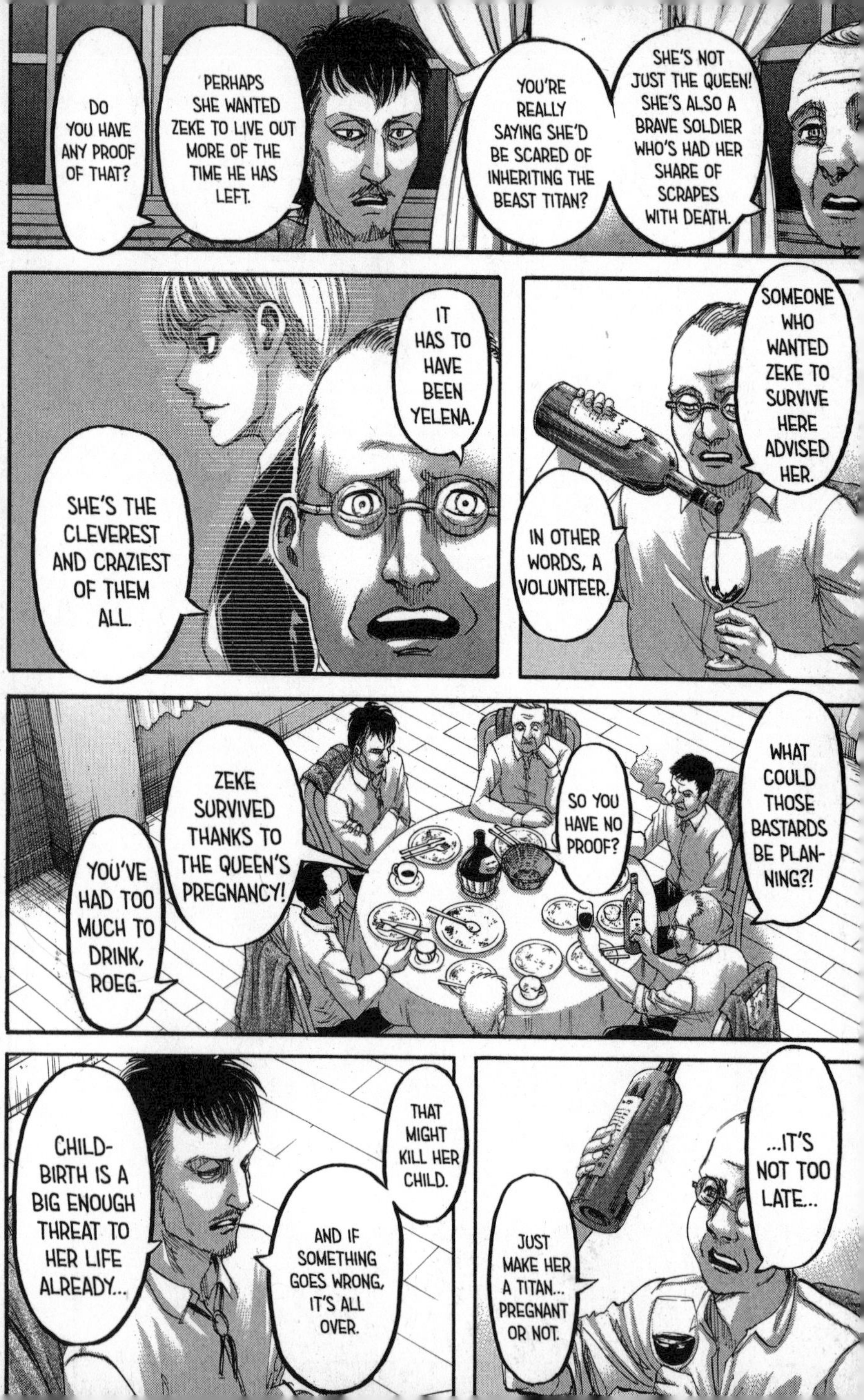
SHE'S NOT JUST THE QUEEN! SHE'S ALSO A BRAVE SOLDIER WHO'S HAD HER SHARE OF SCRAPES WITH DEATH.
YOU'RE REALLY SAYING SHE'D BE SCARED OF INHERITING THE BEAST TITAN?
PERHAPS SHE WANTED ZEKE TO LIVE OUT MORE OF THE TIME HE HAS LEFT.
DO YOU HAVE ANY PROOF OF THAT?
SOMEONE WHO WANTED ZEKE TO SURVIVE HERE ADVISED HER.
IN OTHER WORDS, A VOLUNTEER.
IT HAS TO HAVE BEEN YELENA.
SHE'S THE CLEVEREST AND CRAZIEST OF THEM ALL.
WHAT COULD THOSE BASTARDS BE PLAN-NING?!
SO YOU HAVE NO PROOF?
ZEKE SURVIVED THANKS TO THE QUEEN'S PREGNANCY!
YOU'VE HAD TOO MUCH TO DRINK, ROEG.
...IT'S NOT TOO LATE...
JUST MAKE HER A TITAN... PREGNANT OR NOT.
THAT MIGHT KILL HER CHILD.
AND IF SOMETHING GOES WRONG, IT'S ALL OVER.
CHILD-BIRTH IS A BIG ENOUGH THREAT TO HER LIFE ALREADY...

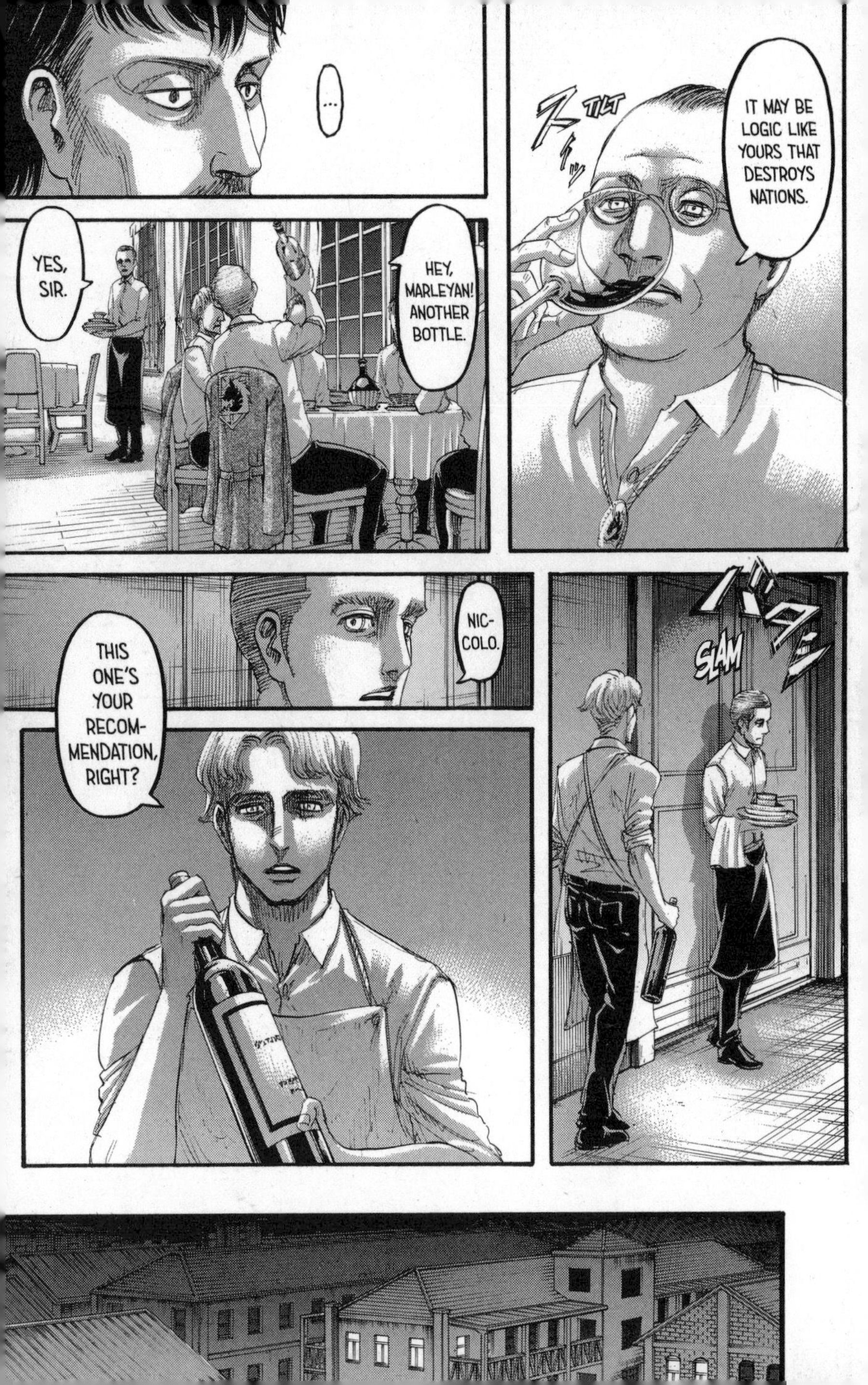
IT MAY BE LOGIC LIKE YOURS THAT DESTROYS NATIONS.
TILT
...
HEY, MARLEYAN! ANOTHER BOTTLE.
YES, SIR.
SLAM
NIC-COLO.
THIS ONE'S YOUR RECOM-MENDATION, RIGHT?

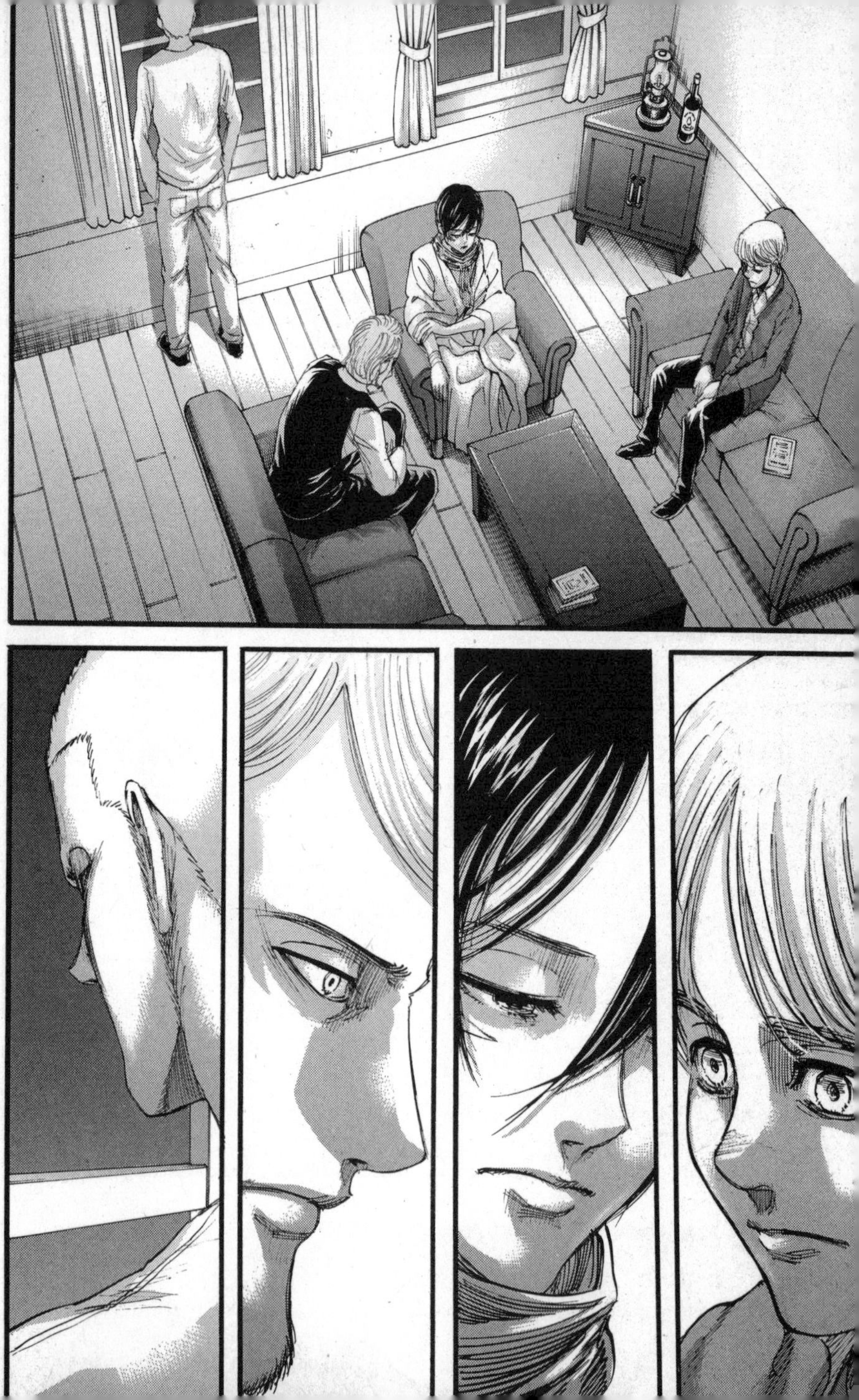

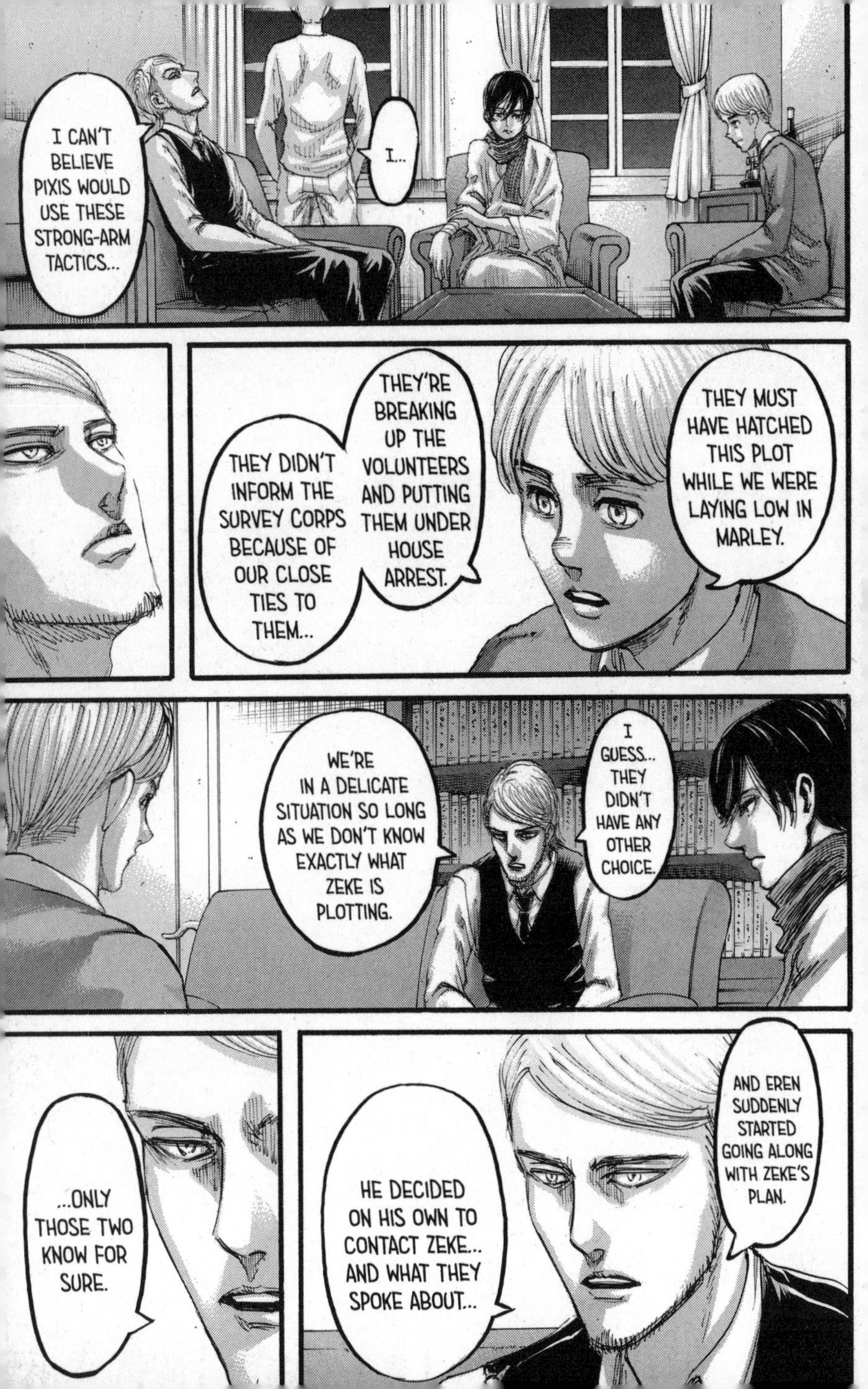
I CAN'T BELIEVE PIXIS WOULD USE THESE STRONG-ARM TACTICS...
I...
THEY MUST HAVE HATCHED THIS PLOT WHILE WE WERE LAYING LOW IN MARLEY.
THEY'RE BREAKING UP THE VOLUNTEERS AND PUTTING THEM UNDER HOUSE ARREST.
THEY DIDN'T INFORM THE SURVEY CORPS BECAUSE OF OUR CLOSE TIES TO THEM...
I GUESS... THEY DIDN'T HAVE ANY OTHER CHOICE.
WE'RE IN A DELICATE SITUATION SO LONG AS WE DON'T KNOW EXACTLY WHAT ZEKE IS PLOTTING.
AND EREN SUDDENLY STARTED GOING ALONG WITH ZEKE'S PLAN.
HE DECIDED ON HIS OWN TO CONTACT ZEKE... AND WHAT THEY SPOKE ABOUT...
...ONLY THOSE TWO KNOW FOR SURE.

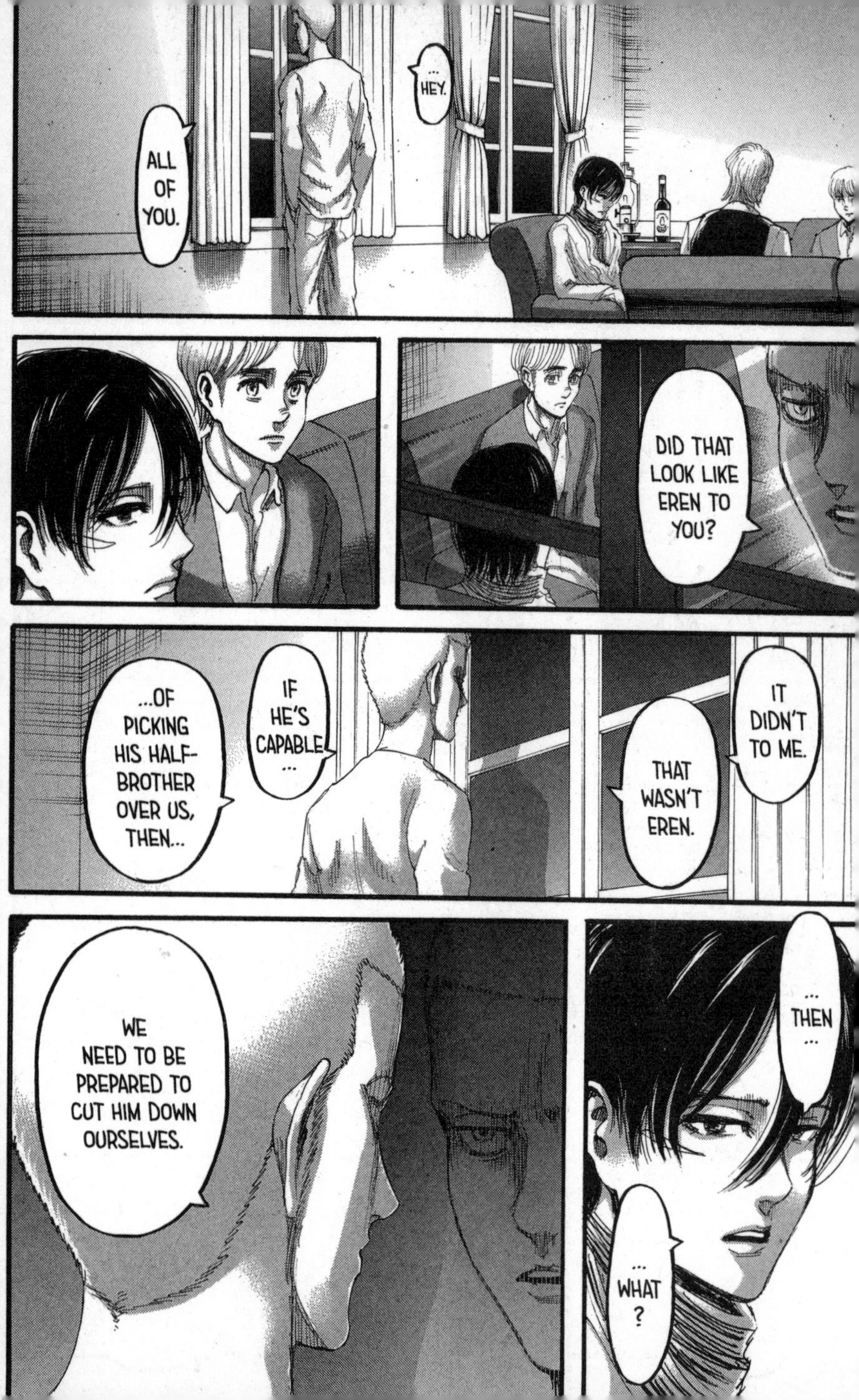
...HEY.
ALL OF YOU.
DID THAT LOOK LIKE EREN TO YOU?
IT DIDN'T TO ME.
THAT WASN'T EREN.
IF HE'S CAPABLE...
...OF PICKING HIS HALF-BROTHER OVER US, THEN...
...THEN...
WE NEED TO BE PREPARED TO CUT HIM DOWN OURSELVES.
...WHAT?

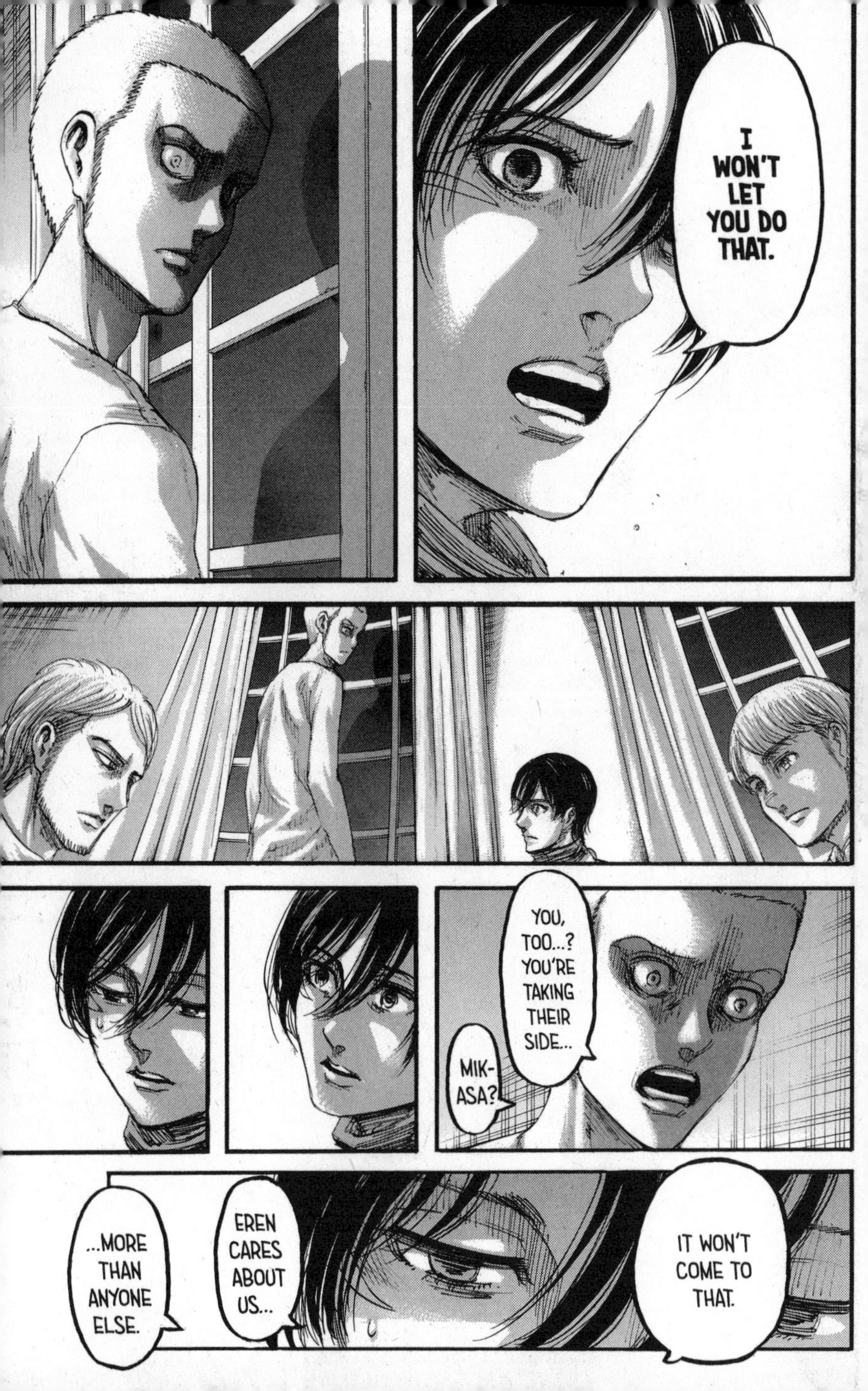
I WON'T LET YOU DO THAT.
YOU, TOO...? YOU'RE TAKING THEIR SIDE...
MIK-ASA?
IT WON'T COME TO THAT.
EREN CARES ABOUT US...
...MORE THAN ANYONE ELSE.

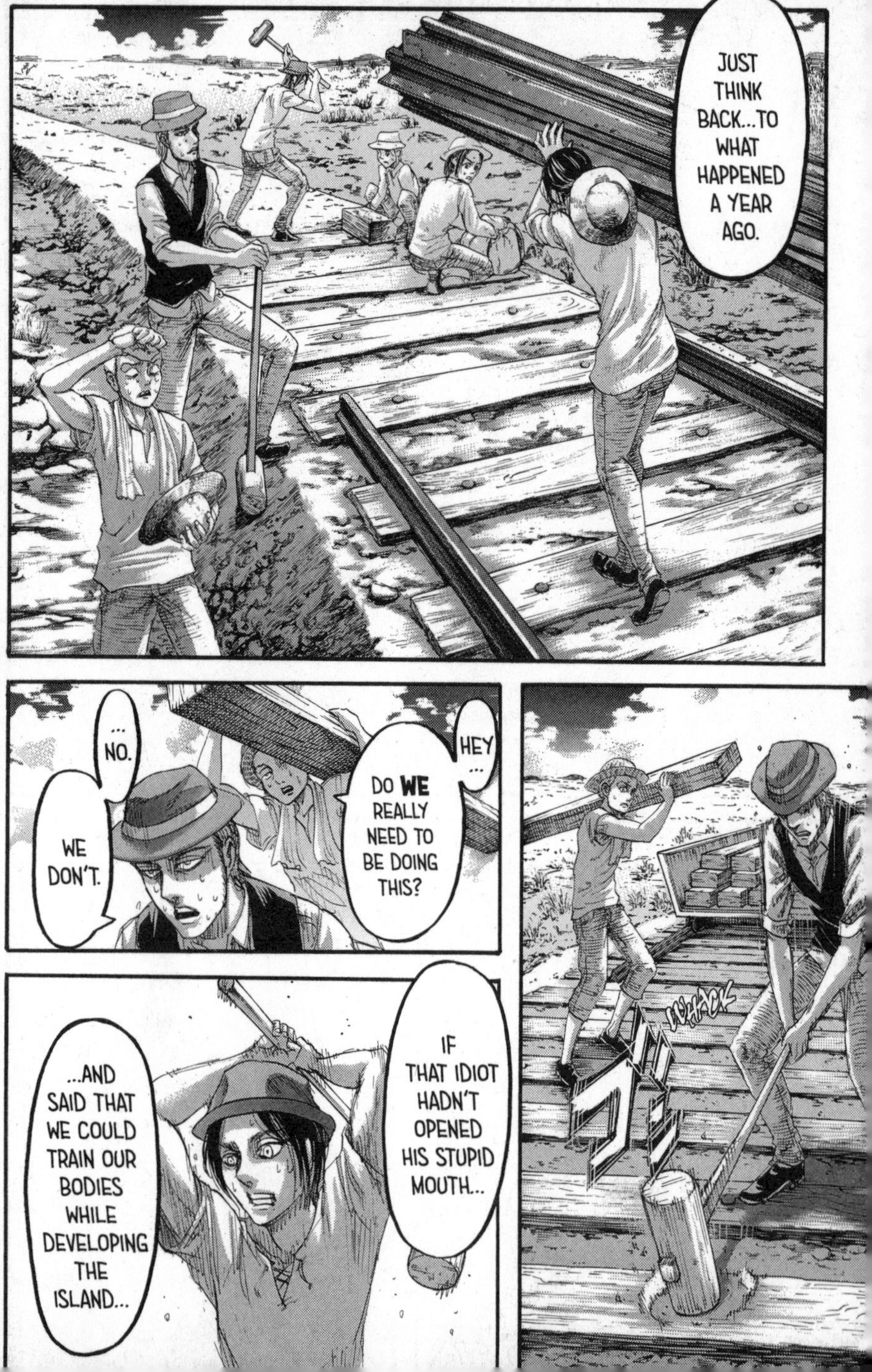
JUST THINK BACK...TO WHAT HAPPENED A YEAR AGO.
HEY...
DO **WE** REALLY NEED TO BE DOING THIS?
...NO.
WE DON'T.
IF THAT IDIOT HADN'T OPENED HIS STUPID MOUTH...
...AND SAID THAT WE COULD TRAIN OUR BODIES WHILE DEVELOPING THE ISLAND...

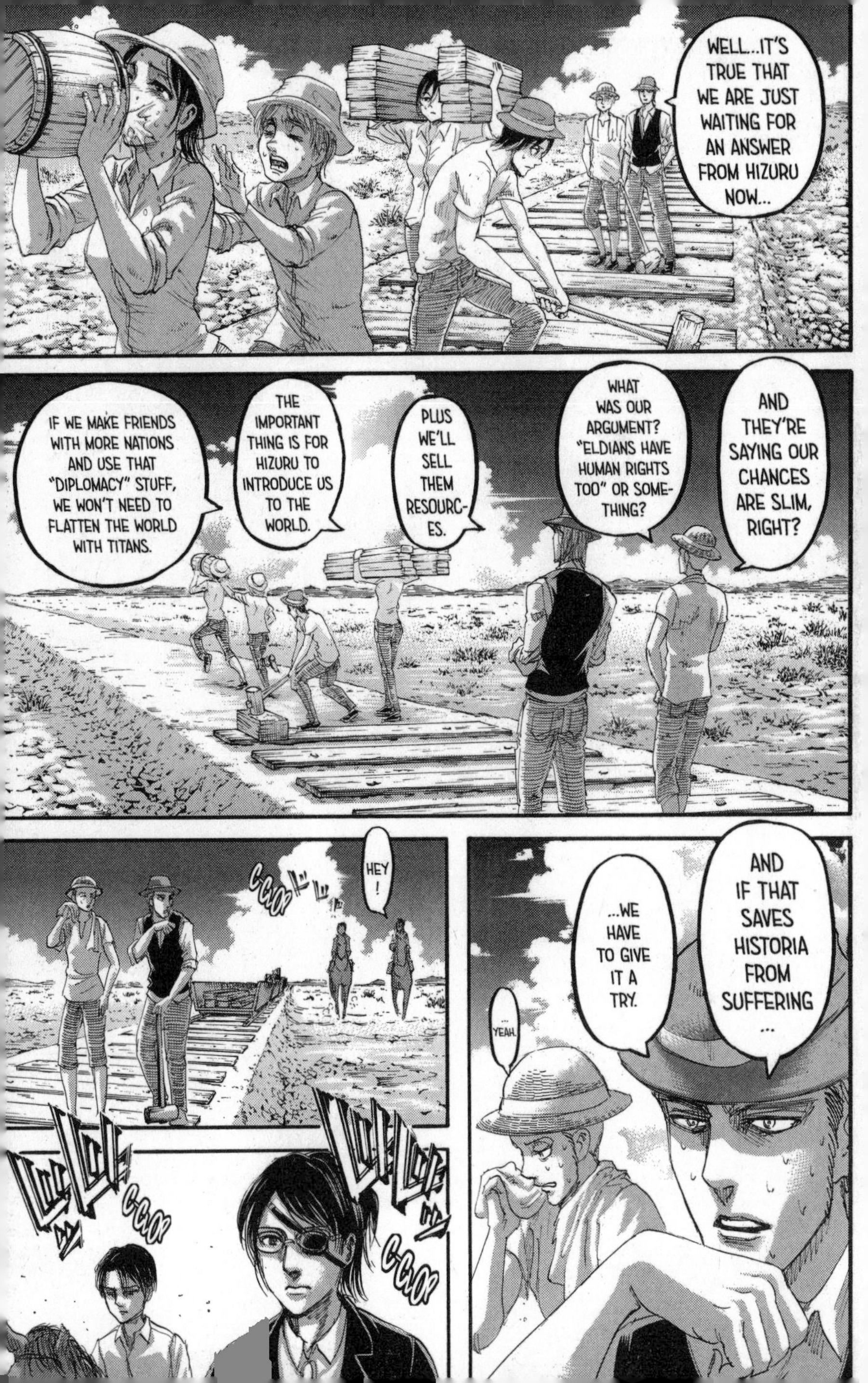
WELL...IT'S TRUE THAT WE ARE JUST WAITING FOR AN ANSWER FROM HIZURU NOW...
AND THEY'RE SAYING OUR CHANCES ARE SLIM, RIGHT?
WHAT WAS OUR ARGUMENT? "ELDIANS HAVE HUMAN RIGHTS TOO" OR SOMETHING?
PLUS WE'LL SELL THEM RESOURCES.
THE IMPORTANT THING IS FOR HIZURU TO INTRODUCE US TO THE WORLD.
IF WE MAKE FRIENDS WITH MORE NATIONS AND USE THAT "DIPLOMACY" STUFF, WE WON'T NEED TO FLATTEN THE WORLD WITH TITANS.
AND IF THAT SAVES HISTORIA FROM SUFFERING...
...WE HAVE TO GIVE IT A TRY.
...YEAH.
HEY!
C-CLOP
C-CLOP
C-CLOP

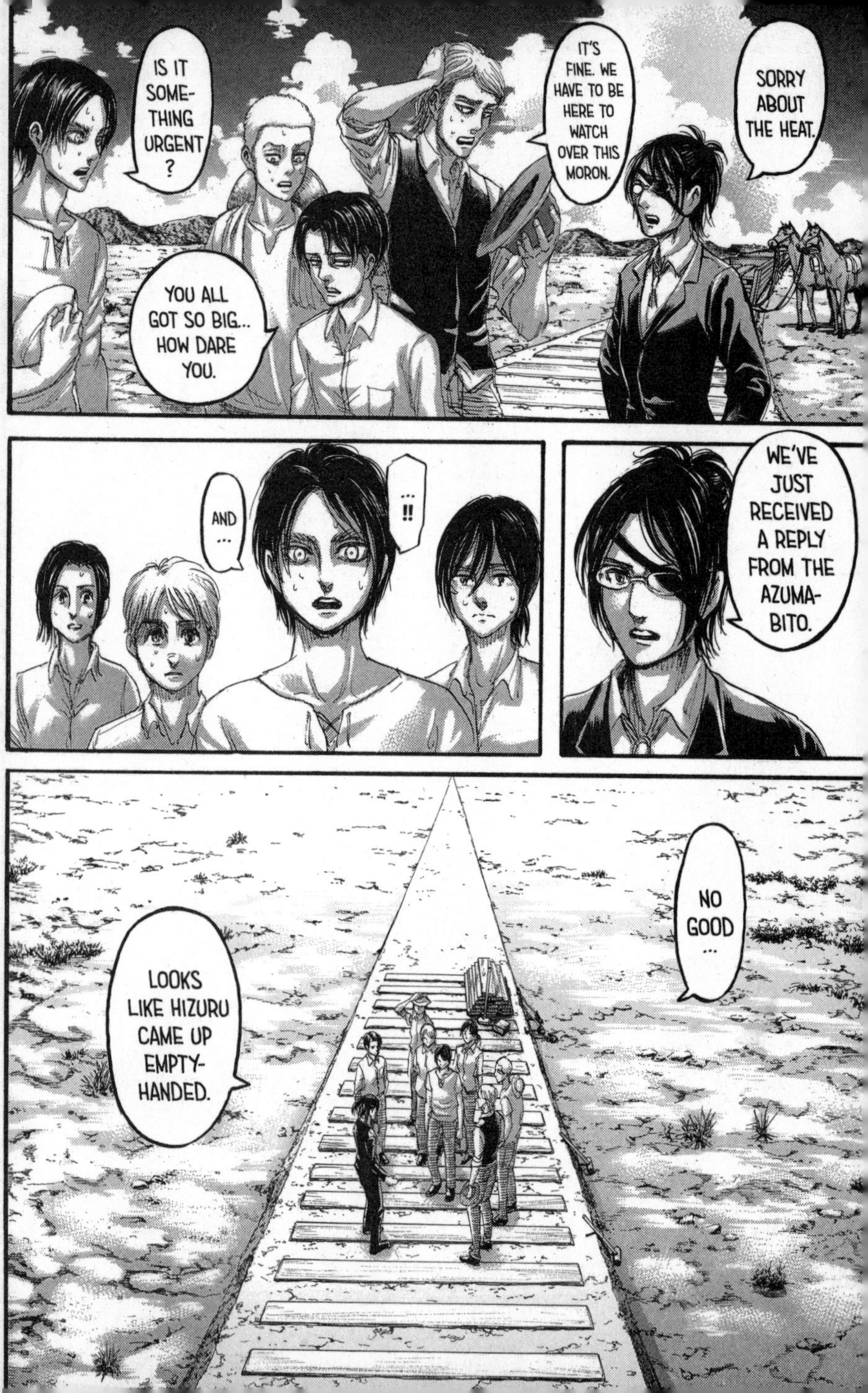
SORRY ABOUT THE HEAT.
IT'S FINE. WE HAVE TO BE HERE TO WATCH OVER THIS MORON.
IS IT SOME-THING URGENT?
YOU ALL GOT SO BIG... HOW DARE YOU.
WE'VE JUST RECEIVED A REPLY FROM THE AZUMA-BITO.
...!!
AND ...
NO GOOD ...
LOOKS LIKE HIZURU CAME UP EMPTY-HANDED.

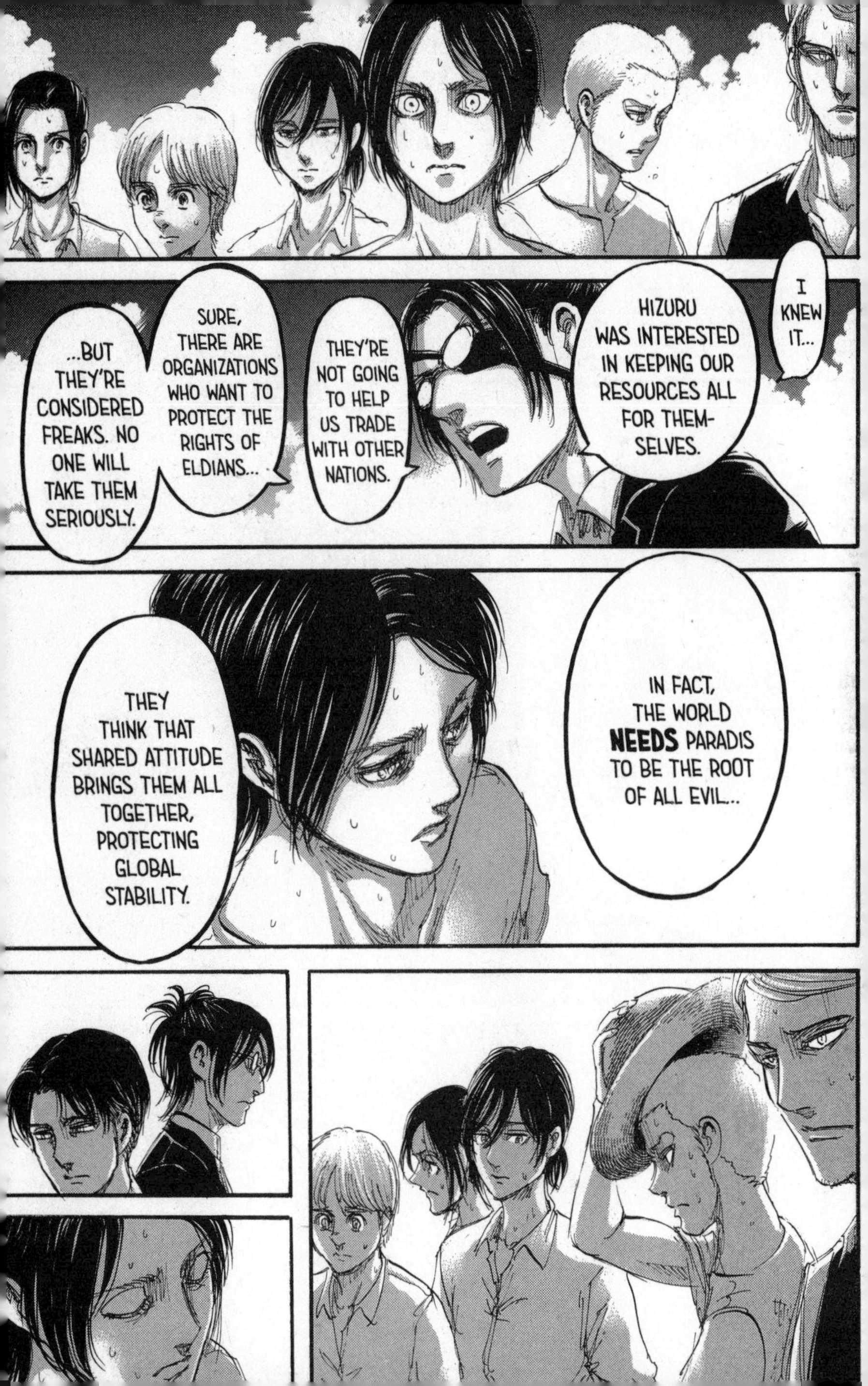
I KNEW IT...
HIZURU WAS INTERESTED IN KEEPING OUR RESOURCES ALL FOR THEM-SELVES.
THEY'RE NOT GOING TO HELP US TRADE WITH OTHER NATIONS.
SURE, THERE ARE ORGANIZATIONS WHO WANT TO PROTECT THE RIGHTS OF ELDIANS...
...BUT THEY'RE CONSIDERED FREAKS. NO ONE WILL TAKE THEM SERIOUSLY.
IN FACT, THE WORLD **NEEDS** PARADIS TO BE THE ROOT OF ALL EVIL...
THEY THINK THAT SHARED ATTITUDE BRINGS THEM ALL TOGETHER, PROTECTING GLOBAL STABILITY.

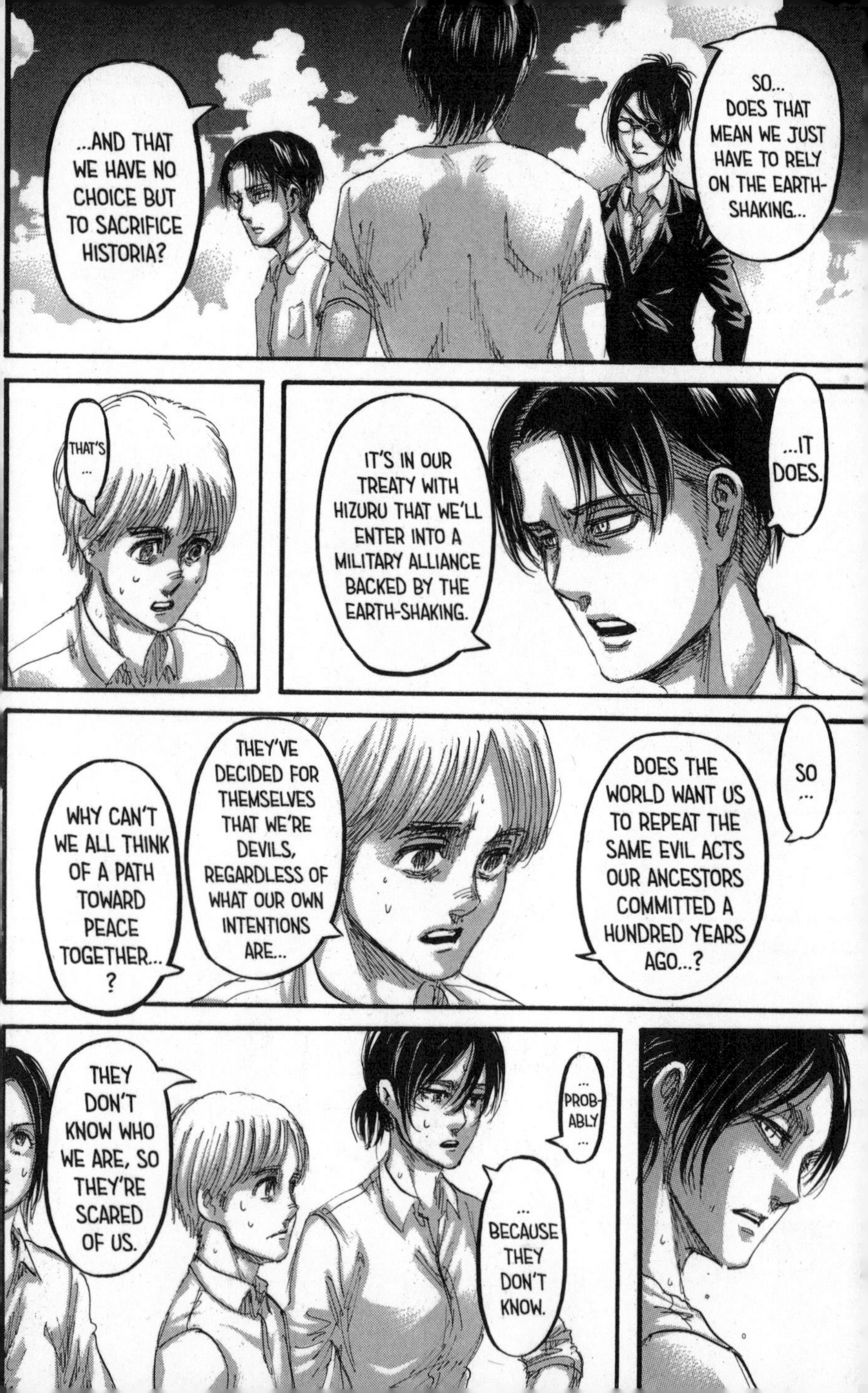
SO... DOES THAT MEAN WE JUST HAVE TO RELY ON THE EARTH-SHAKING...
...AND THAT WE HAVE NO CHOICE BUT TO SACRIFICE HISTORIA?
...IT DOES.
IT'S IN OUR TREATY WITH HIZURU THAT WE'LL ENTER INTO A MILITARY ALLIANCE BACKED BY THE EARTH-SHAKING.
THAT'S ...
SO ...
DOES THE WORLD WANT US TO REPEAT THE SAME EVIL ACTS OUR ANCESTORS COMMITTED A HUNDRED YEARS AGO...?
THEY'VE DECIDED FOR THEMSELVES THAT WE'RE DEVILS, REGARDLESS OF WHAT OUR OWN INTENTIONS ARE...
WHY CAN'T WE ALL THINK OF A PATH TOWARD PEACE TOGETHER... ?
... PROBABLY ...
... BECAUSE THEY DON'T KNOW.
THEY DON'T KNOW WHO WE ARE, SO THEY'RE SCARED OF US.

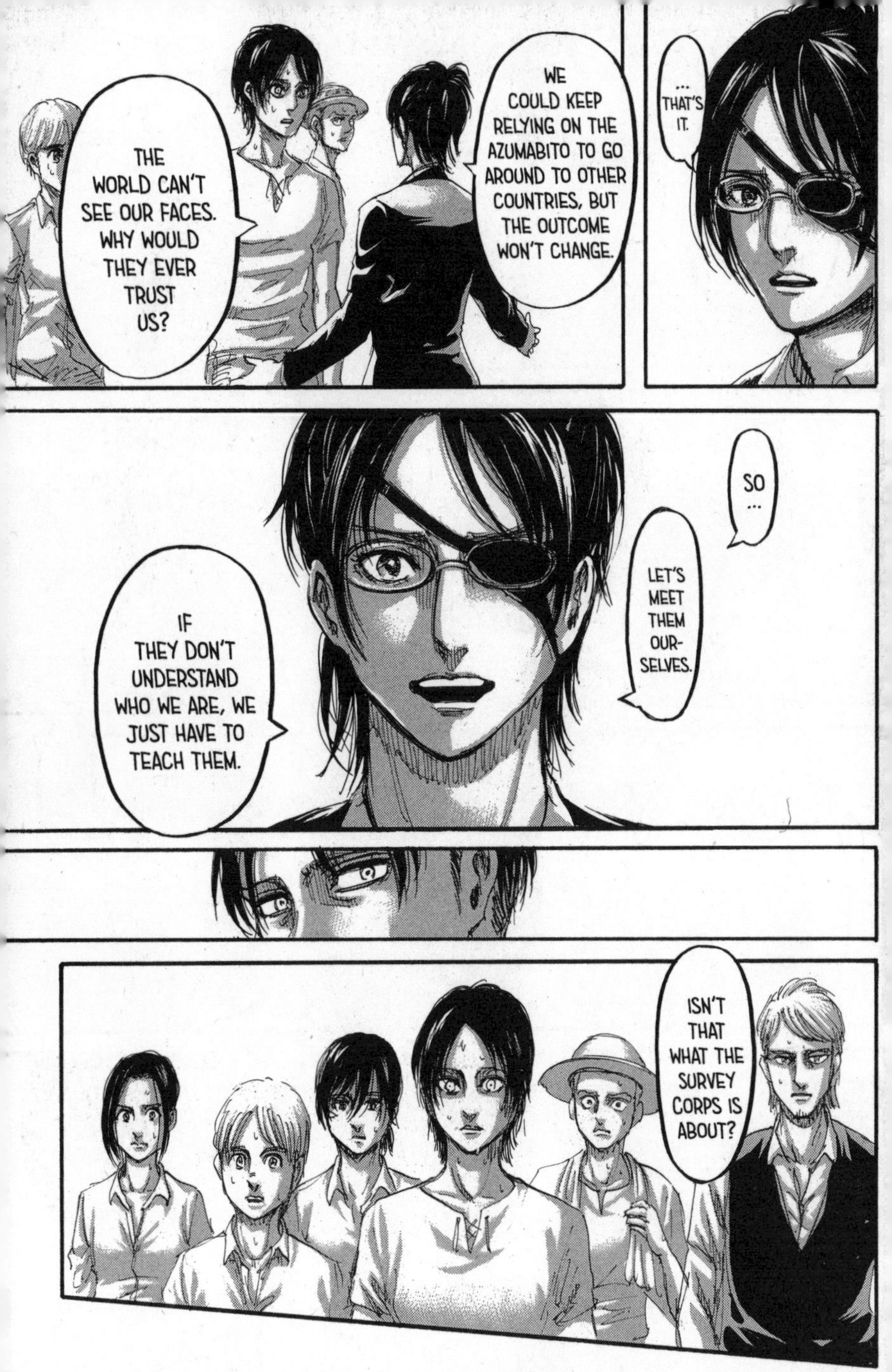
WE COULD KEEP RELYING ON THE AZUMABITO TO GO AROUND TO OTHER COUNTRIES, BUT THE OUTCOME WON'T CHANGE.
THE WORLD CAN'T SEE OUR FACES. WHY WOULD THEY EVER TRUST US?
... THAT'S IT.
SO ...
LET'S MEET THEM OUR-SELVES.
IF THEY DON'T UNDERSTAND WHO WE ARE, WE JUST HAVE TO TEACH THEM.
ISN'T THAT WHAT THE SURVEY CORPS IS ABOUT?

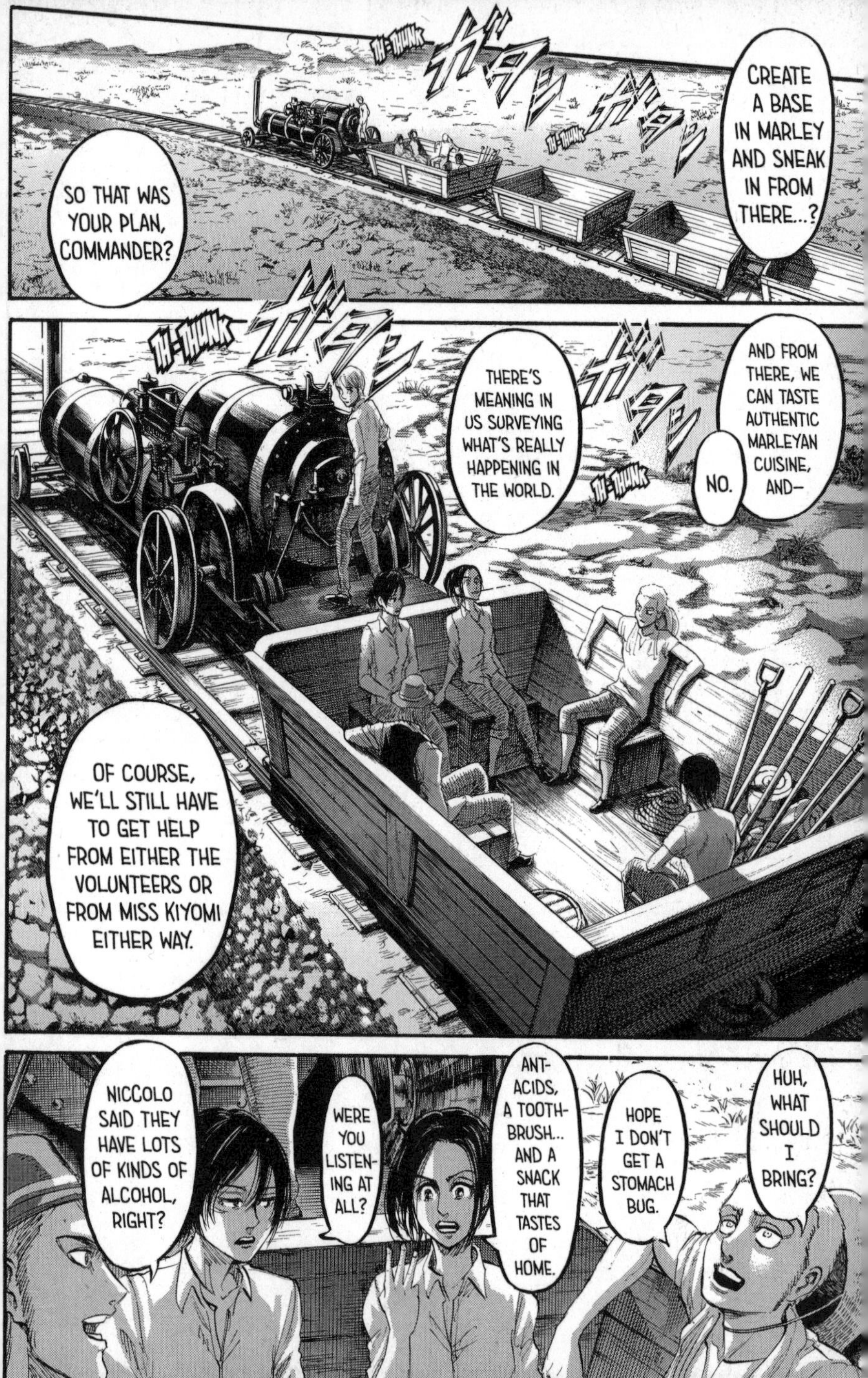
CREATE A BASE IN MARLEY AND SNEAK IN FROM THERE...?
TH-THUNK
TH-THUNK
SO THAT WAS YOUR PLAN, COMMANDER?
AND FROM THERE, WE CAN TASTE AUTHENTIC MARLEYAN CUISINE, AND—
NO.
TH-THUNK
THERE'S MEANING IN US SURVEYING WHAT'S REALLY HAPPENING IN THE WORLD.
TH-THUNK
OF COURSE, WE'LL STILL HAVE TO GET HELP FROM EITHER THE VOLUNTEERS OR FROM MISS KIYOMI EITHER WAY.
HUH, WHAT SHOULD I BRING?
HOPE I DON'T GET A STOMACH BUG.
ANT-ACIDS, A TOOTH-BRUSH... AND A SNACK THAT TASTES OF HOME.
WERE YOU LISTEN-ING AT ALL?
NICCOLO SAID THEY HAVE LOTS OF KINDS OF ALCOHOL, RIGHT?

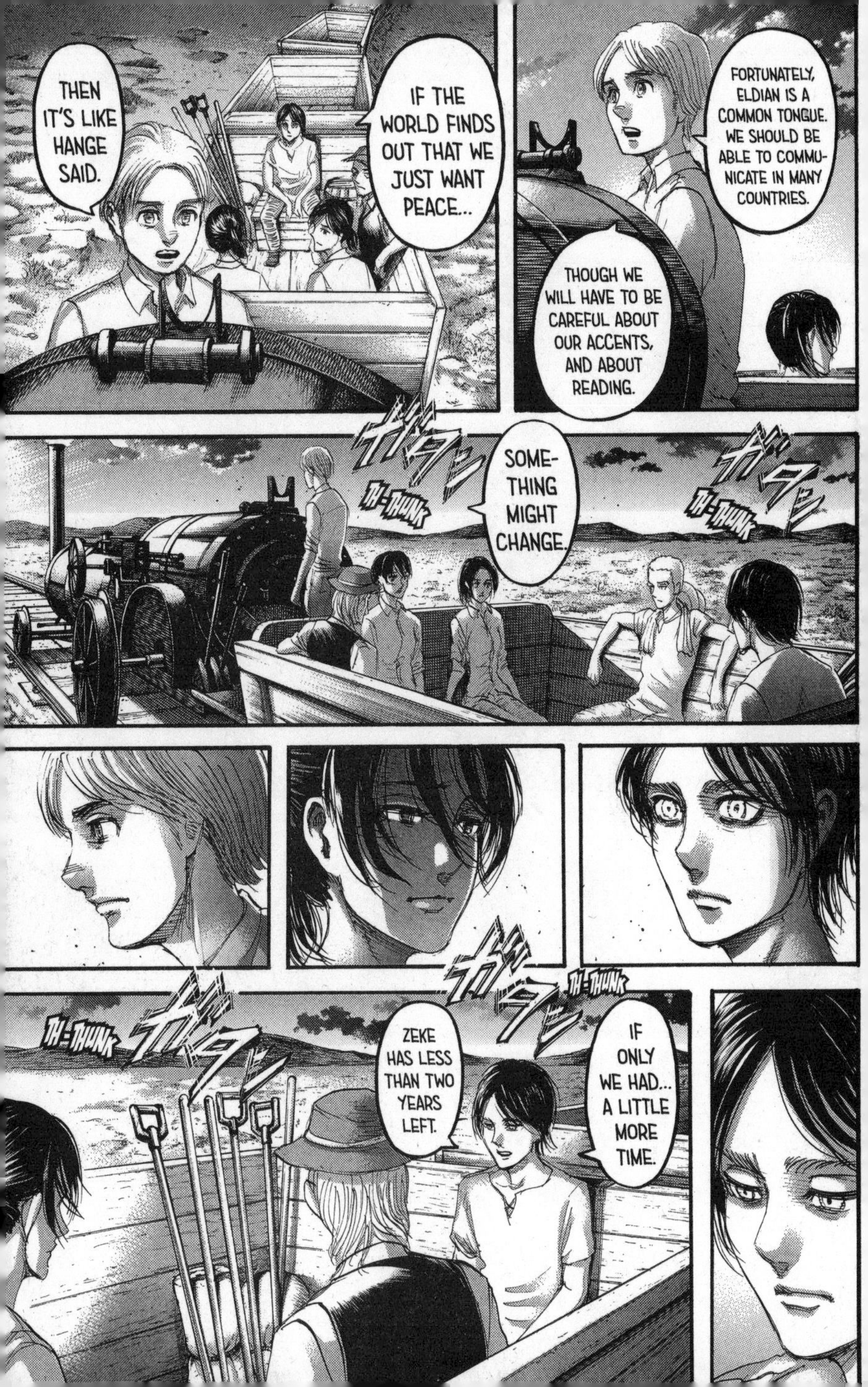
FORTUNATELY, ELDIAN IS A COMMON TONGUE. WE SHOULD BE ABLE TO COMMUNICATE IN MANY COUNTRIES.
THOUGH WE WILL HAVE TO BE CAREFUL ABOUT OUR ACCENTS, AND ABOUT READING.
THEN IT'S LIKE HANGE SAID.
IF THE WORLD FINDS OUT THAT WE JUST WANT PEACE...
TH-THUNK
TH-THUNK
SOMETHING MIGHT CHANGE.
TH-THUNK
TH-THUNK
IF ONLY WE HAD... A LITTLE MORE TIME.
ZEKE HAS LESS THAN TWO YEARS LEFT.

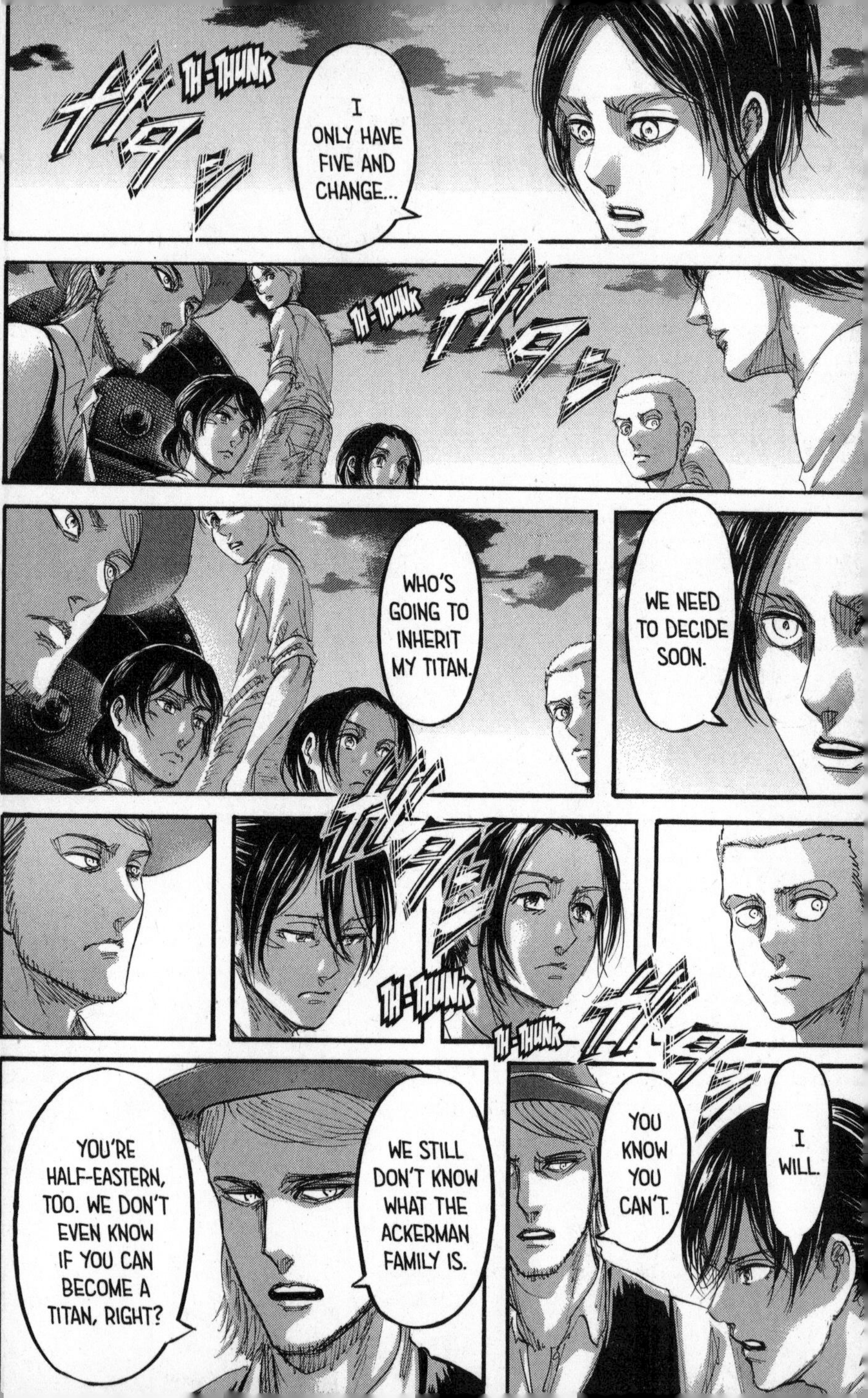
I ONLY HAVE FIVE AND CHANGE...
TH-THUNK
TH-THUNK
WE NEED TO DECIDE SOON.
WHO'S GOING TO INHERIT MY TITAN.
TH-THUNK
TH-THUNK
I WILL.
YOU KNOW YOU CAN'T.
WE STILL DON'T KNOW WHAT THE ACKERMAN FAMILY IS.
YOU'RE HALF-EASTERN, TOO. WE DON'T EVEN KNOW IF YOU CAN BECOME A TITAN, RIGHT?

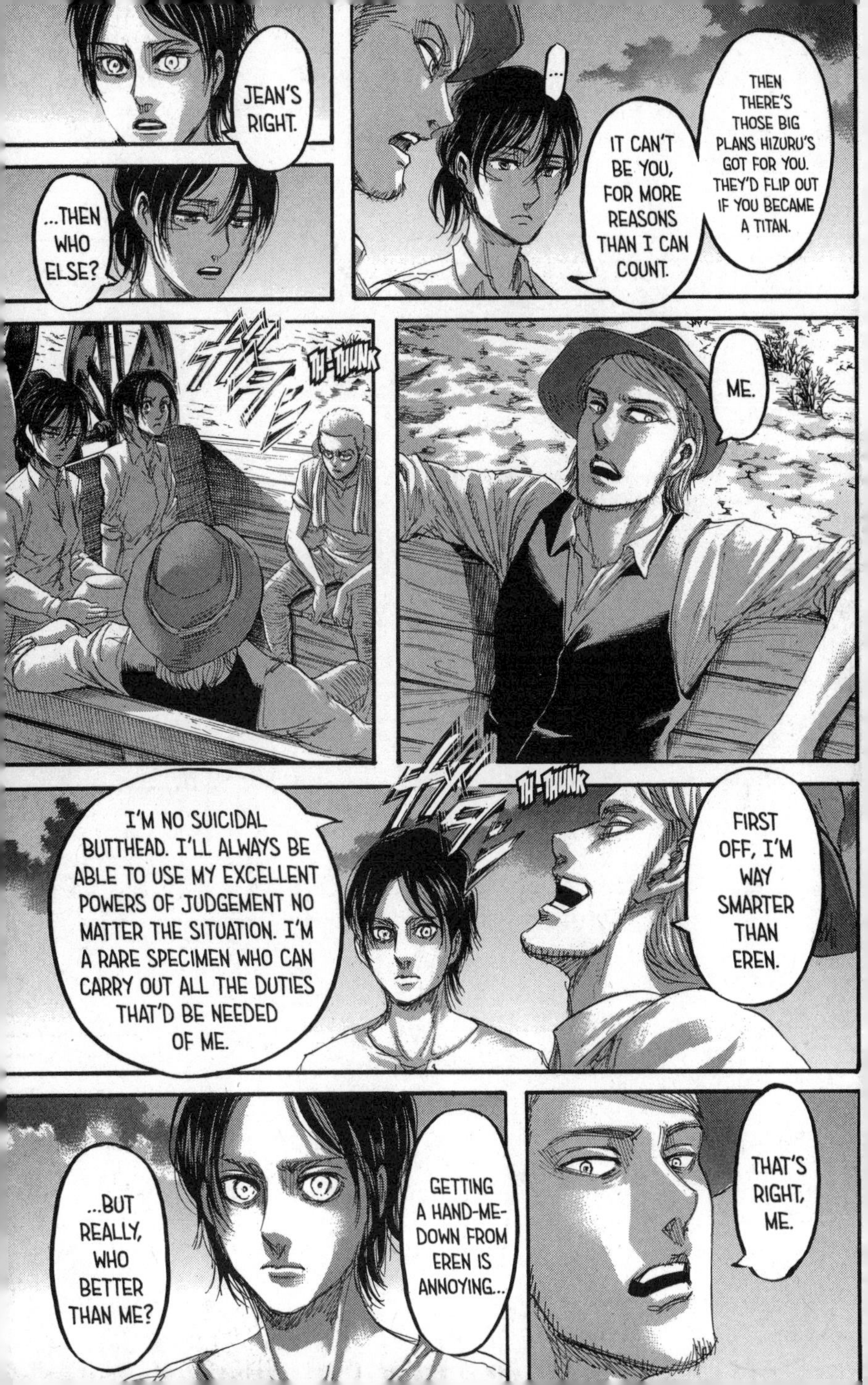
THEN THERE'S THOSE BIG PLANS HIZURU'S GOT FOR YOU. THEY'D FLIP OUT IF YOU BECAME A TITAN.
IT CAN'T BE YOU, FOR MORE REASONS THAN I CAN COUNT.
...
JEAN'S RIGHT.
...THEN WHO ELSE?
ME.
TH-THUNK
TH-THUNK
FIRST OFF, I'M WAY SMARTER THAN EREN.
I'M NO SUICIDAL BUTTHEAD. I'LL ALWAYS BE ABLE TO USE MY EXCELLENT POWERS OF JUDGEMENT NO MATTER THE SITUATION. I'M A RARE SPECIMEN WHO CAN CARRY OUT ALL THE DUTIES THAT'D BE NEEDED OF ME.
THAT'S RIGHT, ME.
GETTING A HAND-ME-DOWN FROM EREN IS ANNOYING...
...BUT REALLY, WHO BETTER THAN ME?

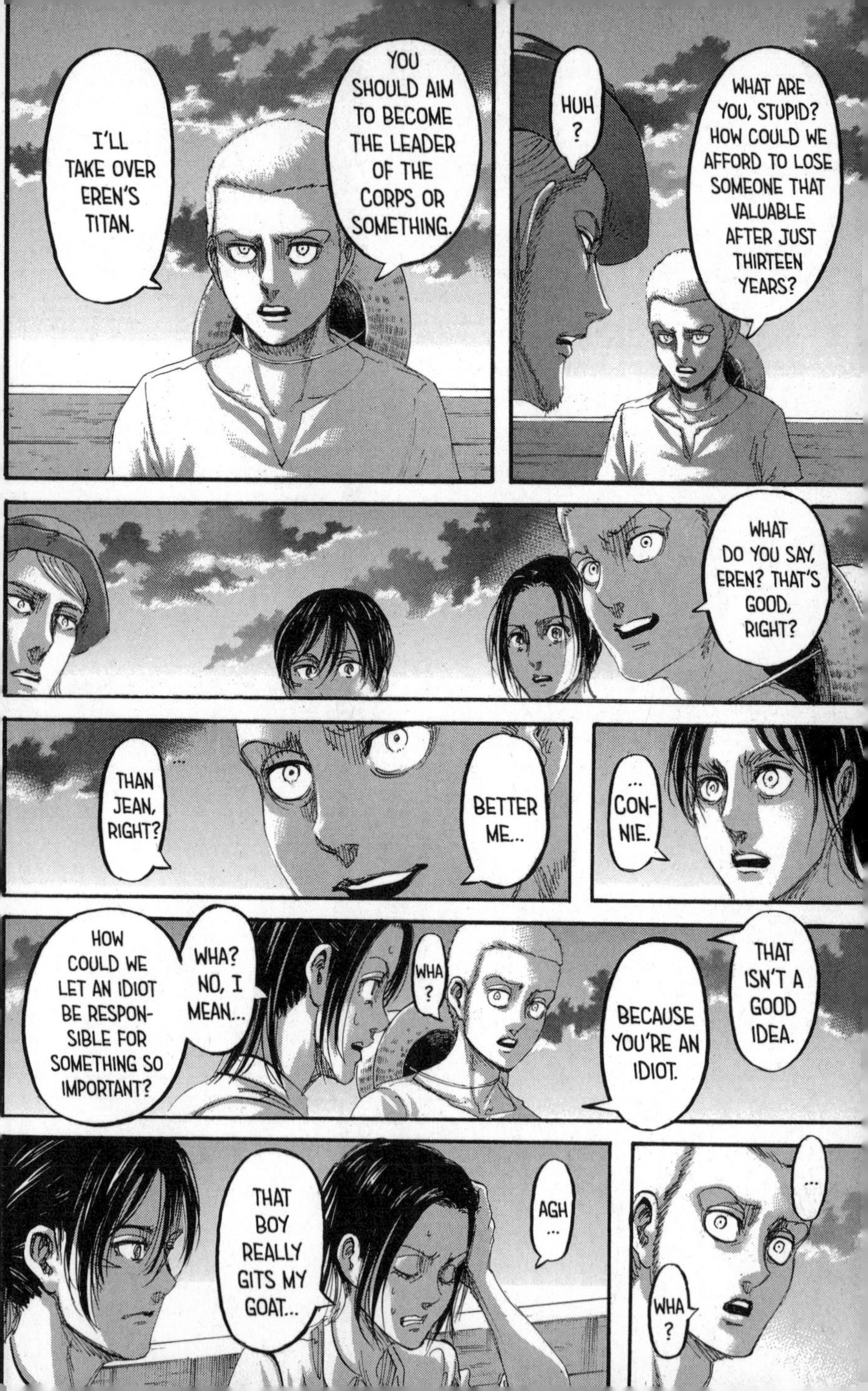
WHAT ARE YOU, STUPID? HOW COULD WE AFFORD TO LOSE SOMEONE THAT VALUABLE AFTER JUST THIRTEEN YEARS?
HUH ?
YOU SHOULD AIM TO BECOME THE LEADER OF THE CORPS OR SOMETHING.
I'LL TAKE OVER EREN'S TITAN.
WHAT DO YOU SAY, EREN? THAT'S GOOD, RIGHT?
... CON-NIE.
BETTER ME...
THAN JEAN, RIGHT?
...
THAT ISN'T A GOOD IDEA.
BECAUSE YOU'RE AN IDIOT.
WHA ?
WHA? NO, I MEAN...
HOW COULD WE LET AN IDIOT BE RESPON-SIBLE FOR SOMETHING SO IMPORTANT?
...
WHA ?
AGH ...
THAT BOY REALLY GITS MY GOAT...

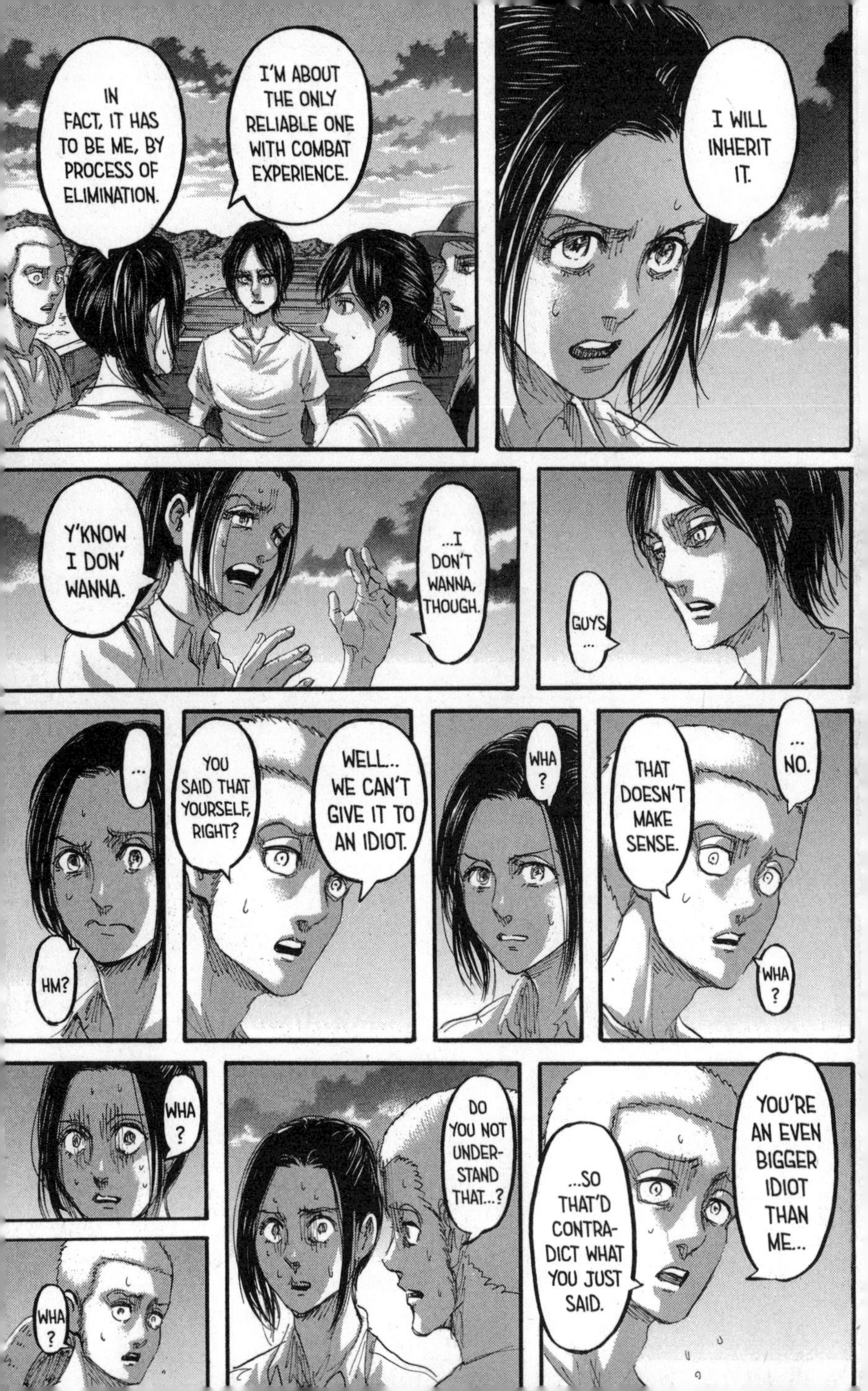

I'M ABOUT THE ONLY RELIABLE ONE WITH COMBAT EXPERIENCE.
IN FACT, IT HAS TO BE ME, BY PROCESS OF ELIMINATION.
I WILL INHERIT IT.
Y'KNOW I DON' WANNA.
...I DON'T WANNA, THOUGH.
GUYS ...
...
HM?
WELL... WE CAN'T GIVE IT TO AN IDIOT.
YOU SAID THAT YOURSELF, RIGHT?
WHA ?
... NO.
THAT DOESN'T MAKE SENSE.
WHA ?
WHA ?
WHA ?
DO YOU NOT UNDER-STAND THAT...?
YOU'RE AN EVEN BIGGER IDIOT THAN ME...
...SO THAT'D CONTRA-DICT WHAT YOU JUST SAID.

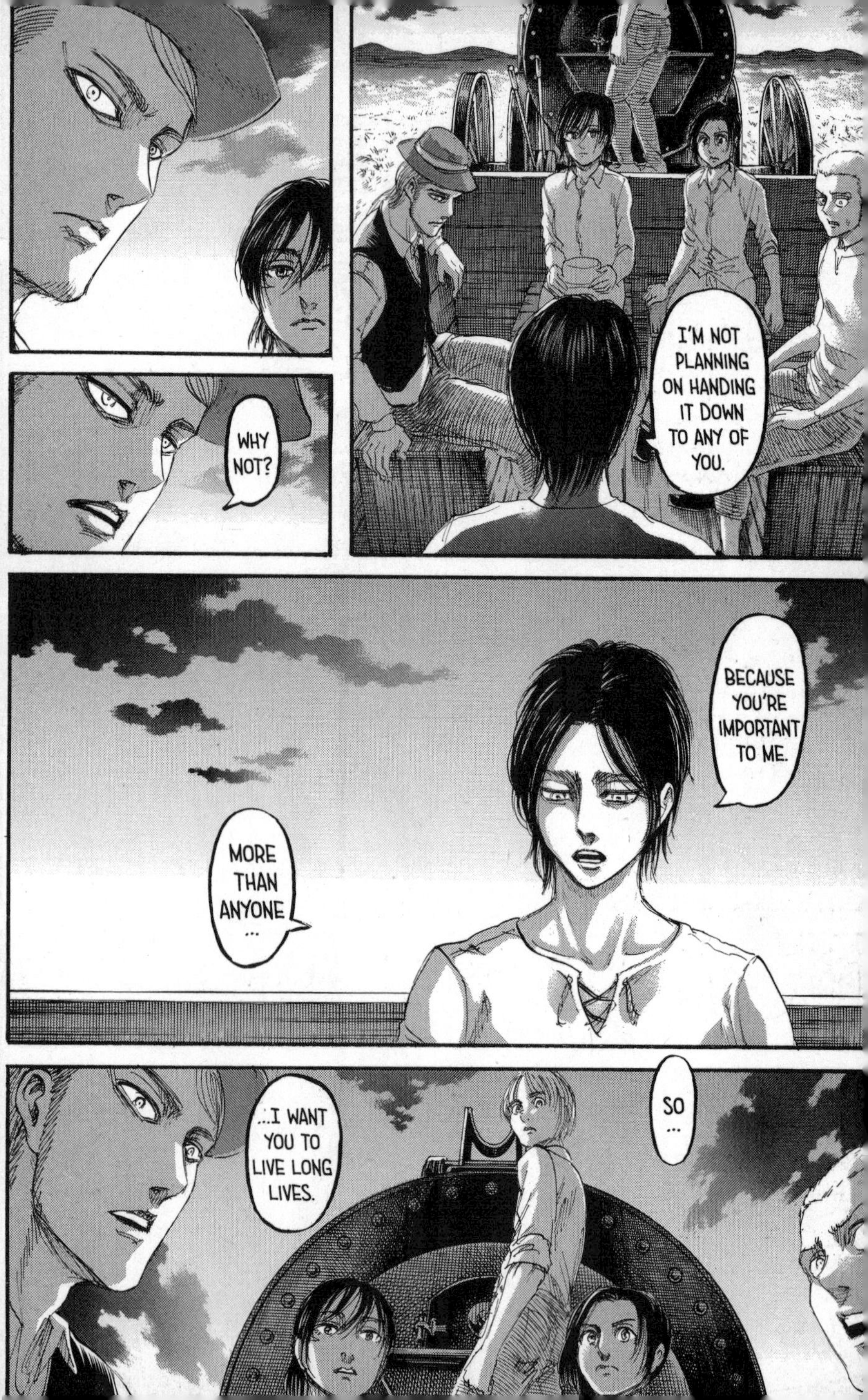
I'M NOT PLANNING ON HANDING IT DOWN TO ANY OF YOU.
WHY NOT?
BECAUSE YOU'RE IMPORTANT TO ME.
MORE THAN ANYONE ...
SO ...
...I WANT YOU TO LIVE LONG LIVES.

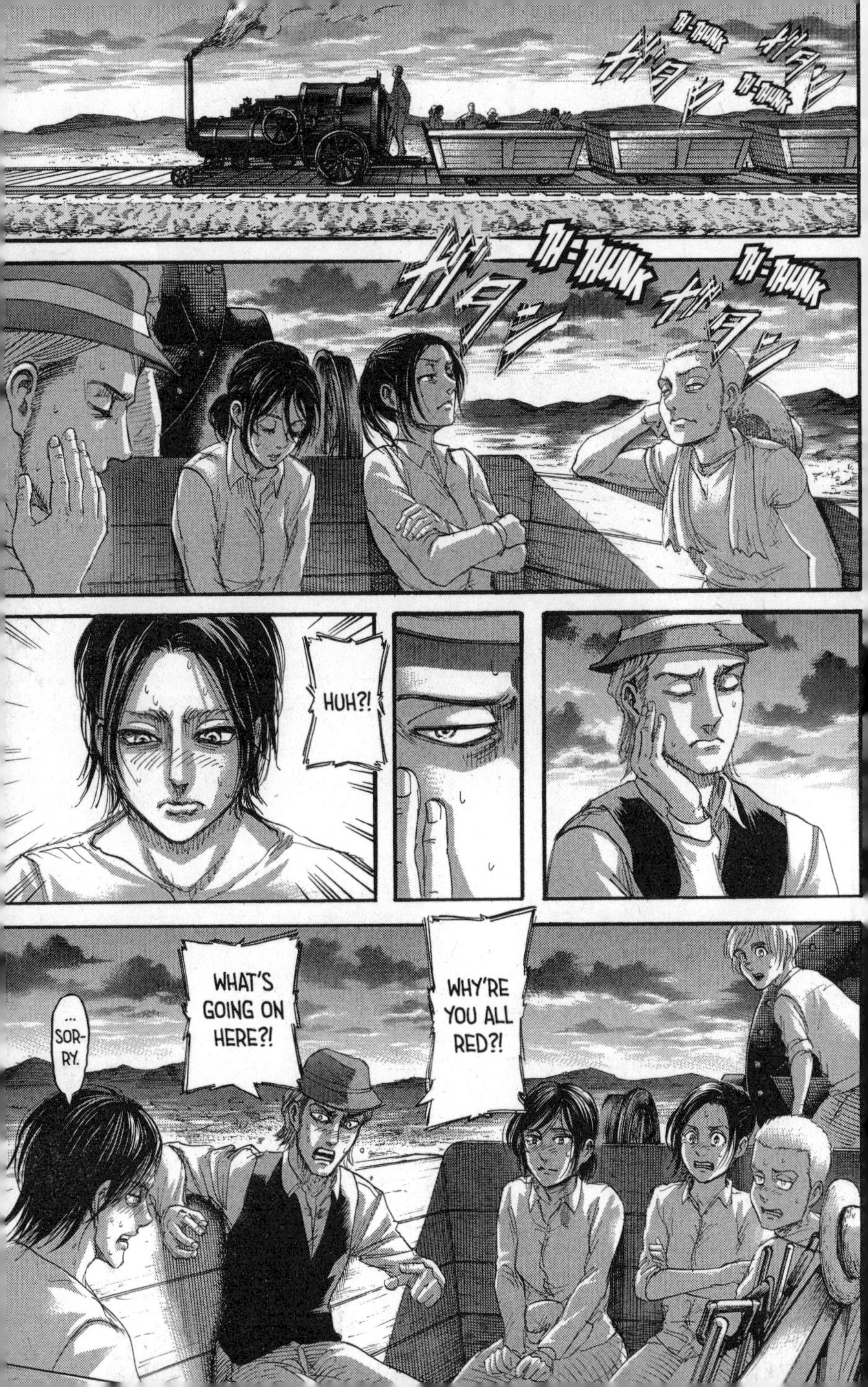
TA-THUNK
TA-THUNK
TA-THUNK
TA-THUNK
HUH?!
WHY'RE YOU ALL RED?!
WHAT'S GOING ON HERE?!
... SOR-RY.

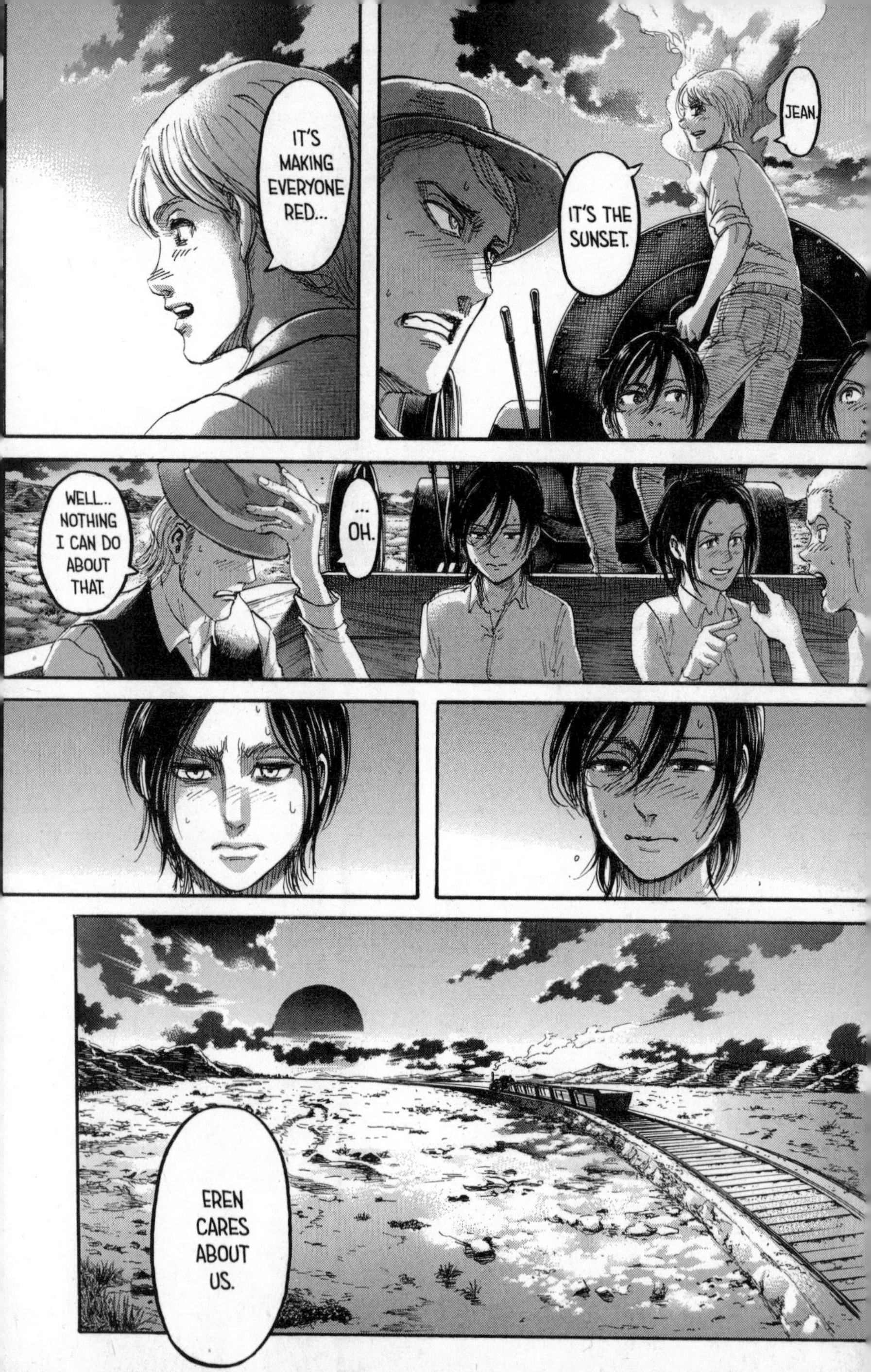
JEAN.
IT'S THE SUNSET.
IT'S MAKING EVERYONE RED...
...OH.
WELL... NOTHING I CAN DO ABOUT THAT.
EREN CARES ABOUT US.

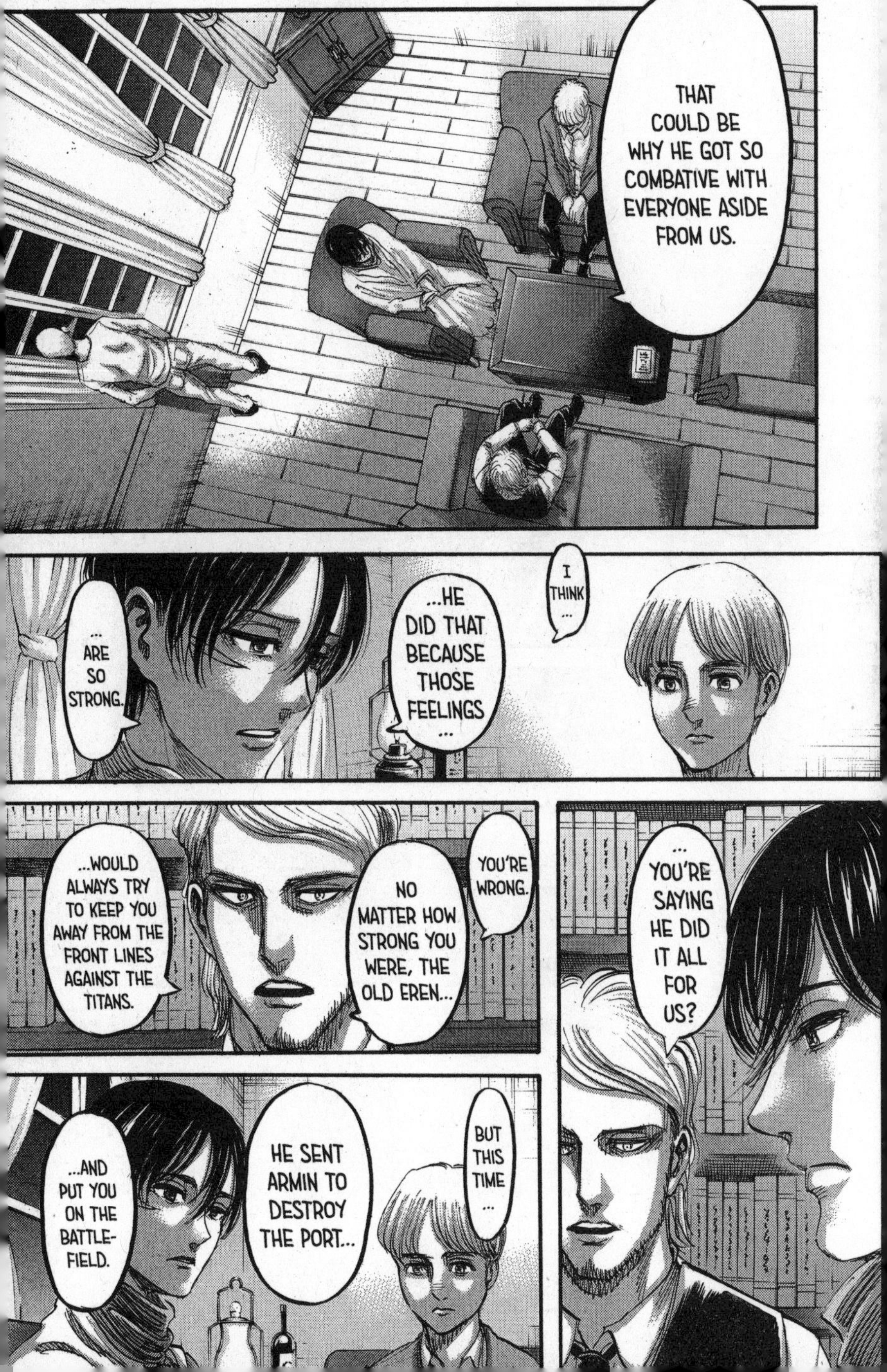
THAT COULD BE WHY HE GOT SO COMBATIVE WITH EVERYONE ASIDE FROM US.
I THINK...
...HE DID THAT BECAUSE THOSE FEELINGS...
...ARE SO STRONG.
...YOU'RE SAYING HE DID IT ALL FOR US?
YOU'RE WRONG.
NO MATTER HOW STRONG YOU WERE, THE OLD EREN...
...WOULD ALWAYS TRY TO KEEP YOU AWAY FROM THE FRONT LINES AGAINST THE TITANS.
BUT THIS TIME...
HE SENT ARMIN TO DESTROY THE PORT...
...AND PUT YOU ON THE BATTLE-FIELD.

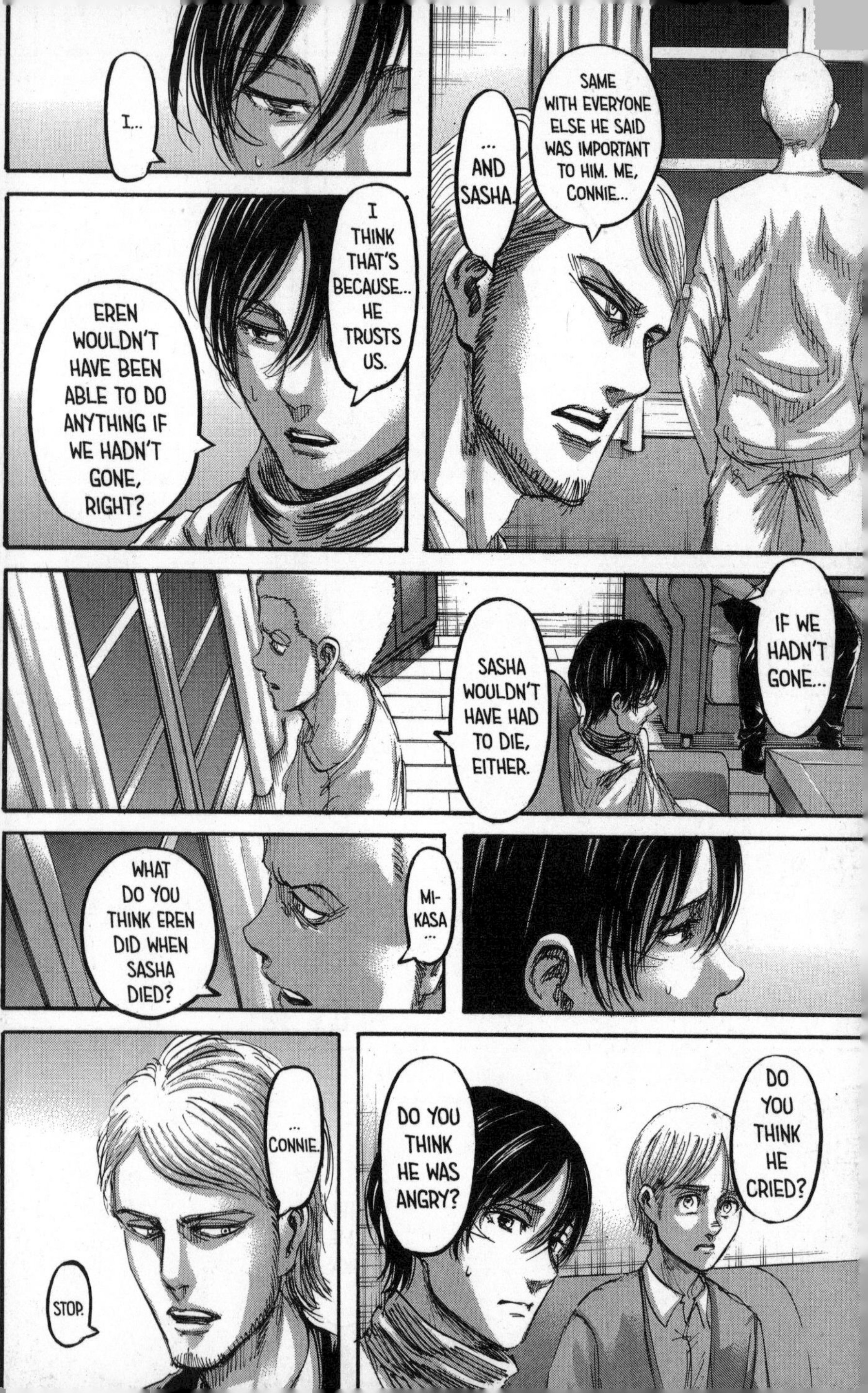

SAME WITH EVERYONE ELSE HE SAID WAS IMPORTANT TO HIM. ME, CONNIE...
... AND SASHA.
I...
I THINK THAT'S BECAUSE... HE TRUSTS US.
EREN WOULDN'T HAVE BEEN ABLE TO DO ANYTHING IF WE HADN'T GONE, RIGHT?
IF WE HADN'T GONE...
SASHA WOULDN'T HAVE HAD TO DIE, EITHER.
MI-KASA...
WHAT DO YOU THINK EREN DID WHEN SASHA DIED?
DO YOU THINK HE CRIED?
DO YOU THINK HE WAS ANGRY?
... CONNIE.
STOP.

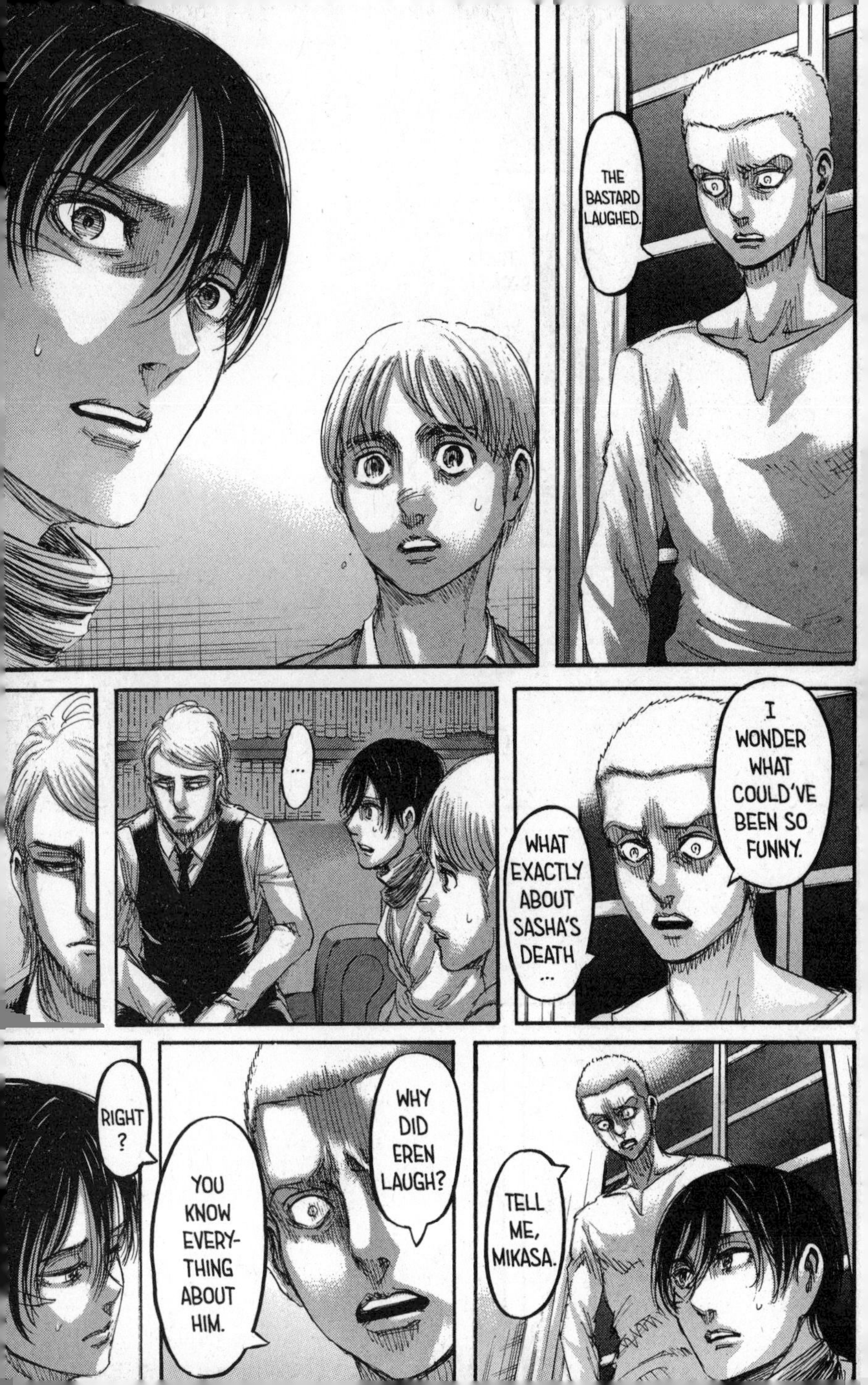
THE BASTARD LAUGHED.
I WONDER WHAT COULD'VE BEEN SO FUNNY.
WHAT EXACTLY ABOUT SASHA'S DEATH ...
...
TELL ME, MIKASA.
WHY DID EREN LAUGH?
YOU KNOW EVERY-THING ABOUT HIM.
RIGHT?

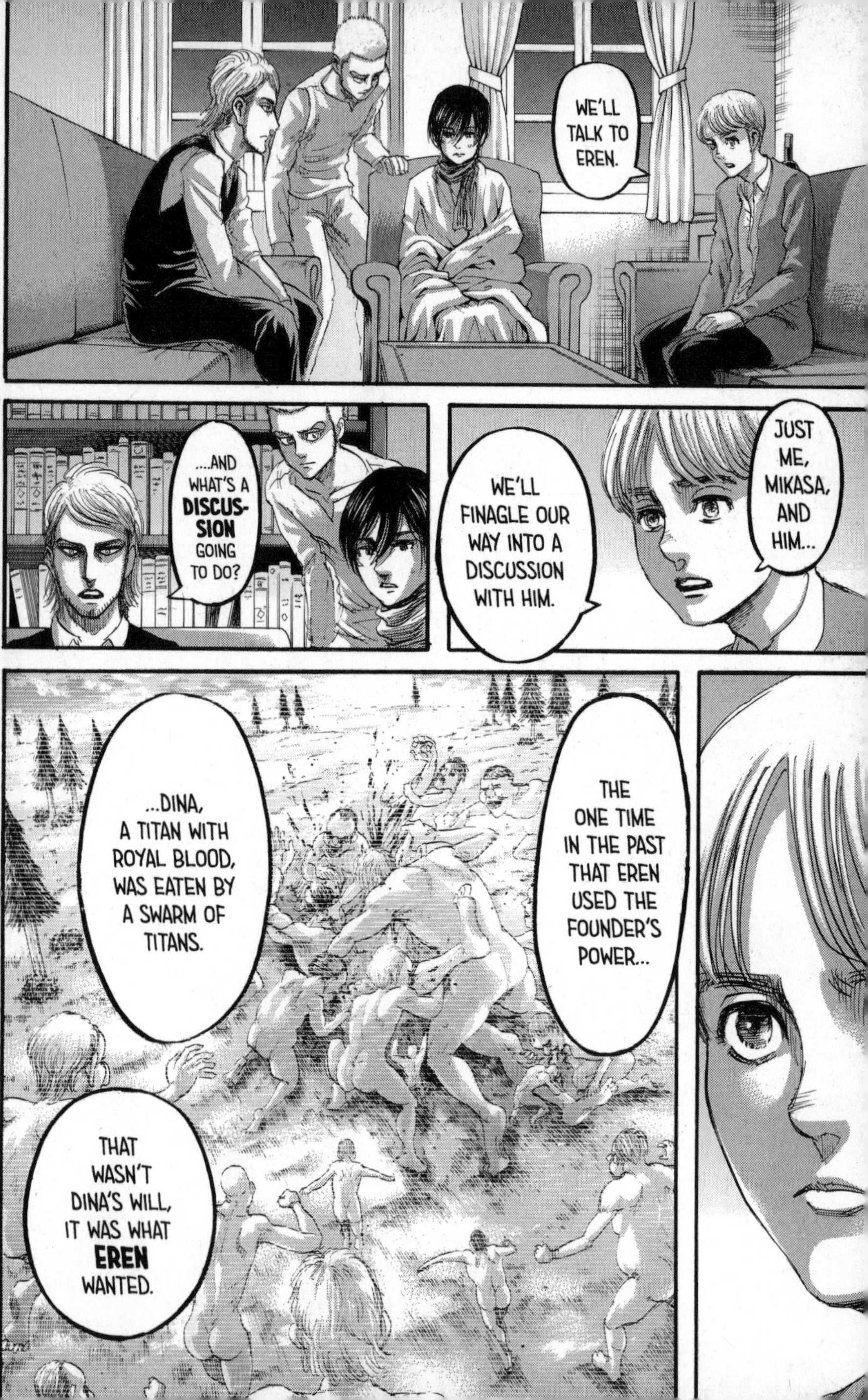
WE'LL TALK TO EREN.
...AND WHAT'S A **DISCUSSION** GOING TO DO?
WE'LL FINAGLE OUR WAY INTO A DISCUSSION WITH HIM.
JUST ME, MIKASA, AND HIM...
...DINA, A TITAN WITH ROYAL BLOOD, WAS EATEN BY A SWARM OF TITANS.
THE ONE TIME IN THE PAST THAT EREN USED THE FOUNDER'S POWER...
THAT WASN'T DINA'S WILL, IT WAS WHAT **EREN** WANTED.

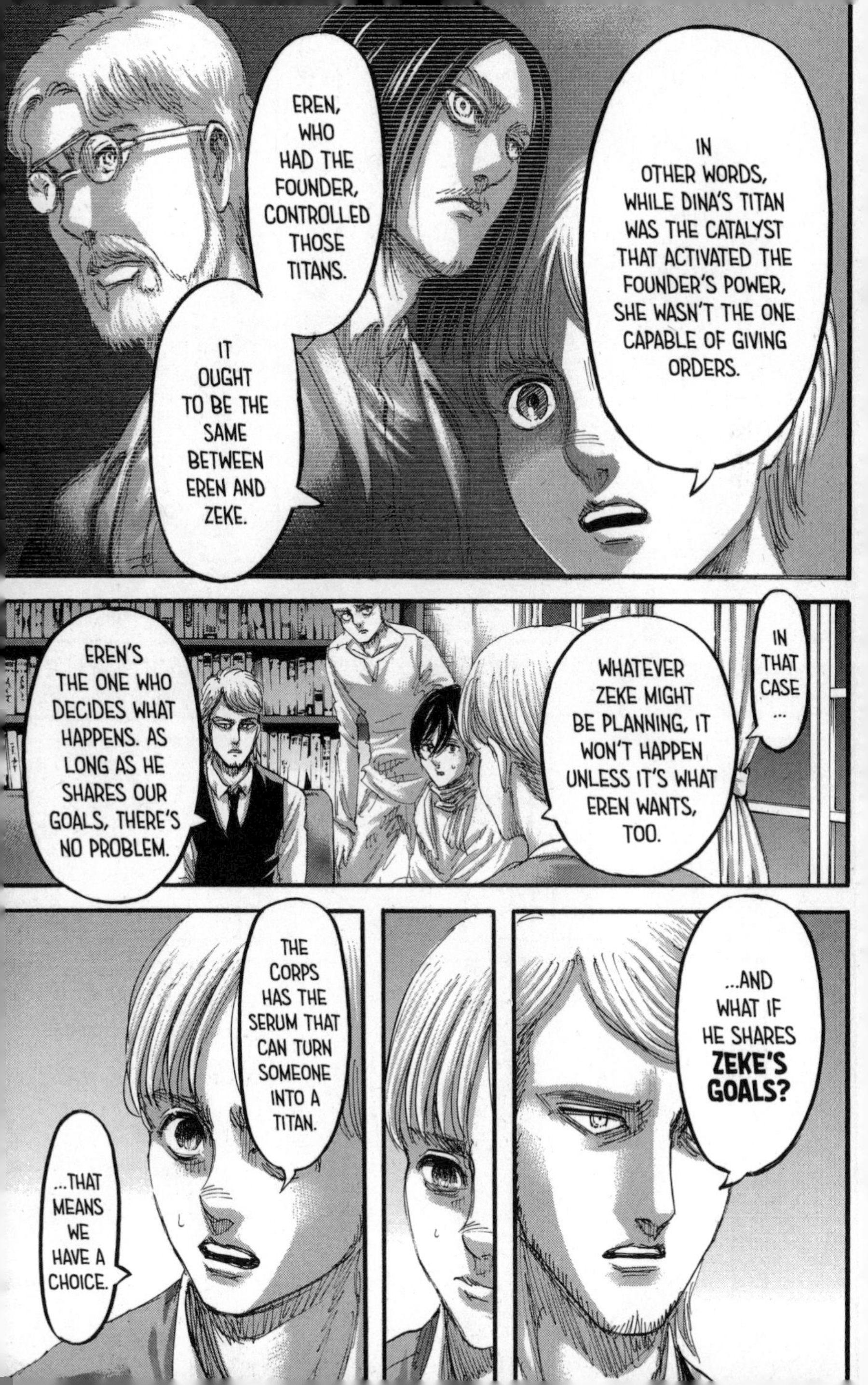
IN OTHER WORDS, WHILE DINA'S TITAN WAS THE CATALYST THAT ACTIVATED THE FOUNDER'S POWER, SHE WASN'T THE ONE CAPABLE OF GIVING ORDERS.
EREN, WHO HAD THE FOUNDER, CONTROLLED THOSE TITANS.
IT OUGHT TO BE THE SAME BETWEEN EREN AND ZEKE.
IN THAT CASE ...
WHATEVER ZEKE MIGHT BE PLANNING, IT WON'T HAPPEN UNLESS IT'S WHAT EREN WANTS, TOO.
EREN'S THE ONE WHO DECIDES WHAT HAPPENS. AS LONG AS HE SHARES OUR GOALS, THERE'S NO PROBLEM.
...AND WHAT IF HE SHARES **ZEKE'S GOALS?**
THE CORPS HAS THE SERUM THAT CAN TURN SOMEONE INTO A TITAN.
...THAT MEANS WE HAVE A CHOICE.

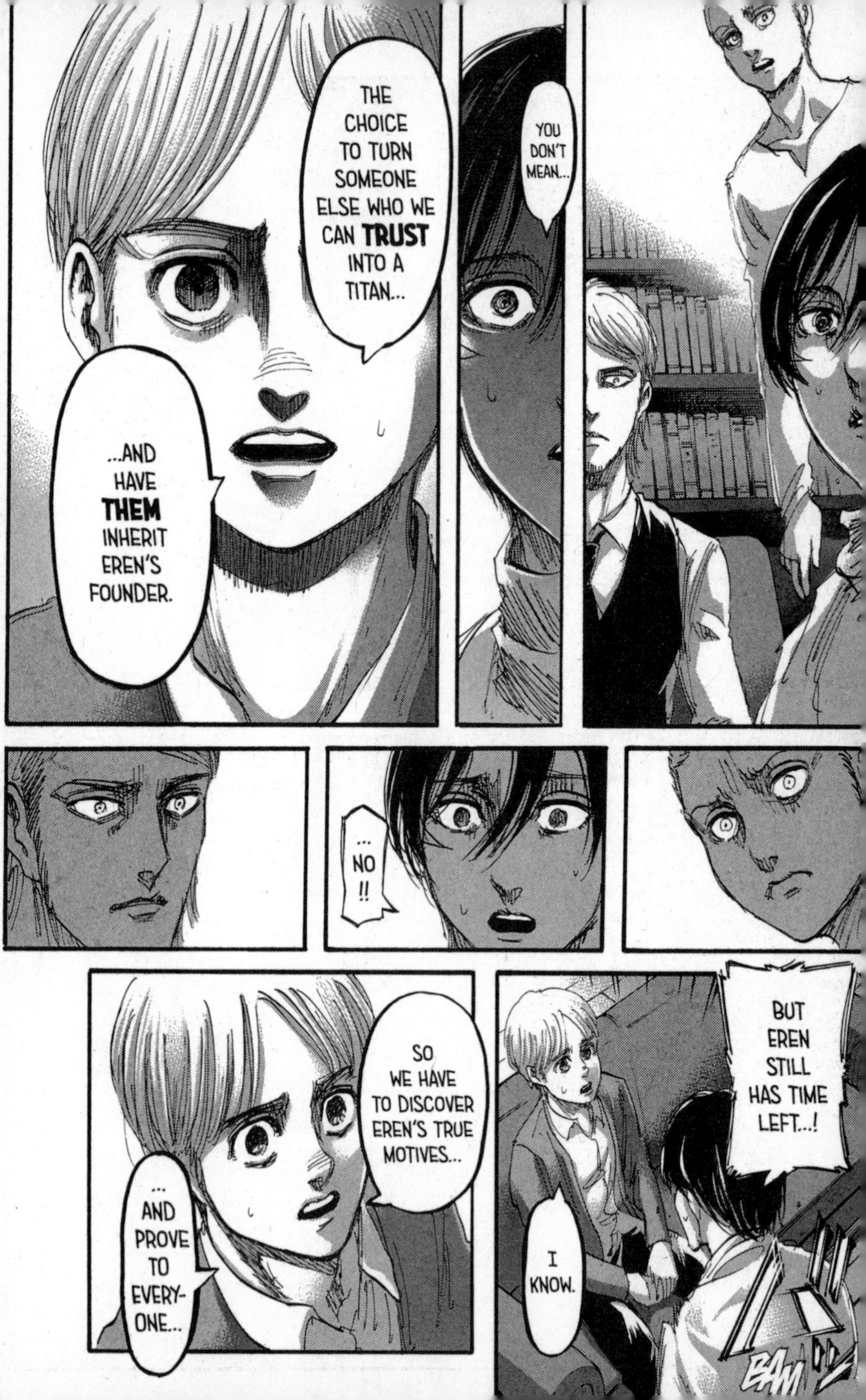
THE CHOICE TO TURN SOMEONE ELSE WHO WE CAN **TRUST** INTO A TITAN...
...AND HAVE **THEM** INHERIT EREN'S FOUNDER.
YOU DON'T MEAN...
... NO !!
SO WE HAVE TO DISCOVER EREN'S TRUE MOTIVES...
... AND PROVE TO EVERYONE...
BUT EREN STILL HAS TIME LEFT...!
I KNOW.
BAM

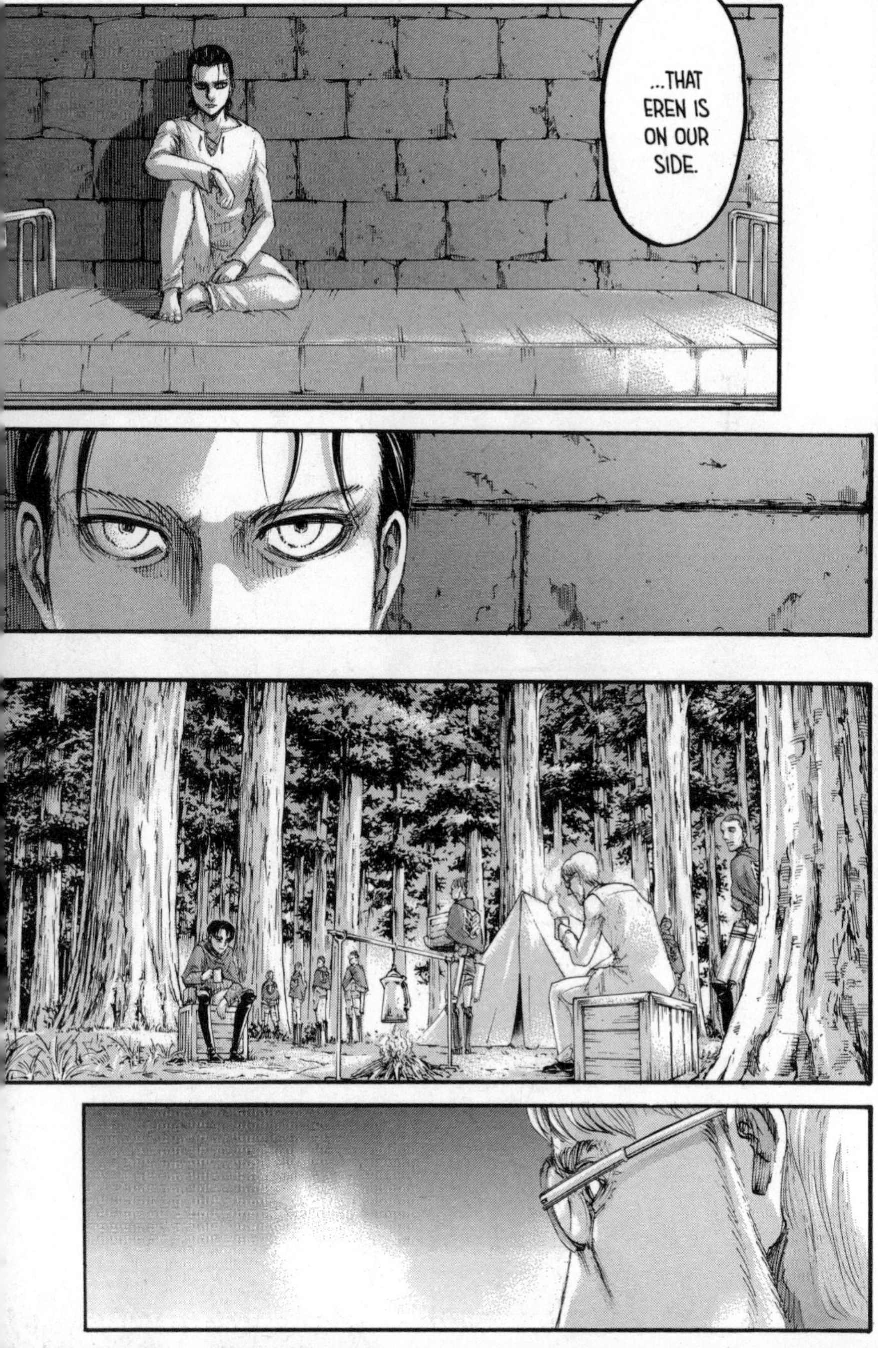
...THAT EREN IS ON OUR SIDE.

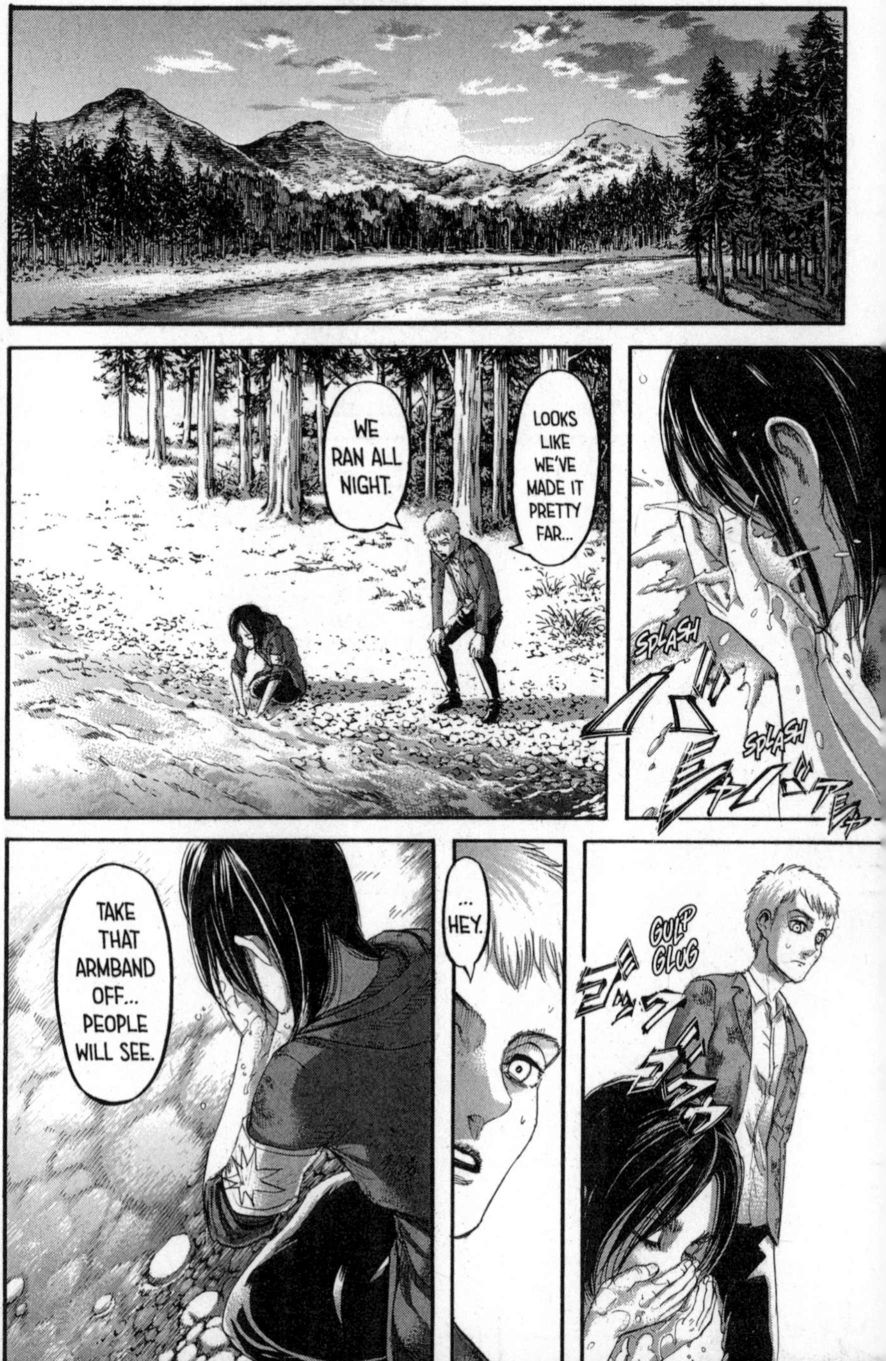
SPLASH
SPLASH
LOOKS LIKE WE'VE MADE IT PRETTY FAR...
WE RAN ALL NIGHT.
GULP GLUG
... HEY.
TAKE THAT ARMBAND OFF... PEOPLE WILL SEE.

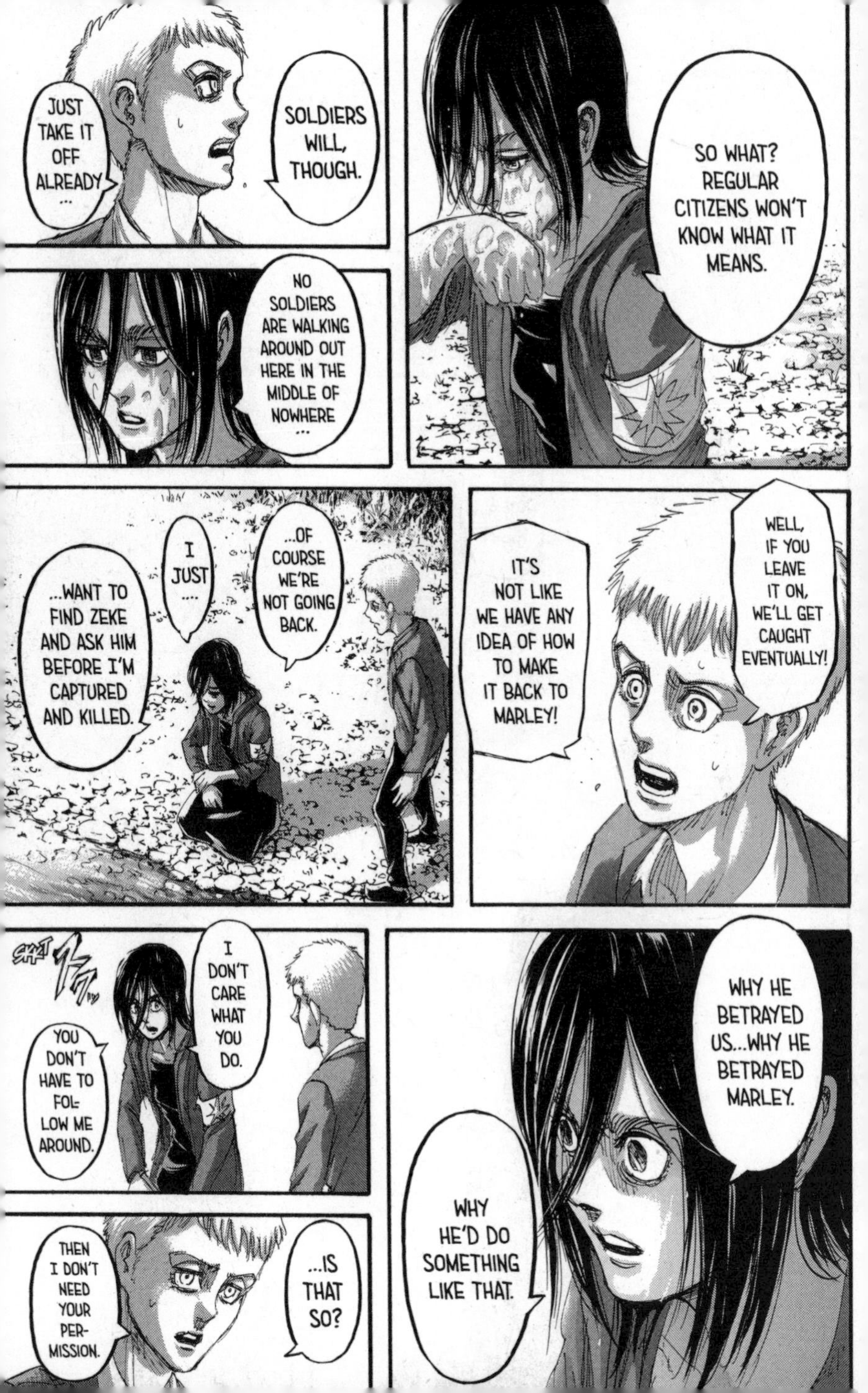
SO WHAT? REGULAR CITIZENS WON'T KNOW WHAT IT MEANS.
SOLDIERS WILL, THOUGH.
JUST TAKE IT OFF ALREADY...
NO SOLDIERS ARE WALKING AROUND OUT HERE IN THE MIDDLE OF NOWHERE...
WELL, IF YOU LEAVE IT ON, WE'LL GET CAUGHT EVENTUALLY!
IT'S NOT LIKE WE HAVE ANY IDEA OF HOW TO MAKE IT BACK TO MARLEY!
...OF COURSE WE'RE NOT GOING BACK.
I JUST...
...WANT TO FIND ZEKE AND ASK HIM BEFORE I'M CAPTURED AND KILLED.
WHY HE BETRAYED US...WHY HE BETRAYED MARLEY.
WHY HE'D DO SOMETHING LIKE THAT.
SHKT
I DON'T CARE WHAT YOU DO.
YOU DON'T HAVE TO FOL-LOW ME AROUND.
...IS THAT SO?
THEN I DON'T NEED YOUR PER-MISSION.

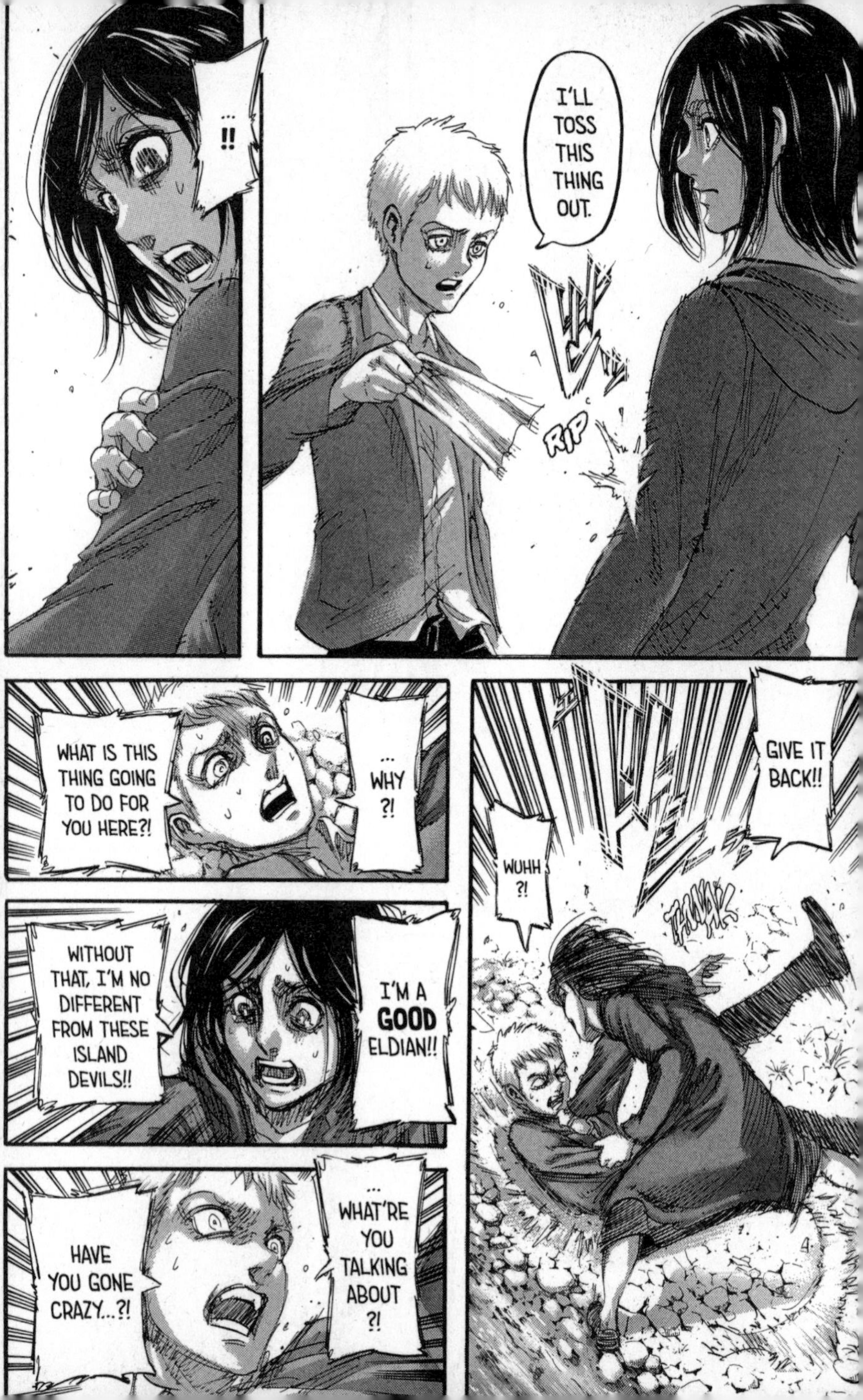
I'LL TOSS THIS THING OUT.
RIP
...!!
GIVE IT BACK!!
WUHH?!
...WHY?!
WHAT IS THIS THING GOING TO DO FOR YOU HERE?!
I'M A GOOD ELDIAN!!
WITHOUT THAT, I'M NO DIFFERENT FROM THESE ISLAND DEVILS!!
...WHAT'RE YOU TALKING ABOUT?!
HAVE YOU GONE CRAZY...?!

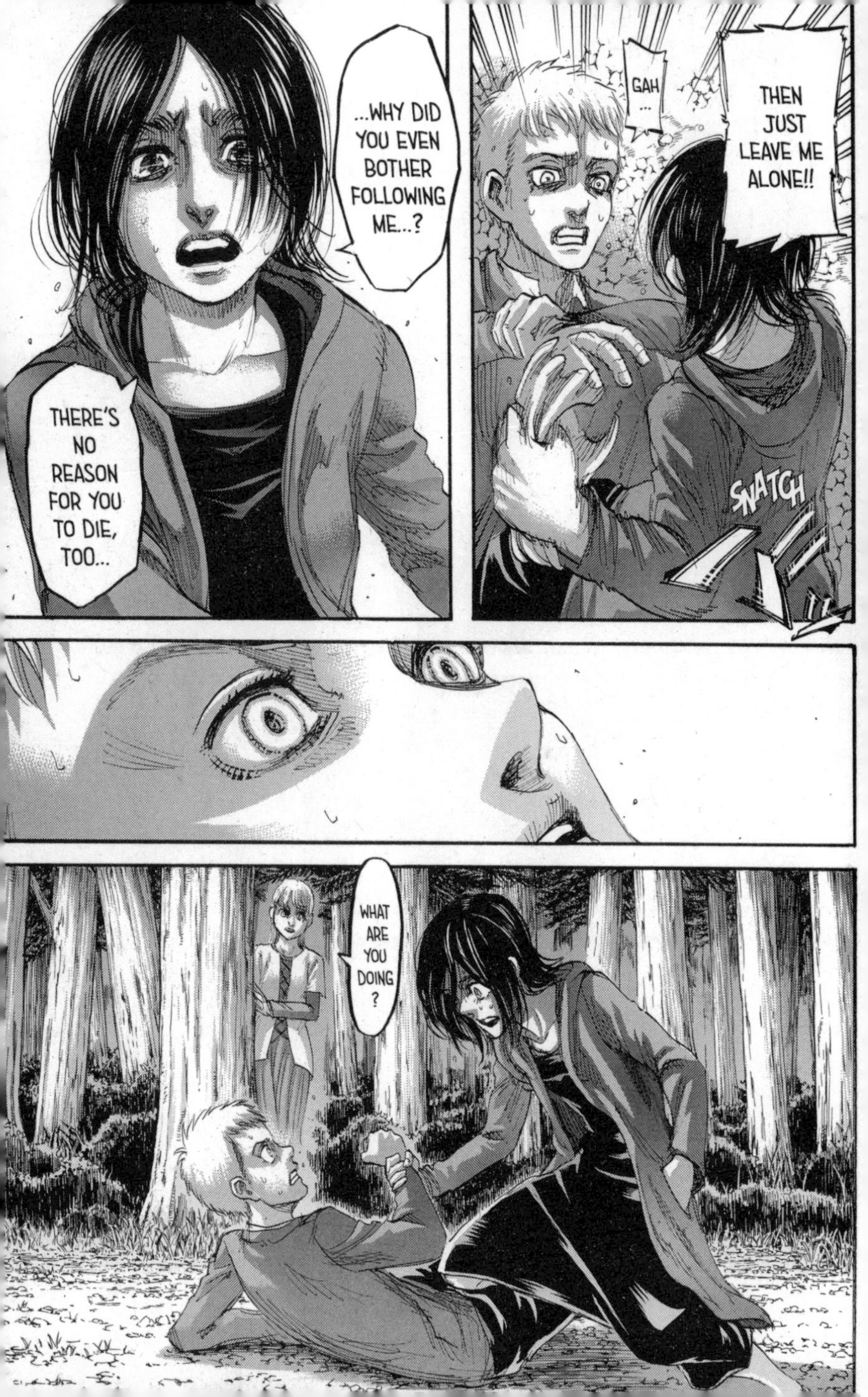
...WHY DID YOU EVEN BOTHER FOLLOWING ME...?
THERE'S NO REASON FOR YOU TO DIE, TOO...
THEN JUST LEAVE ME ALONE!!
GAH ...
SNATCH
WHAT ARE YOU DOING?

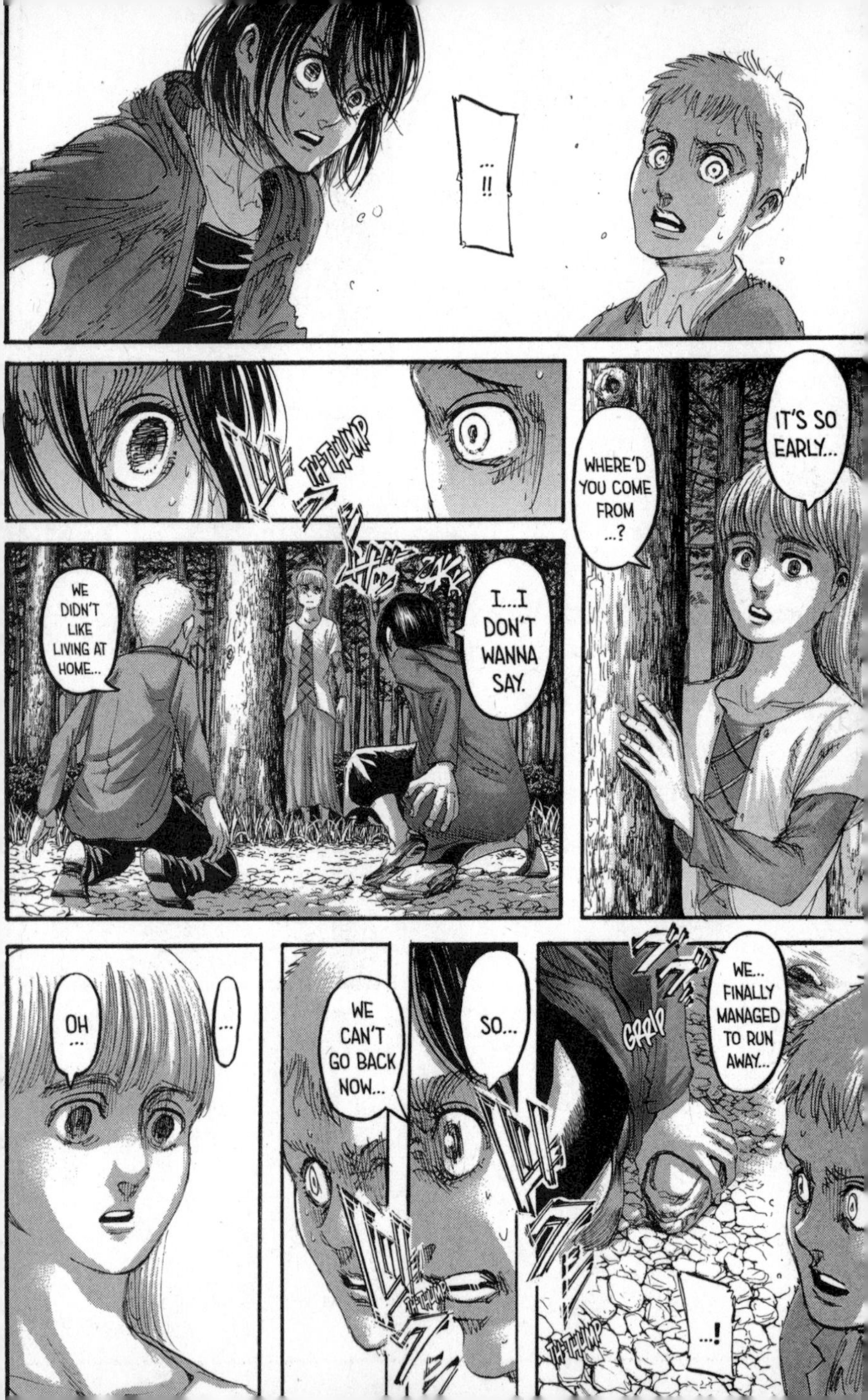
...
!!
IT'S SO EARLY...
WHERE'D YOU COME FROM ...?
TH-THUMP
I...I DON'T WANNA SAY.
WE DIDN'T LIKE LIVING AT HOME...
WE... FINALLY MANAGED TO RUN AWAY...
GRRIP
...!
TH-THUMP
SO...
WE CAN'T GO BACK NOW...
TH-THUMP
...
OH ...

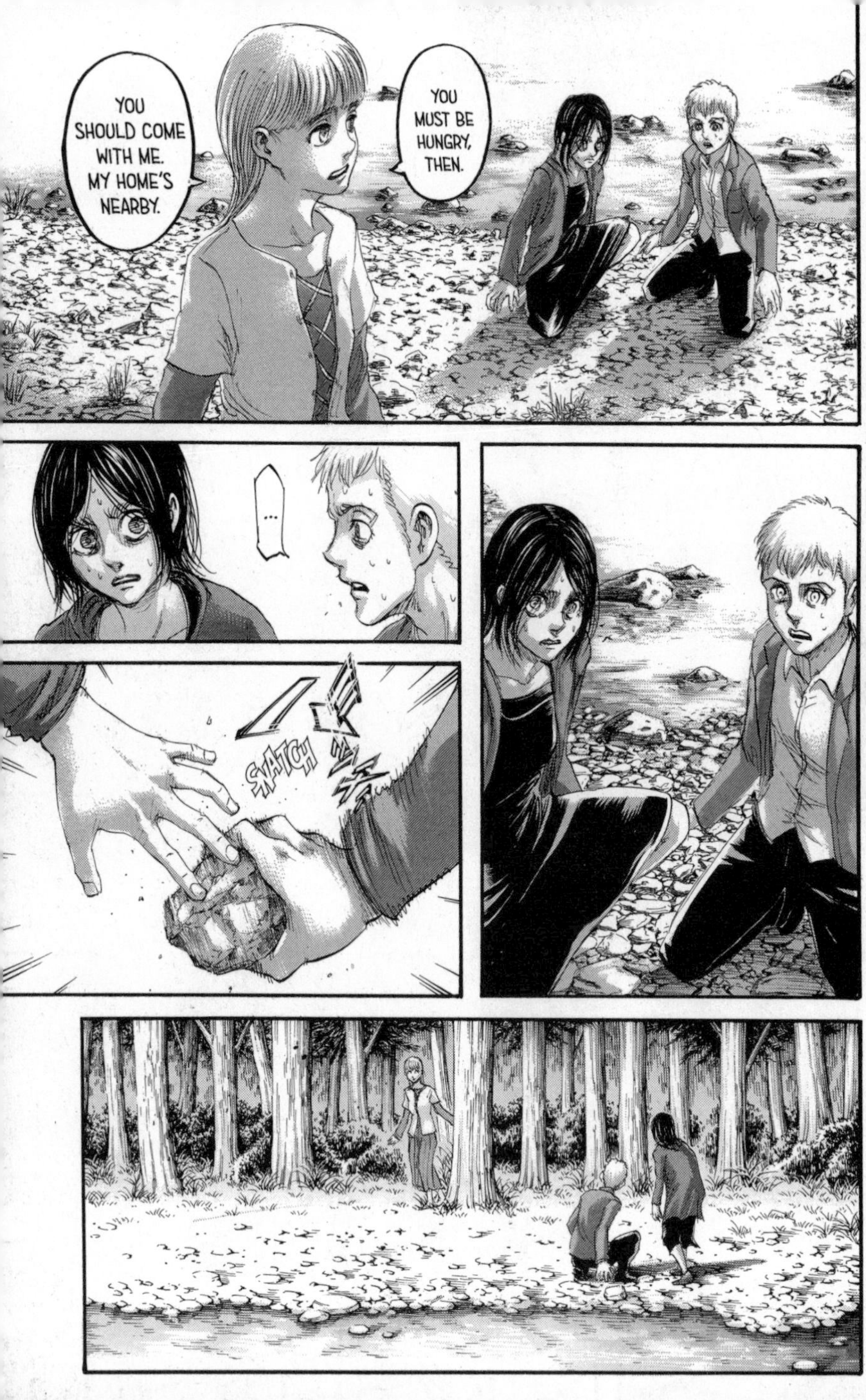
YOU MUST BE HUNGRY, THEN.
YOU SHOULD COME WITH ME. MY HOME'S NEARBY.
...
SNATCH

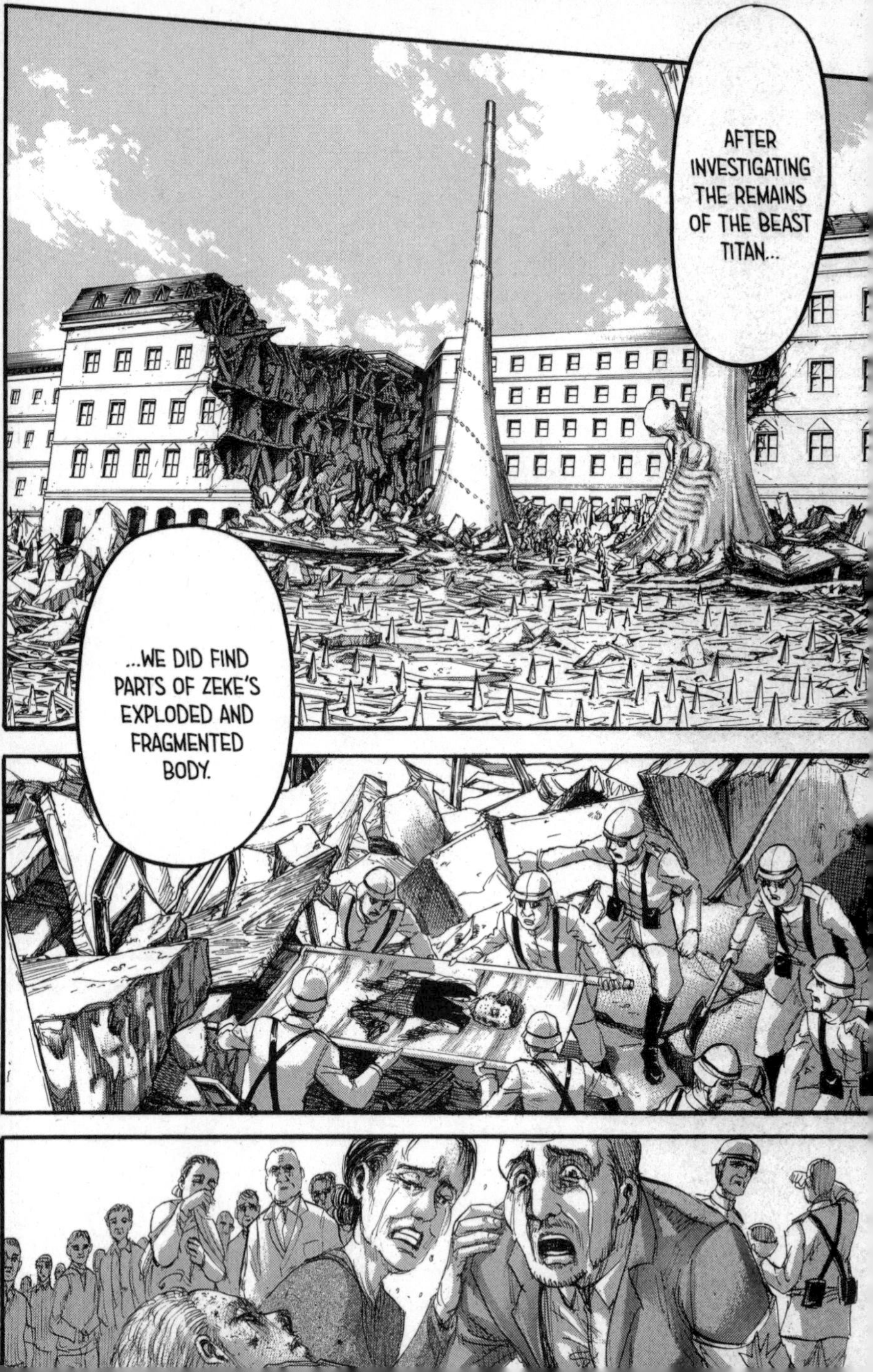
AFTER INVESTIGATING THE REMAINS OF THE BEAST TITAN...
...WE DID FIND PARTS OF ZEKE'S EXPLODED AND FRAGMENTED BODY.

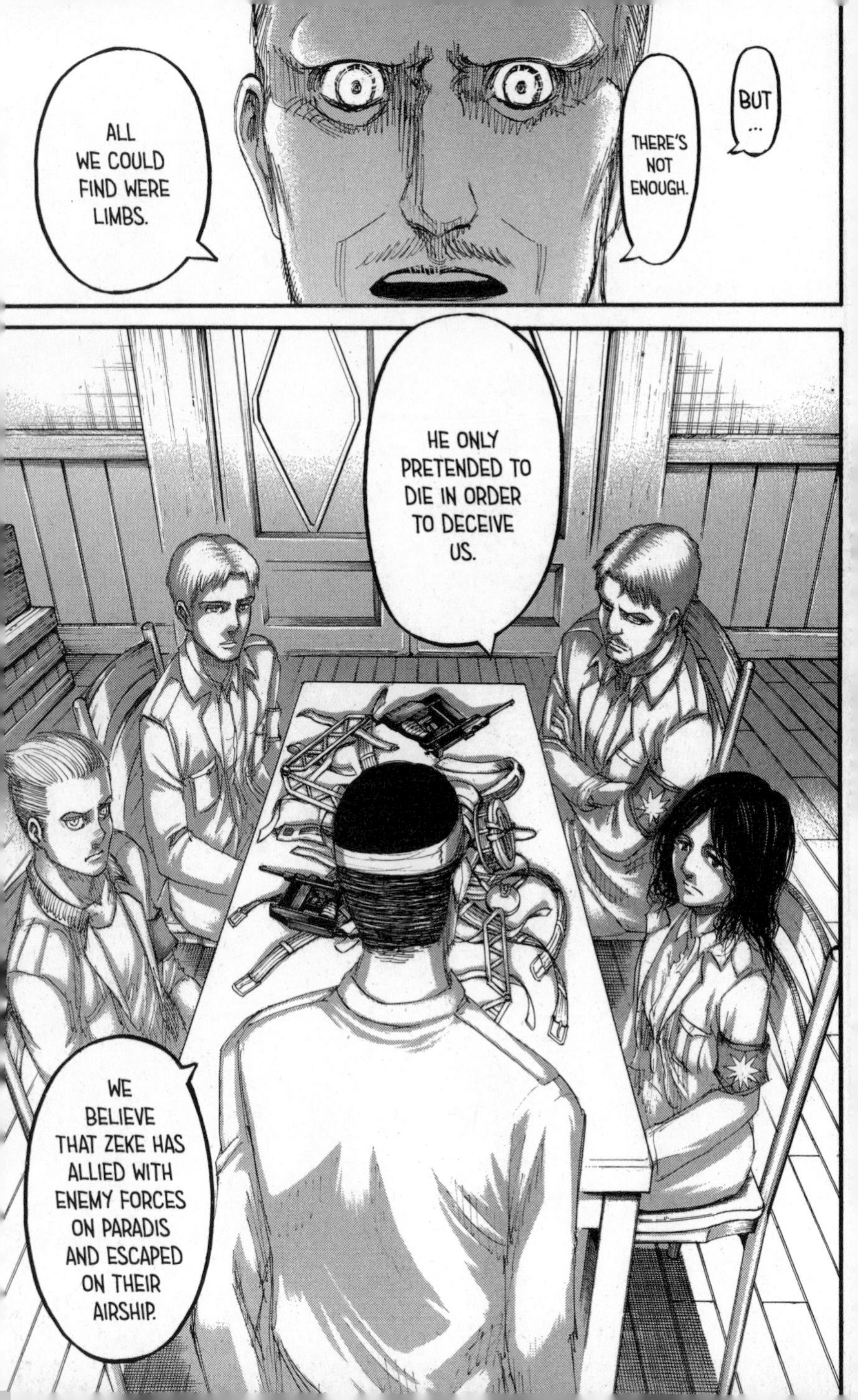
ALL WE COULD FIND WERE LIMBS.
THERE'S NOT ENOUGH.
BUT ...
HE ONLY PRETENDED TO DIE IN ORDER TO DECEIVE US.
WE BELIEVE THAT ZEKE HAS ALLIED WITH ENEMY FORCES ON PARADIS AND ESCAPED ON THEIR AIRSHIP.

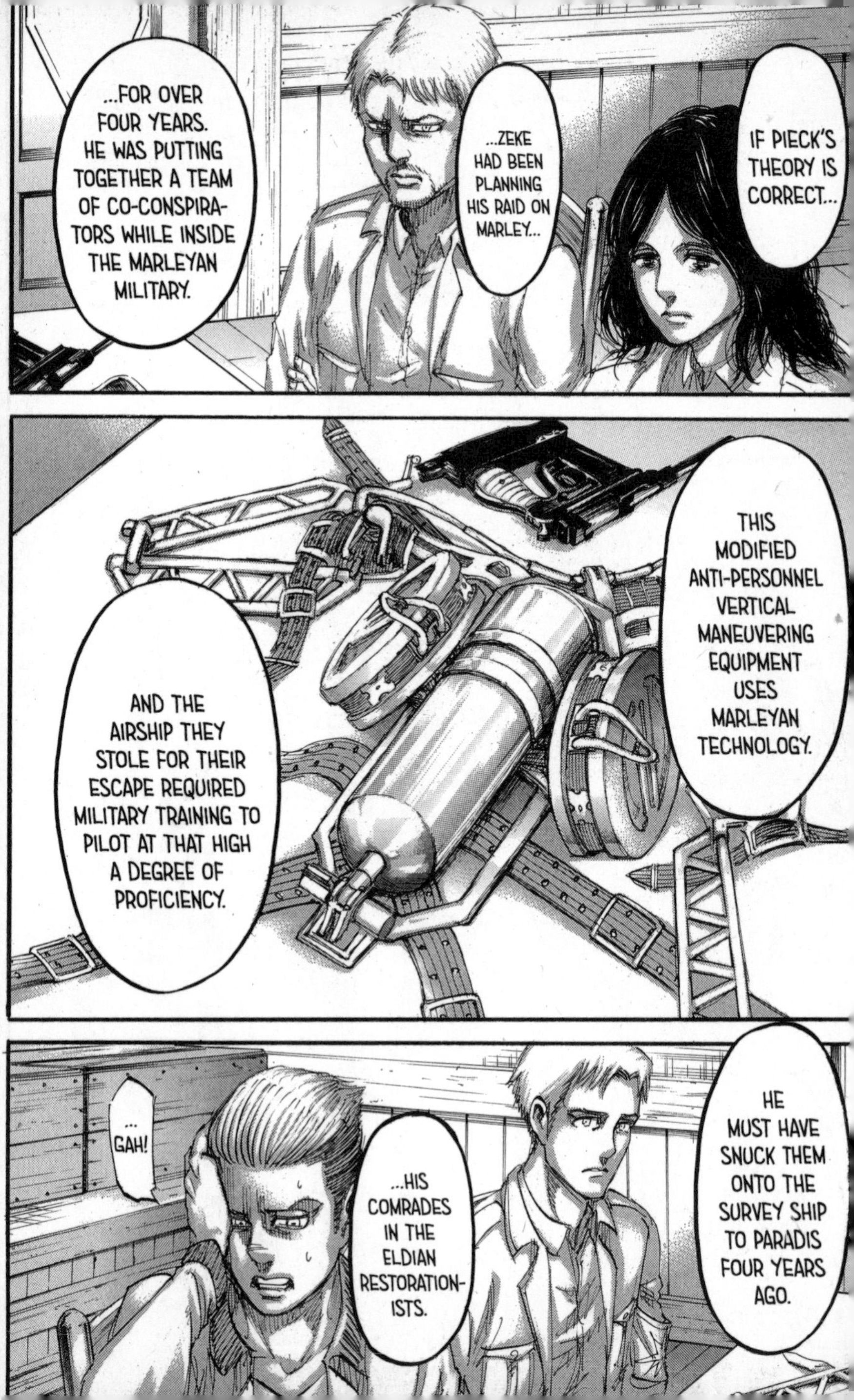
IF PIECK'S THEORY IS CORRECT...
...ZEKE HAD BEEN PLANNING HIS RAID ON MARLEY...
...FOR OVER FOUR YEARS. HE WAS PUTTING TOGETHER A TEAM OF CO-CONSPIRATORS WHILE INSIDE THE MARLEYAN MILITARY.
THIS MODIFIED ANTI-PERSONNEL VERTICAL MANEUVERING EQUIPMENT USES MARLEYAN TECHNOLOGY.
AND THE AIRSHIP THEY STOLE FOR THEIR ESCAPE REQUIRED MILITARY TRAINING TO PILOT AT THAT HIGH A DEGREE OF PROFICIENCY.
HE MUST HAVE SNUCK THEM ONTO THE SURVEY SHIP TO PARADIS FOUR YEARS AGO.
...HIS COMRADES IN THE ELDIAN RESTORATIONISTS.
... GAH!

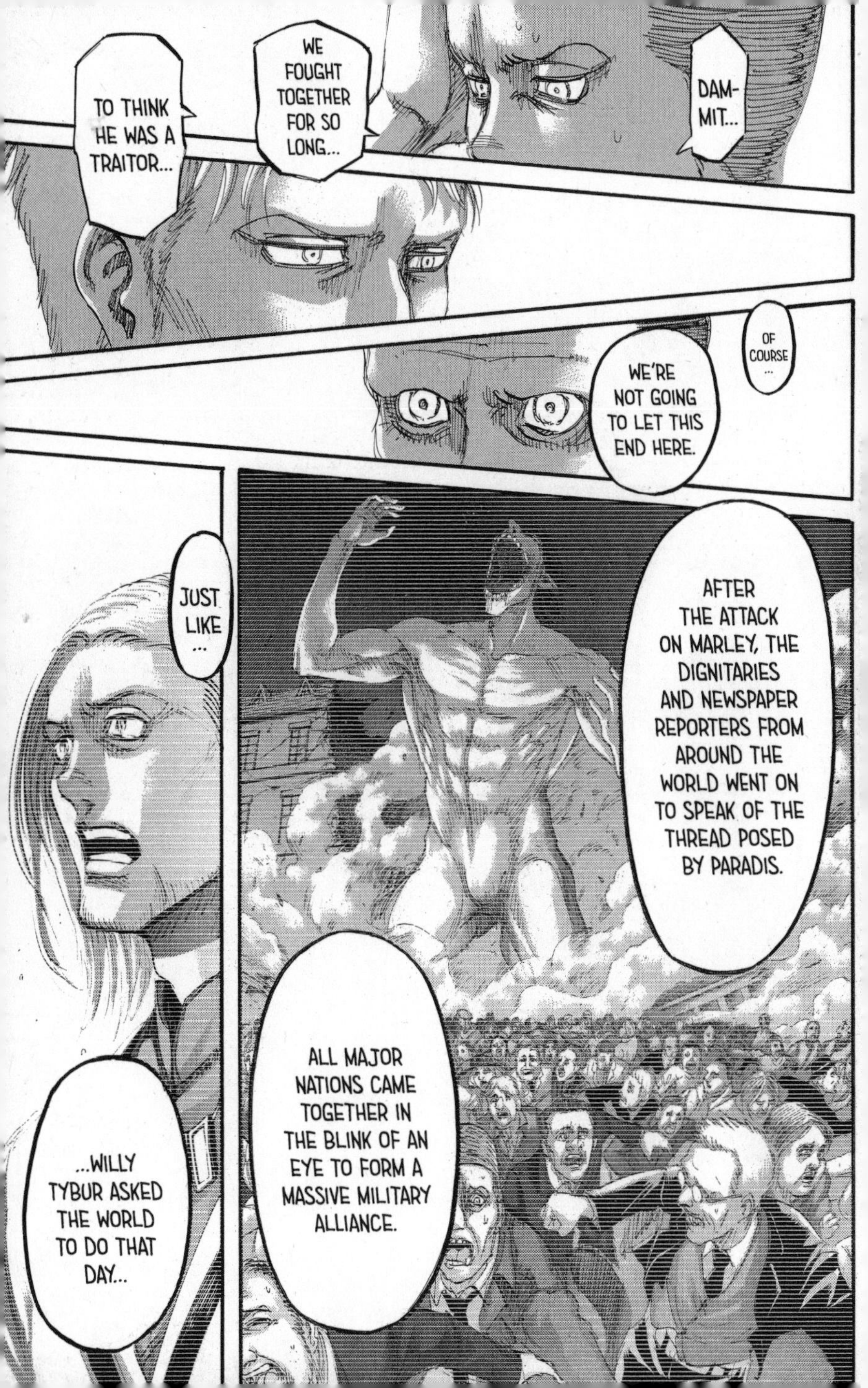
DAM-MIT...
WE FOUGHT TOGETHER FOR SO LONG...
TO THINK HE WAS A TRAITOR...
OF COURSE...
WE'RE NOT GOING TO LET THIS END HERE.
AFTER THE ATTACK ON MARLEY, THE DIGNITARIES AND NEWSPAPER REPORTERS FROM AROUND THE WORLD WENT ON TO SPEAK OF THE THREAD POSED BY PARADIS.
JUST LIKE...
ALL MAJOR NATIONS CAME TOGETHER IN THE BLINK OF AN EYE TO FORM A MASSIVE MILITARY ALLIANCE.
...WILLY TYBUR ASKED THE WORLD TO DO THAT DAY...

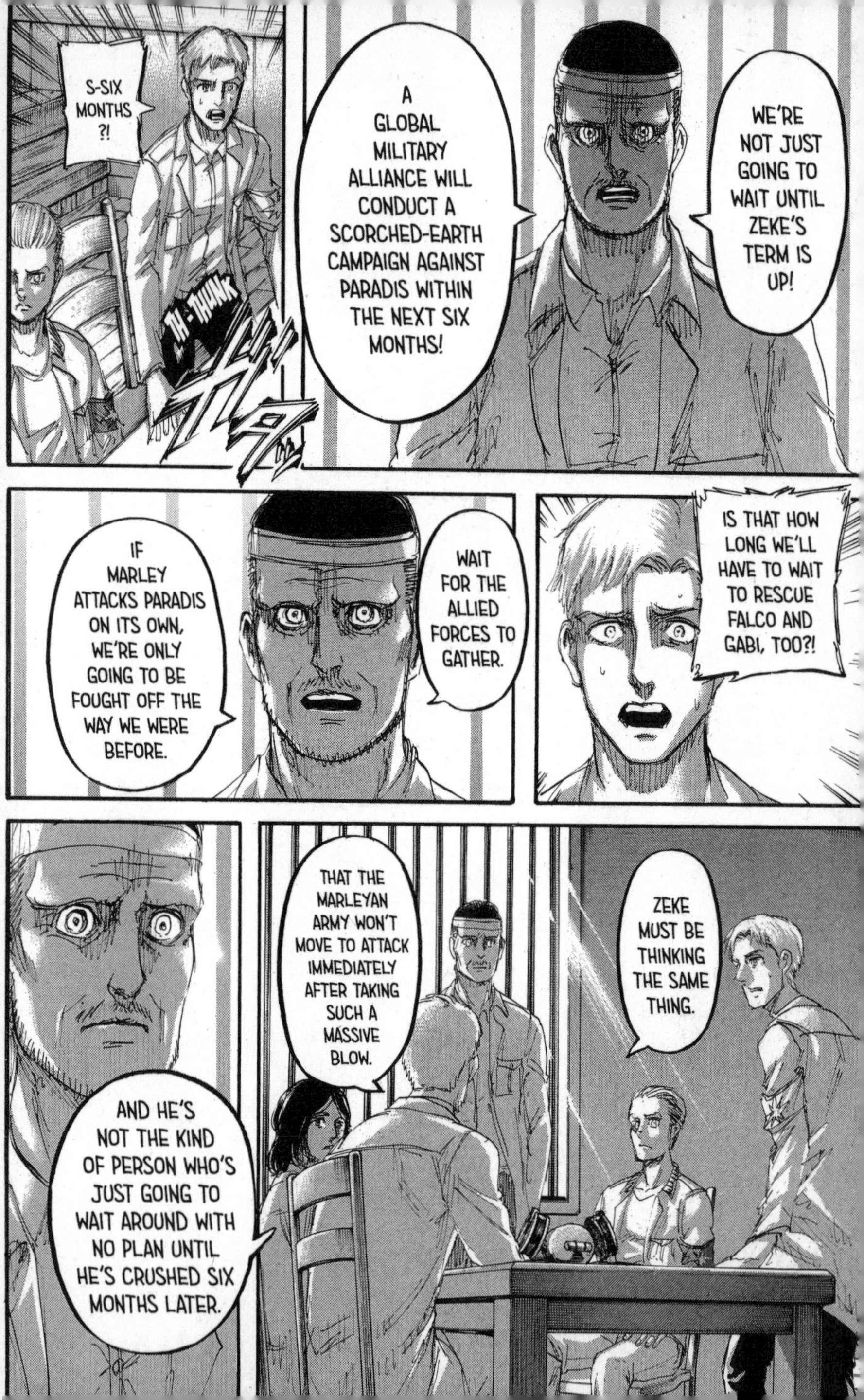

S-SIX MONTHS ?!
TH-THUNK
A GLOBAL MILITARY ALLIANCE WILL CONDUCT A SCORCHED-EARTH CAMPAIGN AGAINST PARADIS WITHIN THE NEXT SIX MONTHS!
WE'RE NOT JUST GOING TO WAIT UNTIL ZEKE'S TERM IS UP!
IF MARLEY ATTACKS PARADIS ON ITS OWN, WE'RE ONLY GOING TO BE FOUGHT OFF THE WAY WE WERE BEFORE.
WAIT FOR THE ALLIED FORCES TO GATHER.
IS THAT HOW LONG WE'LL HAVE TO WAIT TO RESCUE FALCO AND GABI, TOO?!
THAT THE MARLEYAN ARMY WON'T MOVE TO ATTACK IMMEDIATELY AFTER TAKING SUCH A MASSIVE BLOW.
ZEKE MUST BE THINKING THE SAME THING.
AND HE'S NOT THE KIND OF PERSON WHO'S JUST GOING TO WAIT AROUND WITH NO PLAN UNTIL HE'S CRUSHED SIX MONTHS LATER.

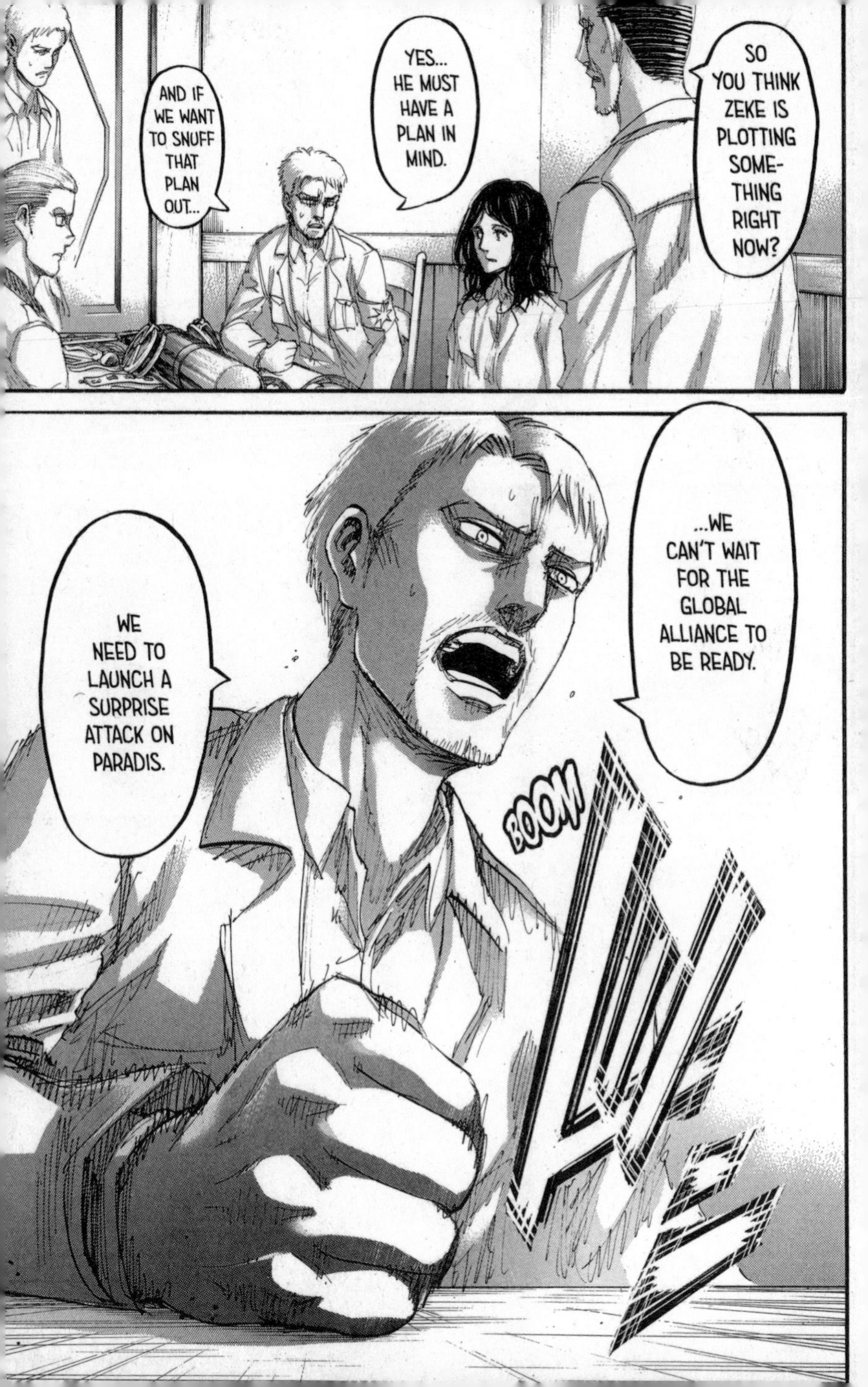
SO YOU THINK ZEKE IS PLOTTING SOME-THING RIGHT NOW?
YES... HE MUST HAVE A PLAN IN MIND.
AND IF WE WANT TO SNUFF THAT PLAN OUT...
...WE CAN'T WAIT FOR THE GLOBAL ALLIANCE TO BE READY.
WE NEED TO LAUNCH A SURPRISE ATTACK ON PARADIS.
BOOM

ATTACK on TITAN

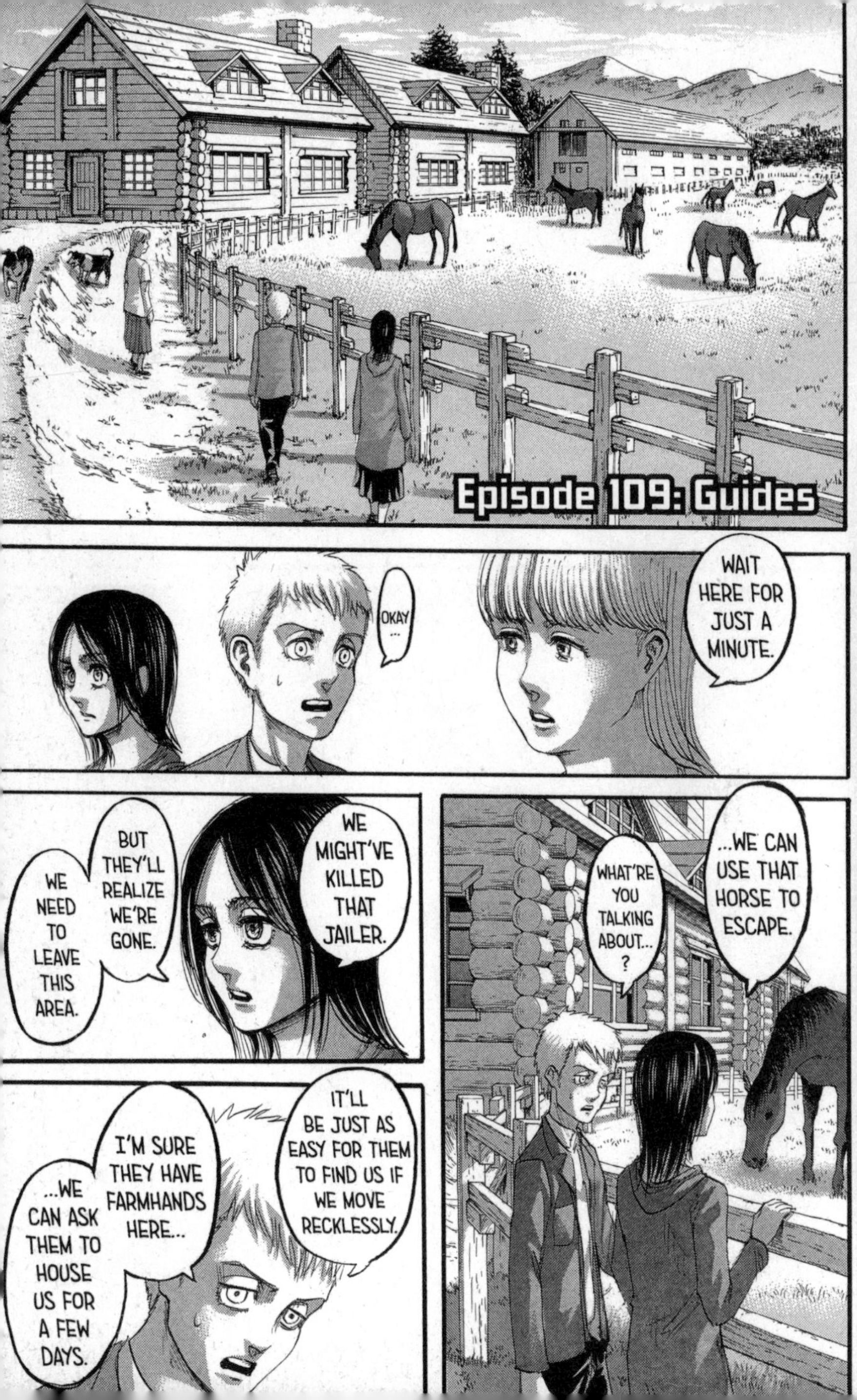
Episode 109: Guides
WAIT HERE FOR JUST A MINUTE.
OKAY...
...WE CAN USE THAT HORSE TO ESCAPE.
WHAT'RE YOU TALKING ABOUT...?
WE MIGHT'VE KILLED THAT JAILER.
BUT THEY'LL REALIZE WE'RE GONE.
WE NEED TO LEAVE THIS AREA.
IT'LL BE JUST AS EASY FOR THEM TO FIND US IF WE MOVE RECKLESSLY.
I'M SURE THEY HAVE FARMHANDS HERE...
...WE CAN ASK THEM TO HOUSE US FOR A FEW DAYS.

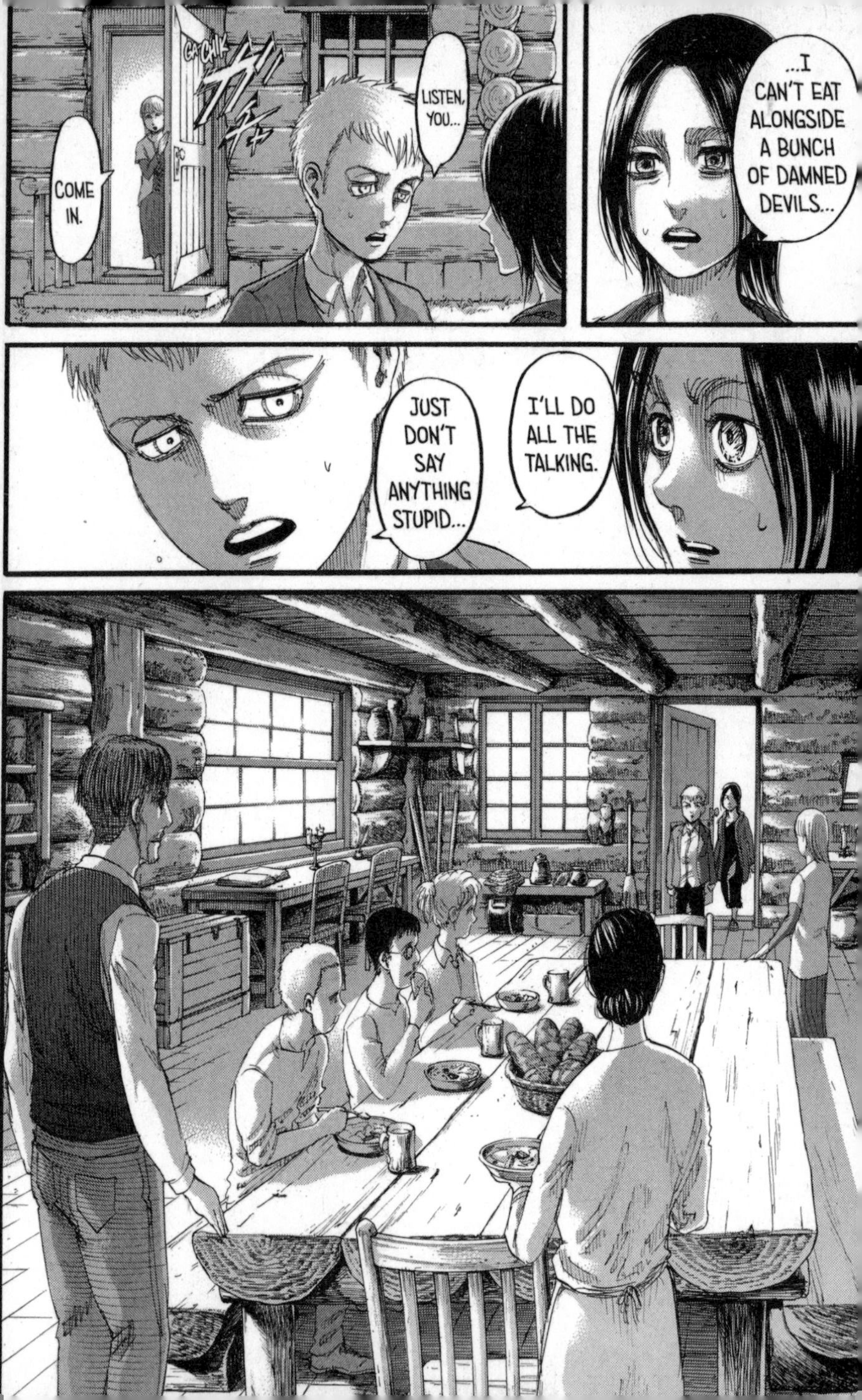
...I CAN'T EAT ALONGSIDE A BUNCH OF DAMNED DEVILS...
LISTEN, YOU...
GA-CHIK
COME IN.
I'LL DO ALL THE TALKING.
JUST DON'T SAY ANYTHING STUPID...

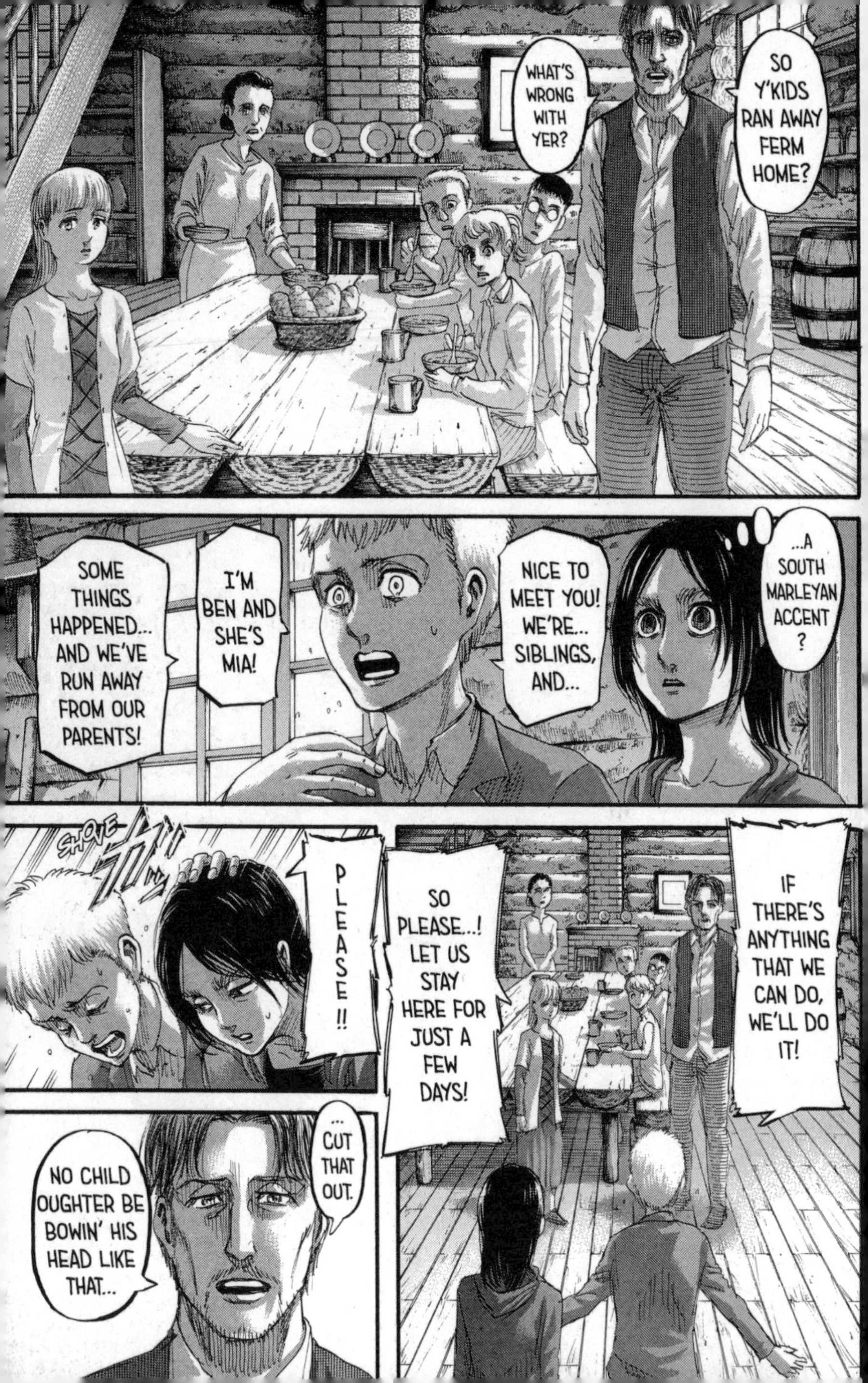
SO Y'KIDS RAN AWAY FERM HOME?
WHAT'S WRONG WITH YER?
...A SOUTH MARLEYAN ACCENT?
NICE TO MEET YOU! WE'RE... SIBLINGS, AND...
I'M BEN AND SHE'S MIA!
SOME THINGS HAPPENED... AND WE'VE RUN AWAY FROM OUR PARENTS!
IF THERE'S ANYTHING THAT WE CAN DO, WE'LL DO IT!
SO PLEASE...! LET US STAY HERE FOR JUST A FEW DAYS!
PLEASE!!
SHOVE
...CUT THAT OUT.
NO CHILD OUGHTER BE BOWIN' HIS HEAD LIKE THAT...

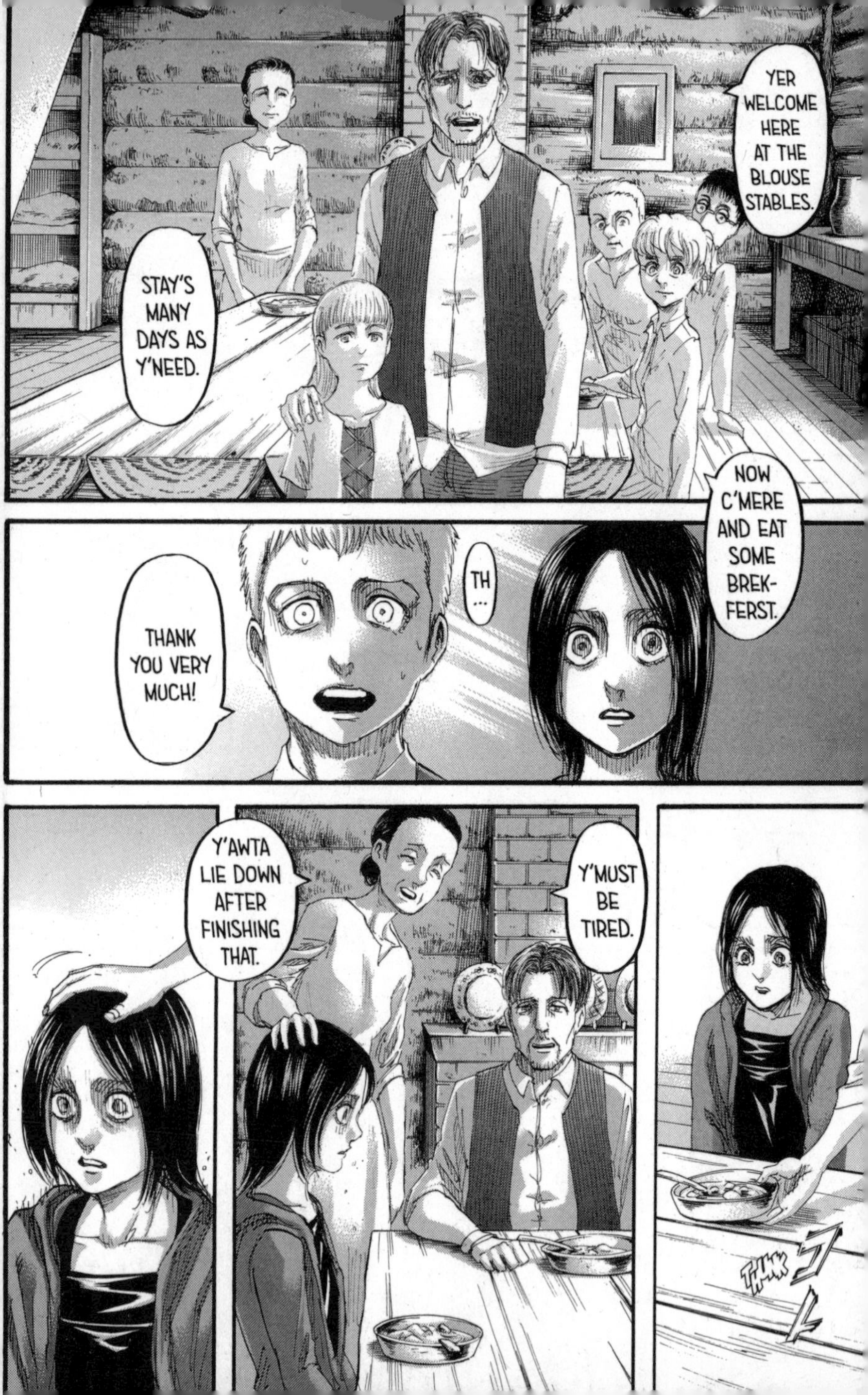
YER WELCOME HERE AT THE BLOUSE STABLES.
STAY'S MANY DAYS AS Y'NEED.
NOW C'MERE AND EAT SOME BREK-FERST.
TH ...
THANK YOU VERY MUCH!
Y'MUST BE TIRED.
Y'AWTA LIE DOWN AFTER FINISHING THAT.
THNK

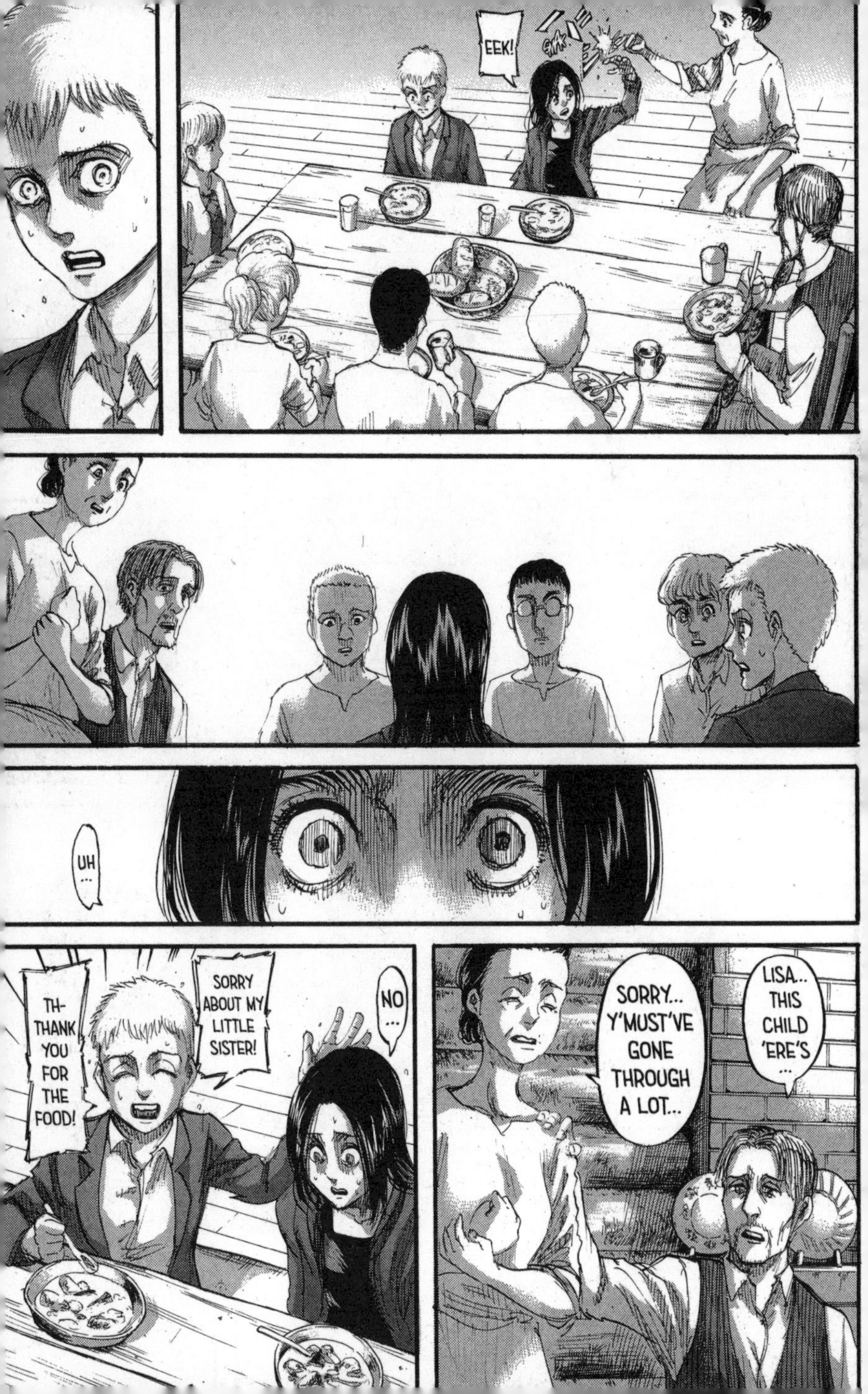EEK!
SMAK
UH...
TH-THANK YOU FOR THE FOOD!
SORRY ABOUT MY LITTLE SISTER!
NO...
LISA... THIS CHILD 'ERE'S...
SORRY... Y'MUST'VE GONE THROUGH A LOT...

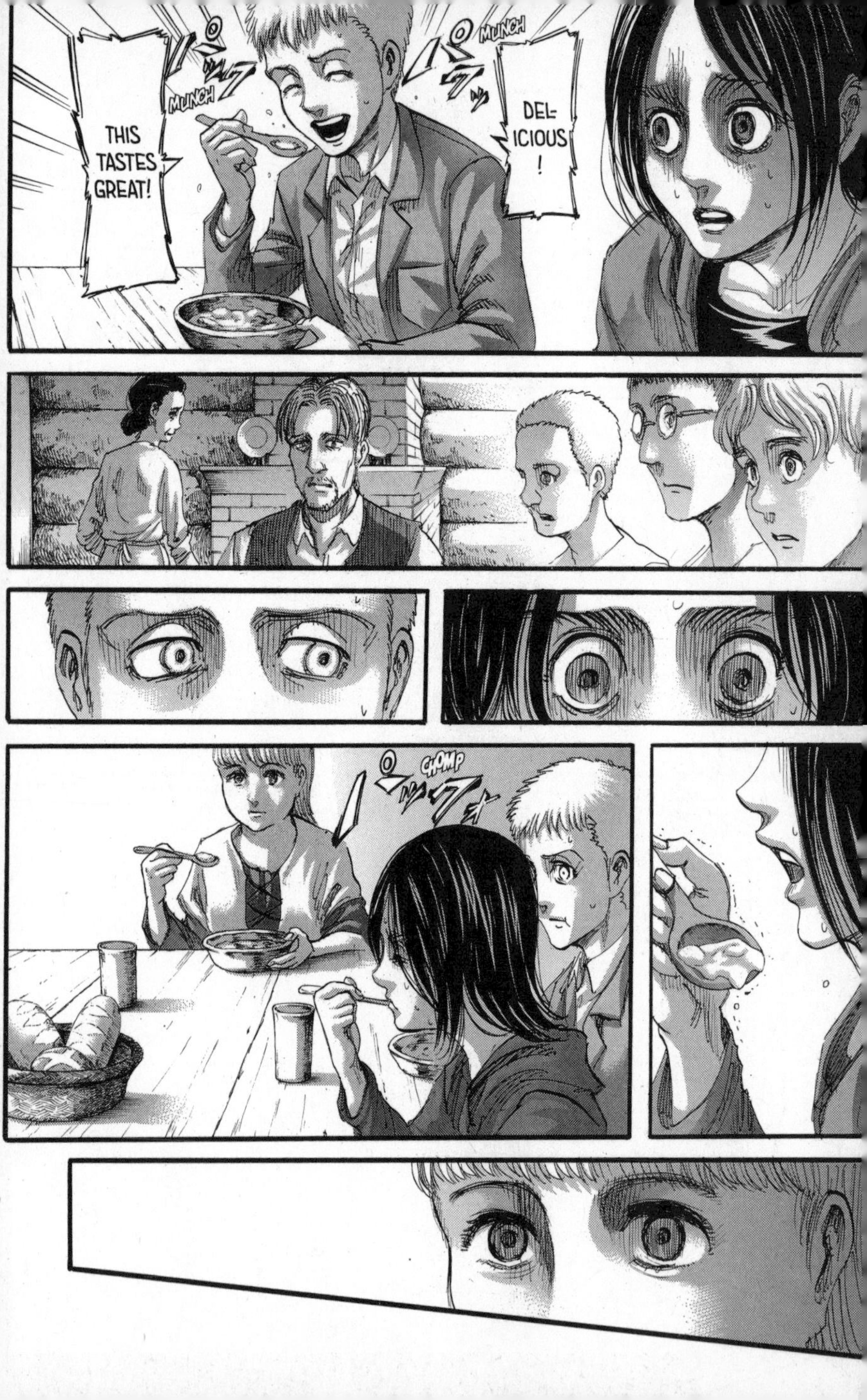
MUNCH
DEL-ICIOUS!
MUNCH
THIS TASTES GREAT!
CHOMP

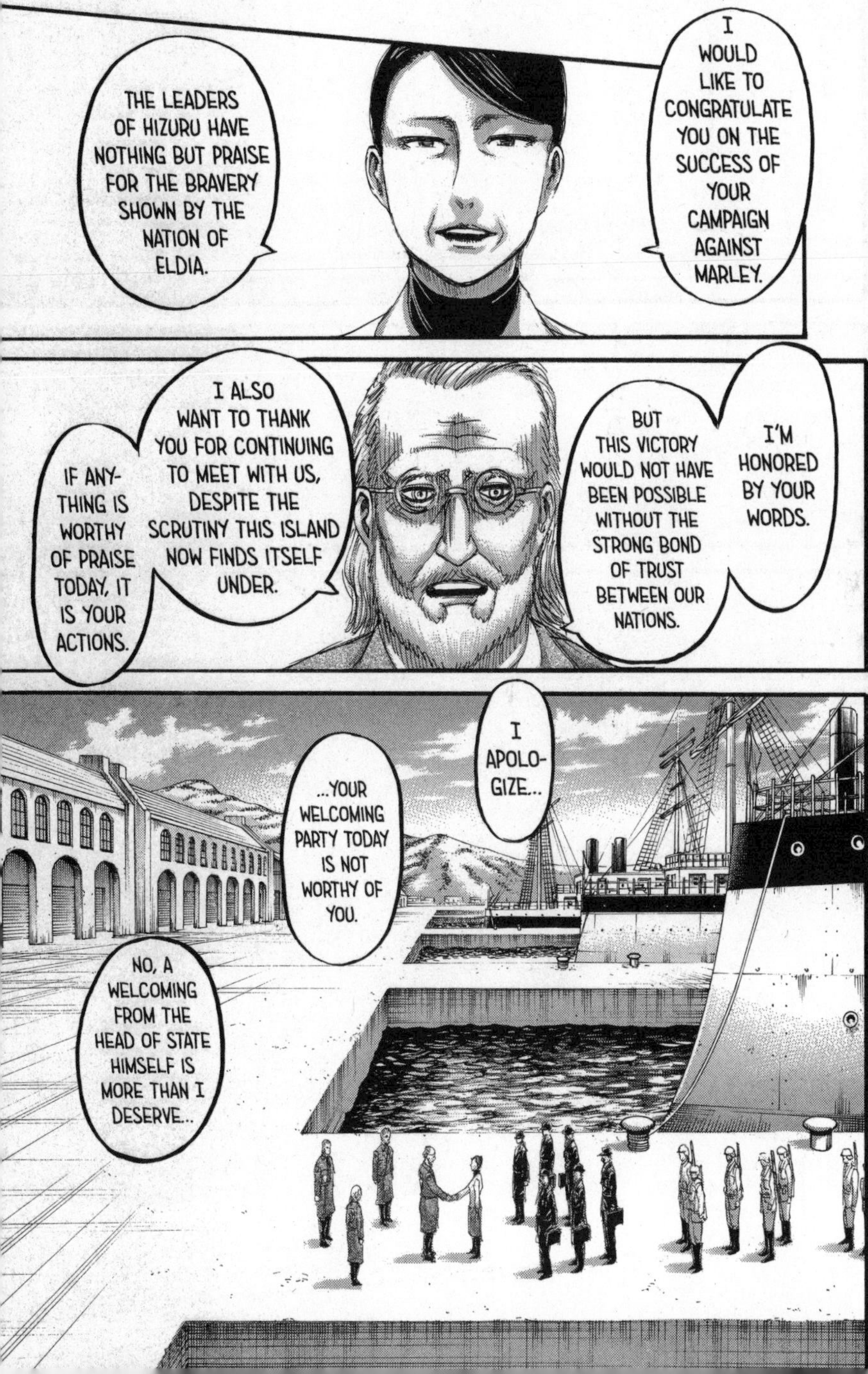
I WOULD LIKE TO CONGRATULATE YOU ON THE SUCCESS OF YOUR CAMPAIGN AGAINST MARLEY.
THE LEADERS OF HIZURU HAVE NOTHING BUT PRAISE FOR THE BRAVERY SHOWN BY THE NATION OF ELDIA.
I'M HONORED BY YOUR WORDS.
BUT THIS VICTORY WOULD NOT HAVE BEEN POSSIBLE WITHOUT THE STRONG BOND OF TRUST BETWEEN OUR NATIONS.
I ALSO WANT TO THANK YOU FOR CONTINUING TO MEET WITH US, DESPITE THE SCRUTINY THIS ISLAND NOW FINDS ITSELF UNDER.
IF ANY-THING IS WORTHY OF PRAISE TODAY, IT IS YOUR ACTIONS.
I APOLO-GIZE...
...YOUR WELCOMING PARTY TODAY IS NOT WORTHY OF YOU.
NO, A WELCOMING FROM THE HEAD OF STATE HIMSELF IS MORE THAN I DESERVE...

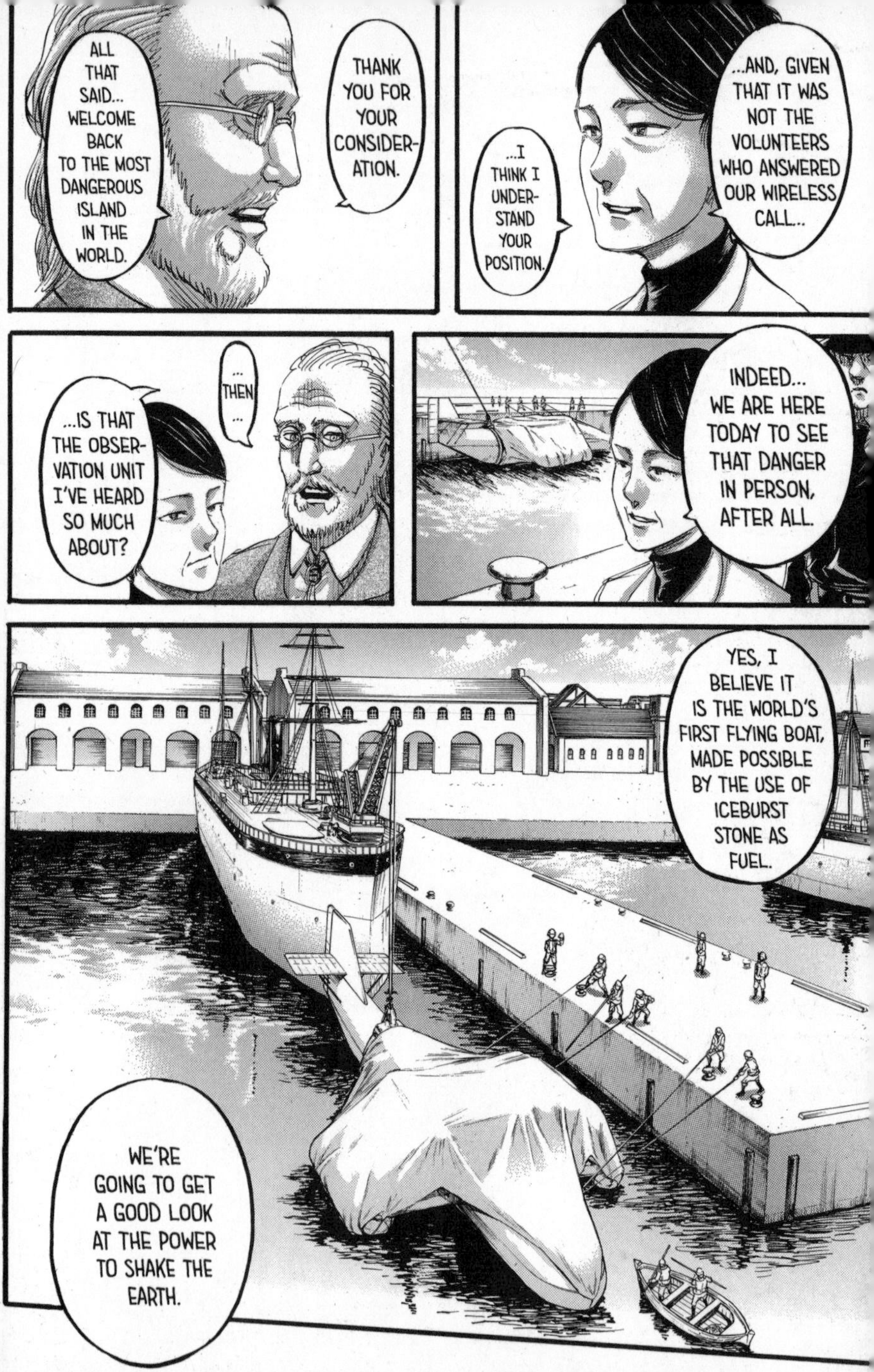
...AND, GIVEN THAT IT WAS NOT THE VOLUNTEERS WHO ANSWERED OUR WIRELESS CALL...
...I THINK I UNDERSTAND YOUR POSITION.
THANK YOU FOR YOUR CONSIDERATION.
ALL THAT SAID... WELCOME BACK TO THE MOST DANGEROUS ISLAND IN THE WORLD.
INDEED... WE ARE HERE TODAY TO SEE THAT DANGER IN PERSON, AFTER ALL.
...THEN...
...IS THAT THE OBSERVATION UNIT I'VE HEARD SO MUCH ABOUT?
YES, I BELIEVE IT IS THE WORLD'S FIRST FLYING BOAT, MADE POSSIBLE BY THE USE OF ICEBURST STONE AS FUEL.
WE'RE GOING TO GET A GOOD LOOK AT THE POWER TO SHAKE THE EARTH.

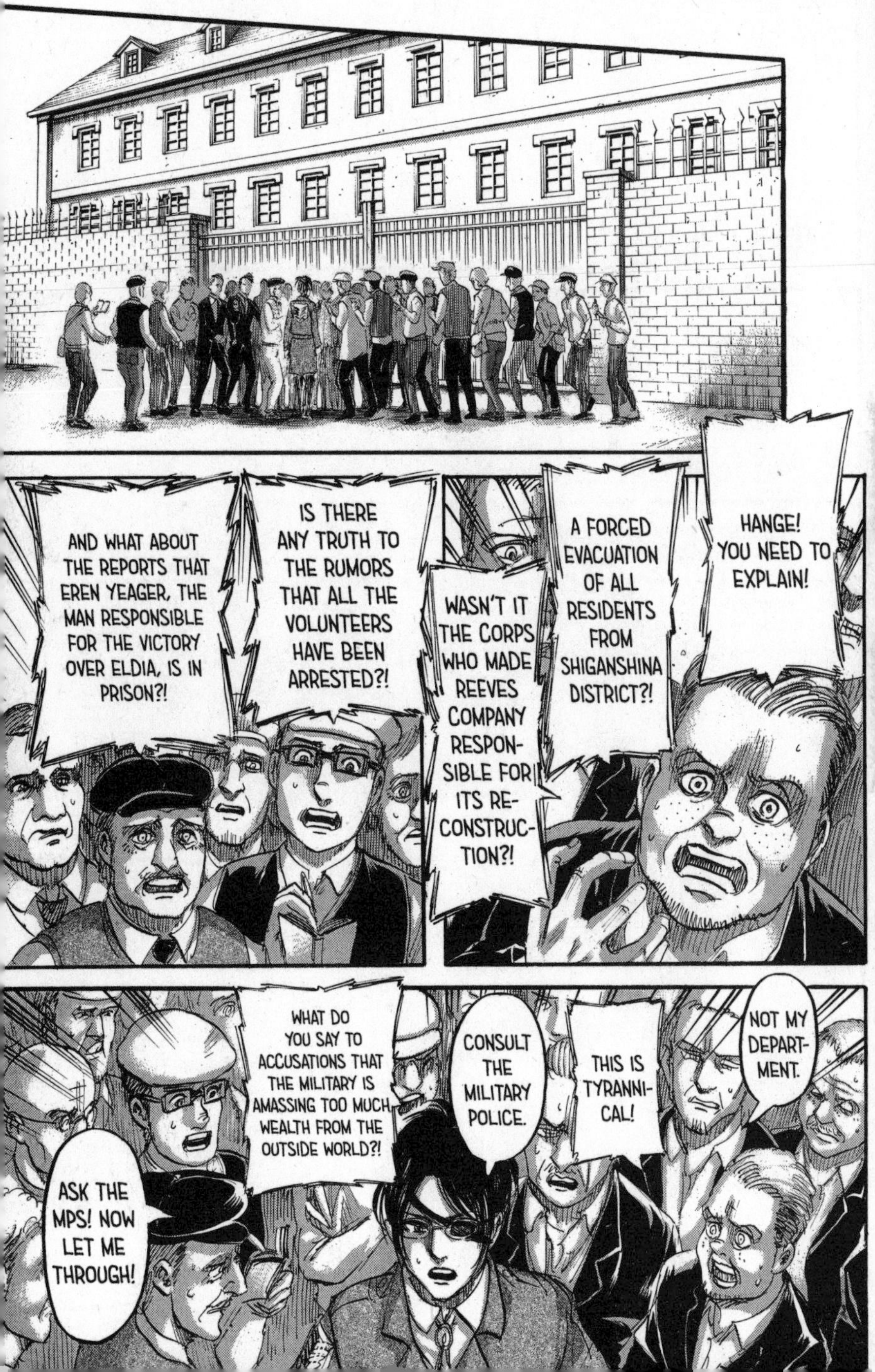
HANGE! YOU NEED TO EXPLAIN!
A FORCED EVACUATION OF ALL RESIDENTS FROM SHIGANSHINA DISTRICT?!
WASN'T IT THE CORPS WHO MADE REEVES COMPANY RESPON-SIBLE FOR ITS RE-CONSTRUC-TION?!
IS THERE ANY TRUTH TO THE RUMORS THAT ALL THE VOLUNTEERS HAVE BEEN ARRESTED?!
AND WHAT ABOUT THE REPORTS THAT EREN YEAGER, THE MAN RESPONSIBLE FOR THE VICTORY OVER ELDIA, IS IN PRISON?!
NOT MY DEPART-MENT.
THIS IS TYRANNI-CAL!
CONSULT THE MILITARY POLICE.
WHAT DO YOU SAY TO ACCUSATIONS THAT THE MILITARY IS AMASSING TOO MUCH WEALTH FROM THE OUTSIDE WORLD?!
ASK THE MPS! NOW LET ME THROUGH!

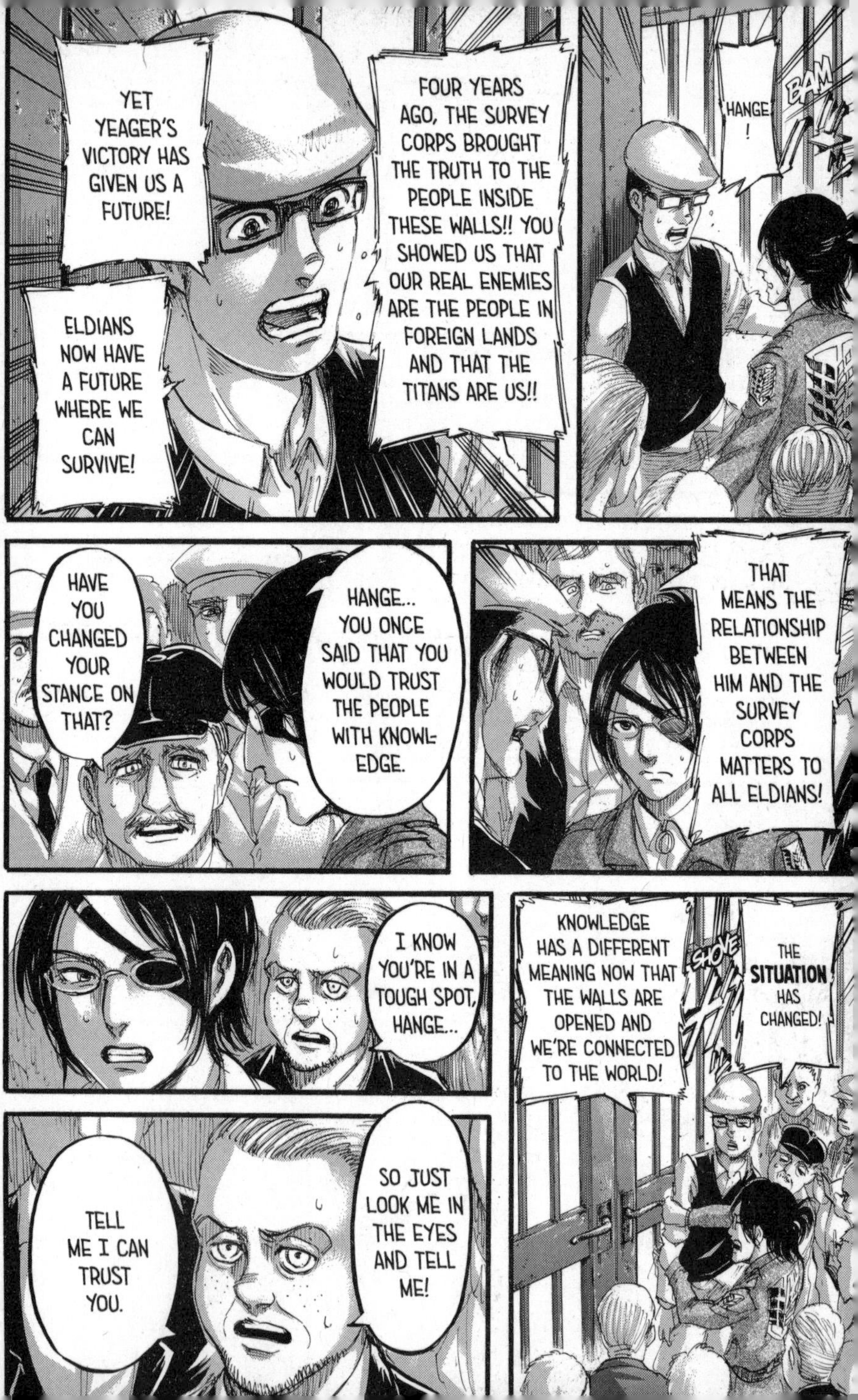
YET YEAGER'S VICTORY HAS GIVEN US A FUTURE!
ELDIANS NOW HAVE A FUTURE WHERE WE CAN SURVIVE!
FOUR YEARS AGO, THE SURVEY CORPS BROUGHT THE TRUTH TO THE PEOPLE INSIDE THESE WALLS!! YOU SHOWED US THAT OUR REAL ENEMIES ARE THE PEOPLE IN FOREIGN LANDS AND THAT THE TITANS ARE US!!
HANGE!
BAM
HAVE YOU CHANGED YOUR STANCE ON THAT?
HANGE... YOU ONCE SAID THAT YOU WOULD TRUST THE PEOPLE WITH KNOWL-EDGE.
THAT MEANS THE RELATIONSHIP BETWEEN HIM AND THE SURVEY CORPS MATTERS TO ALL ELDIANS!
I KNOW YOU'RE IN A TOUGH SPOT, HANGE...
KNOWLEDGE HAS A DIFFERENT MEANING NOW THAT THE WALLS ARE OPENED AND WE'RE CONNECTED TO THE WORLD!
SHOVE
THE SITUATION HAS CHANGED!
TELL ME I CAN TRUST YOU.
SO JUST LOOK ME IN THE EYES AND TELL ME!

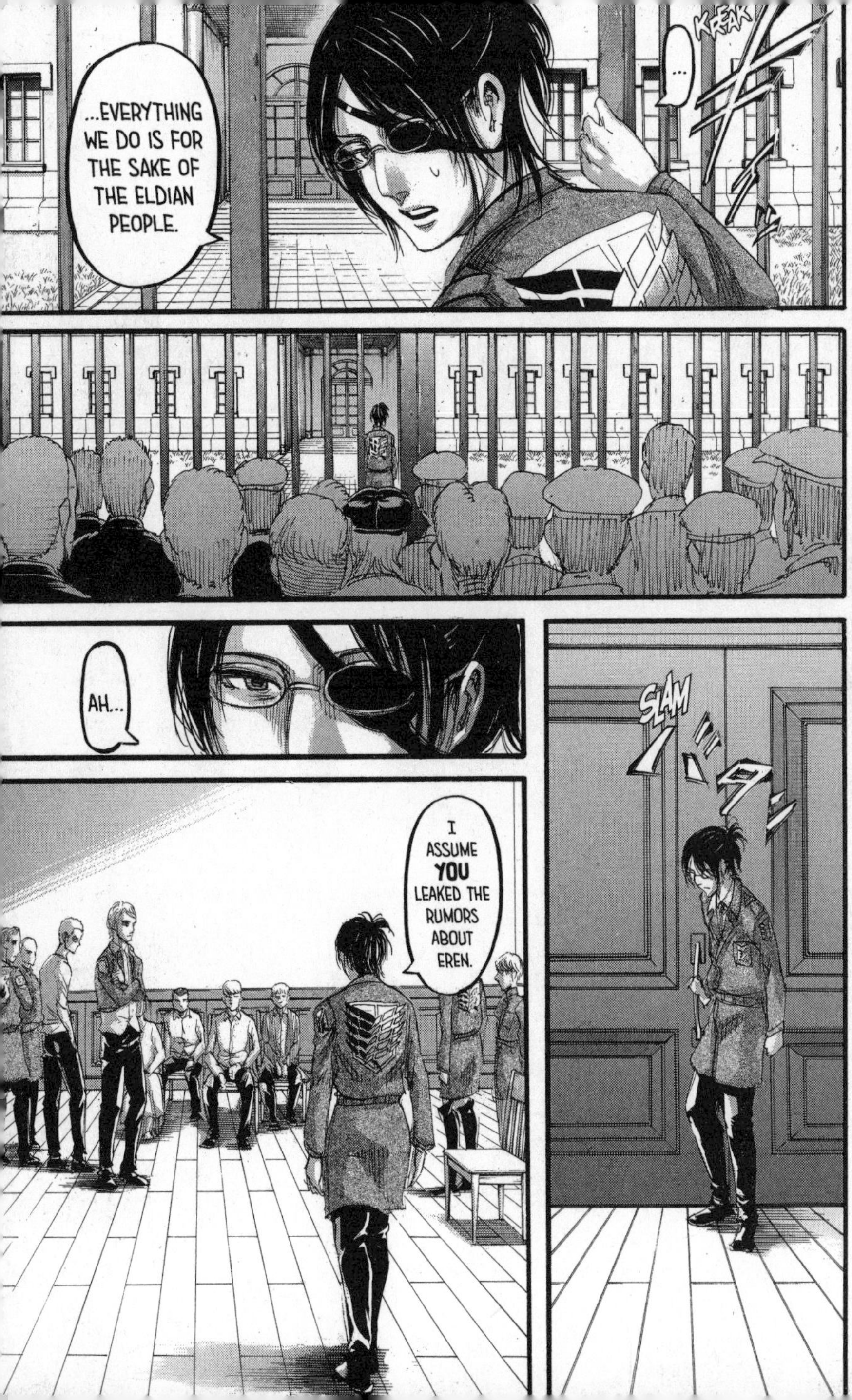
...
KREAK
...EVERYTHING WE DO IS FOR THE SAKE OF THE ELDIAN PEOPLE.
AH...
SLAM
I ASSUME **YOU** LEAKED THE RUMORS ABOUT EREN.

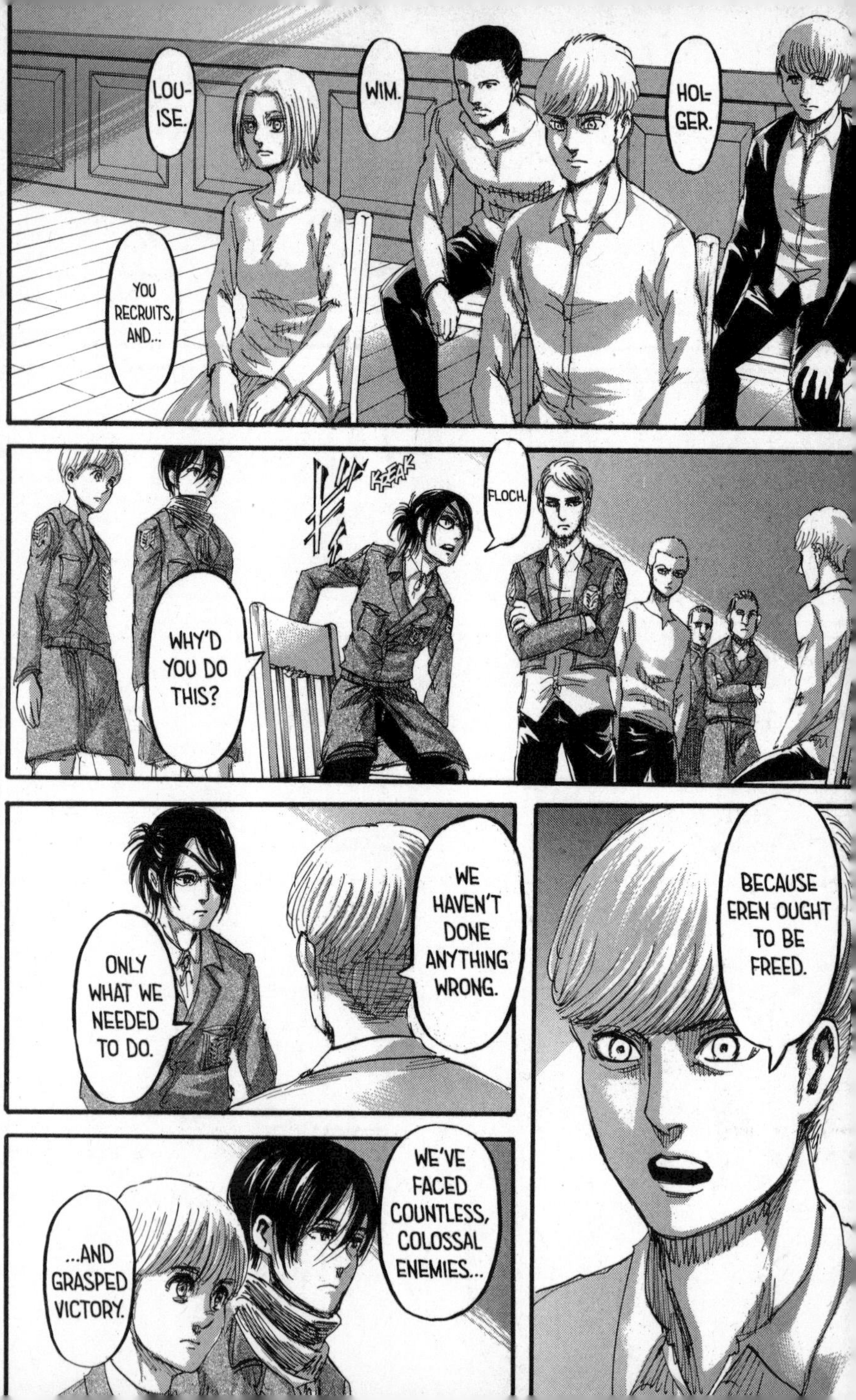
LOU-ISE.
WIM.
HOL-GER.
YOU RECRUITS, AND...
FLOCH.
KREAK
WHY'D YOU DO THIS?
WE HAVEN'T DONE ANYTHING WRONG.
ONLY WHAT WE NEEDED TO DO.
BECAUSE EREN OUGHT TO BE FREED.
WE'VE FACED COUNTLESS, COLOSSAL ENEMIES...
...AND GRASPED VICTORY.

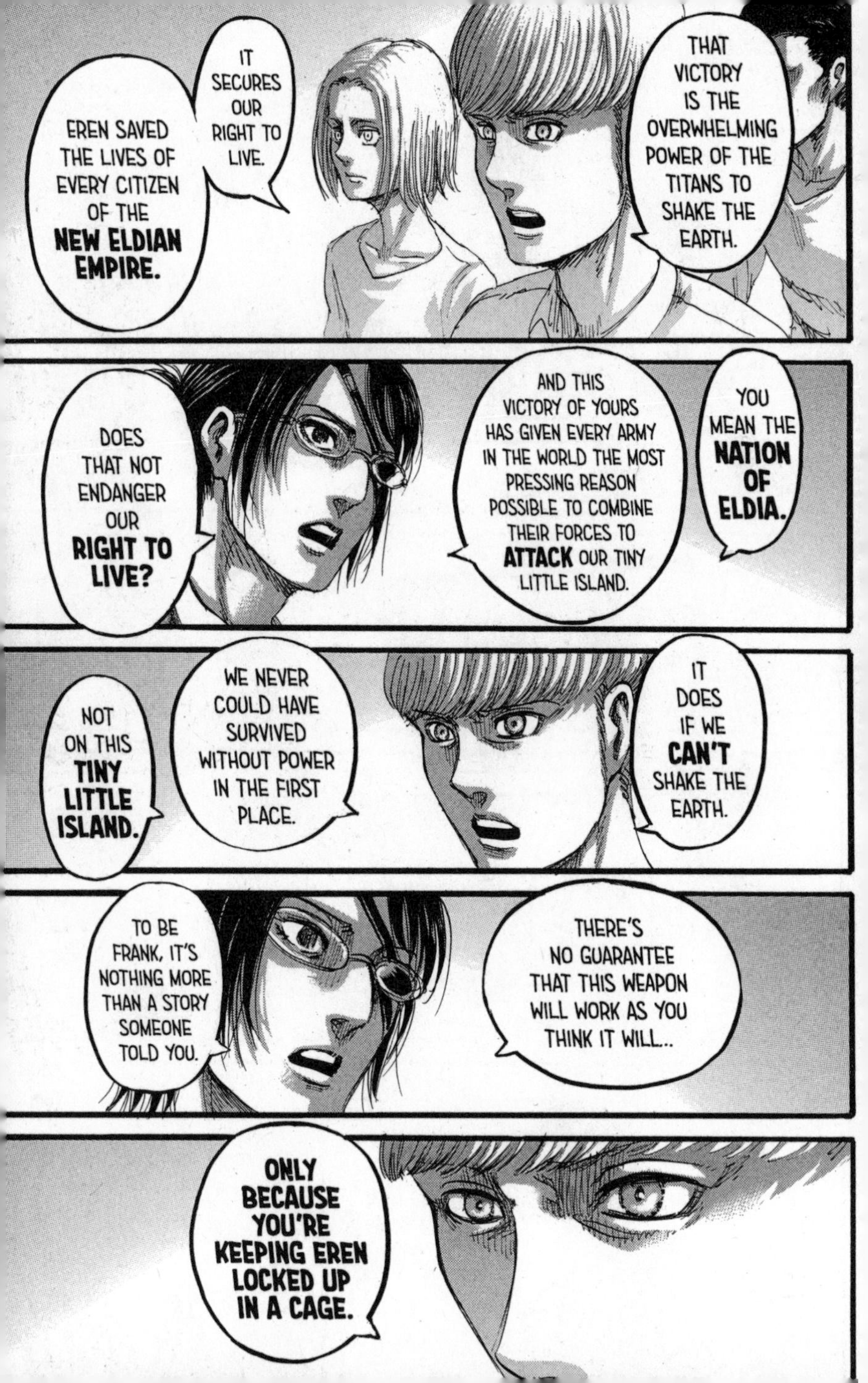
THAT VICTORY IS THE OVERWHELMING POWER OF THE TITANS TO SHAKE THE EARTH.
IT SECURES OUR RIGHT TO LIVE.
EREN SAVED THE LIVES OF EVERY CITIZEN OF THE **NEW ELDIAN EMPIRE.**
YOU MEAN THE **NATION OF ELDIA.**
AND THIS VICTORY OF YOURS HAS GIVEN EVERY ARMY IN THE WORLD THE MOST PRESSING REASON POSSIBLE TO COMBINE THEIR FORCES TO **ATTACK** OUR TINY LITTLE ISLAND.
DOES THAT NOT ENDANGER OUR **RIGHT TO LIVE?**
IT DOES IF WE **CAN'T** SHAKE THE EARTH.
WE NEVER COULD HAVE SURVIVED WITHOUT POWER IN THE FIRST PLACE.
NOT ON THIS **TINY LITTLE ISLAND.**
THERE'S NO GUARANTEE THAT THIS WEAPON WILL WORK AS YOU THINK IT WILL...
TO BE FRANK, IT'S NOTHING MORE THAN A STORY SOMEONE TOLD YOU.
ONLY BECAUSE YOU'RE KEEPING EREN LOCKED UP IN A CAGE.

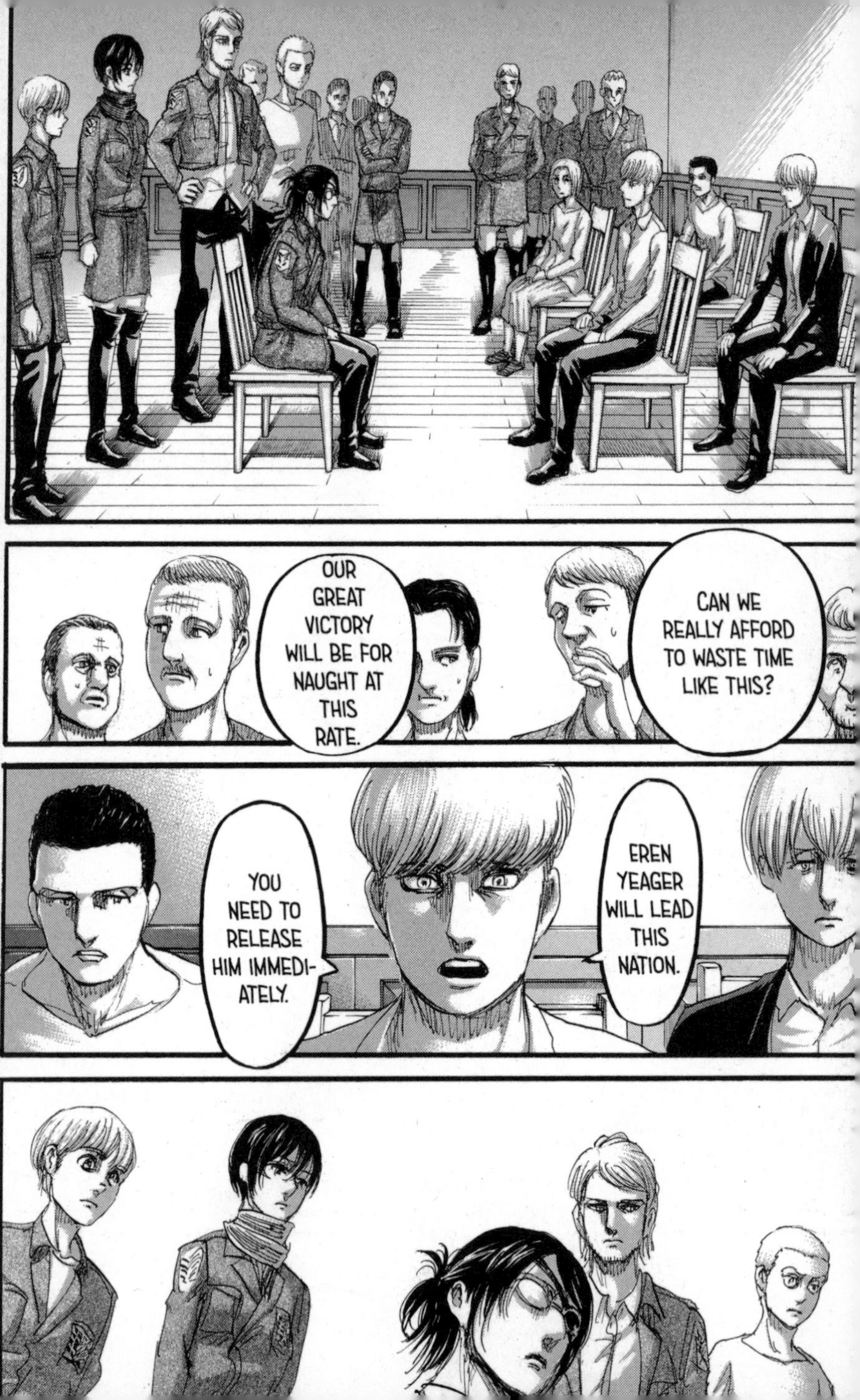
CAN WE REALLY AFFORD TO WASTE TIME LIKE THIS?
OUR GREAT VICTORY WILL BE FOR NAUGHT AT THIS RATE.
EREN YEAGER WILL LEAD THIS NATION.
YOU NEED TO RELEASE HIM IMMEDI-ATELY.

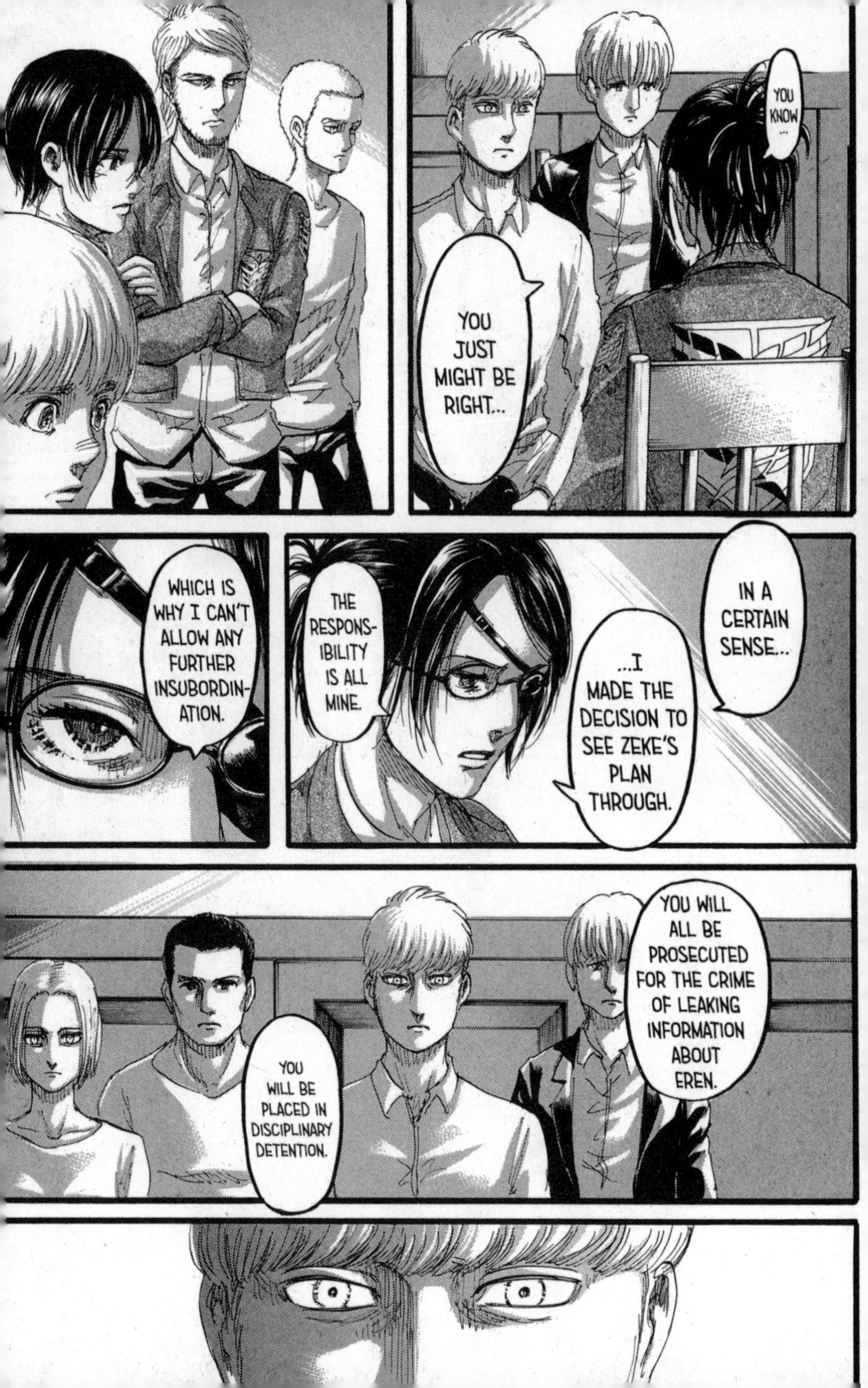
YOU KNOW...
YOU JUST MIGHT BE RIGHT...
IN A CERTAIN SENSE...
...I MADE THE DECISION TO SEE ZEKE'S PLAN THROUGH.
THE RESPONSIBILITY IS ALL MINE.
WHICH IS WHY I CAN'T ALLOW ANY FURTHER INSUBORDINATION.
YOU WILL ALL BE PROSECUTED FOR THE CRIME OF LEAKING INFORMATION ABOUT EREN.
YOU WILL BE PLACED IN DISCIPLINARY DETENTION.

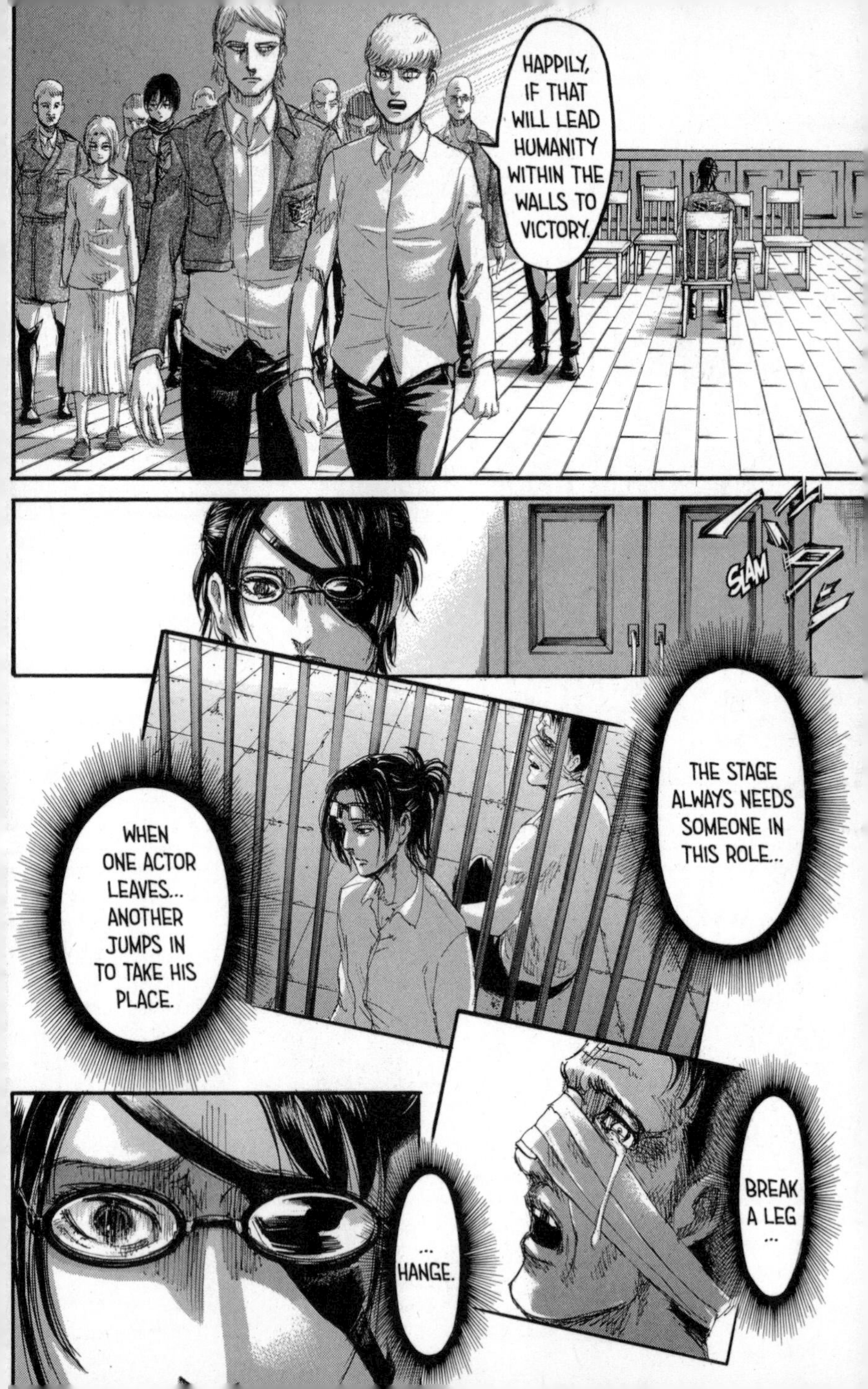
HAPPILY, IF THAT WILL LEAD HUMANITY WITHIN THE WALLS TO VICTORY.
SLAM
THE STAGE ALWAYS NEEDS SOMEONE IN THIS ROLE...
WHEN ONE ACTOR LEAVES... ANOTHER JUMPS IN TO TAKE HIS PLACE.
BREAK A LEG ...
... HANGE.

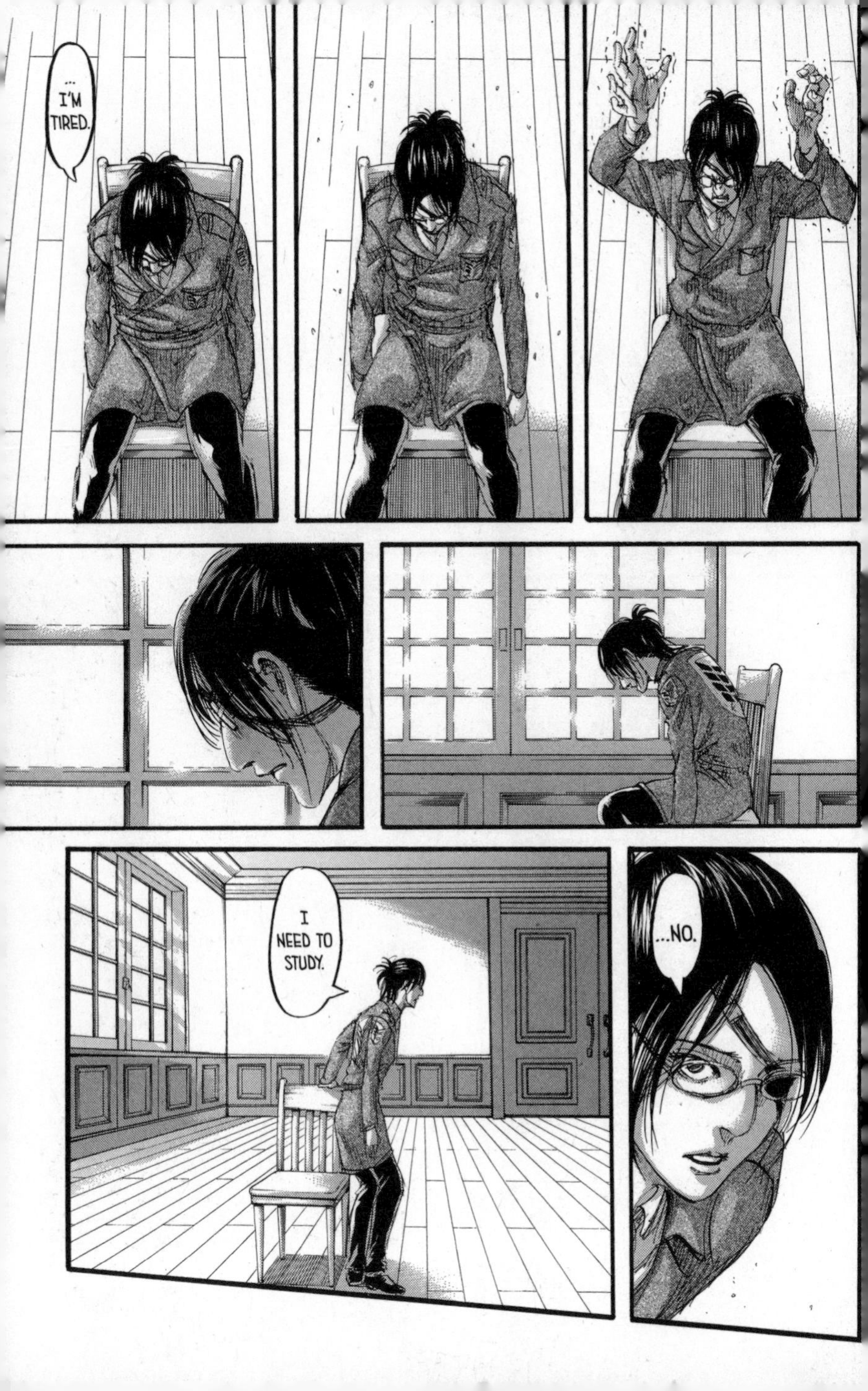
... I'M TIRED.
I NEED TO STUDY.
...NO.

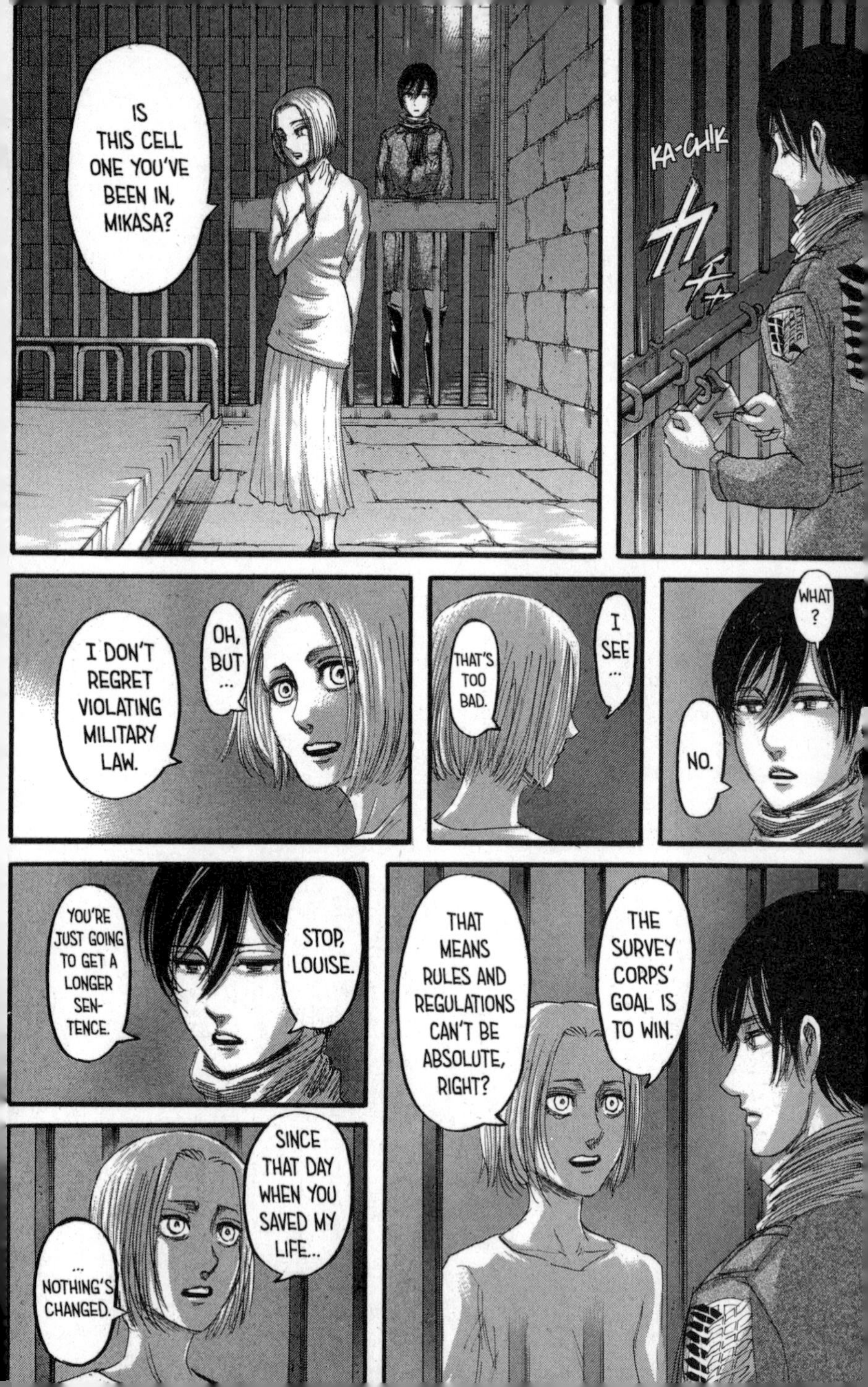
KA-CHIK
カチャ
IS THIS CELL ONE YOU'VE BEEN IN, MIKASA?
WHAT?
NO.
I SEE...
THAT'S TOO BAD.
OH, BUT...
I DON'T REGRET VIOLATING MILITARY LAW.
THE SURVEY CORPS' GOAL IS TO WIN.
THAT MEANS RULES AND REGULATIONS CAN'T BE ABSOLUTE, RIGHT?
STOP, LOUISE.
YOU'RE JUST GOING TO GET A LONGER SEN-TENCE.
SINCE THAT DAY WHEN YOU SAVED MY LIFE...
...NOTHING'S CHANGED.

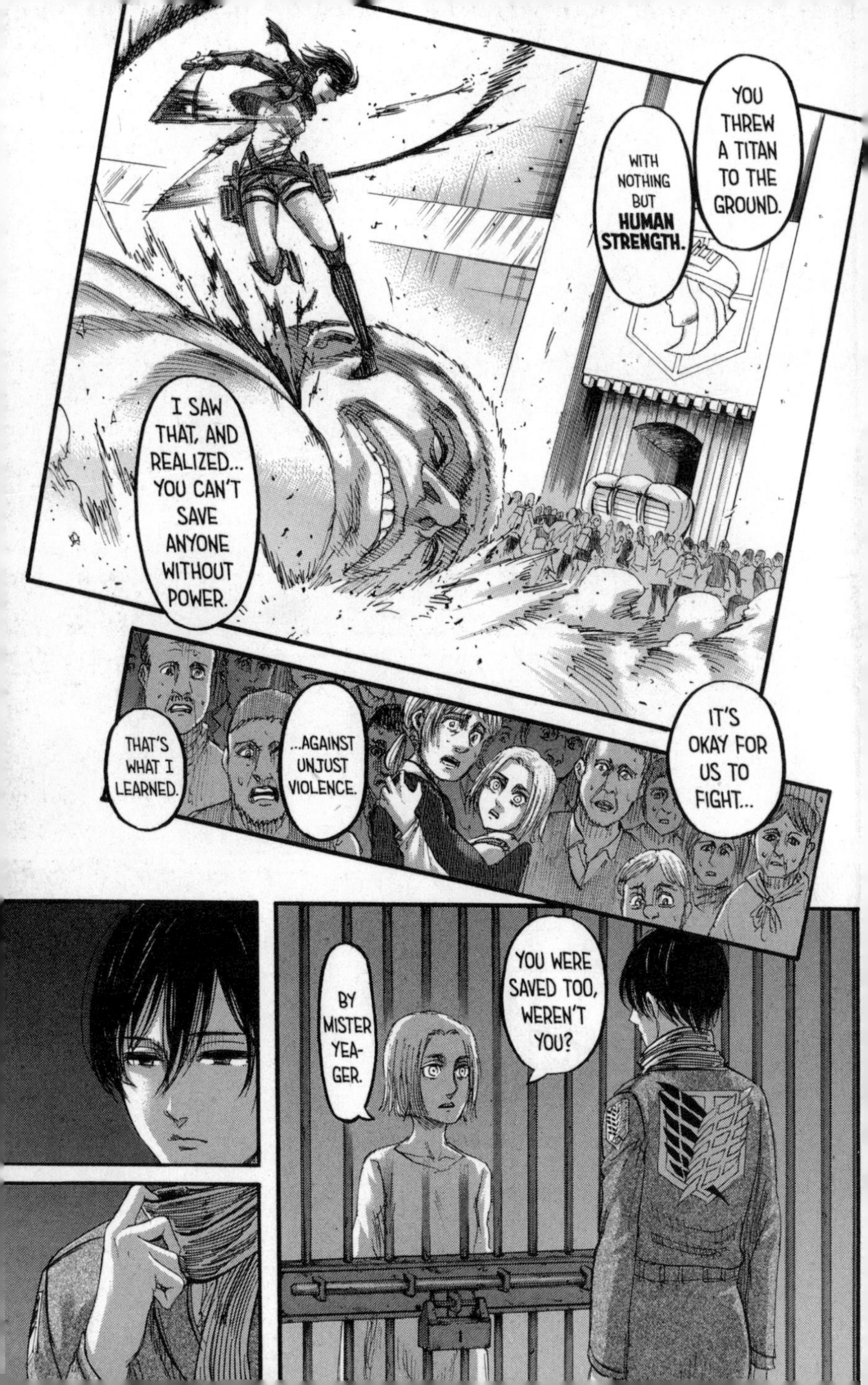
YOU THREW A TITAN TO THE GROUND.
WITH NOTHING BUT HUMAN STRENGTH.
I SAW THAT, AND REALIZED... YOU CAN'T SAVE ANYONE WITHOUT POWER.
IT'S OKAY FOR US TO FIGHT...
...AGAINST UNJUST VIOLENCE.
THAT'S WHAT I LEARNED.
YOU WERE SAVED TOO, WEREN'T YOU?
BY MISTER YEA-GER.

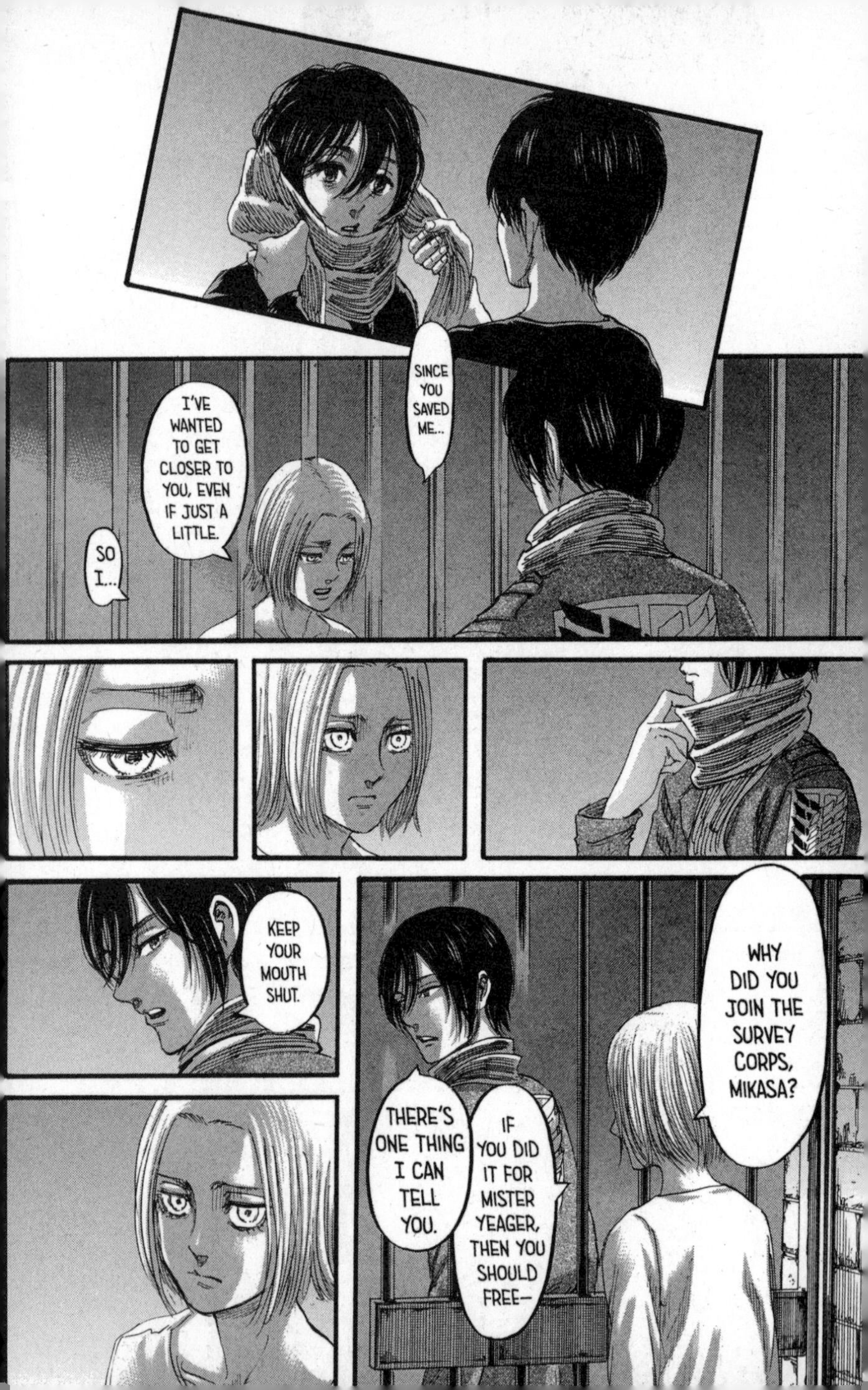
SINCE YOU SAVED ME...
I'VE WANTED TO GET CLOSER TO YOU, EVEN IF JUST A LITTLE.
SO I...
KEEP YOUR MOUTH SHUT.
WHY DID YOU JOIN THE SURVEY CORPS, MIKASA?
IF YOU DID IT FOR MISTER YEAGER, THEN YOU SHOULD FREE—
THERE'S ONE THING I CAN TELL YOU.

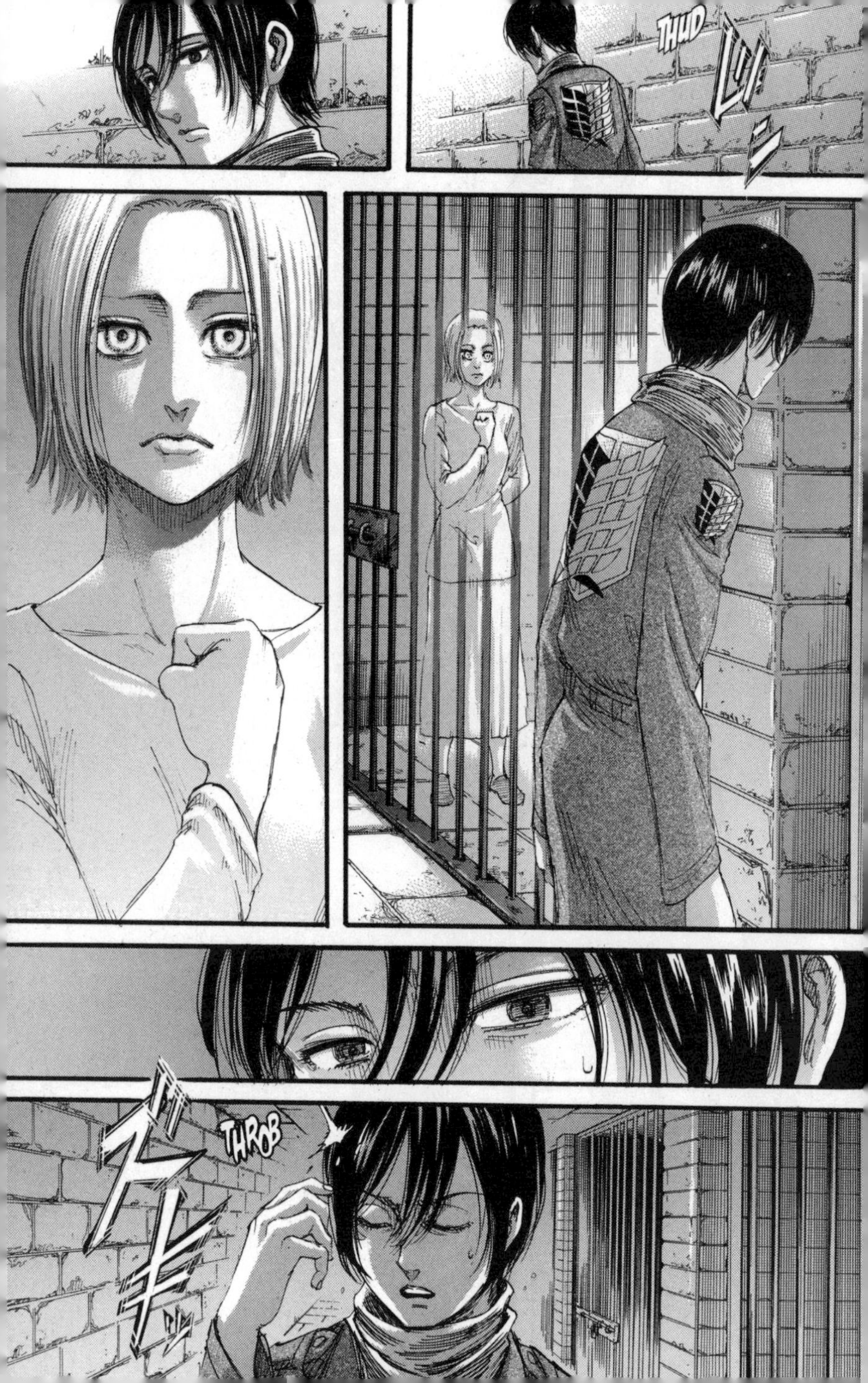
THUD
THROB

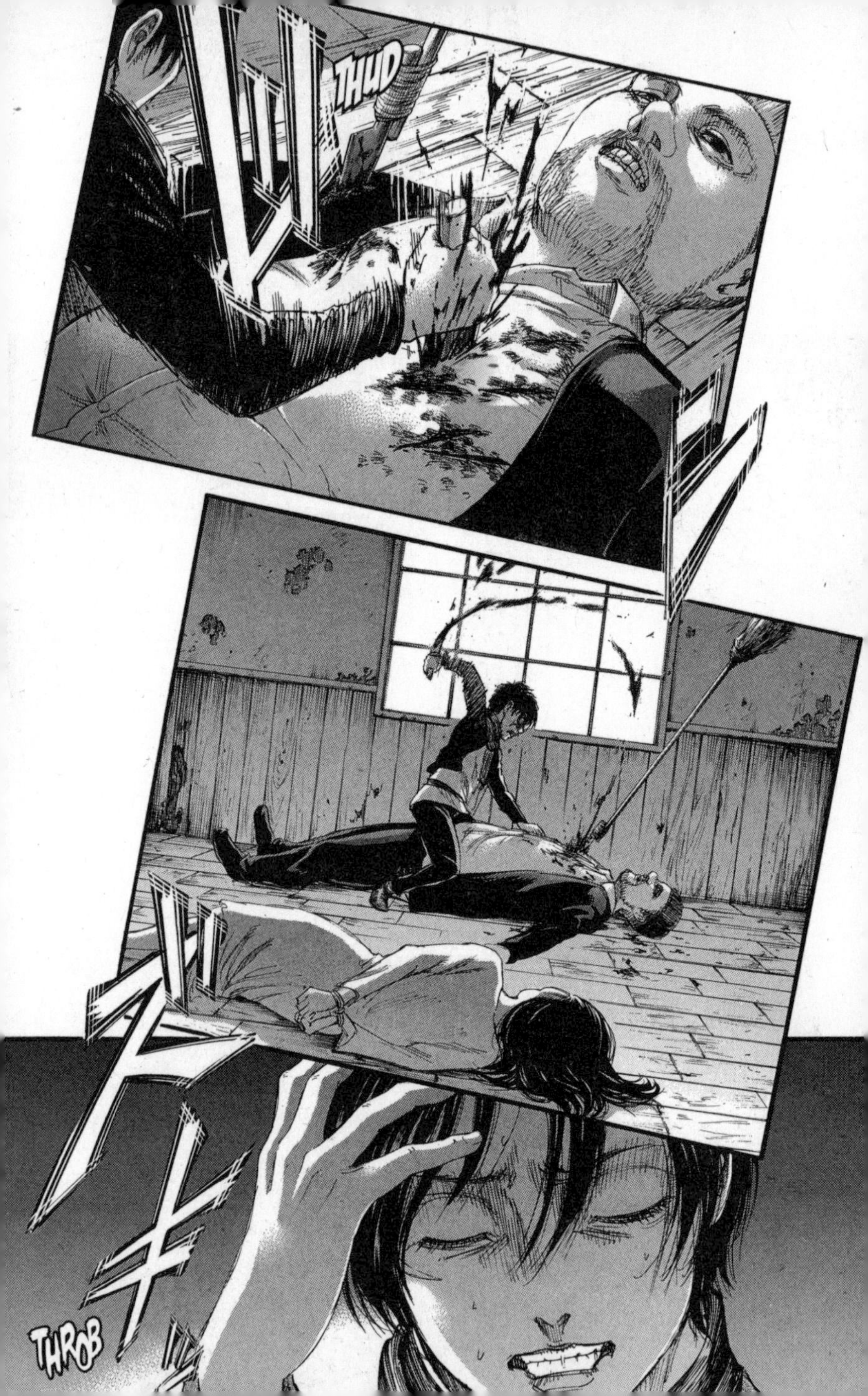
THUD
THROB

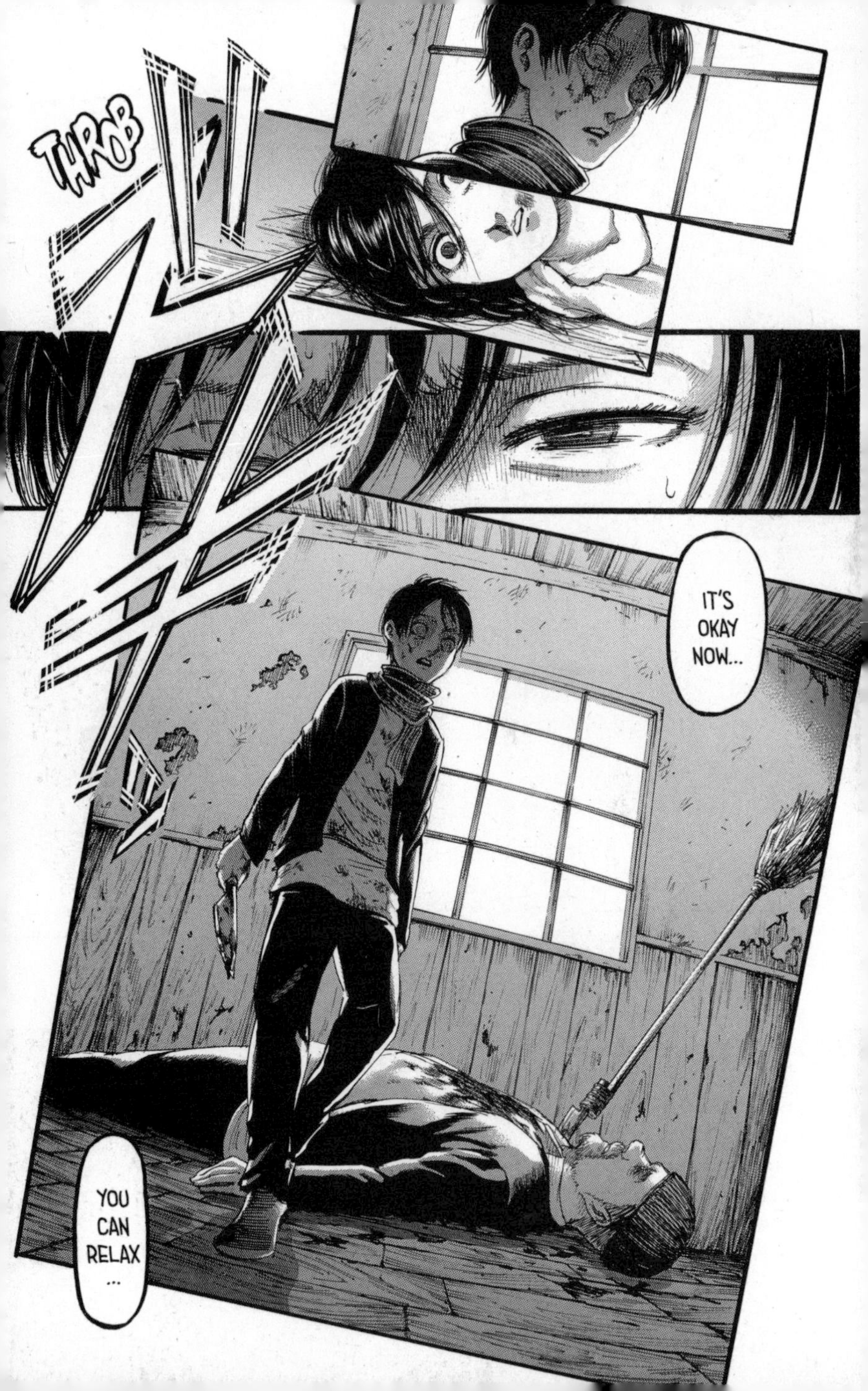
THROB
IT'S OKAY NOW...
YOU CAN RELAX ...

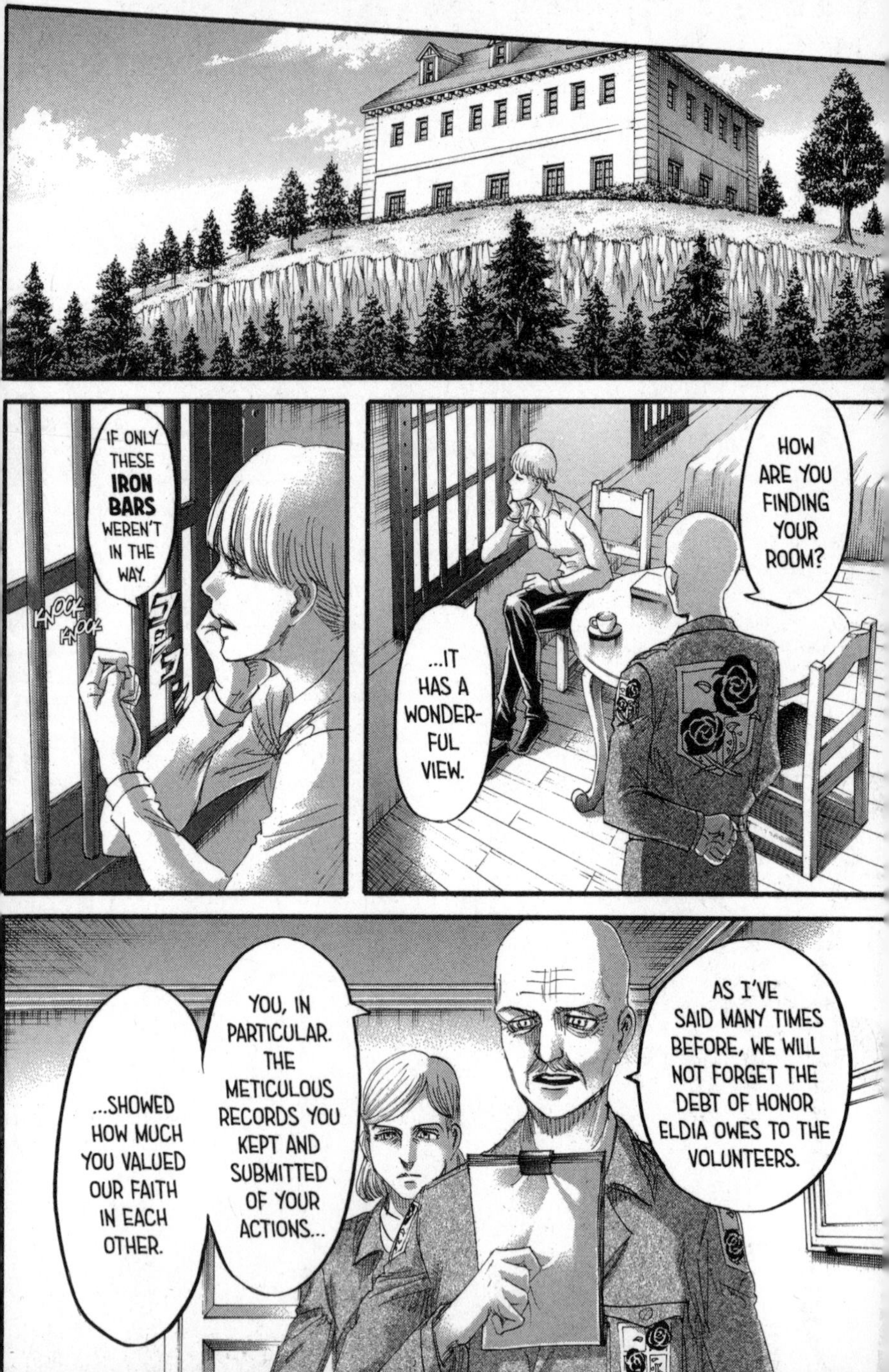
HOW ARE YOU FINDING YOUR ROOM?
...IT HAS A WONDERFUL VIEW.
IF ONLY THESE **IRON BARS** WEREN'T IN THE WAY.
KNOCK KNOCK
AS I'VE SAID MANY TIMES BEFORE, WE WILL NOT FORGET THE DEBT OF HONOR ELDIA OWES TO THE VOLUNTEERS.
YOU, IN PARTICULAR. THE METICULOUS RECORDS YOU KEPT AND SUBMITTED OF YOUR ACTIONS...
...SHOWED HOW MUCH YOU VALUED OUR FAITH IN EACH OTHER.

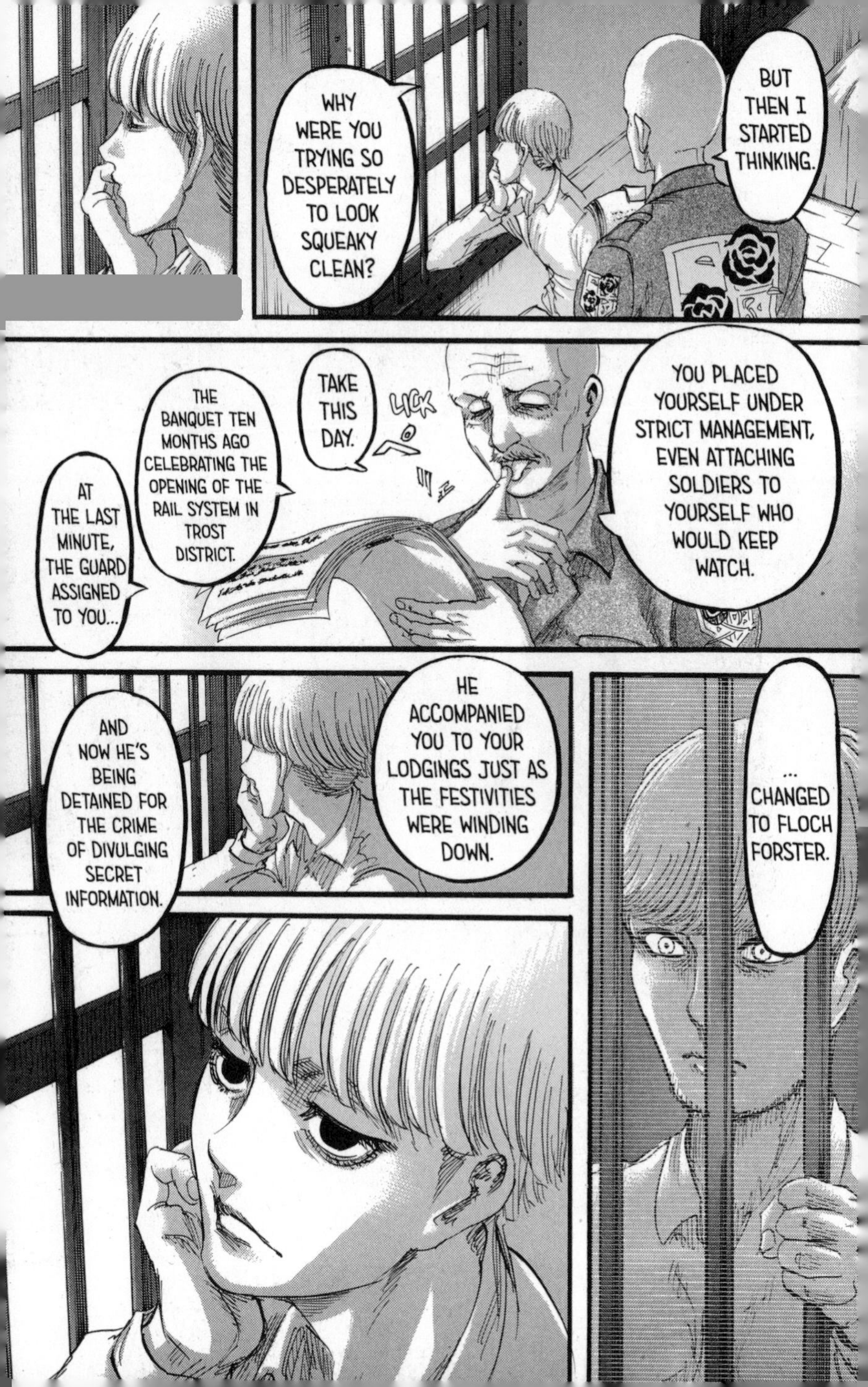
BUT THEN I STARTED THINKING.
WHY WERE YOU TRYING SO DESPERATELY TO LOOK SQUEAKY CLEAN?
YOU PLACED YOURSELF UNDER STRICT MANAGEMENT, EVEN ATTACHING SOLDIERS TO YOURSELF WHO WOULD KEEP WATCH.
LICK
TAKE THIS DAY.
THE BANQUET TEN MONTHS AGO CELEBRATING THE OPENING OF THE RAIL SYSTEM IN TROST DISTRICT.
AT THE LAST MINUTE, THE GUARD ASSIGNED TO YOU...
...CHANGED TO FLOCH FORSTER.
HE ACCOMPANIED YOU TO YOUR LODGINGS JUST AS THE FESTIVITIES WERE WINDING DOWN.
AND NOW HE'S BEING DETAINED FOR THE CRIME OF DIVULGING SECRET INFORMATION.

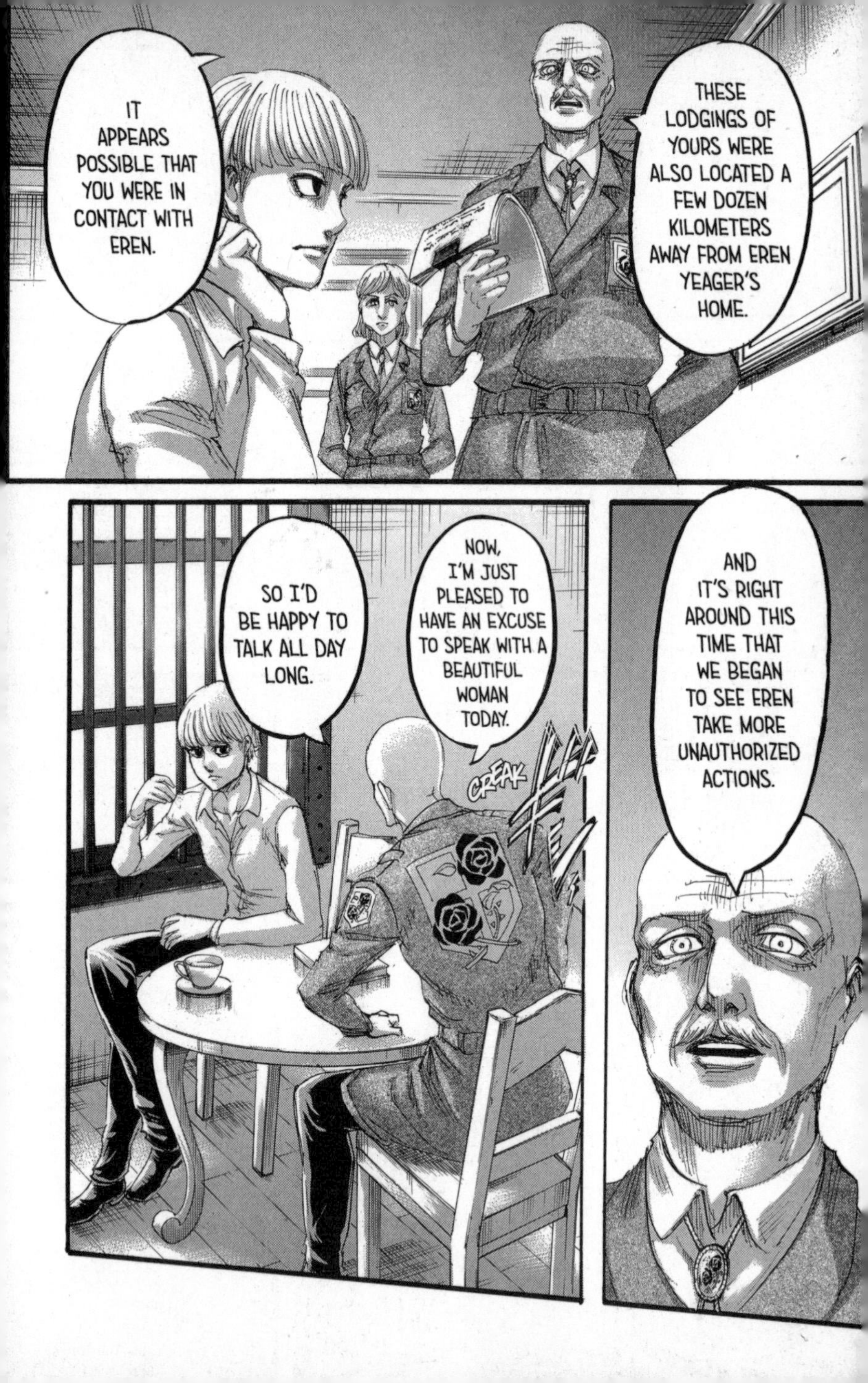
THESE LODGINGS OF YOURS WERE ALSO LOCATED A FEW DOZEN KILOMETERS AWAY FROM EREN YEAGER'S HOME.
IT APPEARS POSSIBLE THAT YOU WERE IN CONTACT WITH EREN.
AND IT'S RIGHT AROUND THIS TIME THAT WE BEGAN TO SEE EREN TAKE MORE UNAUTHORIZED ACTIONS.
NOW, I'M JUST PLEASED TO HAVE AN EXCUSE TO SPEAK WITH A BEAUTIFUL WOMAN TODAY.
CREAK
SO I'D BE HAPPY TO TALK ALL DAY LONG.

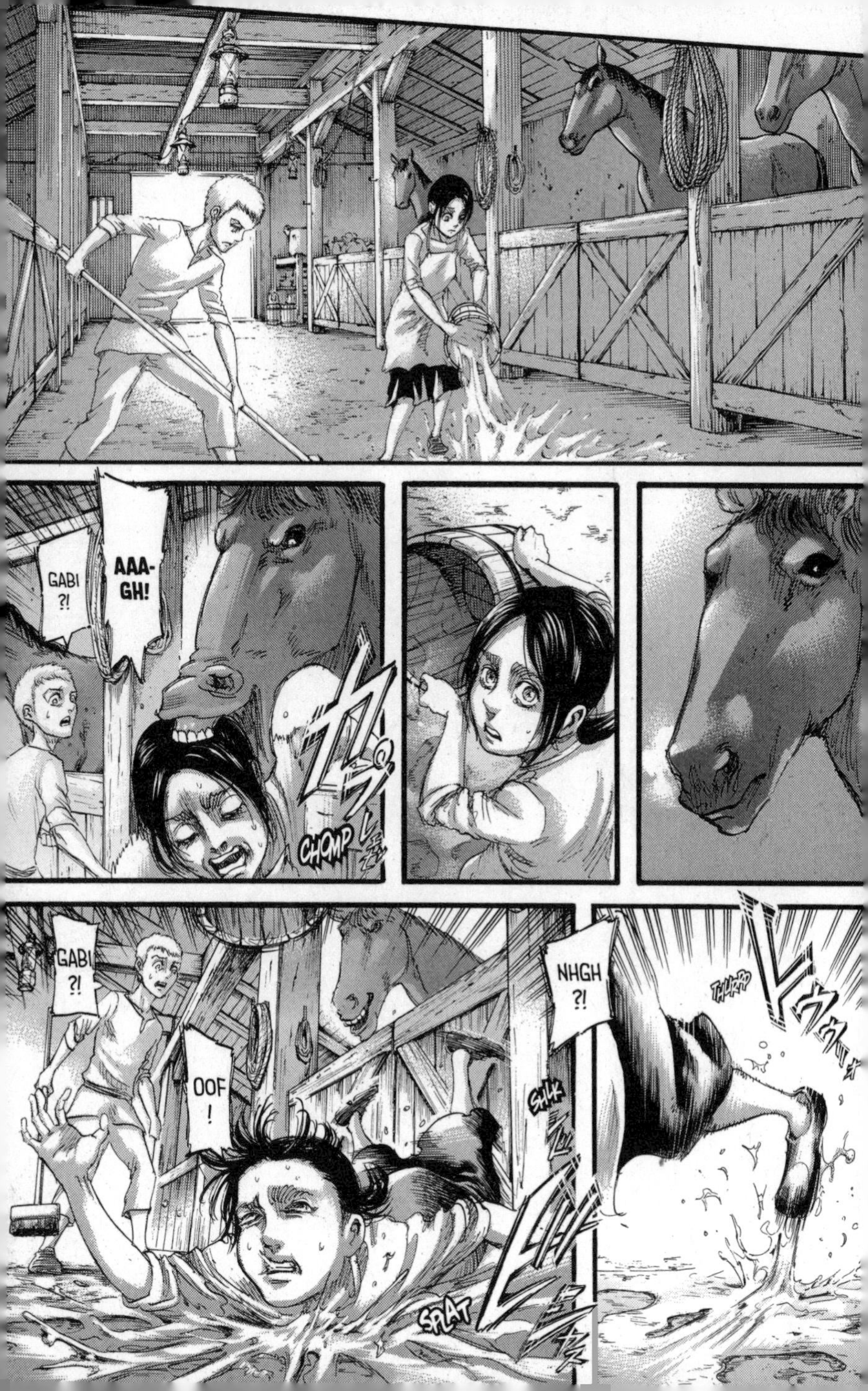
AAA-GH!
GABI ?!
CHOMP
NHGH ?!
THUMP
SHLK
OOF !
GABI ?!
SPLAT

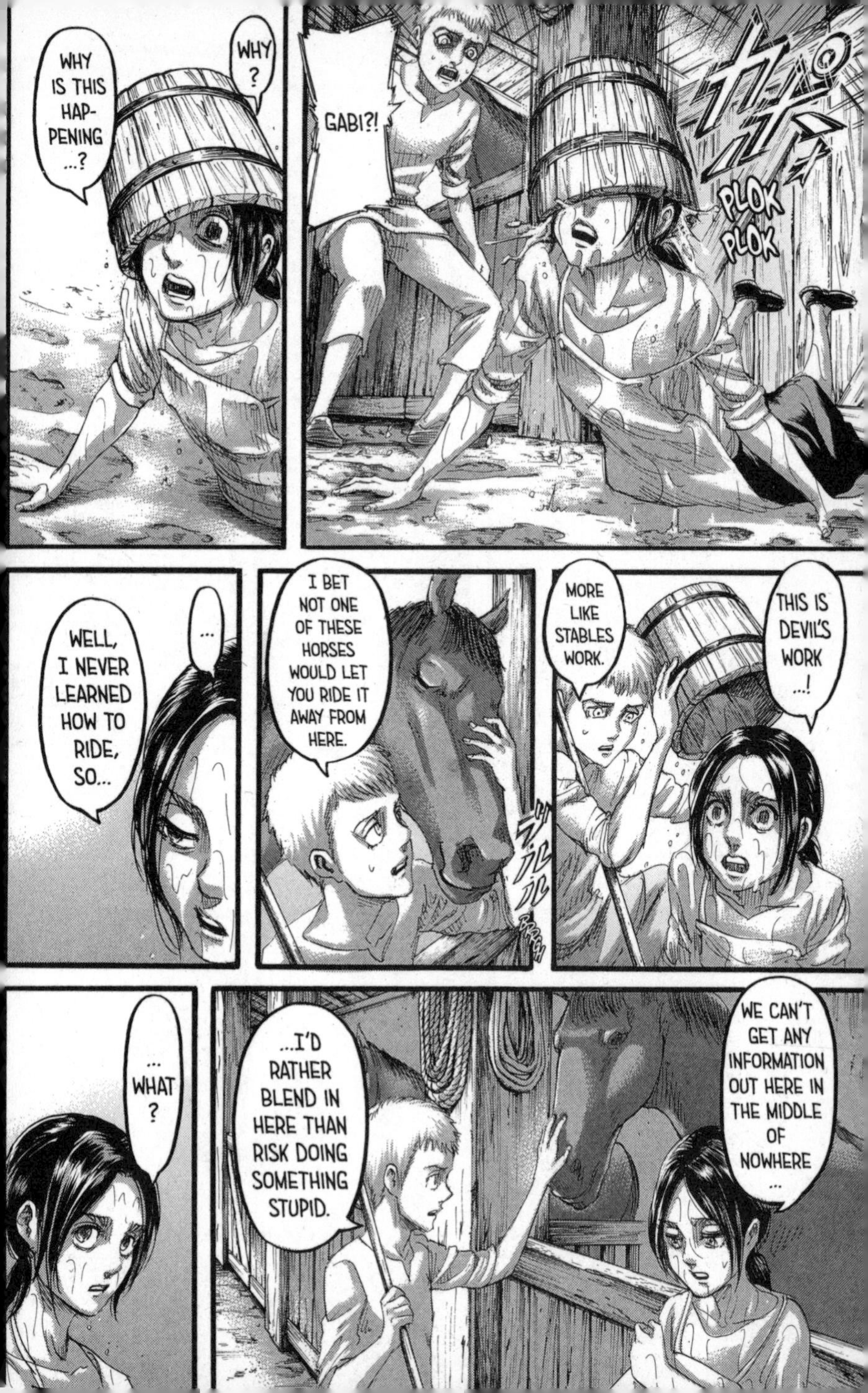
PLOK PLOK
GABI?!
WHY?
WHY IS THIS HAPPENING...?
THIS IS DEVIL'S WORK...!
MORE LIKE STABLES WORK.
I BET NOT ONE OF THESE HORSES WOULD LET YOU RIDE IT AWAY FROM HERE.
...
WELL, I NEVER LEARNED HOW TO RIDE, SO...
WE CAN'T GET ANY INFORMATION OUT HERE IN THE MIDDLE OF NOWHERE...
...I'D RATHER BLEND IN HERE THAN RISK DOING SOMETHING STUPID.
...WHAT?

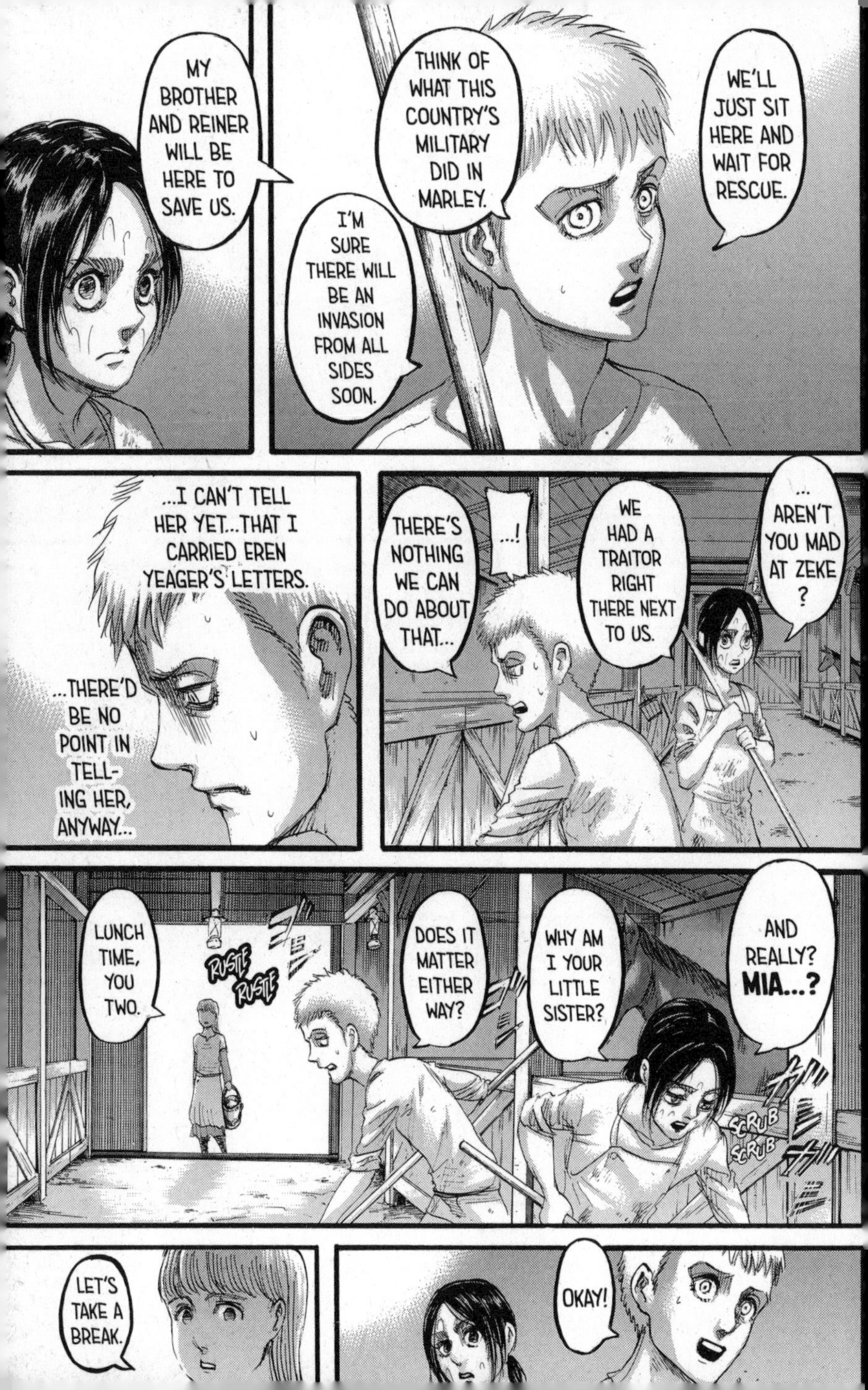
WE'LL JUST SIT HERE AND WAIT FOR RESCUE.
THINK OF WHAT THIS COUNTRY'S MILITARY DID IN MARLEY.
I'M SURE THERE WILL BE AN INVASION FROM ALL SIDES SOON.
MY BROTHER AND REINER WILL BE HERE TO SAVE US.
... AREN'T YOU MAD AT ZEKE?
WE HAD A TRAITOR RIGHT THERE NEXT TO US.
...!
THERE'S NOTHING WE CAN DO ABOUT THAT...
...I CAN'T TELL HER YET...THAT I CARRIED EREN YEAGER'S LETTERS.
...THERE'D BE NO POINT IN TELL-ING HER, ANYWAY...
AND REALLY? **MIA...?**
SCRUB SCRUB
WHY AM I YOUR LITTLE SISTER?
DOES IT MATTER EITHER WAY?
RUSTLE RUSTLE
LUNCH TIME, YOU TWO.
OKAY!
LET'S TAKE A BREAK.

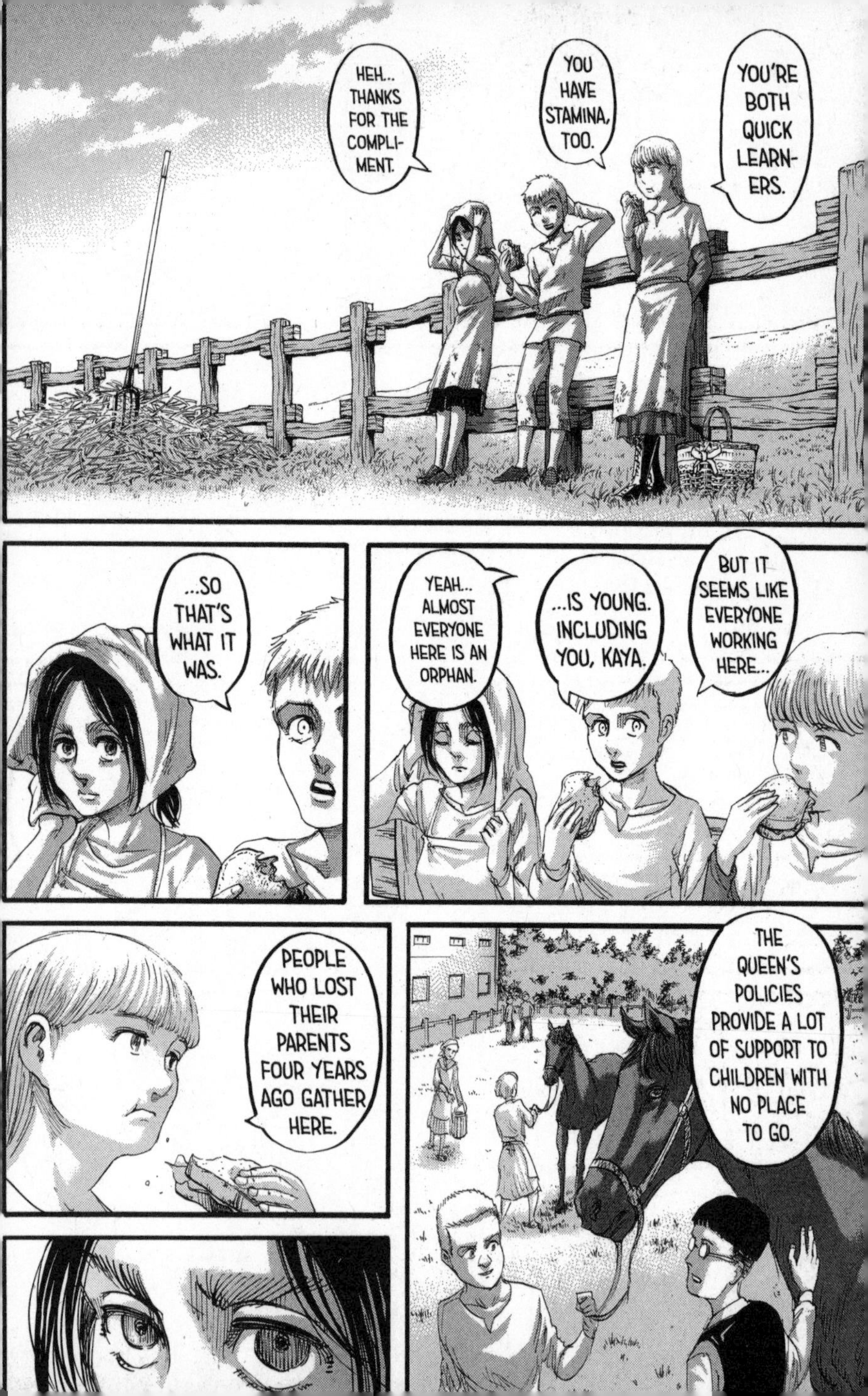
HEH... THANKS FOR THE COMPLI-MENT.
YOU HAVE STAMINA, TOO.
YOU'RE BOTH QUICK LEARN-ERS.
...SO THAT'S WHAT IT WAS.
YEAH... ALMOST EVERYONE HERE IS AN ORPHAN.
...IS YOUNG. INCLUDING YOU, KAYA.
BUT IT SEEMS LIKE EVERYONE WORKING HERE...
PEOPLE WHO LOST THEIR PARENTS FOUR YEARS AGO GATHER HERE.
THE QUEEN'S POLICIES PROVIDE A LOT OF SUPPORT TO CHILDREN WITH NO PLACE TO GO.

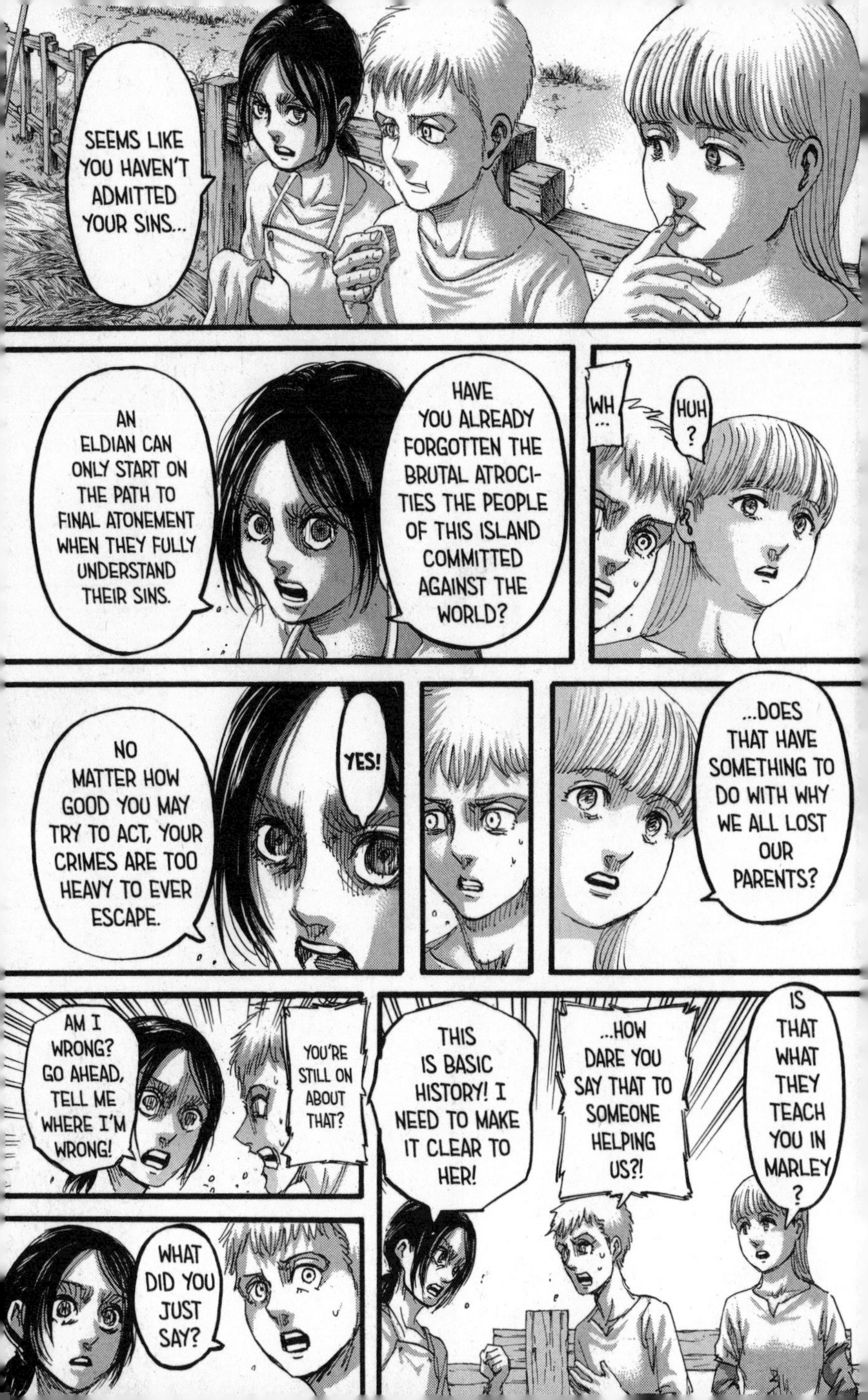
SEEMS LIKE YOU HAVEN'T ADMITTED YOUR SINS...
HUH?
WH...
HAVE YOU ALREADY FORGOTTEN THE BRUTAL ATROCITIES THE PEOPLE OF THIS ISLAND COMMITTED AGAINST THE WORLD?
AN ELDIAN CAN ONLY START ON THE PATH TO FINAL ATONEMENT WHEN THEY FULLY UNDERSTAND THEIR SINS.
...DOES THAT HAVE SOMETHING TO DO WITH WHY WE ALL LOST OUR PARENTS?
YES!
NO MATTER HOW GOOD YOU MAY TRY TO ACT, YOUR CRIMES ARE TOO HEAVY TO EVER ESCAPE.
IS THAT WHAT THEY TEACH YOU IN MARLEY?
...HOW DARE YOU SAY THAT TO SOMEONE HELPING US?!
THIS IS BASIC HISTORY! I NEED TO MAKE IT CLEAR TO HER!
YOU'RE STILL ON ABOUT THAT?
AM I WRONG? GO AHEAD, TELL ME WHERE I'M WRONG!
WHAT DID YOU JUST SAY?

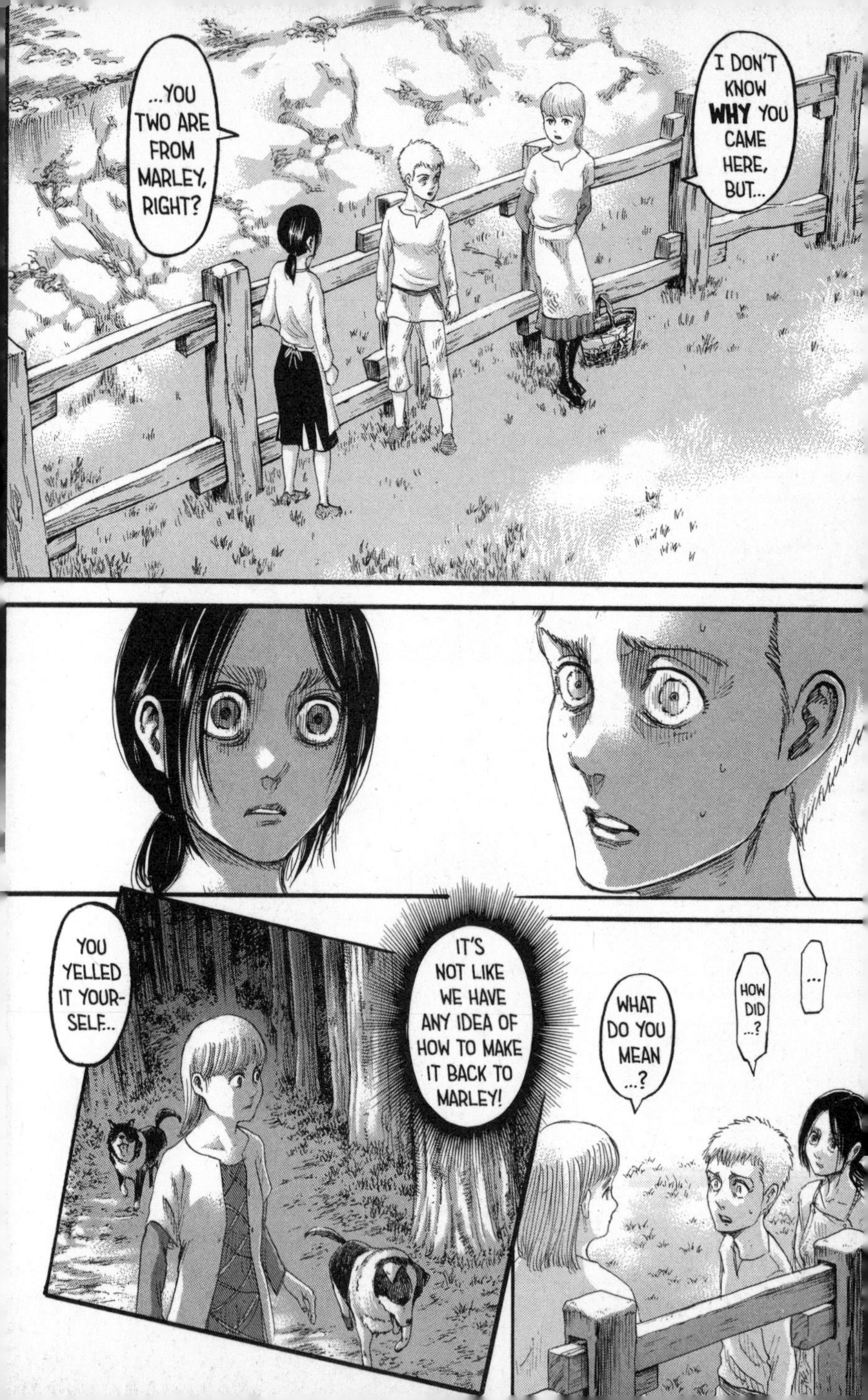
I DON'T KNOW **WHY** YOU CAME HERE, BUT...
...YOU TWO ARE FROM MARLEY, RIGHT?
...
HOW DID ...?
WHAT DO YOU MEAN ...?
IT'S NOT LIKE WE HAVE ANY IDEA OF HOW TO MAKE IT BACK TO MARLEY!
YOU YELLED IT YOUR-SELF...

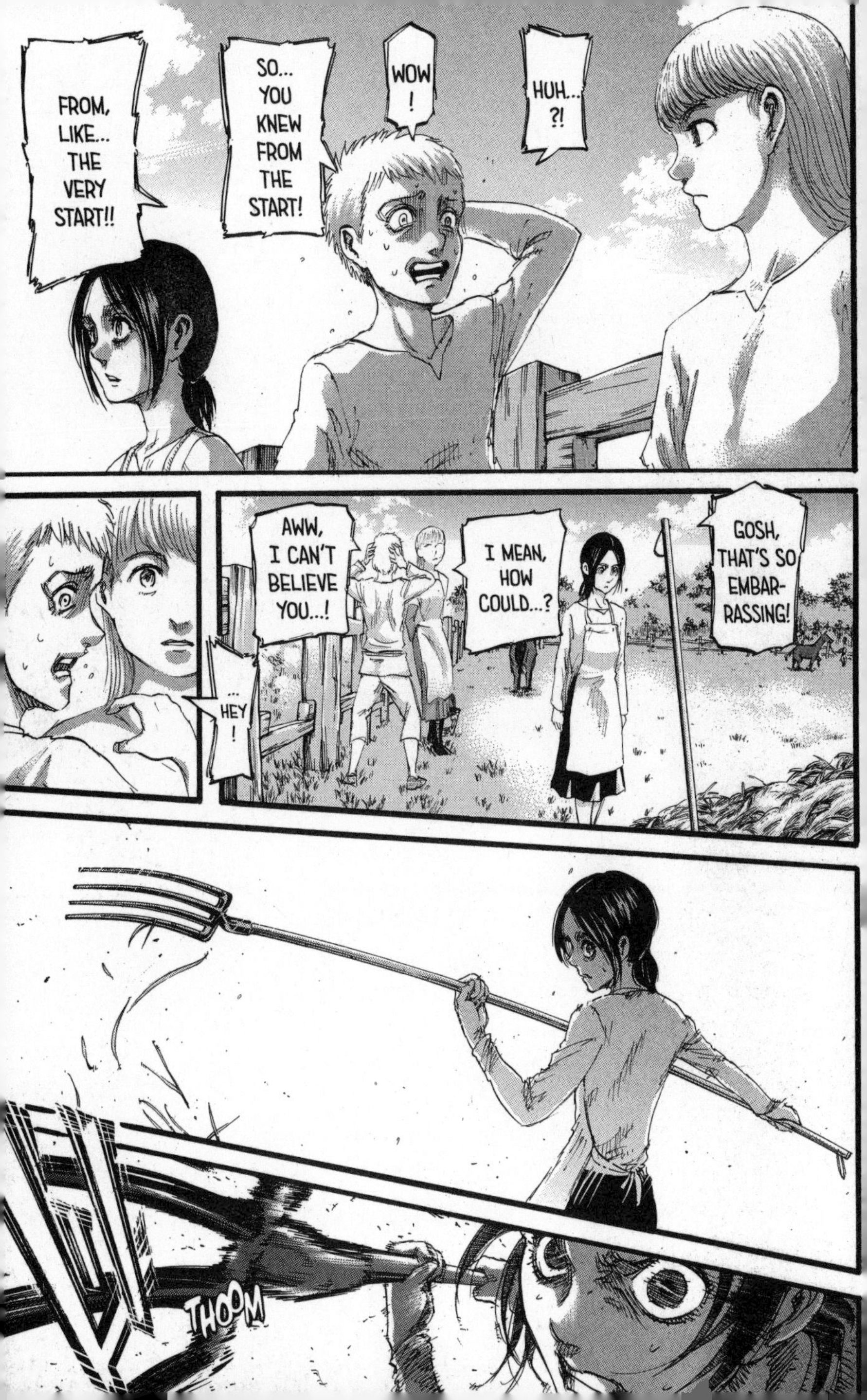
HUH...?!
WOW!
SO... YOU KNEW FROM THE START!
FROM, LIKE... THE VERY START!!
GOSH, THAT'S SO EMBARRASSING!
I MEAN, HOW COULD...?
AWW, I CAN'T BELIEVE YOU...!
...HEY!
THOOM

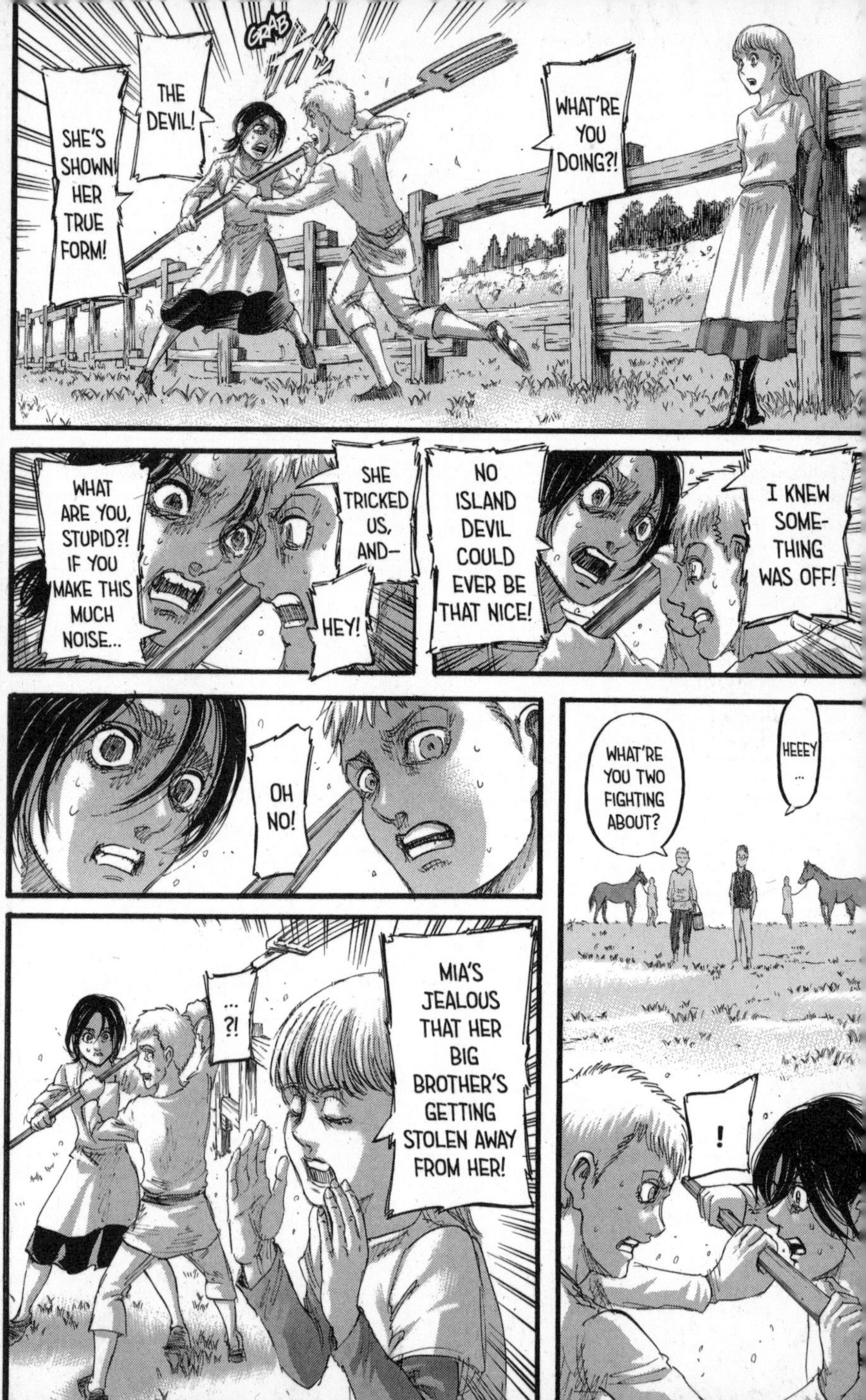
WHAT'RE YOU DOING?!
GRAB
THE DEVIL!
SHE'S SHOWN HER TRUE FORM!
I KNEW SOME-THING WAS OFF!
NO ISLAND DEVIL COULD EVER BE THAT NICE!
SHE TRICKED US, AND—
HEY!
WHAT ARE YOU, STUPID?! IF YOU MAKE THIS MUCH NOISE...
HEEEY...
WHAT'RE YOU TWO FIGHTING ABOUT?
OH NO!
!
...?!
MIA'S JEALOUS THAT HER BIG BROTHER'S GETTING STOLEN AWAY FROM HER!

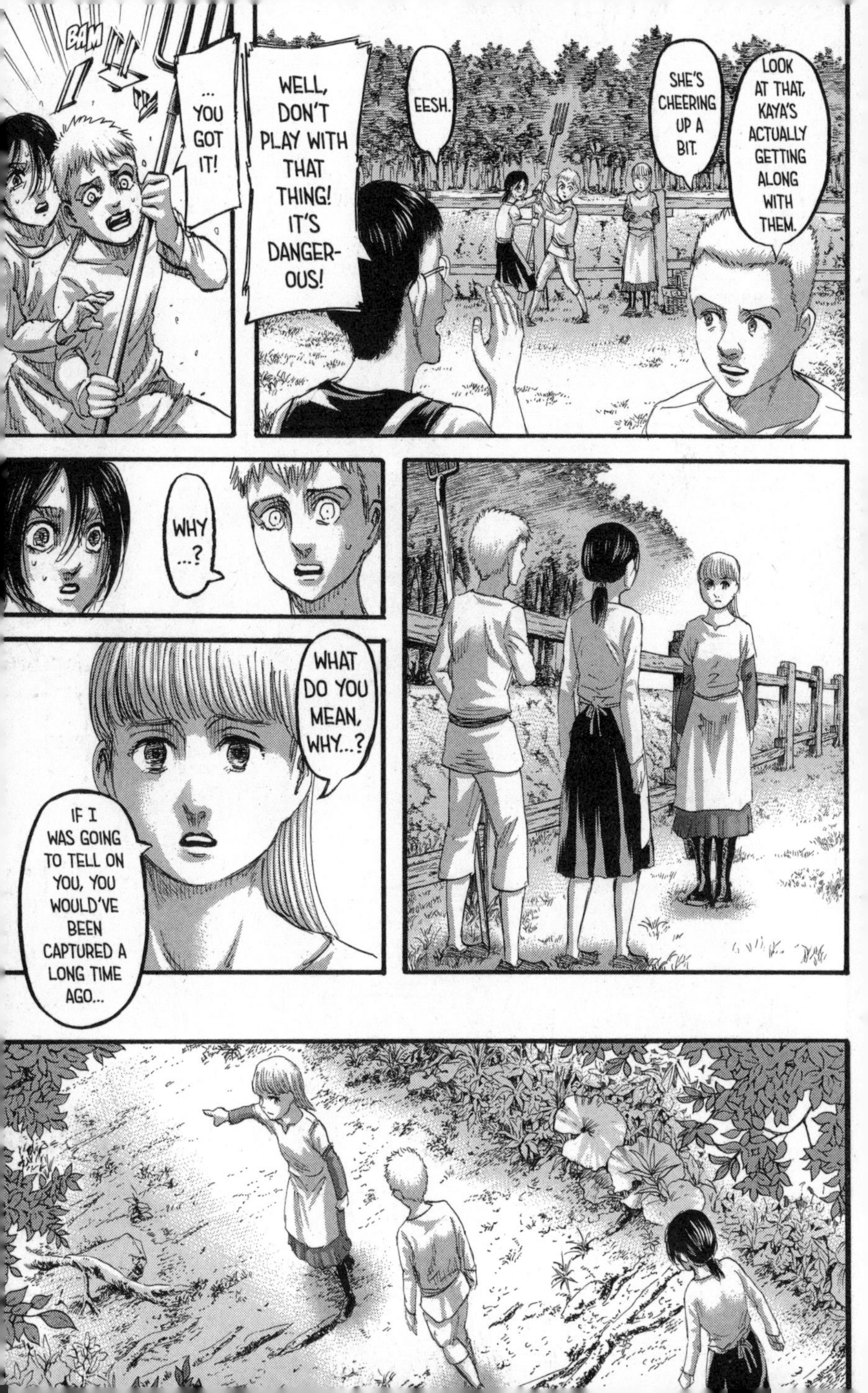
LOOK AT THAT, KAYA'S ACTUALLY GETTING ALONG WITH THEM.
SHE'S CHEERING UP A BIT.
EESH.
WELL, DON'T PLAY WITH THAT THING! IT'S DANGER-OUS!
BAM
... YOU GOT IT!
WHY ...?
WHAT DO YOU MEAN, WHY...?
IF I WAS GOING TO TELL ON YOU, YOU WOULD'VE BEEN CAPTURED A LONG TIME AGO...

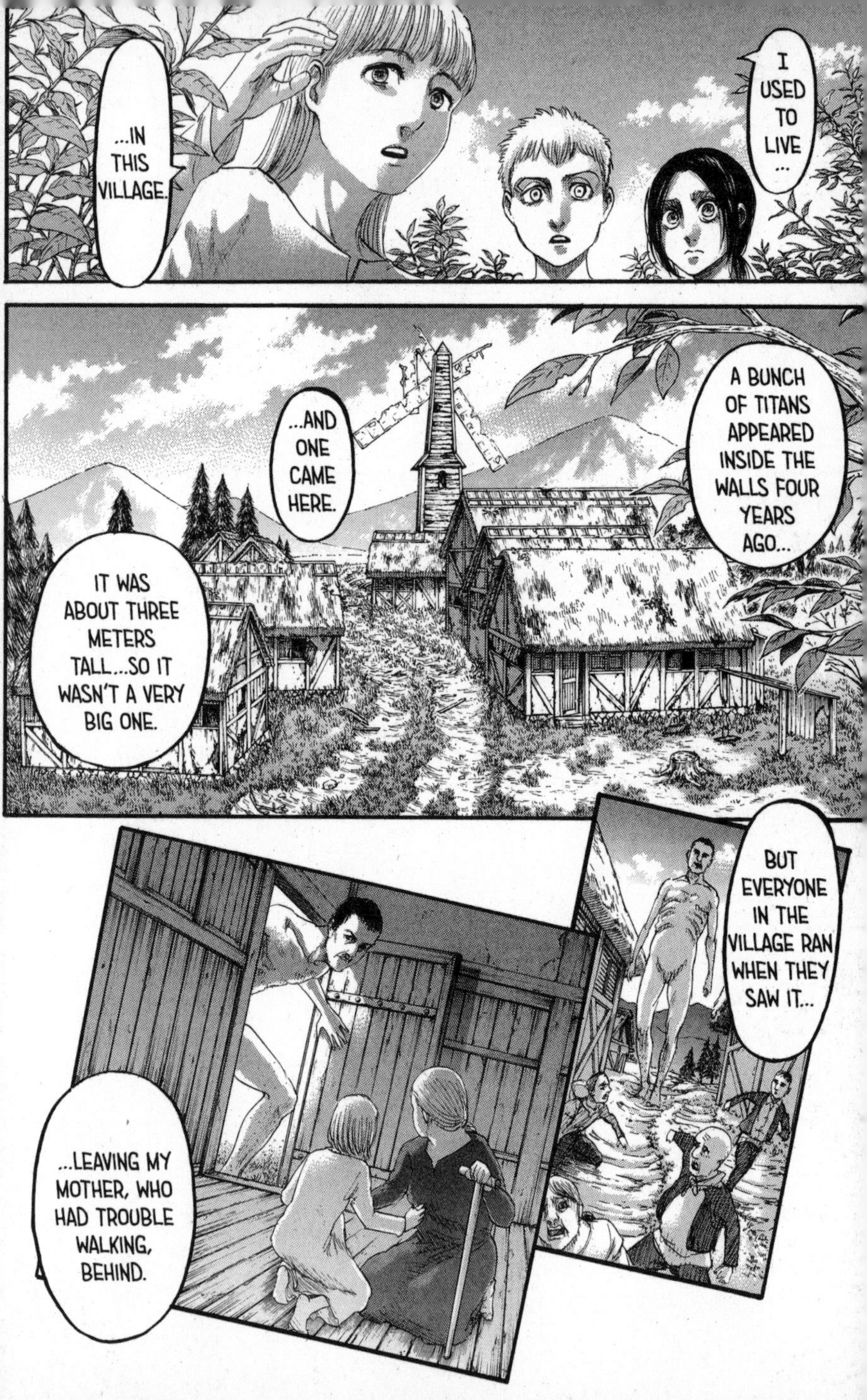
I USED TO LIVE...
...IN THIS VILLAGE.
A BUNCH OF TITANS APPEARED INSIDE THE WALLS FOUR YEARS AGO...
...AND ONE CAME HERE.
IT WAS ABOUT THREE METERS TALL...SO IT WASN'T A VERY BIG ONE.
BUT EVERYONE IN THE VILLAGE RAN WHEN THEY SAW IT...
...LEAVING MY MOTHER, WHO HAD TROUBLE WALKING, BEHIND.

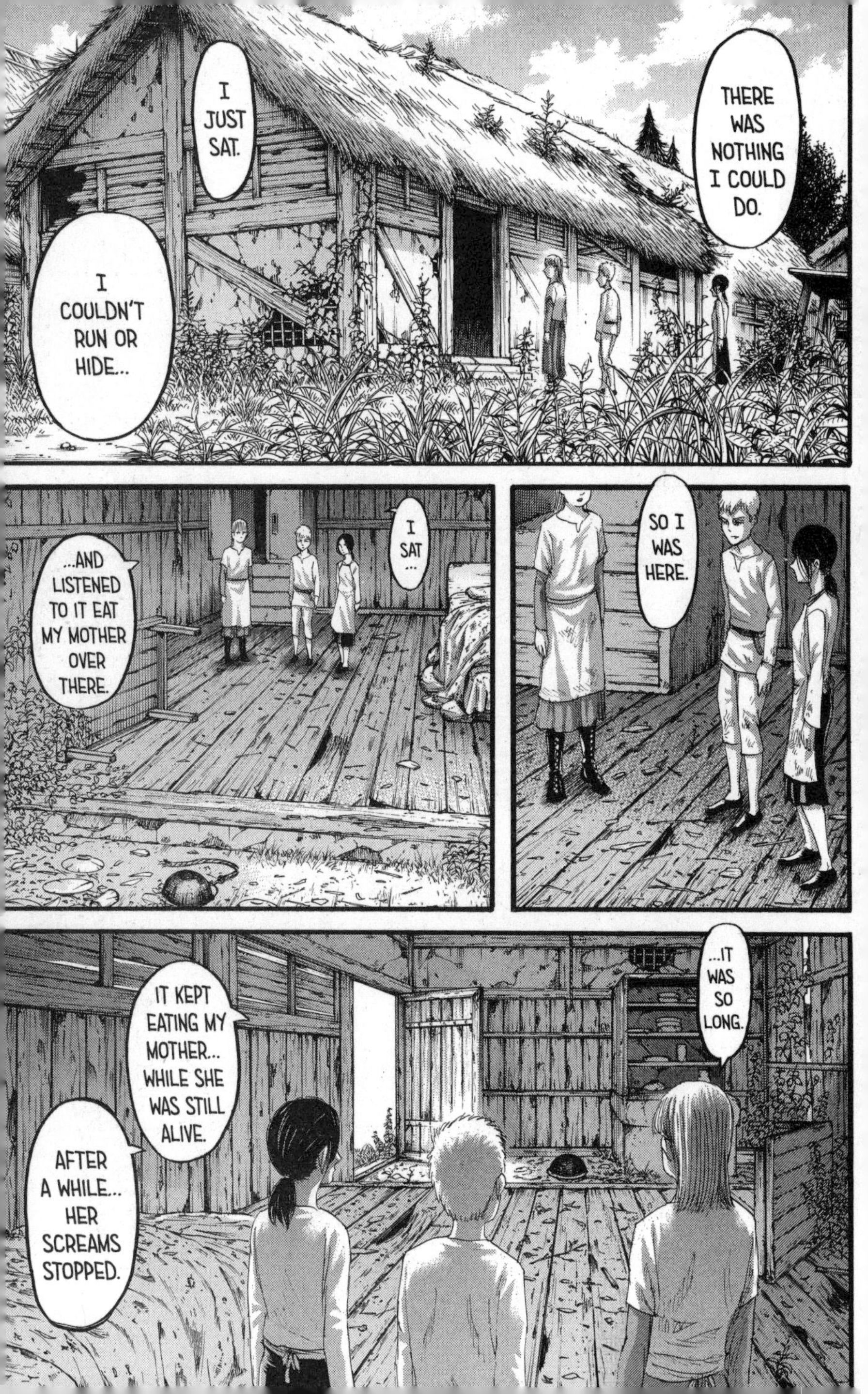
THERE WAS NOTHING I COULD DO.
I JUST SAT.
I COULDN'T RUN OR HIDE...
SO I WAS HERE.
I SAT...
...AND LISTENED TO IT EAT MY MOTHER OVER THERE.
...IT WAS SO LONG.
IT KEPT EATING MY MOTHER... WHILE SHE WAS STILL ALIVE.
AFTER A WHILE... HER SCREAMS STOPPED.

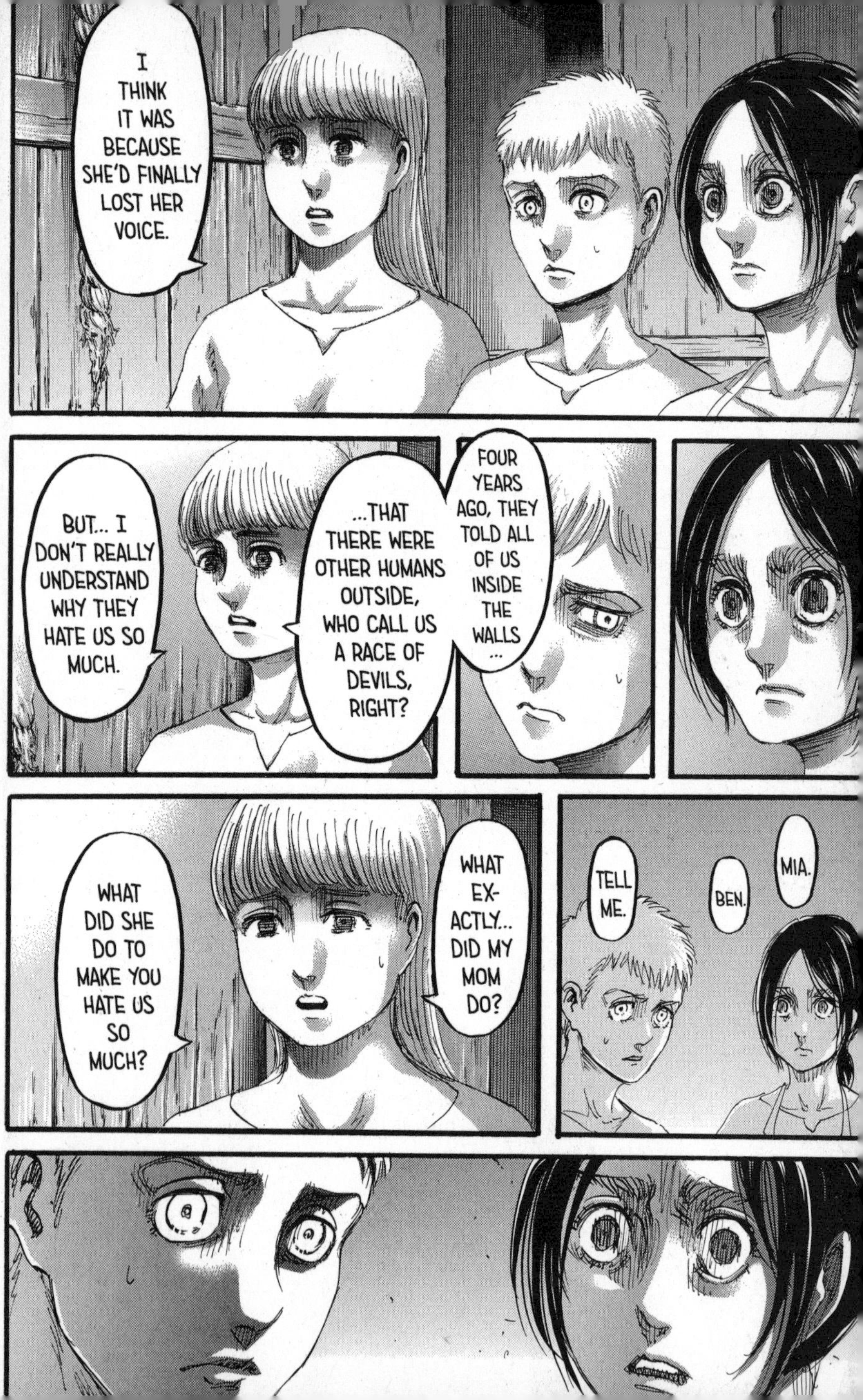
I THINK IT WAS BECAUSE SHE'D FINALLY LOST HER VOICE.
FOUR YEARS AGO, THEY TOLD ALL OF US INSIDE THE WALLS ...
...THAT THERE WERE OTHER HUMANS OUTSIDE, WHO CALL US A RACE OF DEVILS, RIGHT?
BUT... I DON'T REALLY UNDERSTAND WHY THEY HATE US SO MUCH.
MIA.
BEN.
TELL ME.
WHAT EXACTLY... DID MY MOM DO?
WHAT DID SHE DO TO MAKE YOU HATE US SO MUCH?

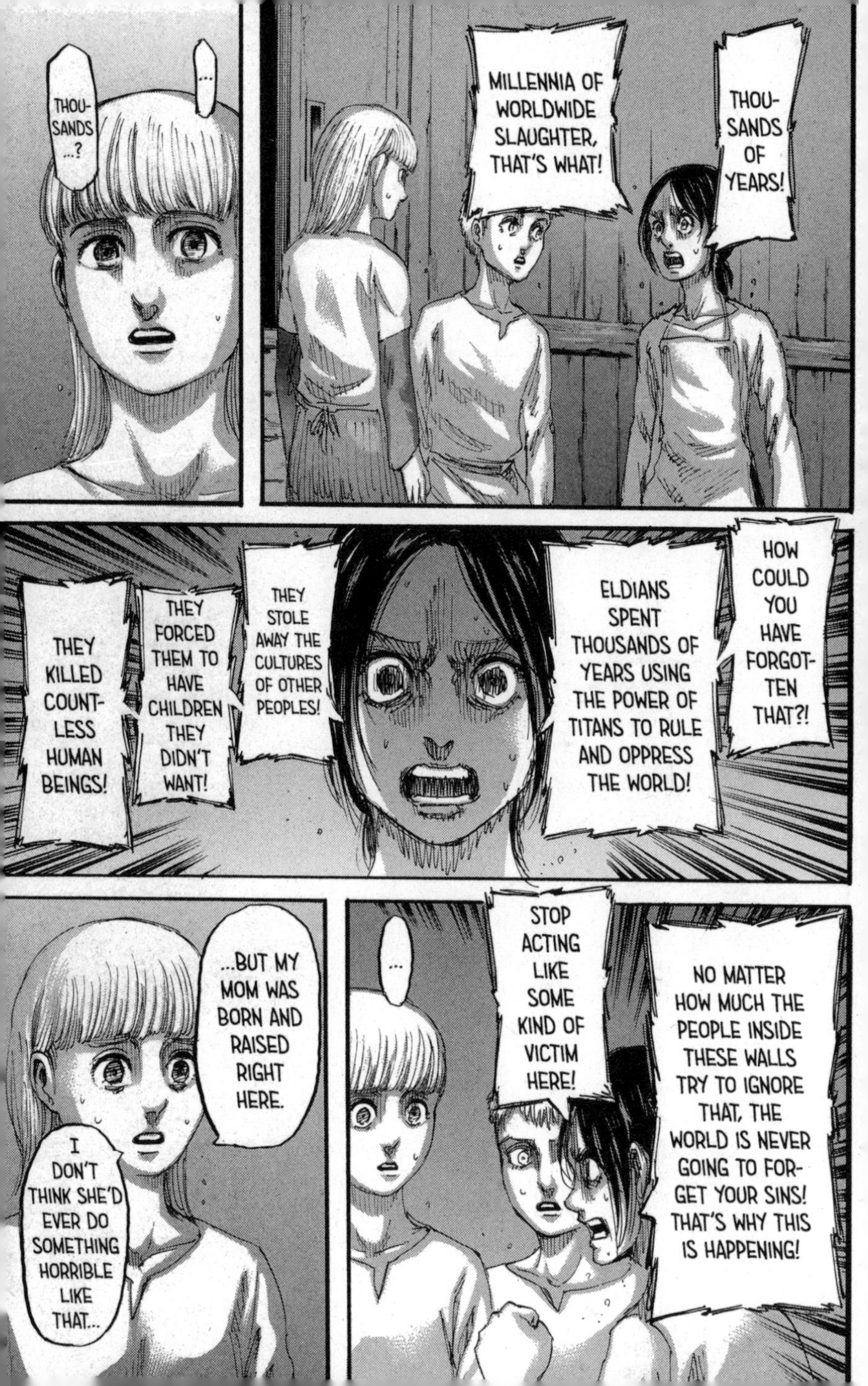

THOUSANDS OF YEARS!
MILLENNIA OF WORLDWIDE SLAUGHTER, THAT'S WHAT!
...
THOUSANDS ...?
HOW COULD YOU HAVE FORGOTTEN THAT?!
ELDIANS SPENT THOUSANDS OF YEARS USING THE POWER OF TITANS TO RULE AND OPPRESS THE WORLD!
THEY STOLE AWAY THE CULTURES OF OTHER PEOPLES!
THEY FORCED THEM TO HAVE CHILDREN THEY DIDN'T WANT!
THEY KILLED COUNTLESS HUMAN BEINGS!
NO MATTER HOW MUCH THE PEOPLE INSIDE THESE WALLS TRY TO IGNORE THAT, THE WORLD IS NEVER GOING TO FORGET YOUR SINS! THAT'S WHY THIS IS HAPPENING!
STOP ACTING LIKE SOME KIND OF VICTIM HERE!
...
...BUT MY MOM WAS BORN AND RAISED RIGHT HERE.
I DON'T THINK SHE'D EVER DO SOMETHING HORRIBLE LIKE THAT...

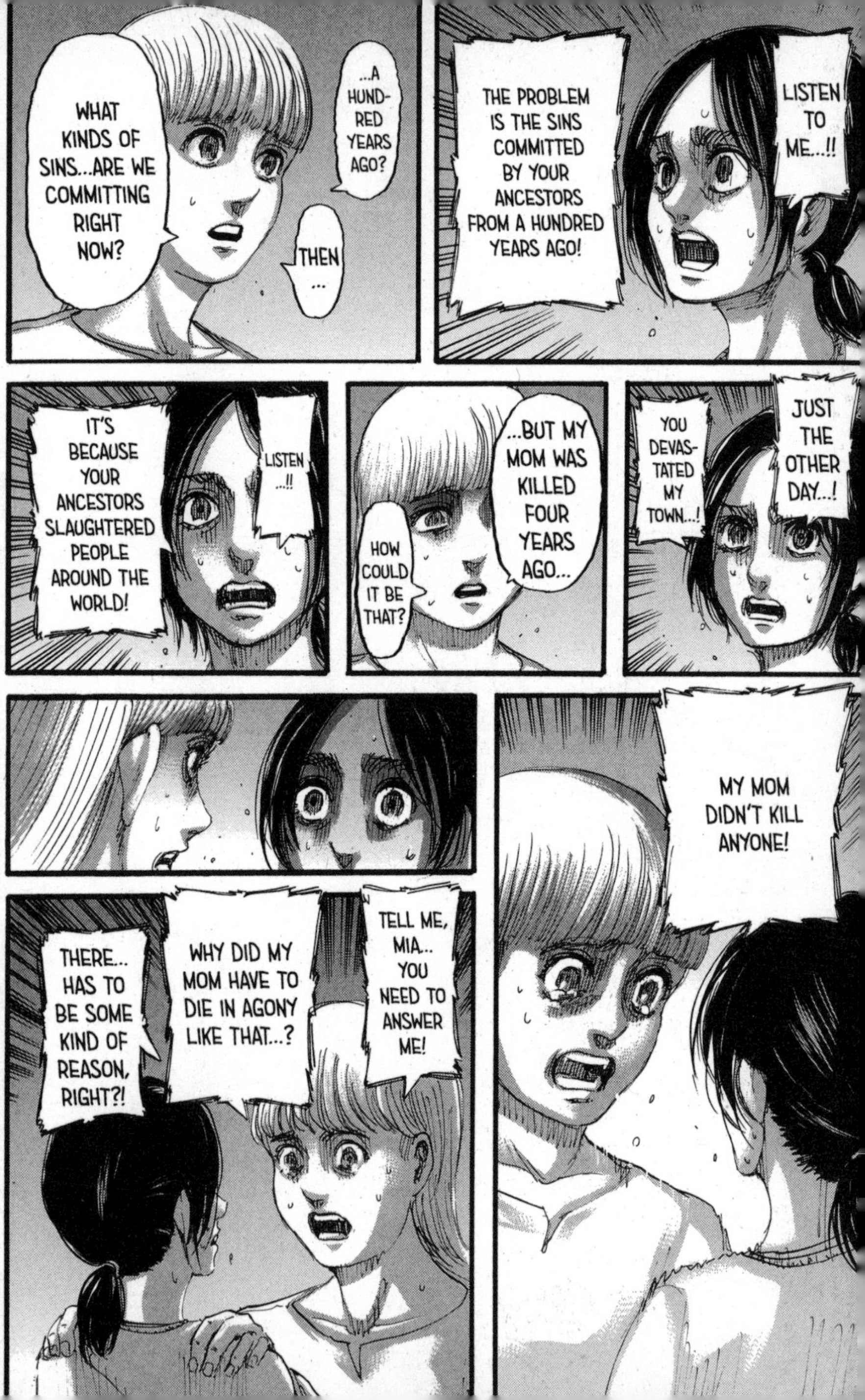
LISTEN TO ME...!!
THE PROBLEM IS THE SINS COMMITTED BY YOUR ANCESTORS FROM A HUNDRED YEARS AGO!
...A HUNDRED YEARS AGO?
THEN...
WHAT KINDS OF SINS...ARE WE COMMITTING RIGHT NOW?
JUST THE OTHER DAY...!
YOU DEVASTATED MY TOWN...!
...BUT MY MOM WAS KILLED FOUR YEARS AGO...
HOW COULD IT BE THAT?
LISTEN...!!
IT'S BECAUSE YOUR ANCESTORS SLAUGHTERED PEOPLE AROUND THE WORLD!
MY MOM DIDN'T KILL ANYONE!
TELL ME, MIA... YOU NEED TO ANSWER ME!
WHY DID MY MOM HAVE TO DIE IN AGONY LIKE THAT...?
THERE... HAS TO BE SOME KIND OF REASON, RIGHT?!

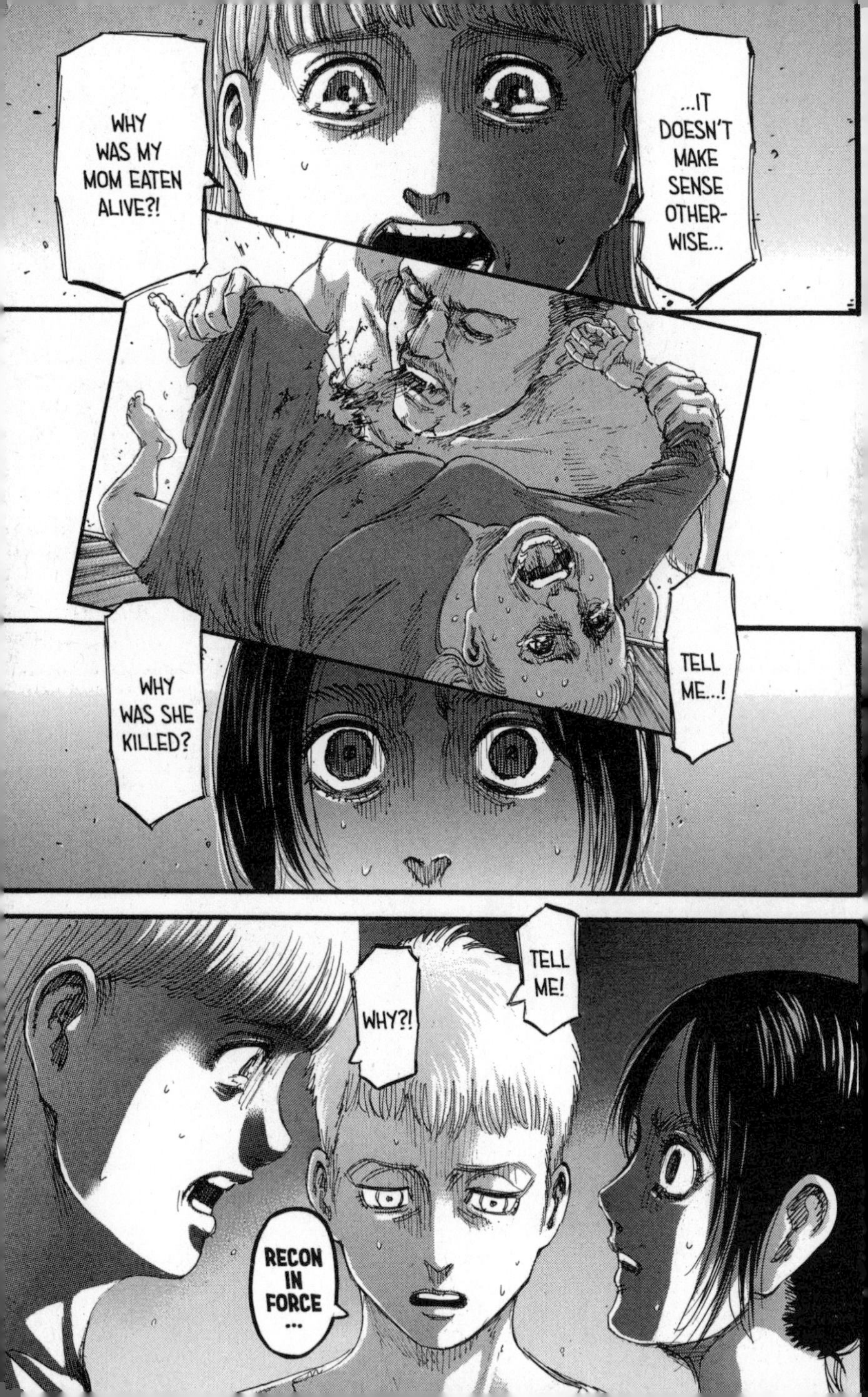
...IT DOESN'T MAKE SENSE OTHER-WISE...
WHY WAS MY MOM EATEN ALIVE?!
TELL ME...!
WHY WAS SHE KILLED?
TELL ME!
WHY?!
RECON IN FORCE...

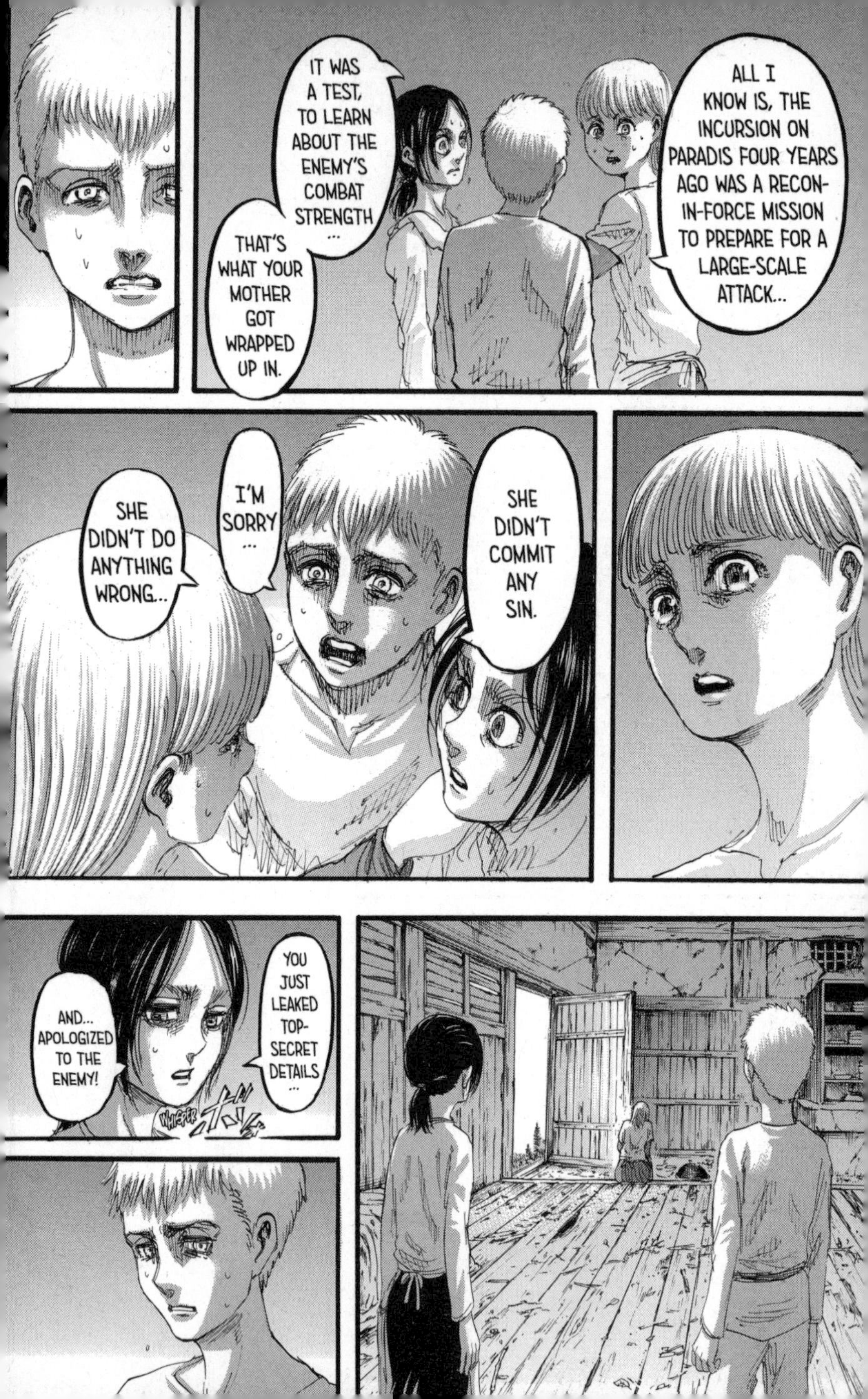
ALL I KNOW IS, THE INCURSION ON PARADIS FOUR YEARS AGO WAS A RECON-IN-FORCE MISSION TO PREPARE FOR A LARGE-SCALE ATTACK...
IT WAS A TEST, TO LEARN ABOUT THE ENEMY'S COMBAT STRENGTH...
THAT'S WHAT YOUR MOTHER GOT WRAPPED UP IN.
SHE DIDN'T COMMIT ANY SIN.
I'M SORRY...
SHE DIDN'T DO ANYTHING WRONG...
YOU JUST LEAKED TOP-SECRET DETAILS...
AND... APOLOGIZED TO THE ENEMY!
WHISPER

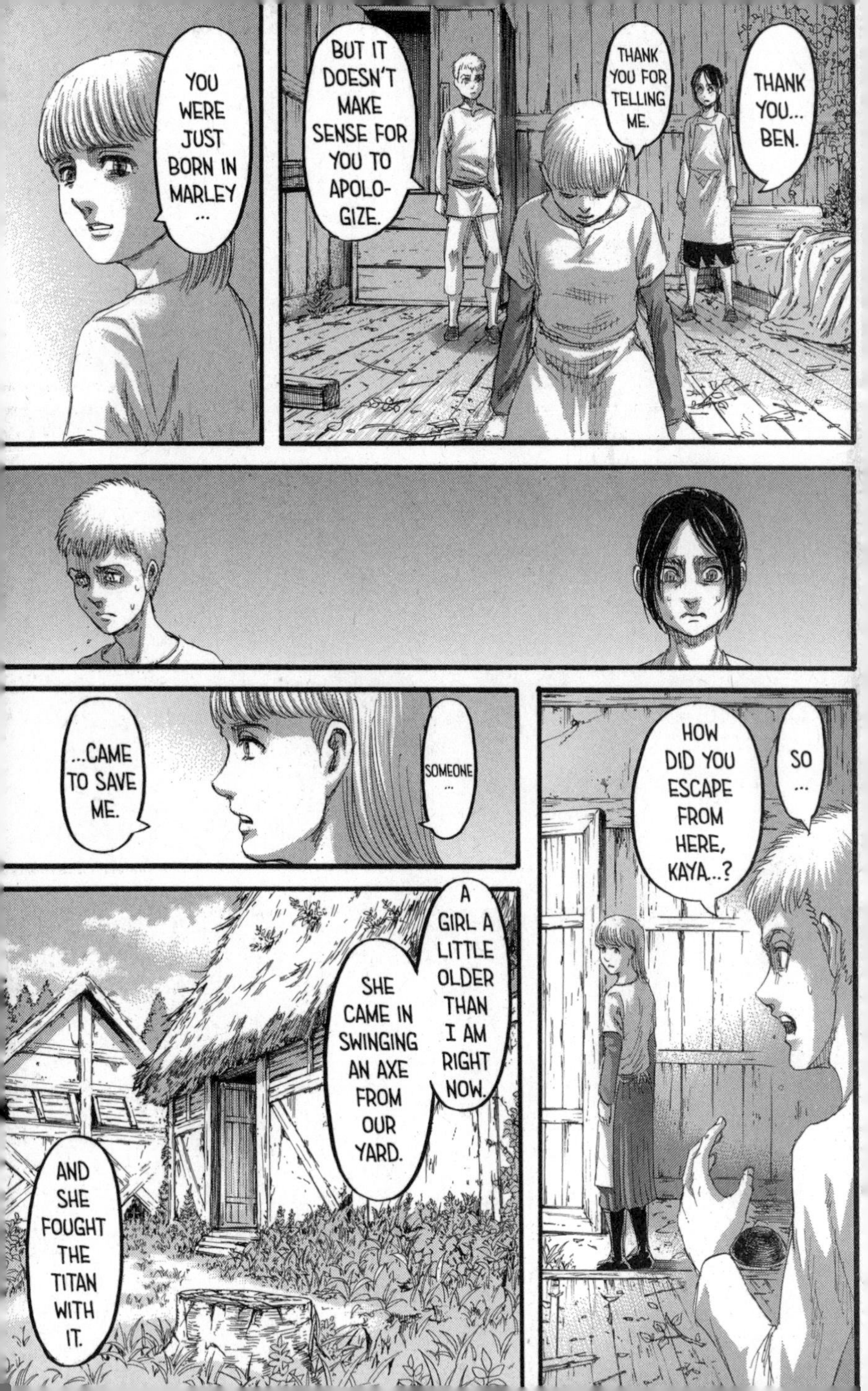
THANK YOU... BEN.
THANK YOU FOR TELLING ME.
BUT IT DOESN'T MAKE SENSE FOR YOU TO APOLOGIZE.
YOU WERE JUST BORN IN MARLEY ...
SO ...
HOW DID YOU ESCAPE FROM HERE, KAYA...?
SOMEONE ...
...CAME TO SAVE ME.
A GIRL A LITTLE OLDER THAN I AM RIGHT NOW.
SHE CAME IN SWINGING AN AXE FROM OUR YARD.
AND SHE FOUGHT THE TITAN WITH IT.

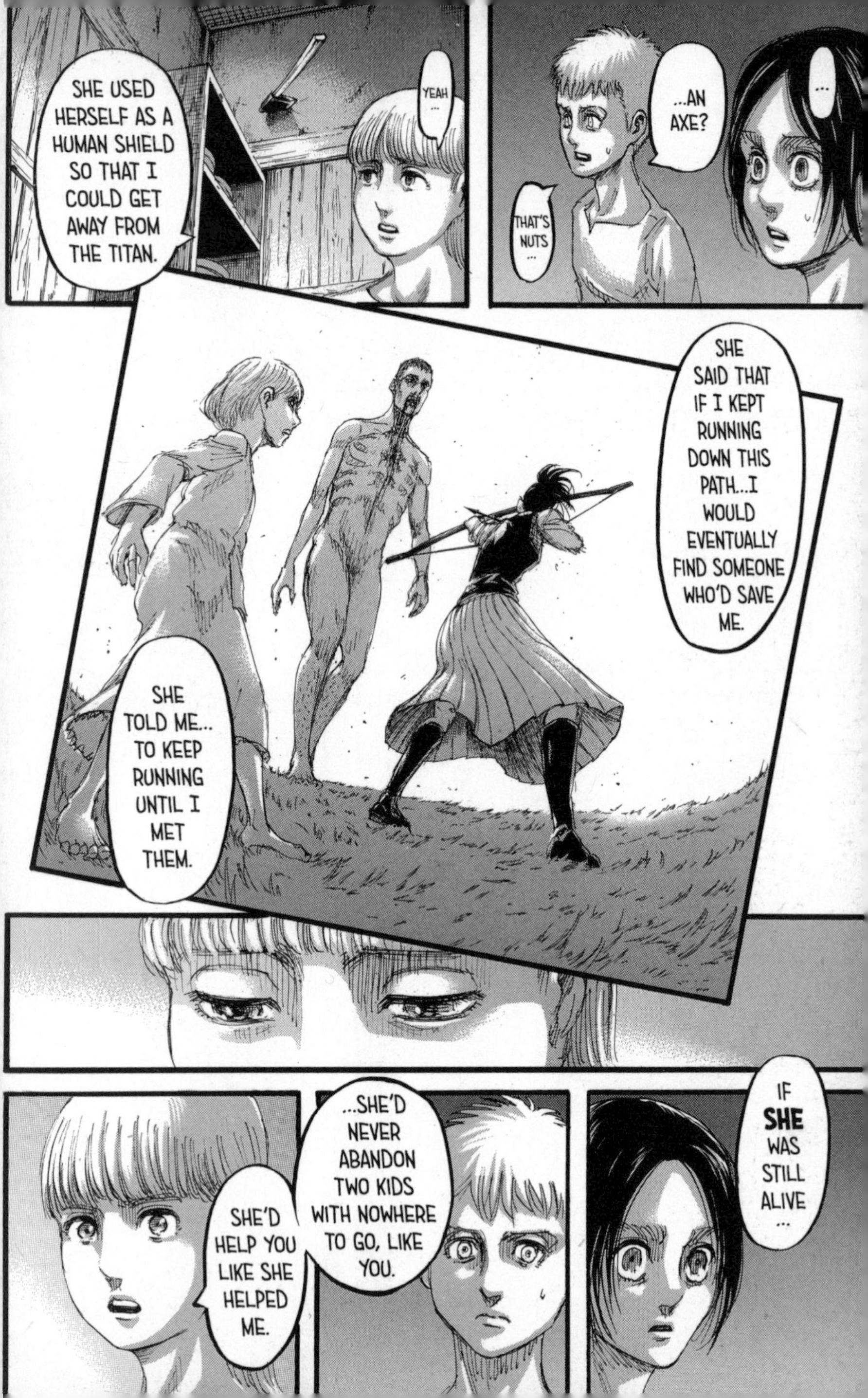
...
...AN AXE?
THAT'S NUTS...
YEAH...
SHE USED HERSELF AS A HUMAN SHIELD SO THAT I COULD GET AWAY FROM THE TITAN.
SHE SAID THAT IF I KEPT RUNNING DOWN THIS PATH...I WOULD EVENTUALLY FIND SOMEONE WHO'D SAVE ME.
SHE TOLD ME... TO KEEP RUNNING UNTIL I MET THEM.
IF **SHE** WAS STILL ALIVE...
...SHE'D NEVER ABANDON TWO KIDS WITH NOWHERE TO GO, LIKE YOU.
SHE'D HELP YOU LIKE SHE HELPED ME.

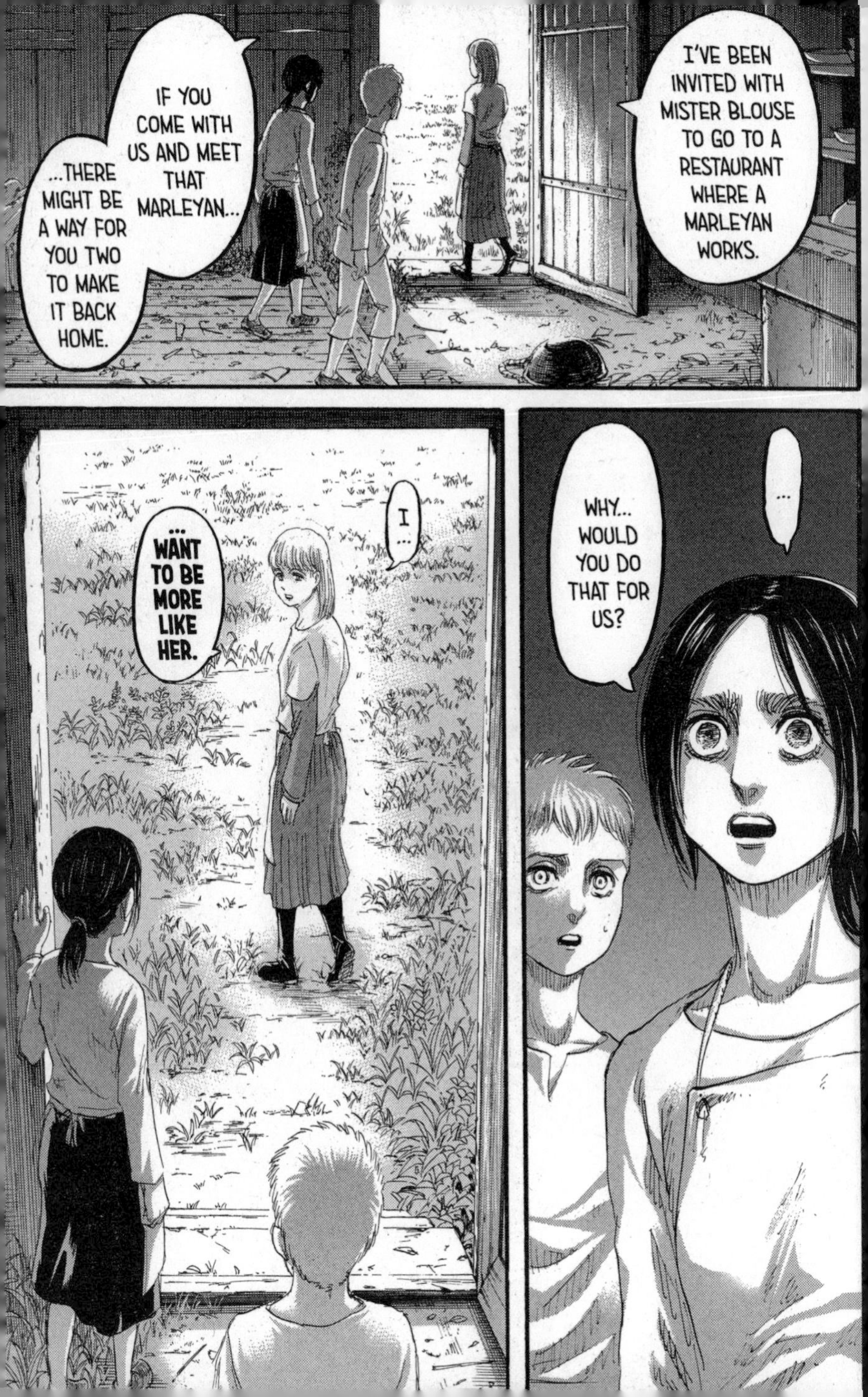

I'VE BEEN INVITED WITH MISTER BLOUSE TO GO TO A RESTAURANT WHERE A MARLEYAN WORKS.
IF YOU COME WITH US AND MEET THAT MARLEYAN...
...THERE MIGHT BE A WAY FOR YOU TWO TO MAKE IT BACK HOME.
...
WHY... WOULD YOU DO THAT FOR US?
I...
...WANT TO BE MORE LIKE HER.

ATTACK on TITAN

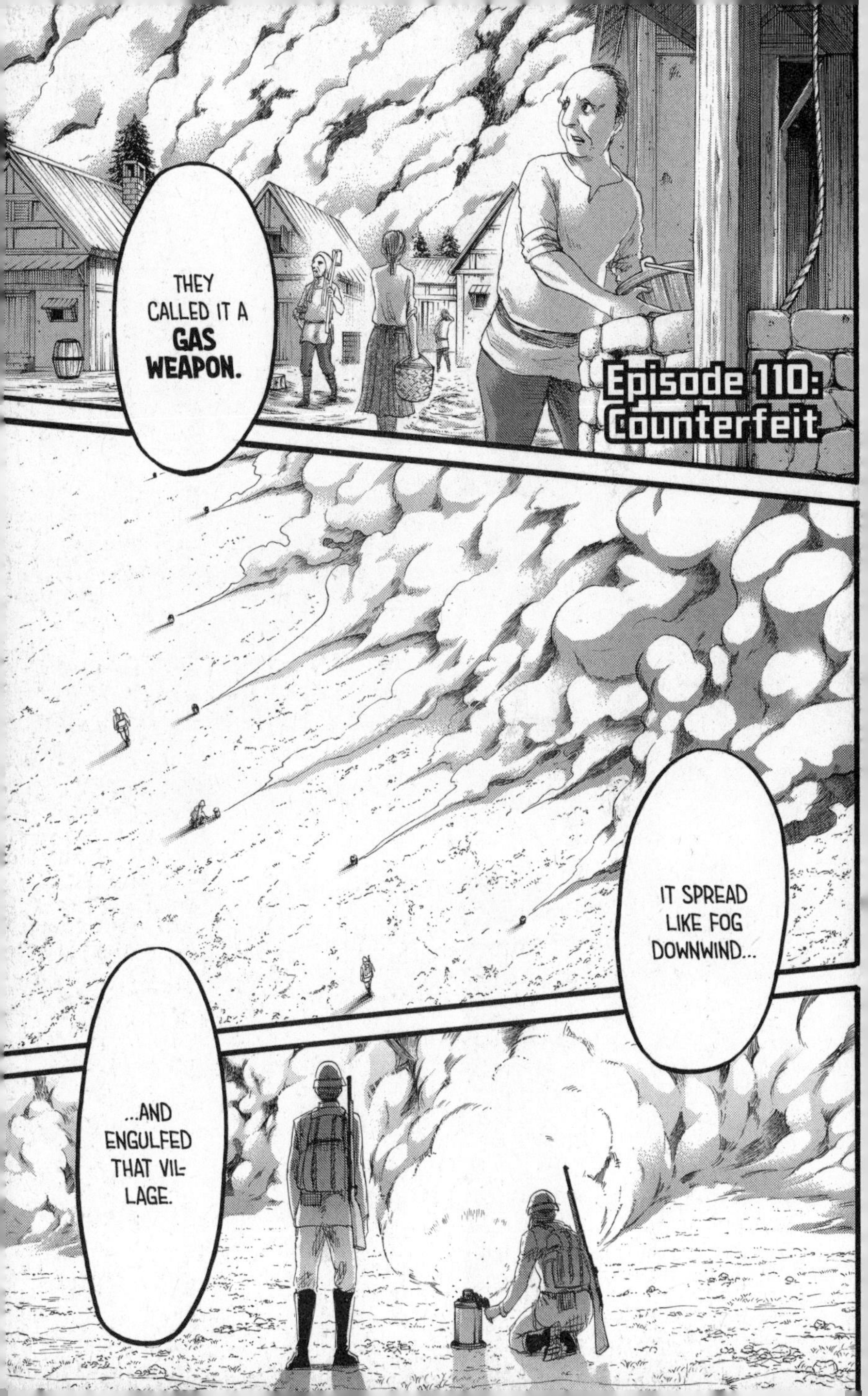
THEY CALLED IT A GAS WEAPON.
Episode 110: Counterfeit
IT SPREAD LIKE FOG DOWNWIND...
...AND ENGULFED THAT VIL-LAGE.

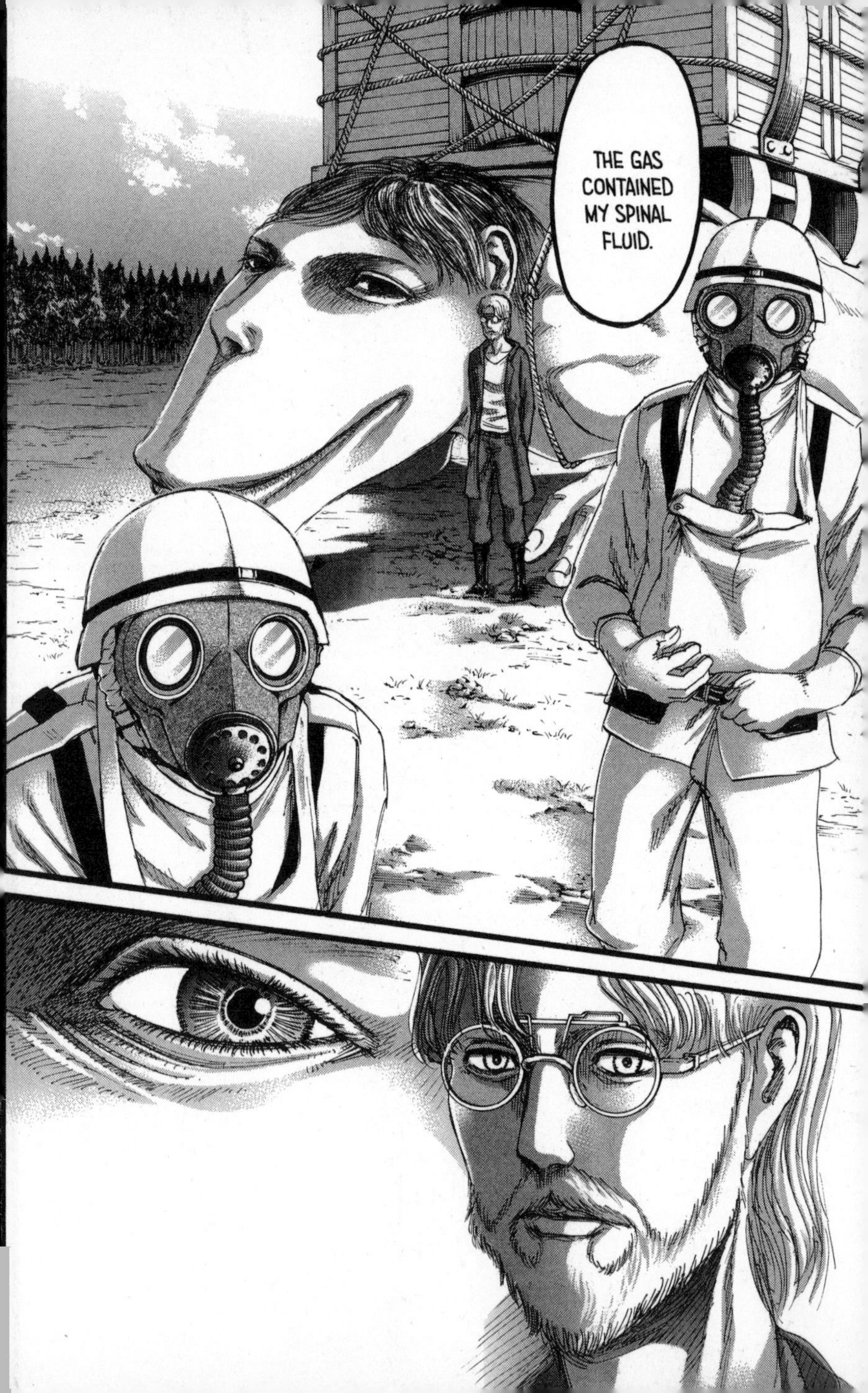
THE GAS CONTAINED MY SPINAL FLUID.

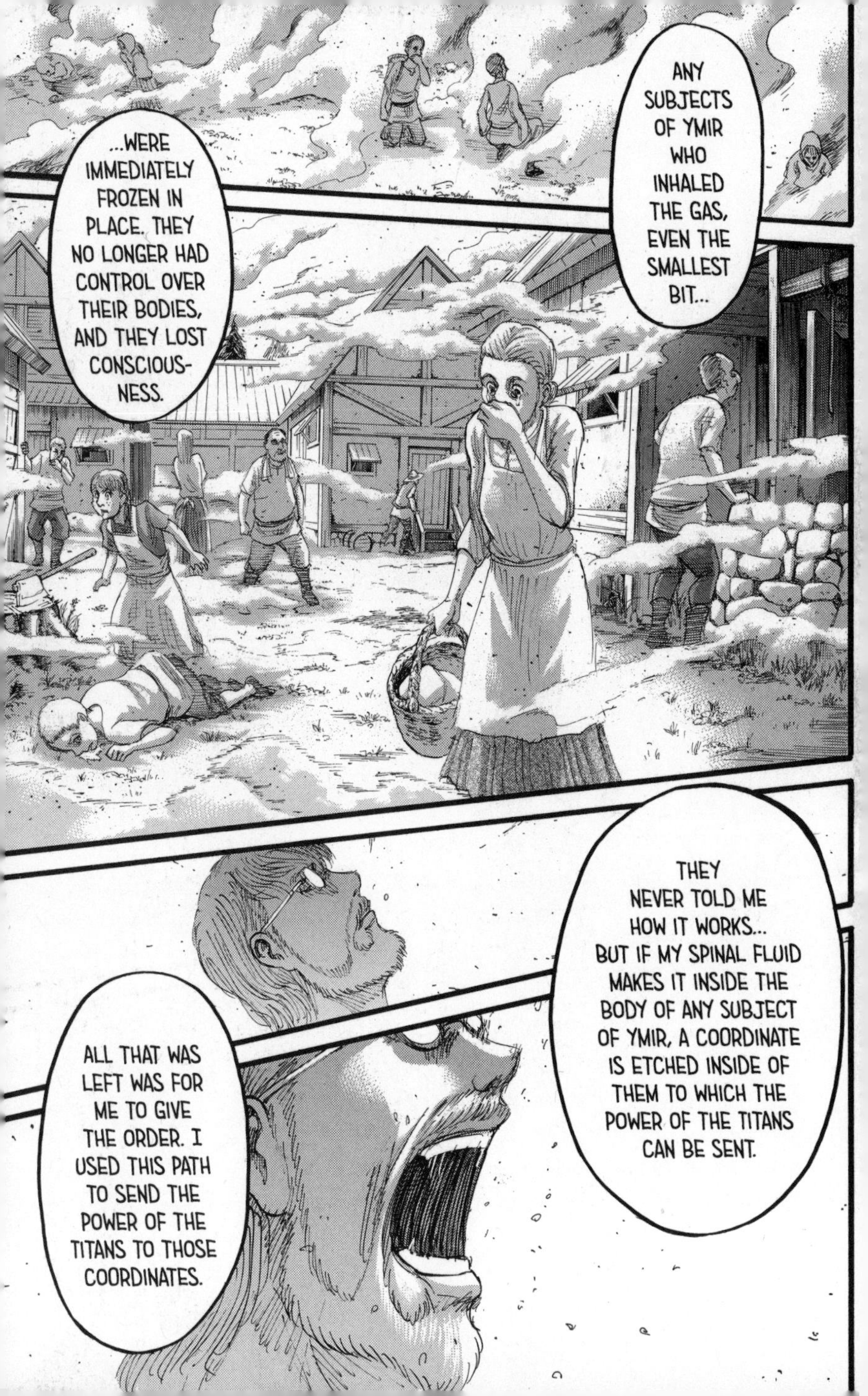
ANY SUBJECTS OF YMIR WHO INHALED THE GAS, EVEN THE SMALLEST BIT...
...WERE IMMEDIATELY FROZEN IN PLACE. THEY NO LONGER HAD CONTROL OVER THEIR BODIES, AND THEY LOST CONSCIOUS-NESS.
THEY NEVER TOLD ME HOW IT WORKS... BUT IF MY SPINAL FLUID MAKES IT INSIDE THE BODY OF ANY SUBJECT OF YMIR, A COORDINATE IS ETCHED INSIDE OF THEM TO WHICH THE POWER OF THE TITANS CAN BE SENT.
ALL THAT WAS LEFT WAS FOR ME TO GIVE THE ORDER. I USED THIS PATH TO SEND THE POWER OF THE TITANS TO THOSE COORDINATES.

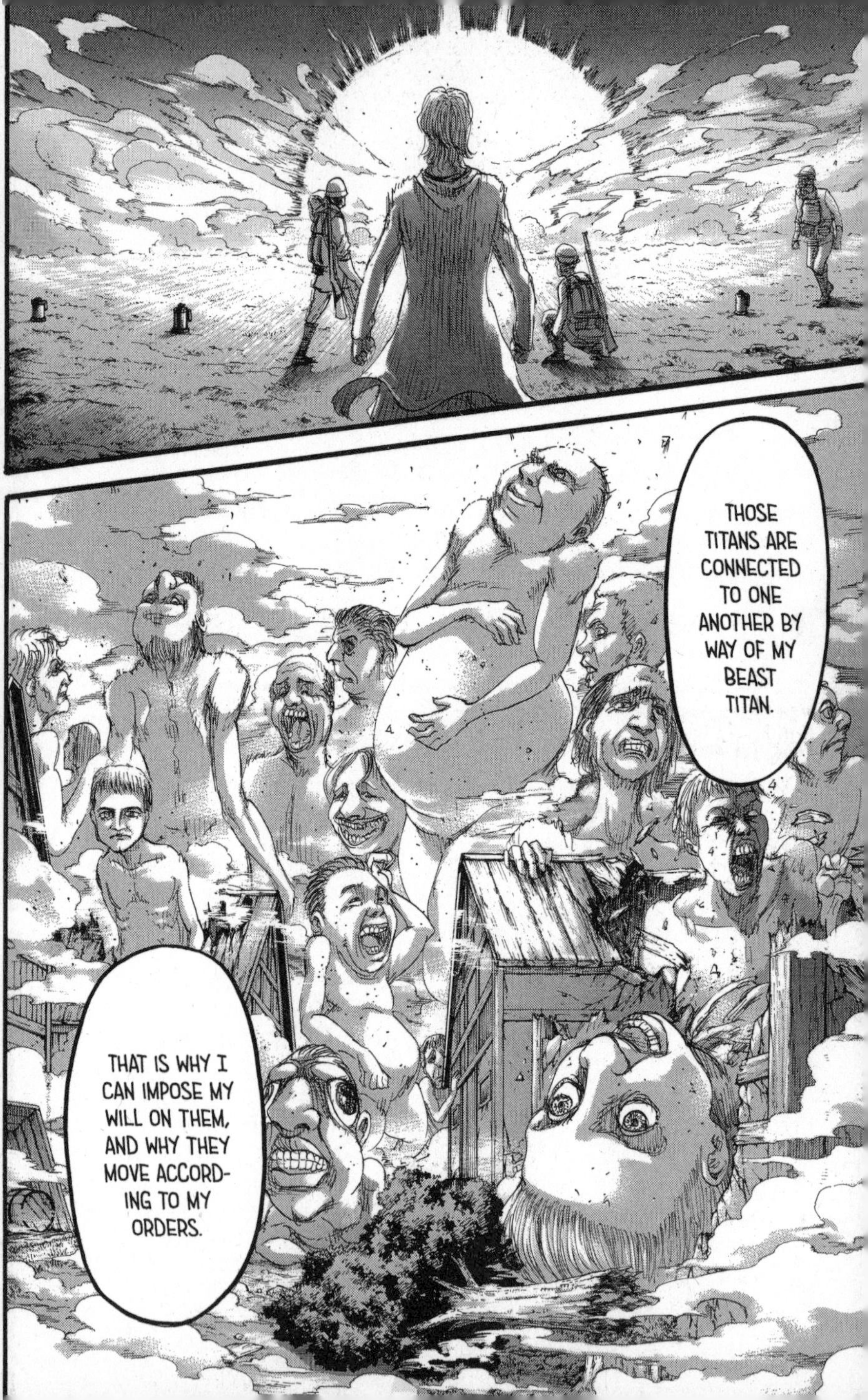
THOSE TITANS ARE CONNECTED TO ONE ANOTHER BY WAY OF MY BEAST TITAN.
THAT IS WHY I CAN IMPOSE MY WILL ON THEM, AND WHY THEY MOVE ACCORD-ING TO MY ORDERS.

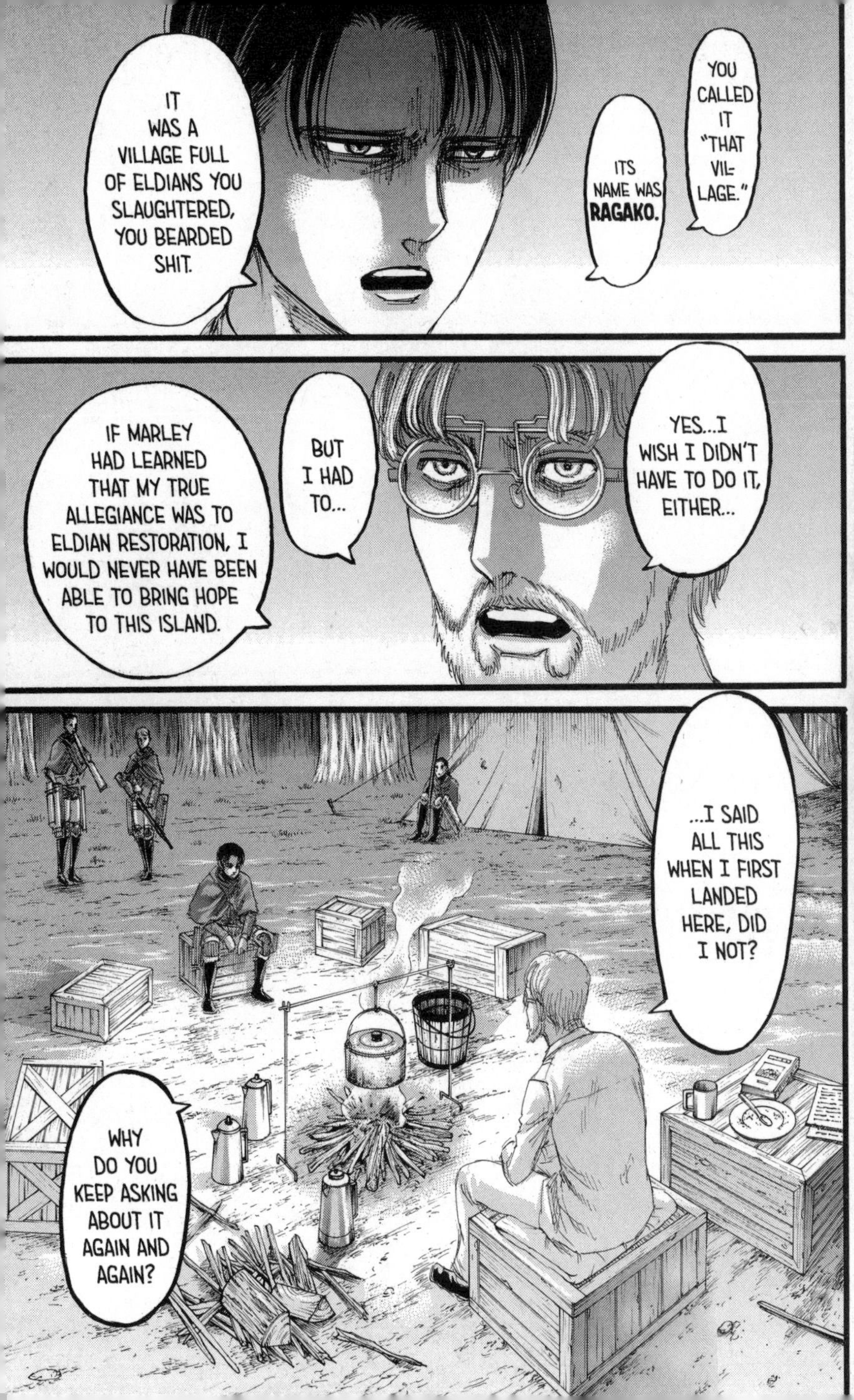
YOU CALLED IT "THAT VIL-LAGE."
ITS NAME WAS **RAGAKO.**
IT WAS A VILLAGE FULL OF ELDIANS YOU SLAUGHTERED, YOU BEARDED SHIT.
YES...I WISH I DIDN'T HAVE TO DO IT, EITHER...
BUT I HAD TO...
IF MARLEY HAD LEARNED THAT MY TRUE ALLEGIANCE WAS TO ELDIAN RESTORATION, I WOULD NEVER HAVE BEEN ABLE TO BRING HOPE TO THIS ISLAND.
...I SAID ALL THIS WHEN I FIRST LANDED HERE, DID I NOT?
WHY DO YOU KEEP ASKING ABOUT IT AGAIN AND AGAIN?

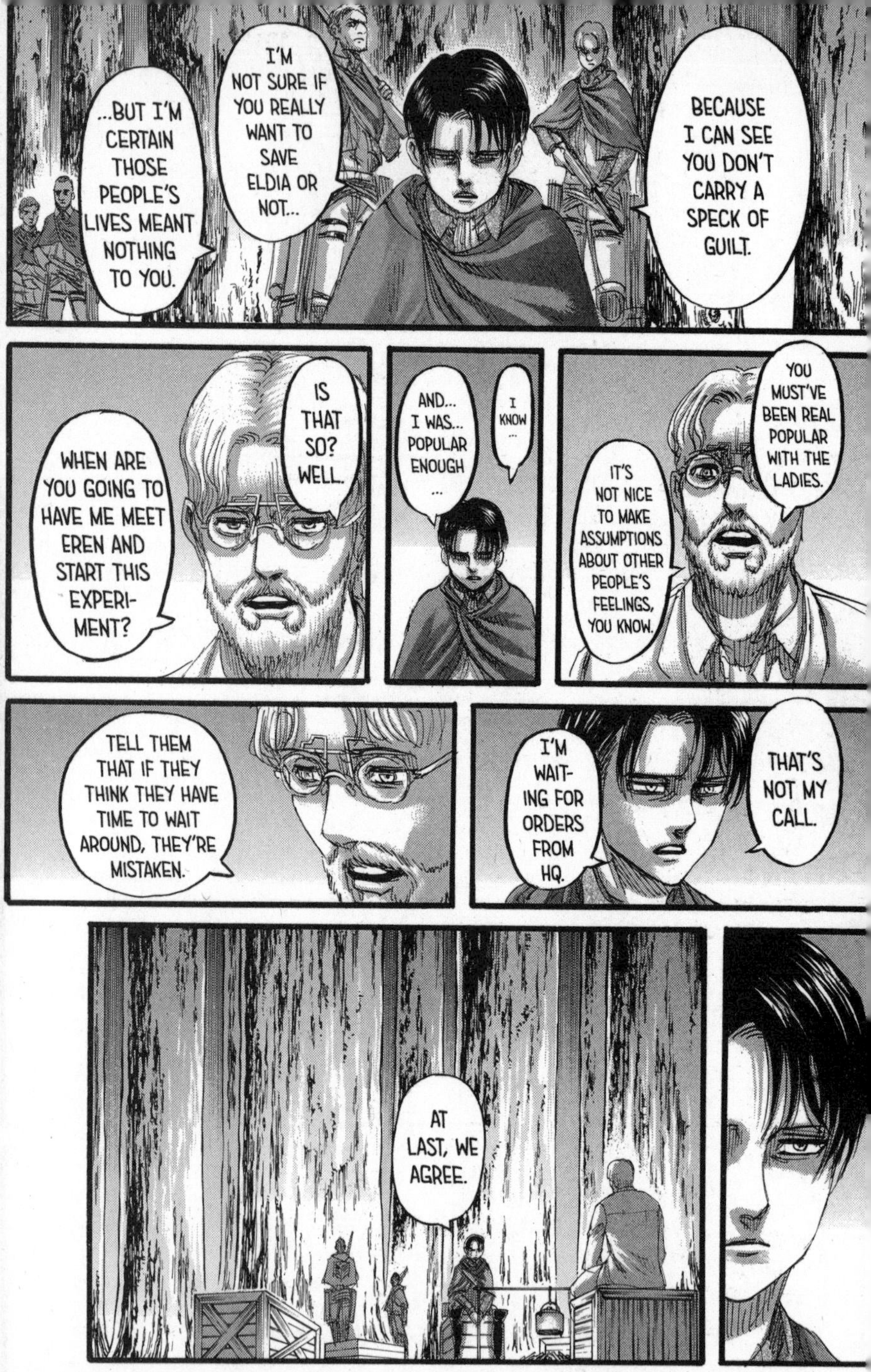
BECAUSE I CAN SEE YOU DON'T CARRY A SPECK OF GUILT.
I'M NOT SURE IF YOU REALLY WANT TO SAVE ELDIA OR NOT...
...BUT I'M CERTAIN THOSE PEOPLE'S LIVES MEANT NOTHING TO YOU.
YOU MUST'VE BEEN REAL POPULAR WITH THE LADIES.
IT'S NOT NICE TO MAKE ASSUMPTIONS ABOUT OTHER PEOPLE'S FEELINGS, YOU KNOW.
I KNOW...
AND... I WAS... POPULAR ENOUGH...
IS THAT SO? WELL.
WHEN ARE YOU GOING TO HAVE ME MEET EREN AND START THIS EXPERIMENT?
THAT'S NOT MY CALL.
I'M WAITING FOR ORDERS FROM HQ.
TELL THEM THAT IF THEY THINK THEY HAVE TIME TO WAIT AROUND, THEY'RE MISTAKEN.
AT LAST, WE AGREE.

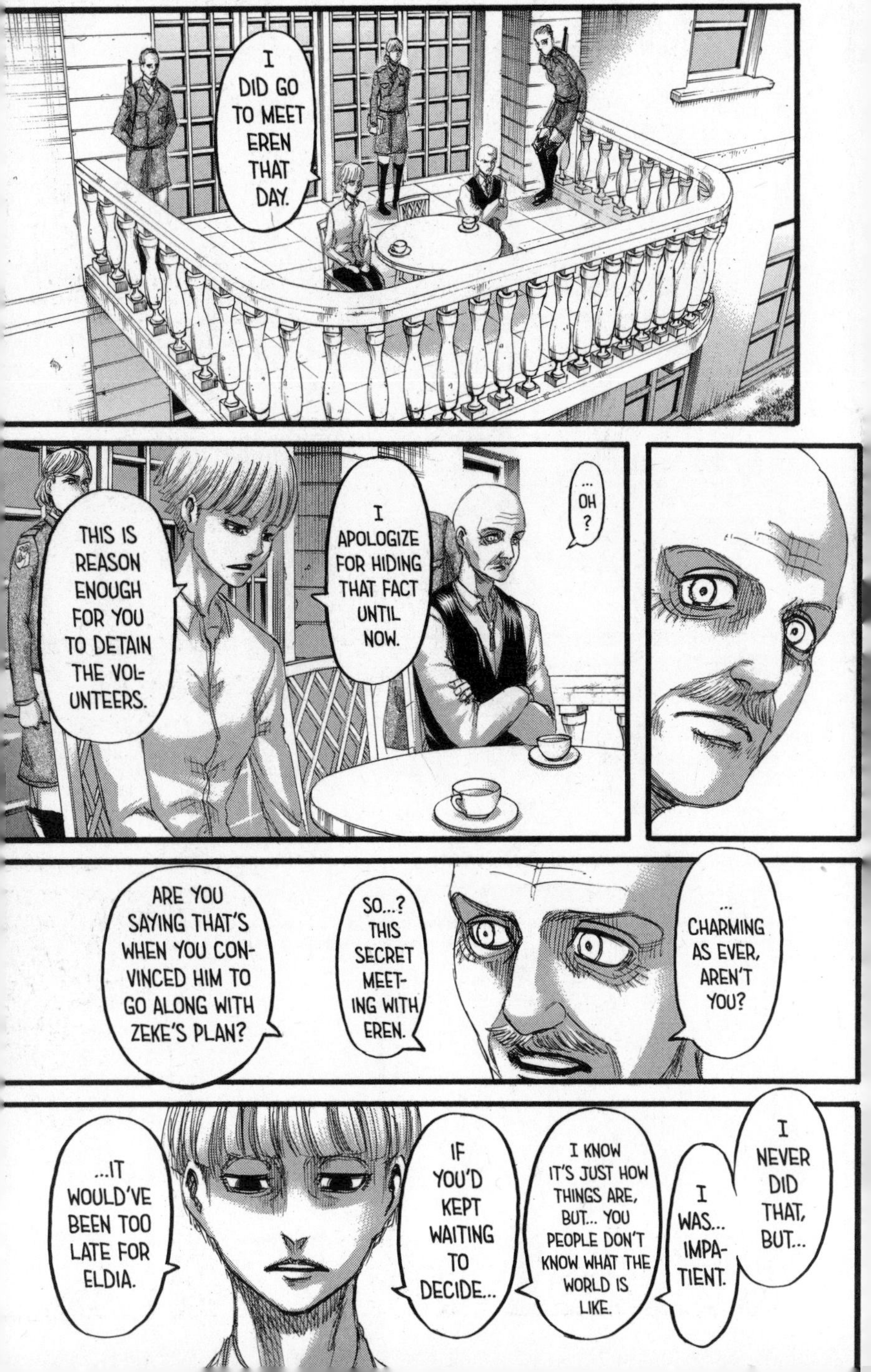
I DID GO TO MEET EREN THAT DAY.
THIS IS REASON ENOUGH FOR YOU TO DETAIN THE VOLUNTEERS.
I APOLOGIZE FOR HIDING THAT FACT UNTIL NOW.
...OH?
ARE YOU SAYING THAT'S WHEN YOU CONVINCED HIM TO GO ALONG WITH ZEKE'S PLAN?
SO...? THIS SECRET MEETING WITH EREN.
...CHARMING AS EVER, AREN'T YOU?
...IT WOULD'VE BEEN TOO LATE FOR ELDIA.
IF YOU'D KEPT WAITING TO DECIDE...
I KNOW IT'S JUST HOW THINGS ARE, BUT... YOU PEOPLE DON'T KNOW WHAT THE WORLD IS LIKE.
I WAS... IMPATIENT.
I NEVER DID THAT, BUT...

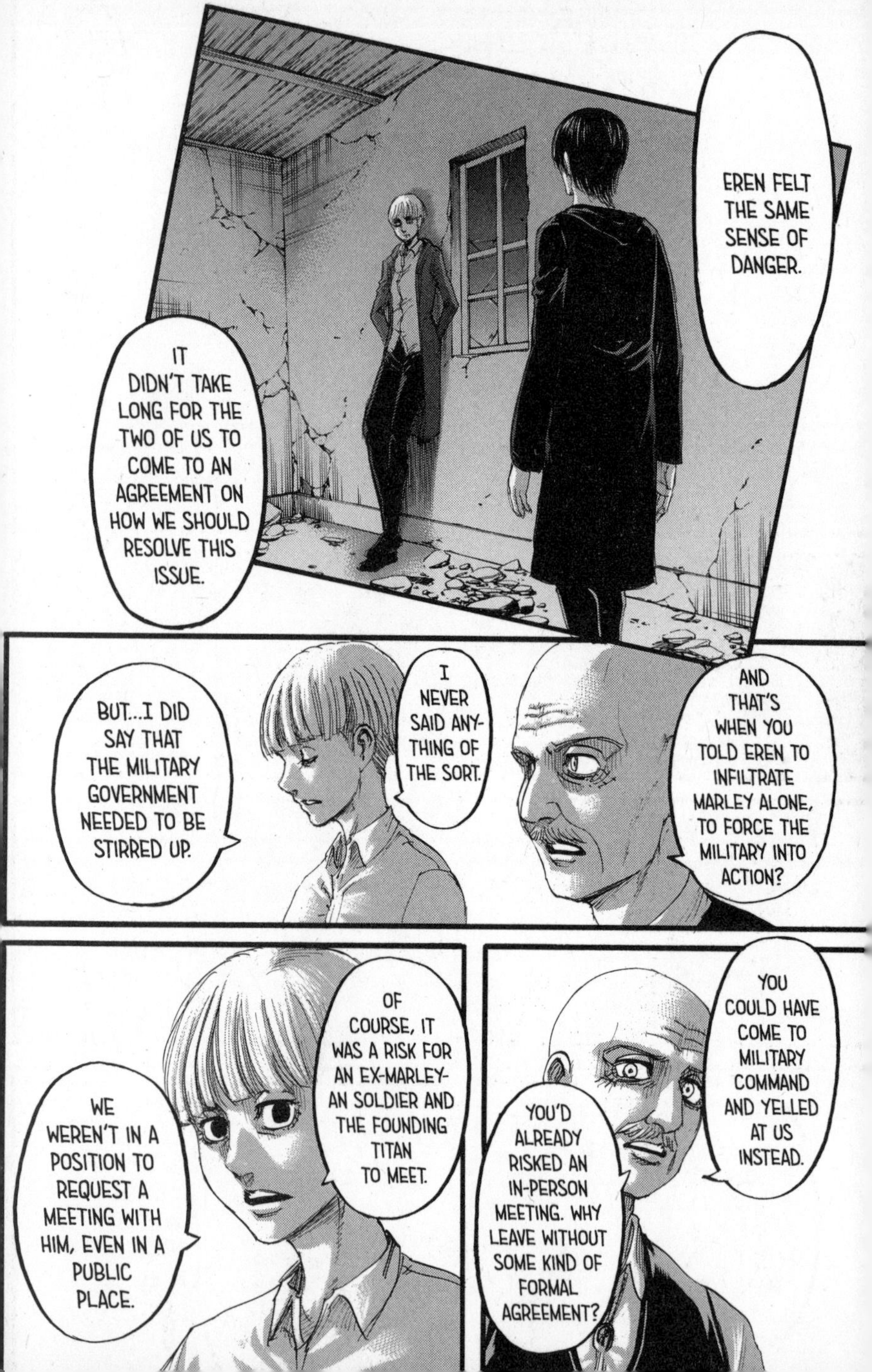
EREN FELT THE SAME SENSE OF DANGER.
IT DIDN'T TAKE LONG FOR THE TWO OF US TO COME TO AN AGREEMENT ON HOW WE SHOULD RESOLVE THIS ISSUE.
AND THAT'S WHEN YOU TOLD EREN TO INFILTRATE MARLEY ALONE, TO FORCE THE MILITARY INTO ACTION?
I NEVER SAID ANY-THING OF THE SORT.
BUT...I DID SAY THAT THE MILITARY GOVERNMENT NEEDED TO BE STIRRED UP.
YOU COULD HAVE COME TO MILITARY COMMAND AND YELLED AT US INSTEAD.
YOU'D ALREADY RISKED AN IN-PERSON MEETING. WHY LEAVE WITHOUT SOME KIND OF FORMAL AGREEMENT?
OF COURSE, IT WAS A RISK FOR AN EX-MARLEY-AN SOLDIER AND THE FOUNDING TITAN TO MEET.
WE WEREN'T IN A POSITION TO REQUEST A MEETING WITH HIM, EVEN IN A PUBLIC PLACE.

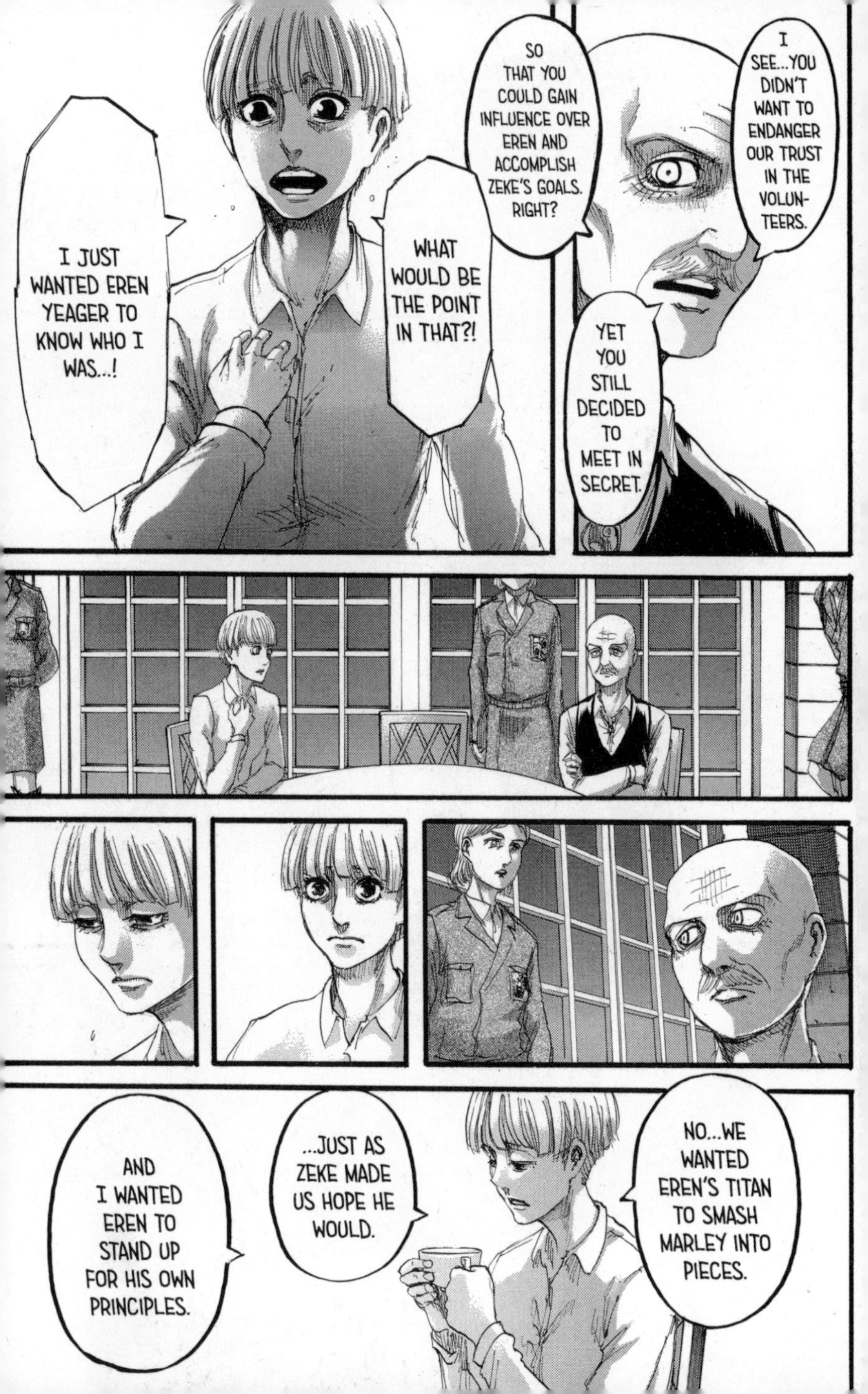

I SEE...YOU DIDN'T WANT TO ENDANGER OUR TRUST IN THE VOLUNTEERS.
YET YOU STILL DECIDED TO MEET IN SECRET.
SO THAT YOU COULD GAIN INFLUENCE OVER EREN AND ACCOMPLISH ZEKE'S GOALS. RIGHT?
WHAT WOULD BE THE POINT IN THAT?!
I JUST WANTED EREN YEAGER TO KNOW WHO I WAS...!
NO...WE WANTED EREN'S TITAN TO SMASH MARLEY INTO PIECES.
...JUST AS ZEKE MADE US HOPE HE WOULD.
AND I WANTED EREN TO STAND UP FOR HIS OWN PRINCIPLES.

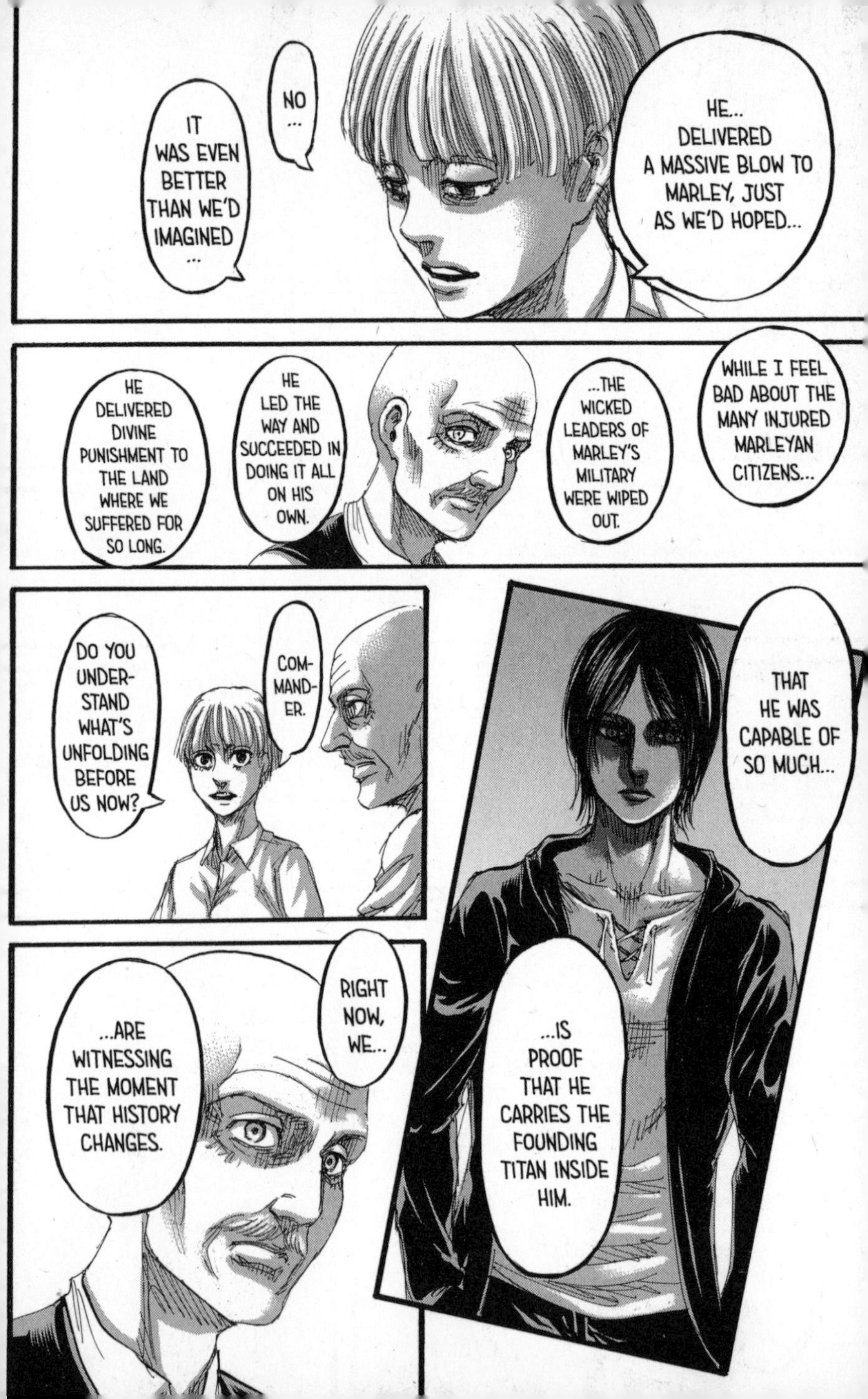
HE... DELIVERED A MASSIVE BLOW TO MARLEY, JUST AS WE'D HOPED...
NO ...
IT WAS EVEN BETTER THAN WE'D IMAGINED ...
WHILE I FEEL BAD ABOUT THE MANY INJURED MARLEYAN CITIZENS...
...THE WICKED LEADERS OF MARLEY'S MILITARY WERE WIPED OUT.
HE LED THE WAY AND SUCCEEDED IN DOING IT ALL ON HIS OWN.
HE DELIVERED DIVINE PUNISHMENT TO THE LAND WHERE WE SUFFERED FOR SO LONG.
THAT HE WAS CAPABLE OF SO MUCH...
...IS PROOF THAT HE CARRIES THE FOUNDING TITAN INSIDE HIM.
COM-MAND-ER.
DO YOU UNDER-STAND WHAT'S UNFOLDING BEFORE US NOW?
RIGHT NOW, WE...
...ARE WITNESSING THE MOMENT THAT HISTORY CHANGES.

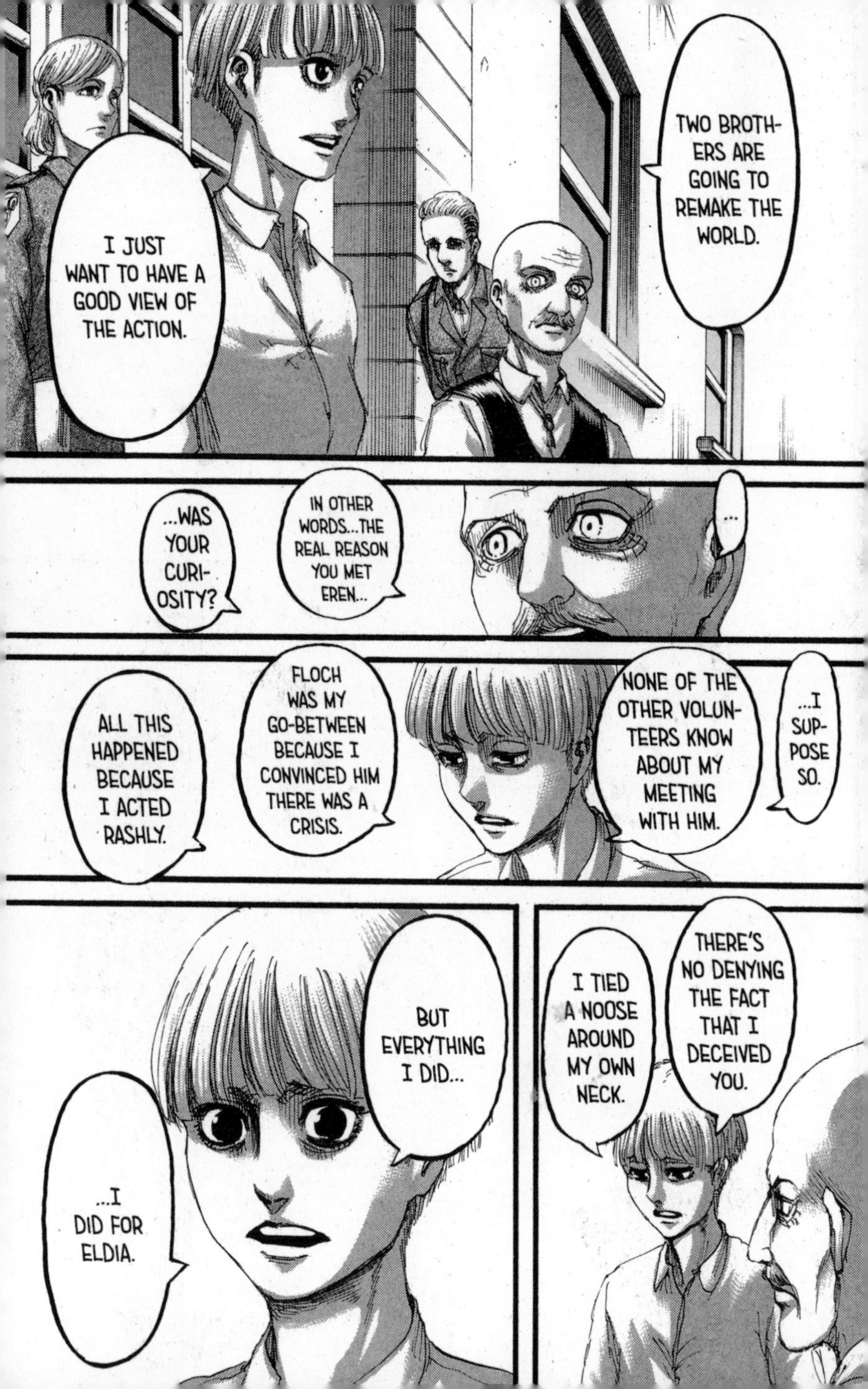
TWO BROTHERS ARE GOING TO REMAKE THE WORLD.
I JUST WANT TO HAVE A GOOD VIEW OF THE ACTION.
...
IN OTHER WORDS...THE REAL REASON YOU MET EREN...
...WAS YOUR CURIOSITY?
...I SUPPOSE SO.
NONE OF THE OTHER VOLUNTEERS KNOW ABOUT MY MEETING WITH HIM.
FLOCH WAS MY GO-BETWEEN BECAUSE I CONVINCED HIM THERE WAS A CRISIS.
ALL THIS HAPPENED BECAUSE I ACTED RASHLY.
THERE'S NO DENYING THE FACT THAT I DECEIVED YOU.
I TIED A NOOSE AROUND MY OWN NECK.
BUT EVERYTHING I DID...
...I DID FOR ELDIA.

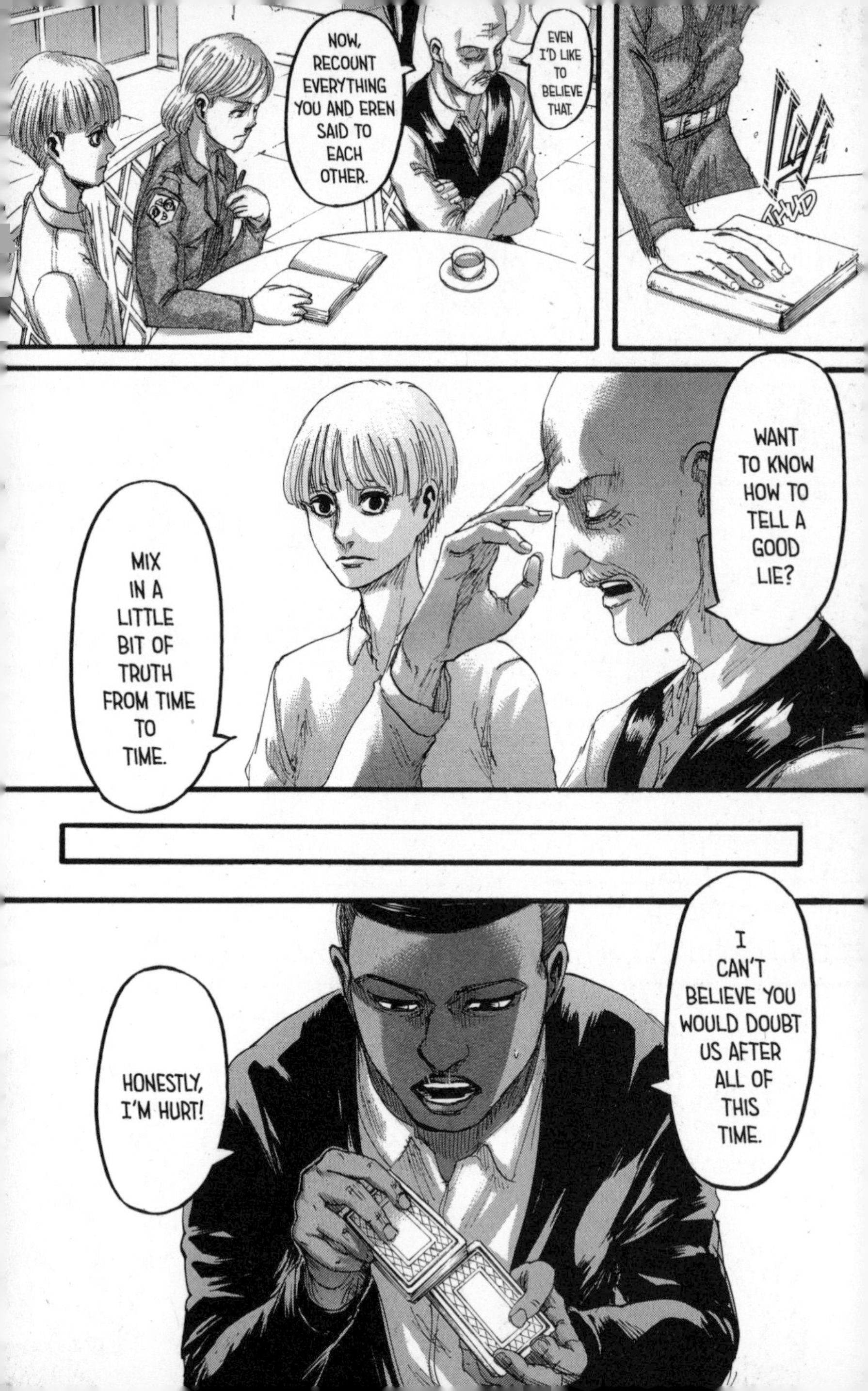
NOW, RECOUNT EVERYTHING YOU AND EREN SAID TO EACH OTHER.
EVEN I'D LIKE TO BELIEVE THAT.
THUD
WANT TO KNOW HOW TO TELL A GOOD LIE?
MIX IN A LITTLE BIT OF TRUTH FROM TIME TO TIME.
HONESTLY, I'M HURT!
I CAN'T BELIEVE YOU WOULD DOUBT US AFTER ALL OF THIS TIME.

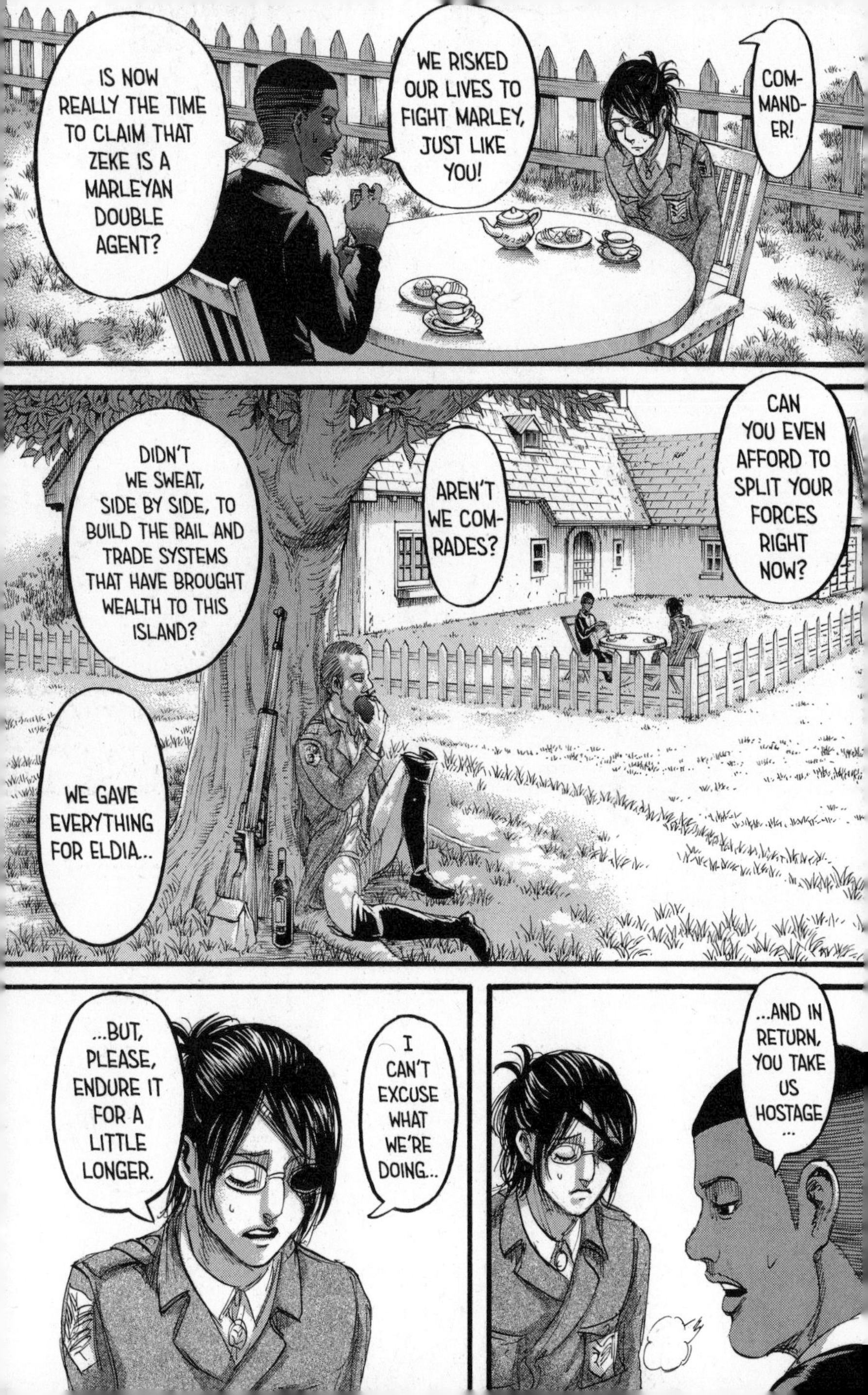
COMMANDER!
WE RISKED OUR LIVES TO FIGHT MARLEY, JUST LIKE YOU!
IS NOW REALLY THE TIME TO CLAIM THAT ZEKE IS A MARLEYAN DOUBLE AGENT?
CAN YOU EVEN AFFORD TO SPLIT YOUR FORCES RIGHT NOW?
AREN'T WE COMRADES?
DIDN'T WE SWEAT, SIDE BY SIDE, TO BUILD THE RAIL AND TRADE SYSTEMS THAT HAVE BROUGHT WEALTH TO THIS ISLAND?
WE GAVE EVERYTHING FOR ELDIA...
...AND IN RETURN, YOU TAKE US HOSTAGE...
I CAN'T EXCUSE WHAT WE'RE DOING...
...BUT, PLEASE, ENDURE IT FOR A LITTLE LONGER.

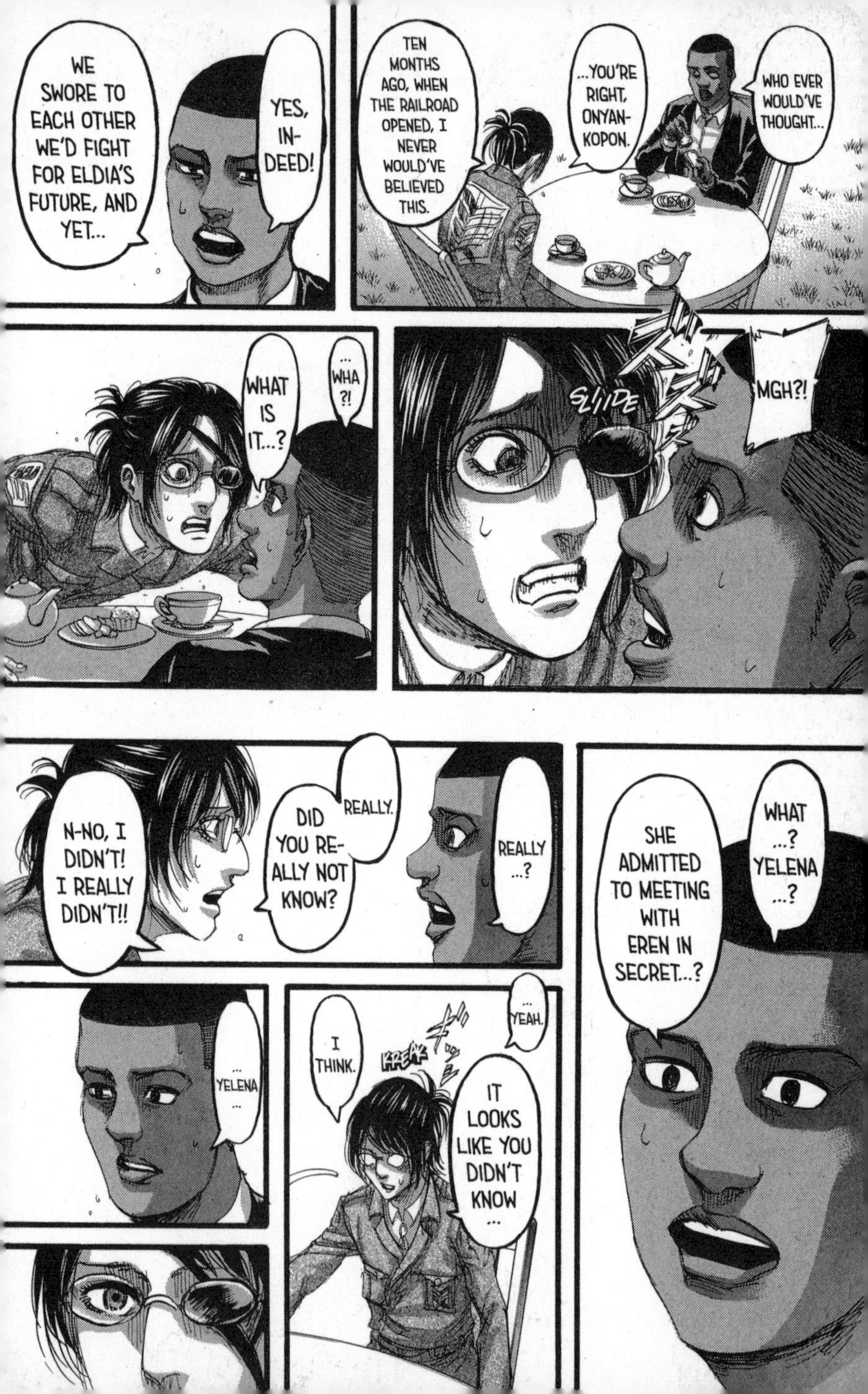
WE SWORE TO EACH OTHER WE'D FIGHT FOR ELDIA'S FUTURE, AND YET...
YES, IN-DEED!
TEN MONTHS AGO, WHEN THE RAILROAD OPENED, I NEVER WOULD'VE BELIEVED THIS.
...YOU'RE RIGHT, ONYAN-KOPON.
WHO EVER WOULD'VE THOUGHT...
WHAT IS IT...?
...WHA ?!
SLIIDE
MGH?!
N-NO, I DIDN'T! I REALLY DIDN'T!!
DID YOU RE-ALLY NOT KNOW?
REALLY.
REALLY ...?
SHE ADMITTED TO MEETING WITH EREN IN SECRET...?
WHAT ...? YELENA ...?
... YELENA ...
I THINK.
KREAK
... YEAH.
IT LOOKS LIKE YOU DIDN'T KNOW ...

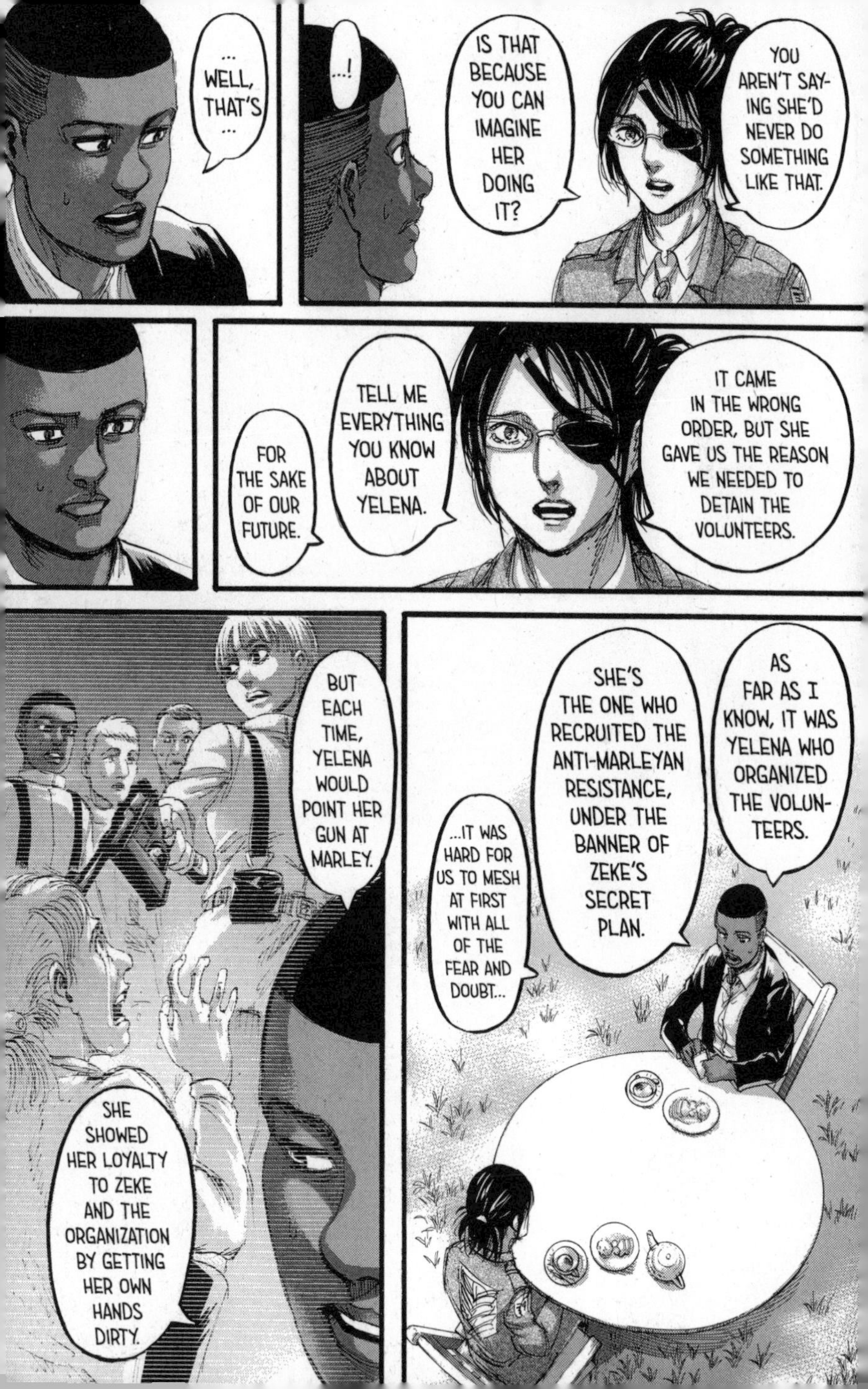

YOU AREN'T SAYING SHE'D NEVER DO SOMETHING LIKE THAT.
IS THAT BECAUSE YOU CAN IMAGINE HER DOING IT?
...!
... WELL, THAT'S ...
IT CAME IN THE WRONG ORDER, BUT SHE GAVE US THE REASON WE NEEDED TO DETAIN THE VOLUNTEERS.
TELL ME EVERYTHING YOU KNOW ABOUT YELENA.
FOR THE SAKE OF OUR FUTURE.
AS FAR AS I KNOW, IT WAS YELENA WHO ORGANIZED THE VOLUNTEERS.
SHE'S THE ONE WHO RECRUITED THE ANTI-MARLEYAN RESISTANCE, UNDER THE BANNER OF ZEKE'S SECRET PLAN.
...IT WAS HARD FOR US TO MESH AT FIRST WITH ALL OF THE FEAR AND DOUBT...
BUT EACH TIME, YELENA WOULD POINT HER GUN AT MARLEY.
SHE SHOWED HER LOYALTY TO ZEKE AND THE ORGANIZATION BY GETTING HER OWN HANDS DIRTY.

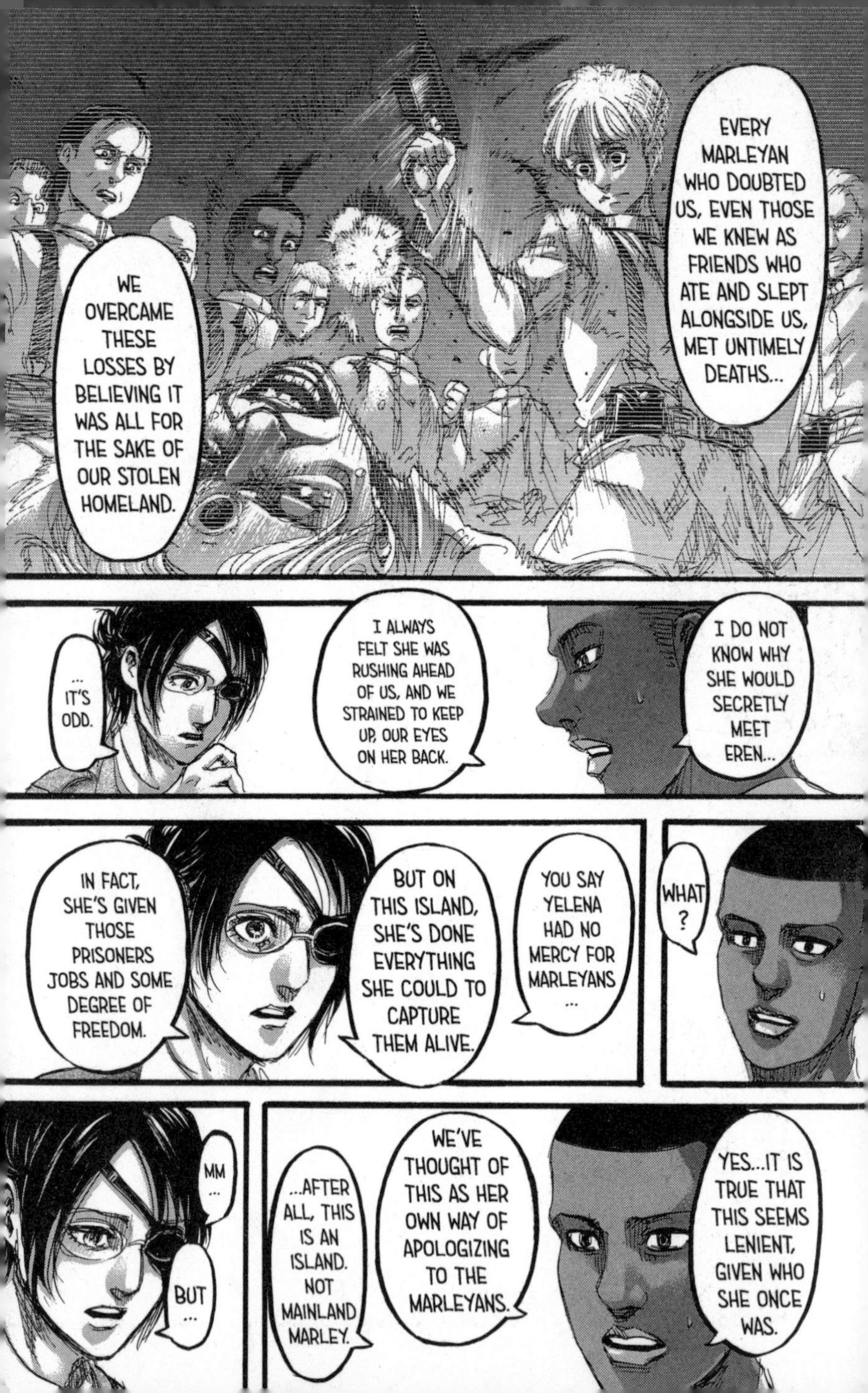
WE OVERCAME THESE LOSSES BY BELIEVING IT WAS ALL FOR THE SAKE OF OUR STOLEN HOMELAND.
EVERY MARLEYAN WHO DOUBTED US, EVEN THOSE WE KNEW AS FRIENDS WHO ATE AND SLEPT ALONGSIDE US, MET UNTIMELY DEATHS...
... IT'S ODD.
I ALWAYS FELT SHE WAS RUSHING AHEAD OF US, AND WE STRAINED TO KEEP UP, OUR EYES ON HER BACK.
I DO NOT KNOW WHY SHE WOULD SECRETLY MEET EREN...
IN FACT, SHE'S GIVEN THOSE PRISONERS JOBS AND SOME DEGREE OF FREEDOM.
BUT ON THIS ISLAND, SHE'S DONE EVERYTHING SHE COULD TO CAPTURE THEM ALIVE.
YOU SAY YELENA HAD NO MERCY FOR MARLEYANS ...
WHAT ?
MM ...
BUT ...
...AFTER ALL, THIS IS AN ISLAND. NOT MAINLAND MARLEY.
WE'VE THOUGHT OF THIS AS HER OWN WAY OF APOLOGIZING TO THE MARLEYANS.
YES...IT IS TRUE THAT THIS SEEMS LENIENT, GIVEN WHO SHE ONCE WAS.

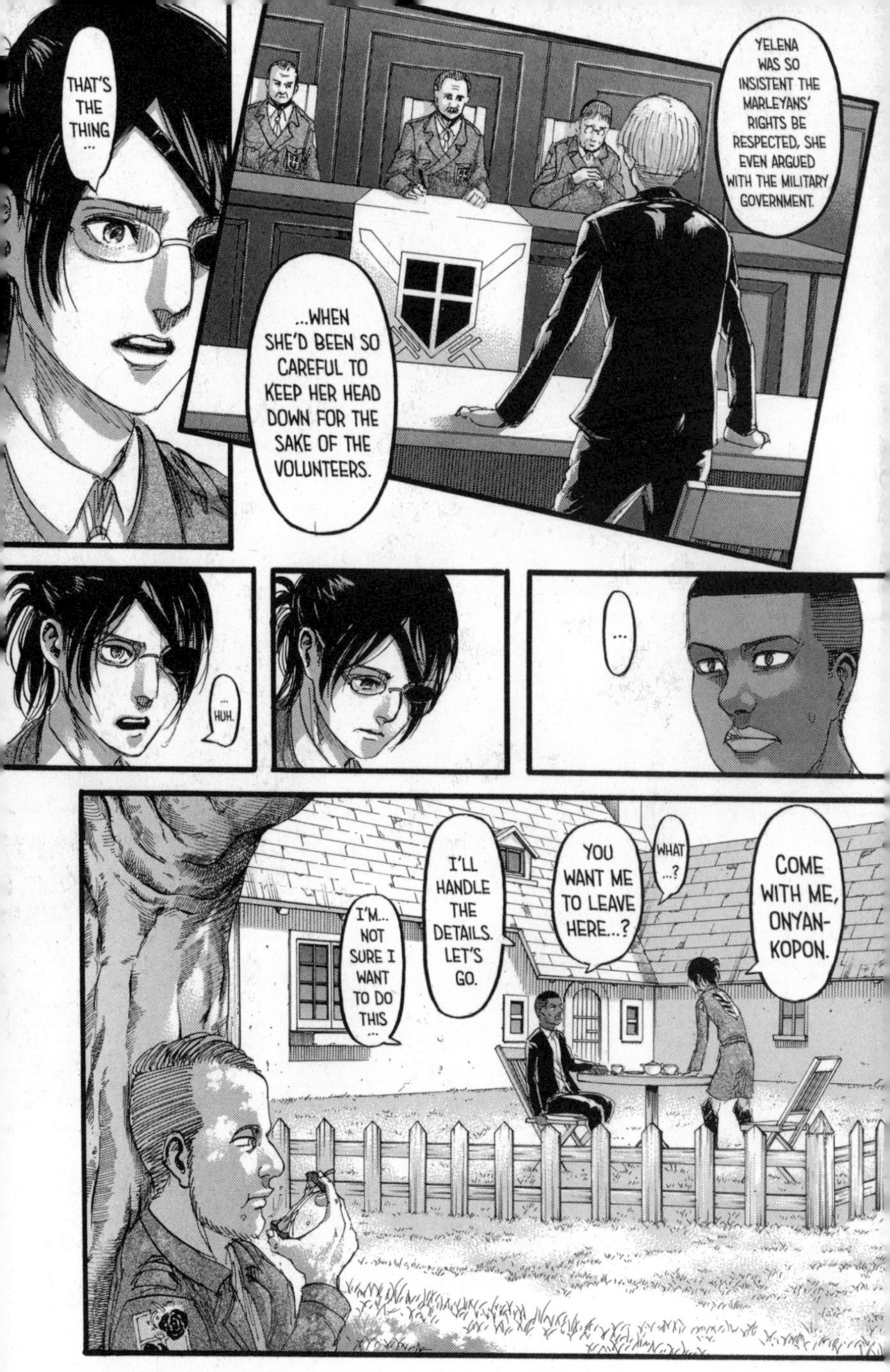
THAT'S THE THING ...
YELENA WAS SO INSISTENT THE MARLEYANS' RIGHTS BE RESPECTED, SHE EVEN ARGUED WITH THE MILITARY GOVERNMENT.
...WHEN SHE'D BEEN SO CAREFUL TO KEEP HER HEAD DOWN FOR THE SAKE OF THE VOLUNTEERS.
... HUH.
...
COME WITH ME, ONYAN-KOPON.
WHAT ...?
YOU WANT ME TO LEAVE HERE...?
I'LL HANDLE THE DETAILS. LET'S GO.
I'M... NOT SURE I WANT TO DO THIS ...

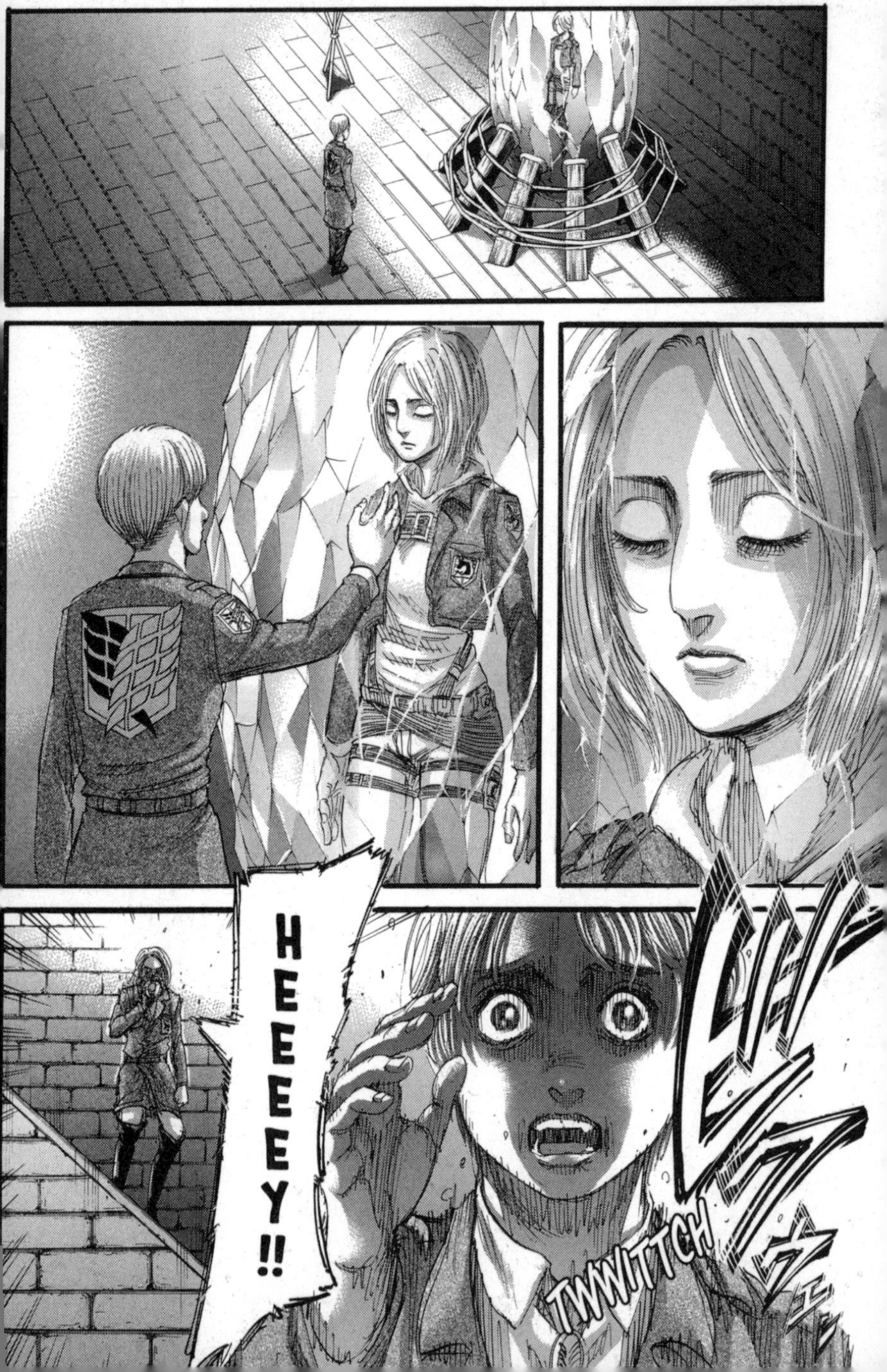

HEEEEEY!!
TWWITTCH

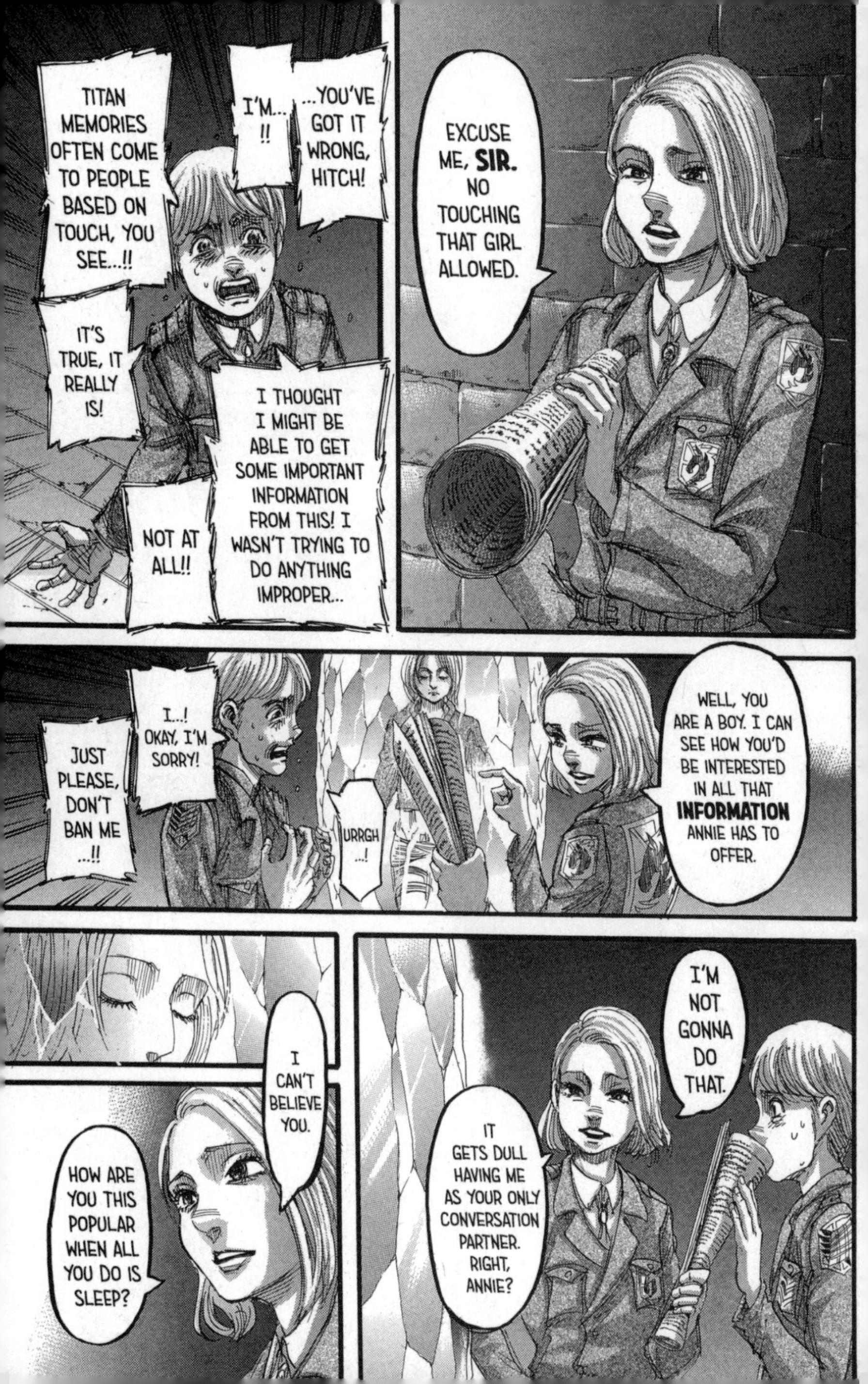
TITAN MEMORIES OFTEN COME TO PEOPLE BASED ON TOUCH, YOU SEE...!!
I'M... !!
...YOU'VE GOT IT WRONG, HITCH!
IT'S TRUE, IT REALLY IS!
I THOUGHT I MIGHT BE ABLE TO GET SOME IMPORTANT INFORMATION FROM THIS! I WASN'T TRYING TO DO ANYTHING IMPROPER...
NOT AT ALL!!
EXCUSE ME, SIR. NO TOUCHING THAT GIRL ALLOWED.
I...! OKAY, I'M SORRY!
JUST PLEASE, DON'T BAN ME ...!!
URRGH ...!
WELL, YOU ARE A BOY. I CAN SEE HOW YOU'D BE INTERESTED IN ALL THAT INFORMATION ANNIE HAS TO OFFER.
I CAN'T BELIEVE YOU.
HOW ARE YOU THIS POPULAR WHEN ALL YOU DO IS SLEEP?
I'M NOT GONNA DO THAT.
IT GETS DULL HAVING ME AS YOUR ONLY CONVERSATION PARTNER. RIGHT, ANNIE?

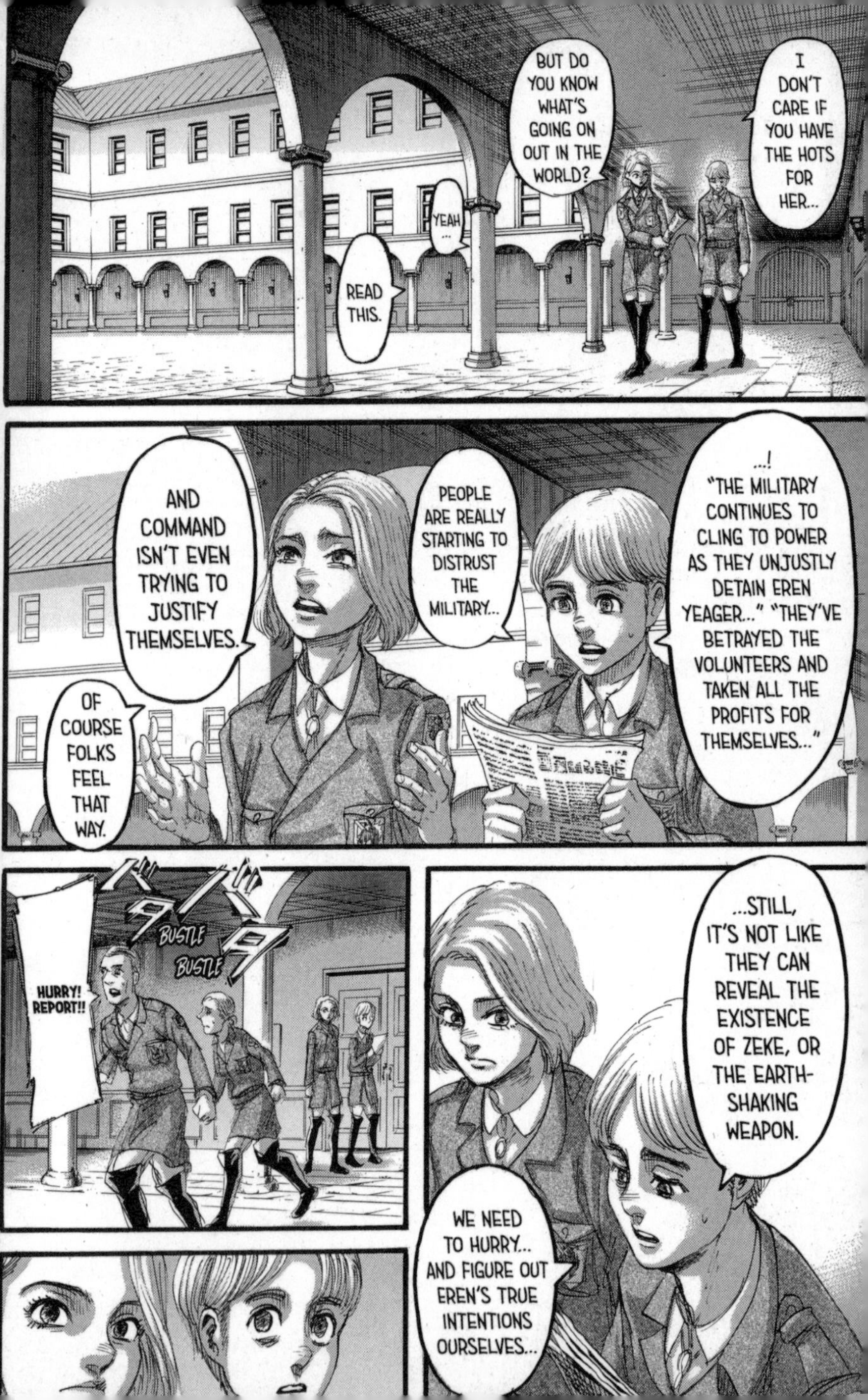

I DON'T CARE IF YOU HAVE THE HOTS FOR HER...
BUT DO YOU KNOW WHAT'S GOING ON OUT IN THE WORLD?
YEAH ...
READ THIS.
...! "THE MILITARY CONTINUES TO CLING TO POWER AS THEY UNJUSTLY DETAIN EREN YEAGER..." "THEY'VE BETRAYED THE VOLUNTEERS AND TAKEN ALL THE PROFITS FOR THEMSELVES..."
PEOPLE ARE REALLY STARTING TO DISTRUST THE MILITARY...
AND COMMAND ISN'T EVEN TRYING TO JUSTIFY THEMSELVES.
OF COURSE FOLKS FEEL THAT WAY.
...STILL, IT'S NOT LIKE THEY CAN REVEAL THE EXISTENCE OF ZEKE, OR THE EARTH-SHAKING WEAPON.
WE NEED TO HURRY... AND FIGURE OUT EREN'S TRUE INTENTIONS OURSELVES...
BUSTLE
BUSTLE
HURRY! REPORT!!

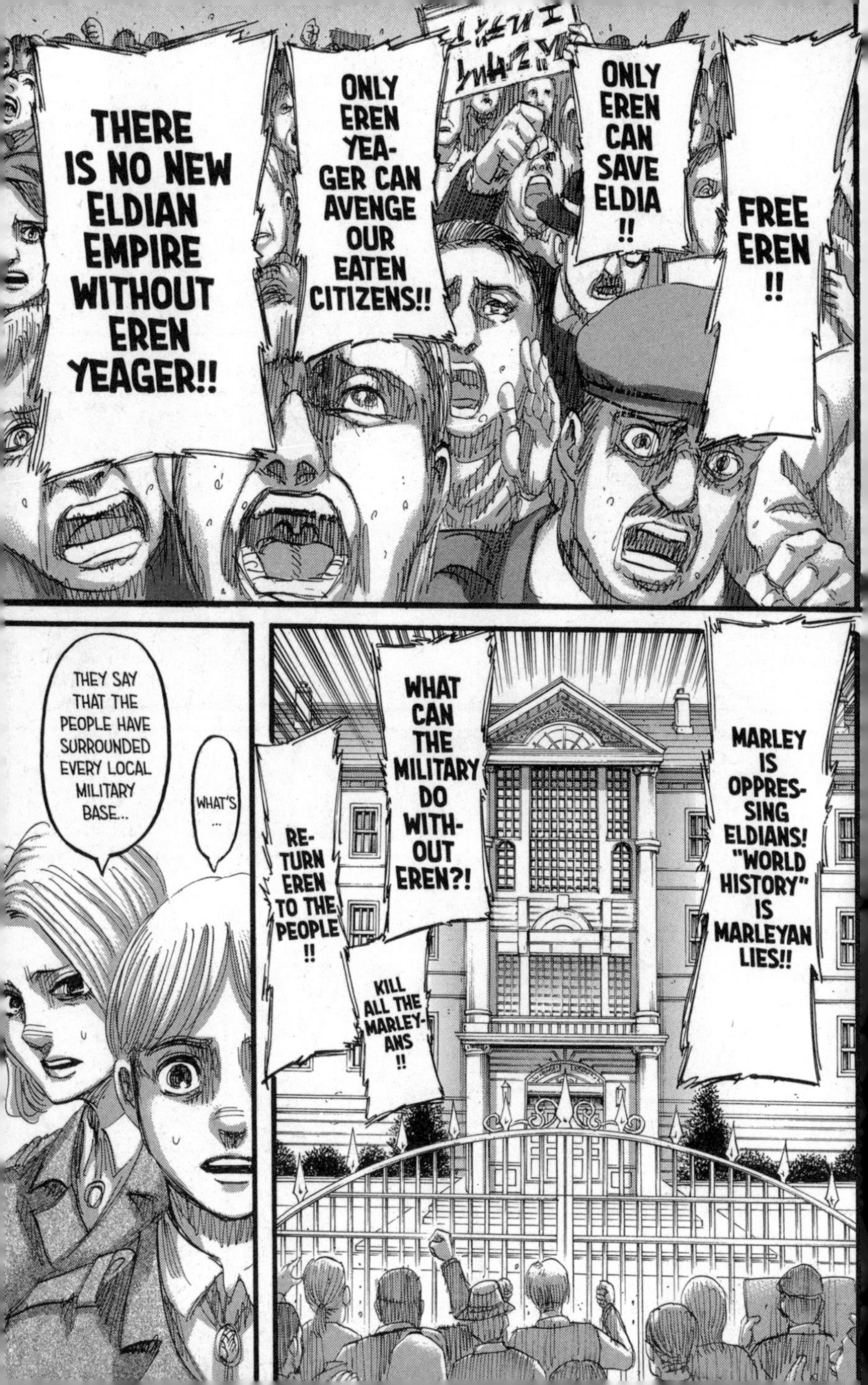
FREE EREN!!
ONLY EREN CAN SAVE ELDIA!!
ONLY EREN YEAGER CAN AVENGE OUR EATEN CITIZENS!!
THERE IS NO NEW ELDIAN EMPIRE WITHOUT EREN YEAGER!!
MARLEY IS OPPRESSING ELDIANS! "WORLD HISTORY" IS MARLEYAN LIES!!
WHAT CAN THE MILITARY DO WITHOUT EREN?!
RETURN EREN TO THE PEOPLE!!
KILL ALL THE MARLEYANS!!
WHAT'S...
THEY SAY THAT THE PEOPLE HAVE SURROUNDED EVERY LOCAL MILITARY BASE...

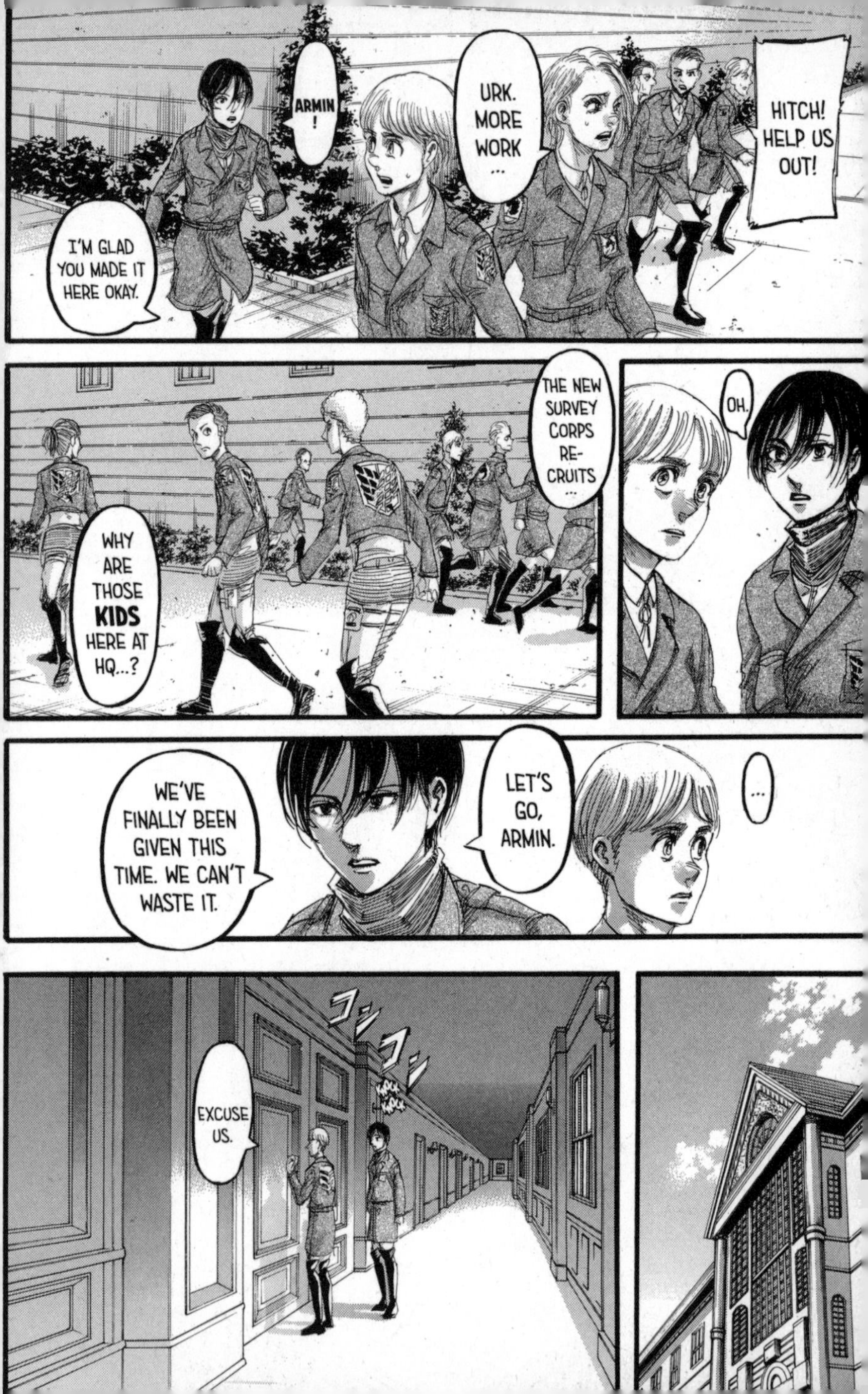
ARMIN!
I'M GLAD YOU MADE IT HERE OKAY.
URK. MORE WORK...
HITCH! HELP US OUT!
WHY ARE THOSE KIDS HERE AT HQ...?
THE NEW SURVEY CORPS RE-CRUITS...
OH.
WE'VE FINALLY BEEN GIVEN THIS TIME. WE CAN'T WASTE IT.
LET'S GO, ARMIN.
...
EXCUSE US.

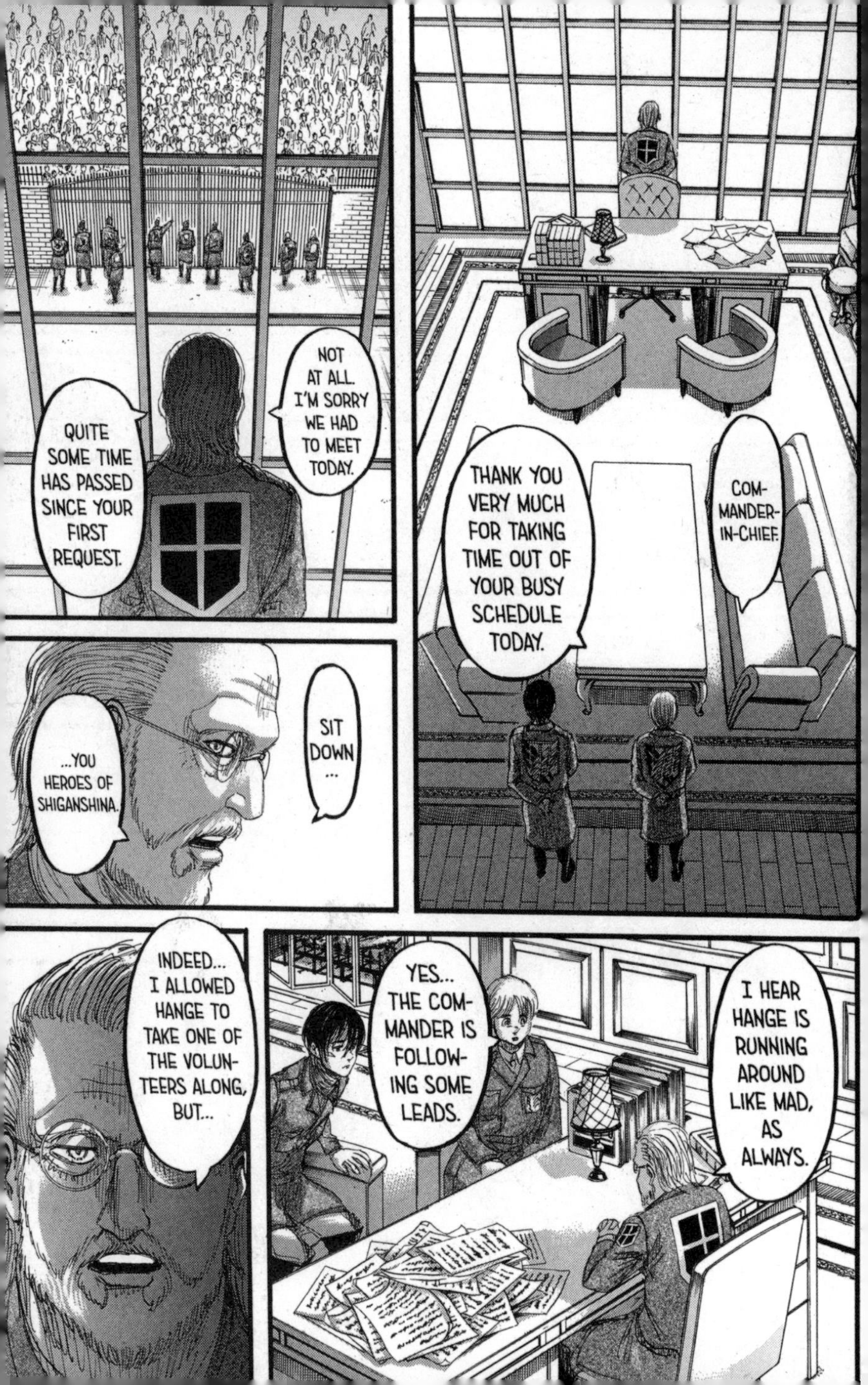
COM-MANDER-IN-CHIEF.
THANK YOU VERY MUCH FOR TAKING TIME OUT OF YOUR BUSY SCHEDULE TODAY.
NOT AT ALL. I'M SORRY WE HAD TO MEET TODAY.
QUITE SOME TIME HAS PASSED SINCE YOUR FIRST REQUEST.
SIT DOWN...
...YOU HEROES OF SHIGANSHINA.
I HEAR HANGE IS RUNNING AROUND LIKE MAD, AS ALWAYS.
YES... THE COM-MANDER IS FOLLOW-ING SOME LEADS.
INDEED... I ALLOWED HANGE TO TAKE ONE OF THE VOLUN-TEERS ALONG, BUT...

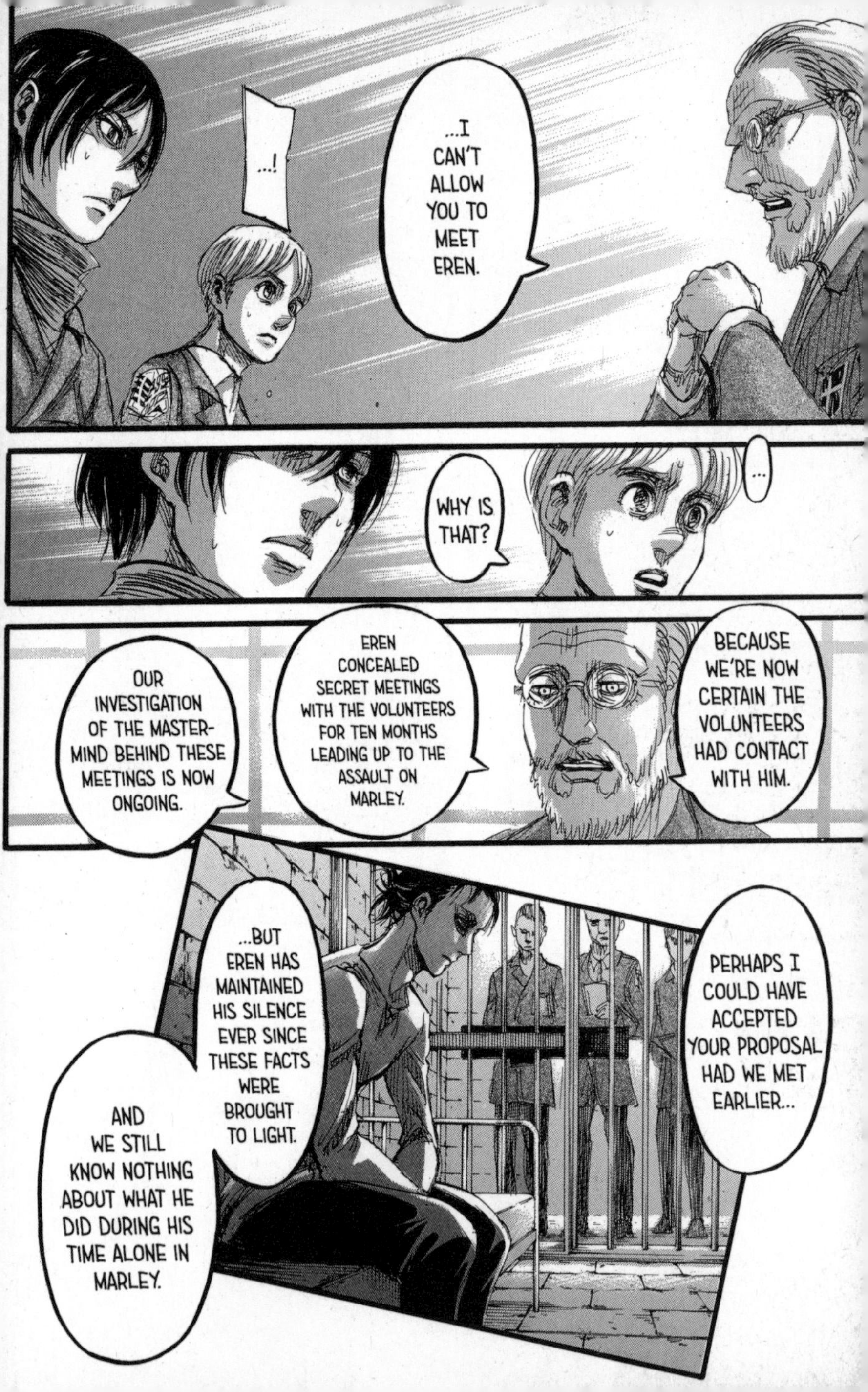
...I CAN'T ALLOW YOU TO MEET EREN.
...!
...
WHY IS THAT?
BECAUSE WE'RE NOW CERTAIN THE VOLUNTEERS HAD CONTACT WITH HIM.
EREN CONCEALED SECRET MEETINGS WITH THE VOLUNTEERS FOR TEN MONTHS LEADING UP TO THE ASSAULT ON MARLEY.
OUR INVESTIGATION OF THE MASTER-MIND BEHIND THESE MEETINGS IS NOW ONGOING.
PERHAPS I COULD HAVE ACCEPTED YOUR PROPOSAL HAD WE MET EARLIER...
...BUT EREN HAS MAINTAINED HIS SILENCE EVER SINCE THESE FACTS WERE BROUGHT TO LIGHT.
AND WE STILL KNOW NOTHING ABOUT WHAT HE DID DURING HIS TIME ALONE IN MARLEY.

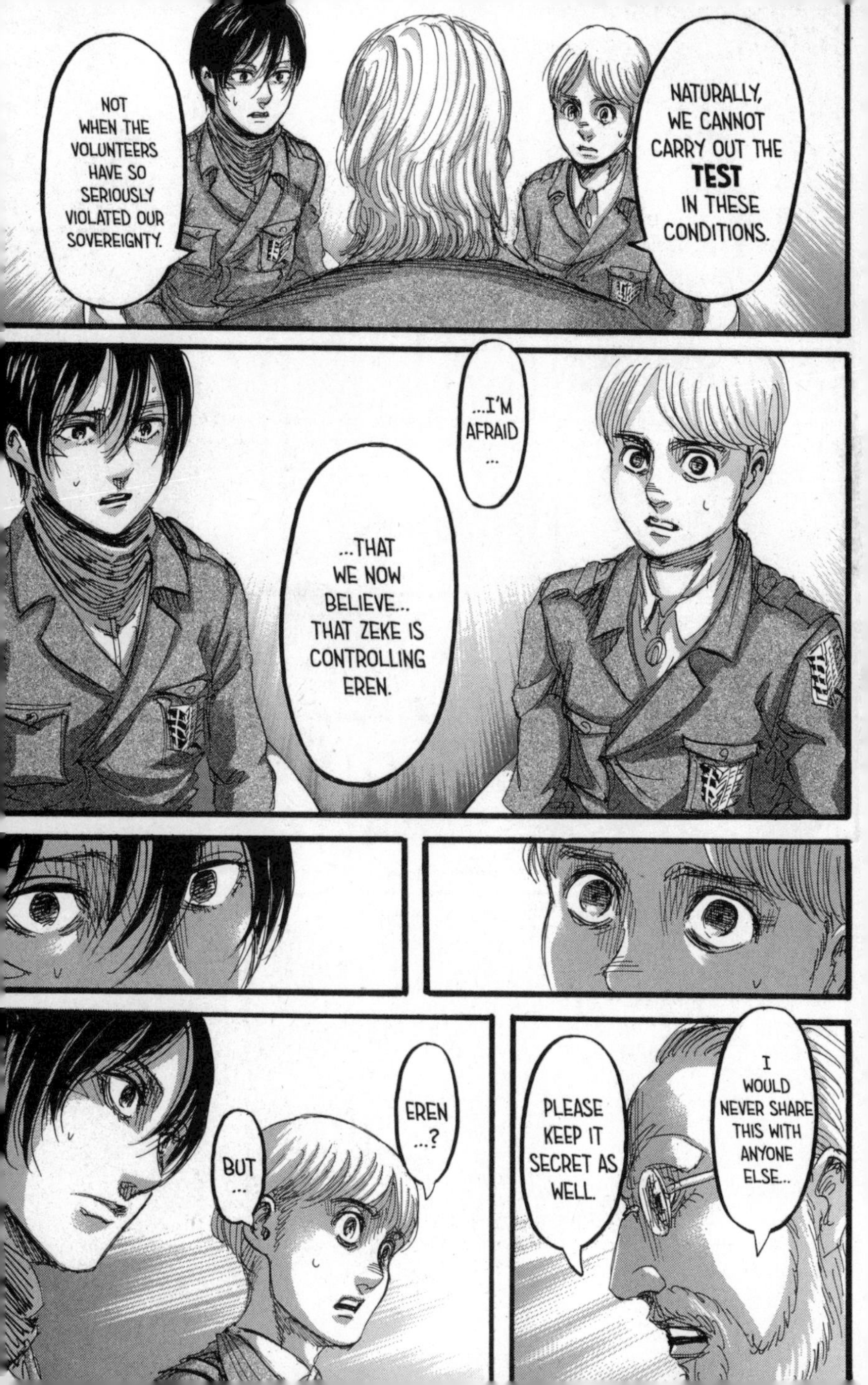
NATURALLY, WE CANNOT CARRY OUT THE **TEST** IN THESE CONDITIONS.
NOT WHEN THE VOLUNTEERS HAVE SO SERIOUSLY VIOLATED OUR SOVEREIGNTY.
...I'M AFRAID ...
...THAT WE NOW BELIEVE... THAT ZEKE IS CONTROLLING EREN.
I WOULD NEVER SHARE THIS WITH ANYONE ELSE...
PLEASE KEEP IT SECRET AS WELL.
EREN ...?
BUT ...

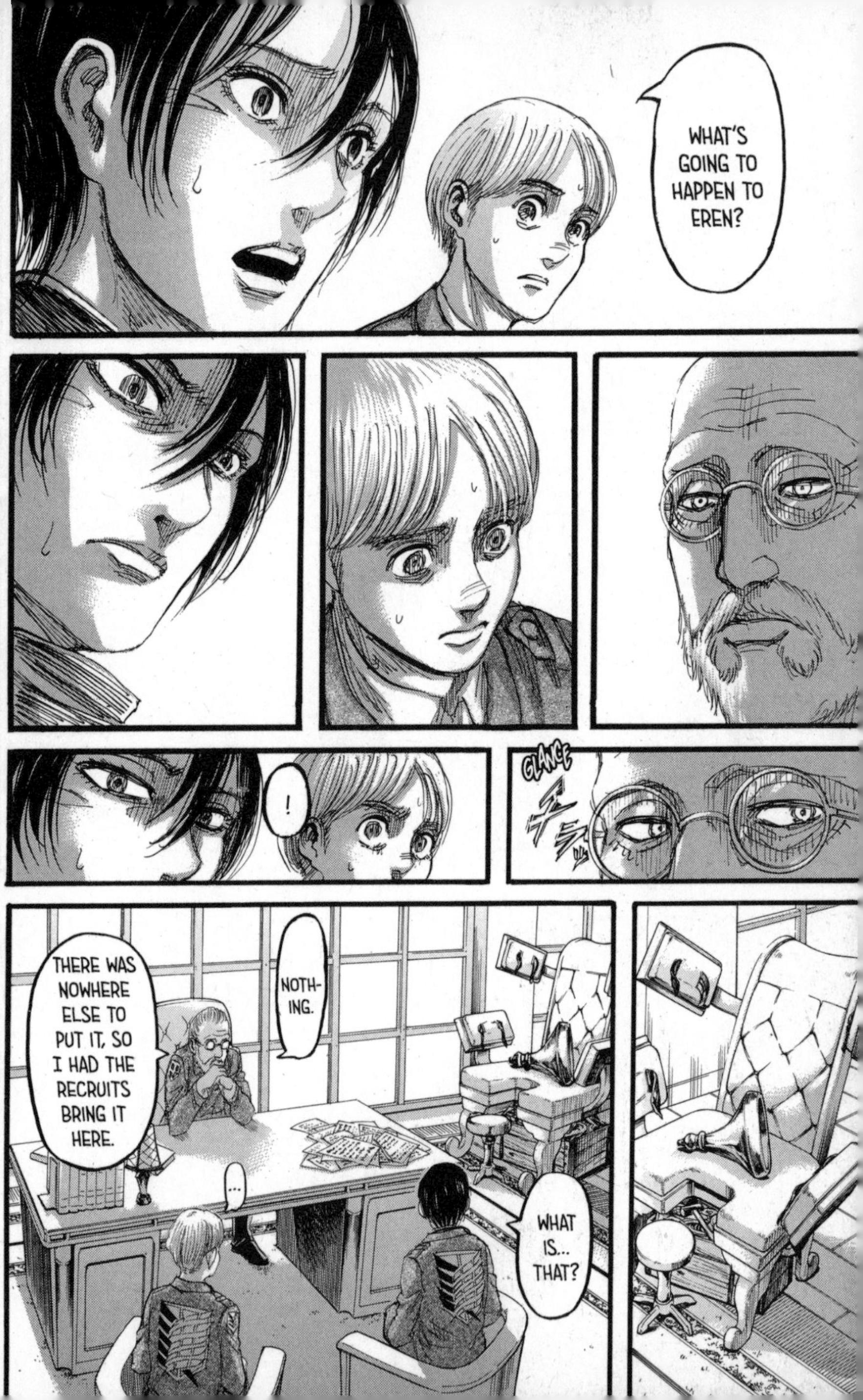

WHAT'S GOING TO HAPPEN TO EREN?
!
GLANCE
THERE WAS NOWHERE ELSE TO PUT IT, SO I HAD THE RECRUITS BRING IT HERE.
NOTH-ING.
...
WHAT IS... THAT?

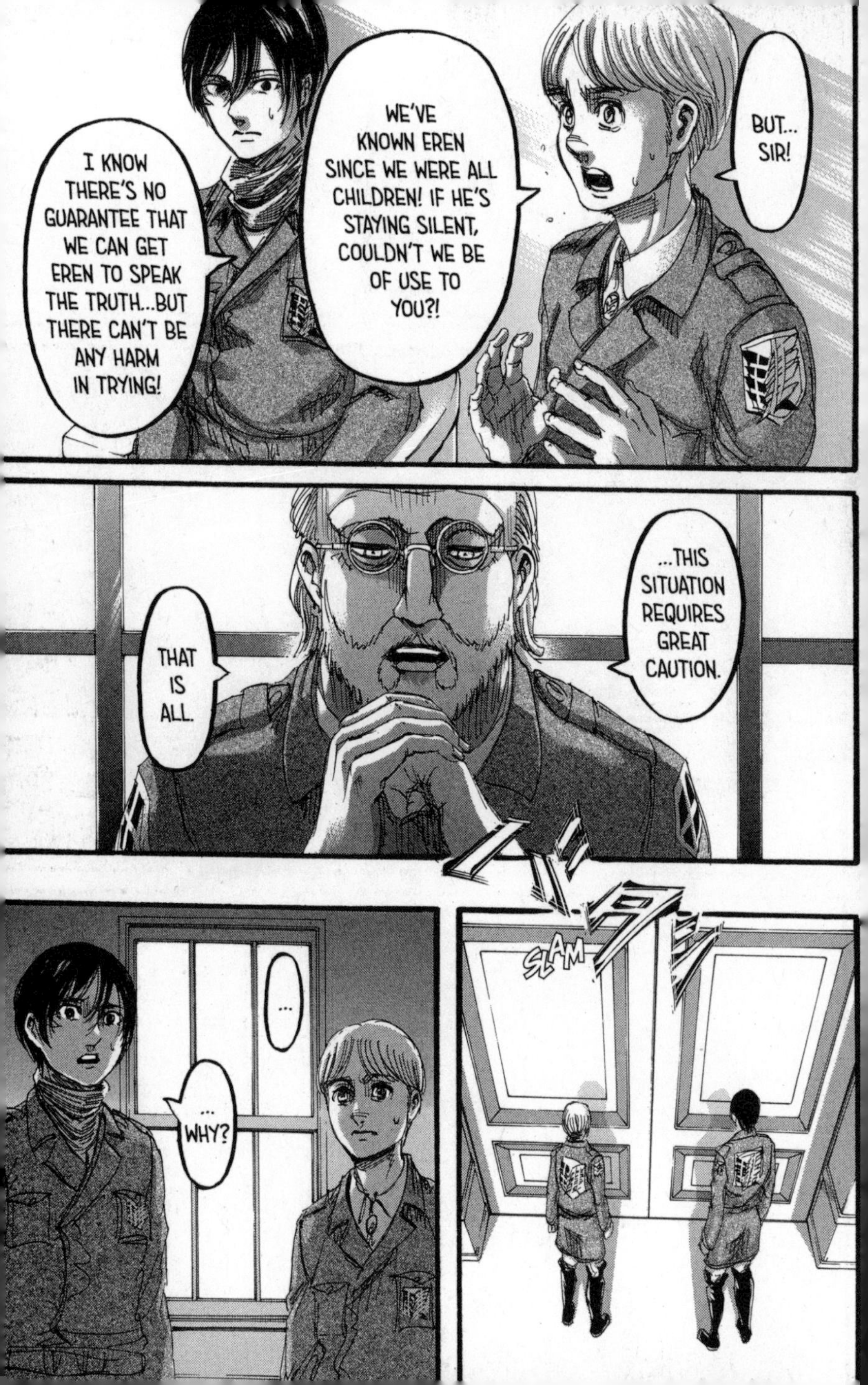
BUT... SIR!
WE'VE KNOWN EREN SINCE WE WERE ALL CHILDREN! IF HE'S STAYING SILENT, COULDN'T WE BE OF USE TO YOU?!
I KNOW THERE'S NO GUARANTEE THAT WE CAN GET EREN TO SPEAK THE TRUTH...BUT THERE CAN'T BE ANY HARM IN TRYING!
...THIS SITUATION REQUIRES GREAT CAUTION.
THAT IS ALL.
SLAM
...
... WHY?

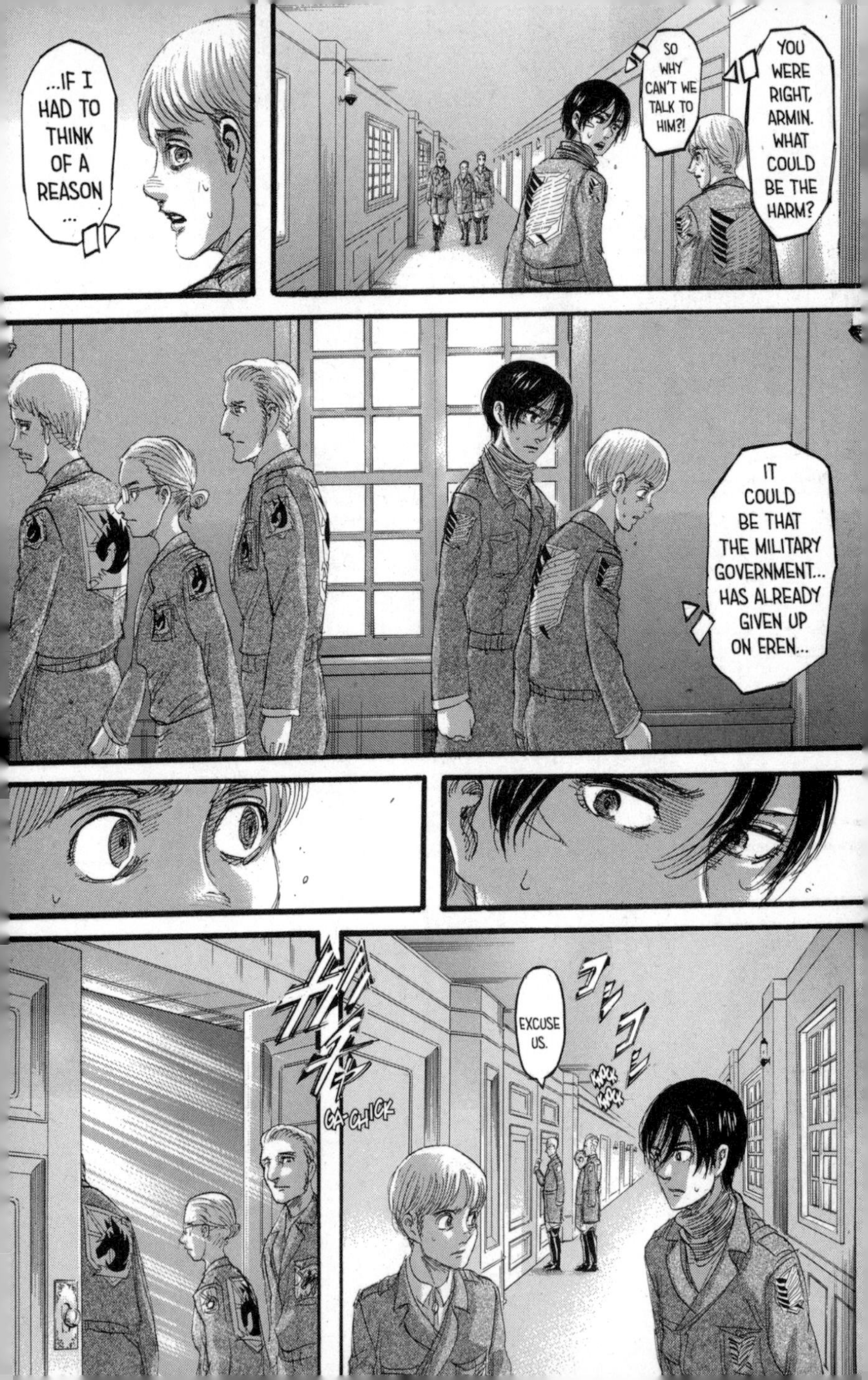
YOU WERE RIGHT, ARMIN. WHAT COULD BE THE HARM?
SO WHY CAN'T WE TALK TO HIM?!
...IF I HAD TO THINK OF A REASON ...
IT COULD BE THAT THE MILITARY GOVERNMENT... HAS ALREADY GIVEN UP ON EREN...
KNOCK KNOCK
EXCUSE US.
GA-CHICK

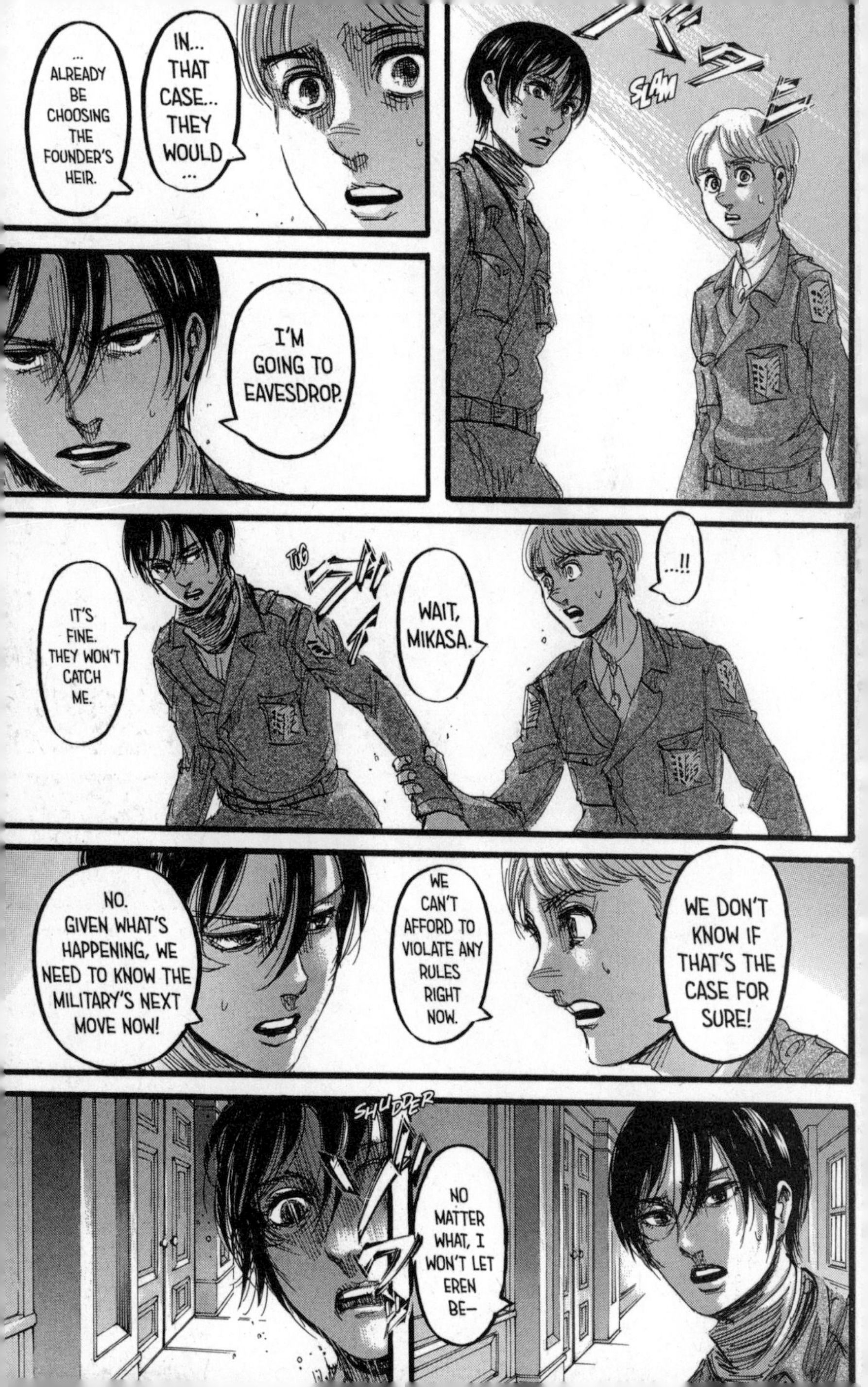
IN... THAT CASE... THEY WOULD ...
... ALREADY BE CHOOSING THE FOUNDER'S HEIR.
SLAM
I'M GOING TO EAVESDROP.
...!!
WAIT, MIKASA.
TUG
IT'S FINE. THEY WON'T CATCH ME.
WE DON'T KNOW IF THAT'S THE CASE FOR SURE!
WE CAN'T AFFORD TO VIOLATE ANY RULES RIGHT NOW.
NO. GIVEN WHAT'S HAPPENING, WE NEED TO KNOW THE MILITARY'S NEXT MOVE NOW!
SHUDDER
NO MATTER WHAT, I WON'T LET EREN BE—

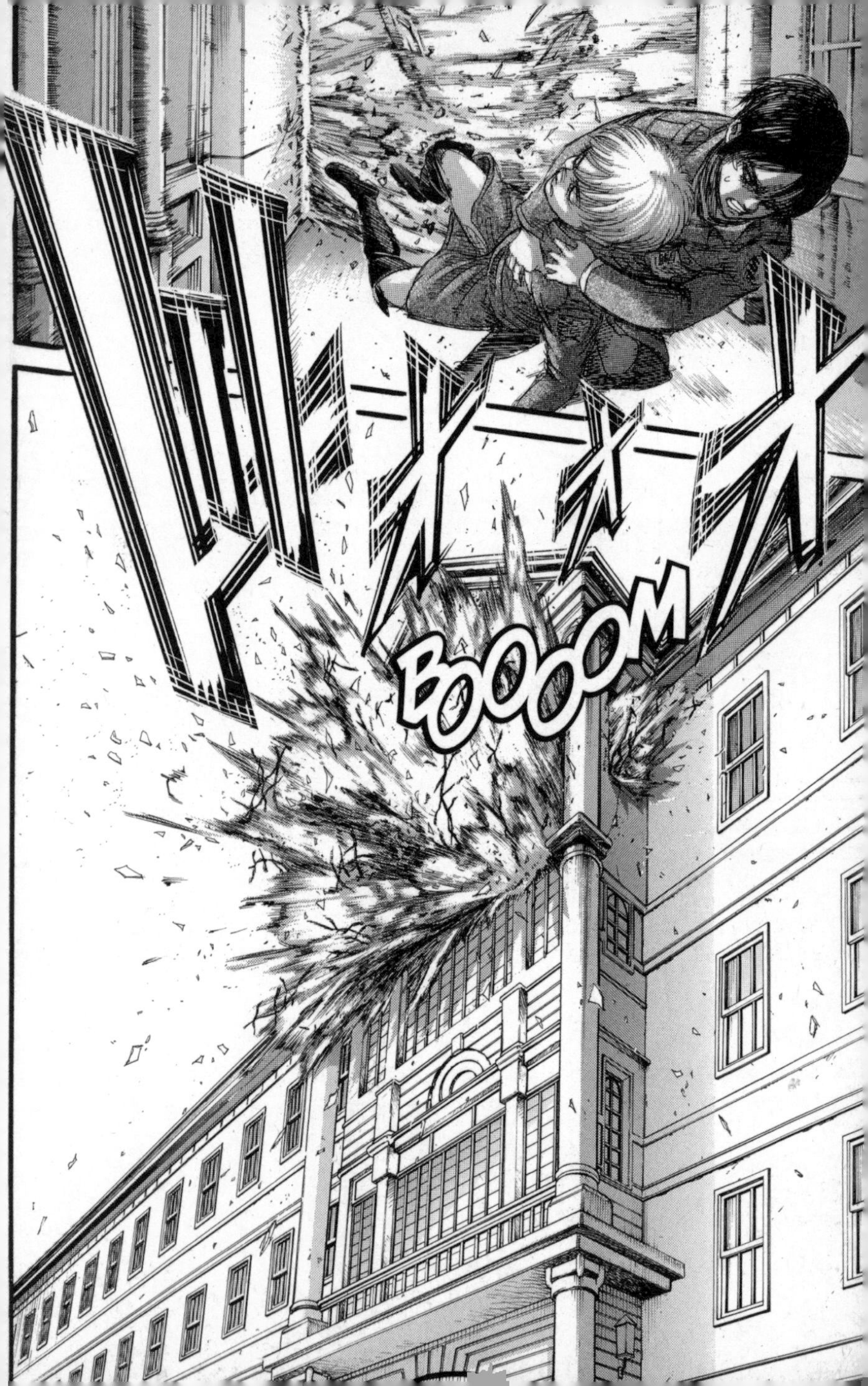
BOOOOM

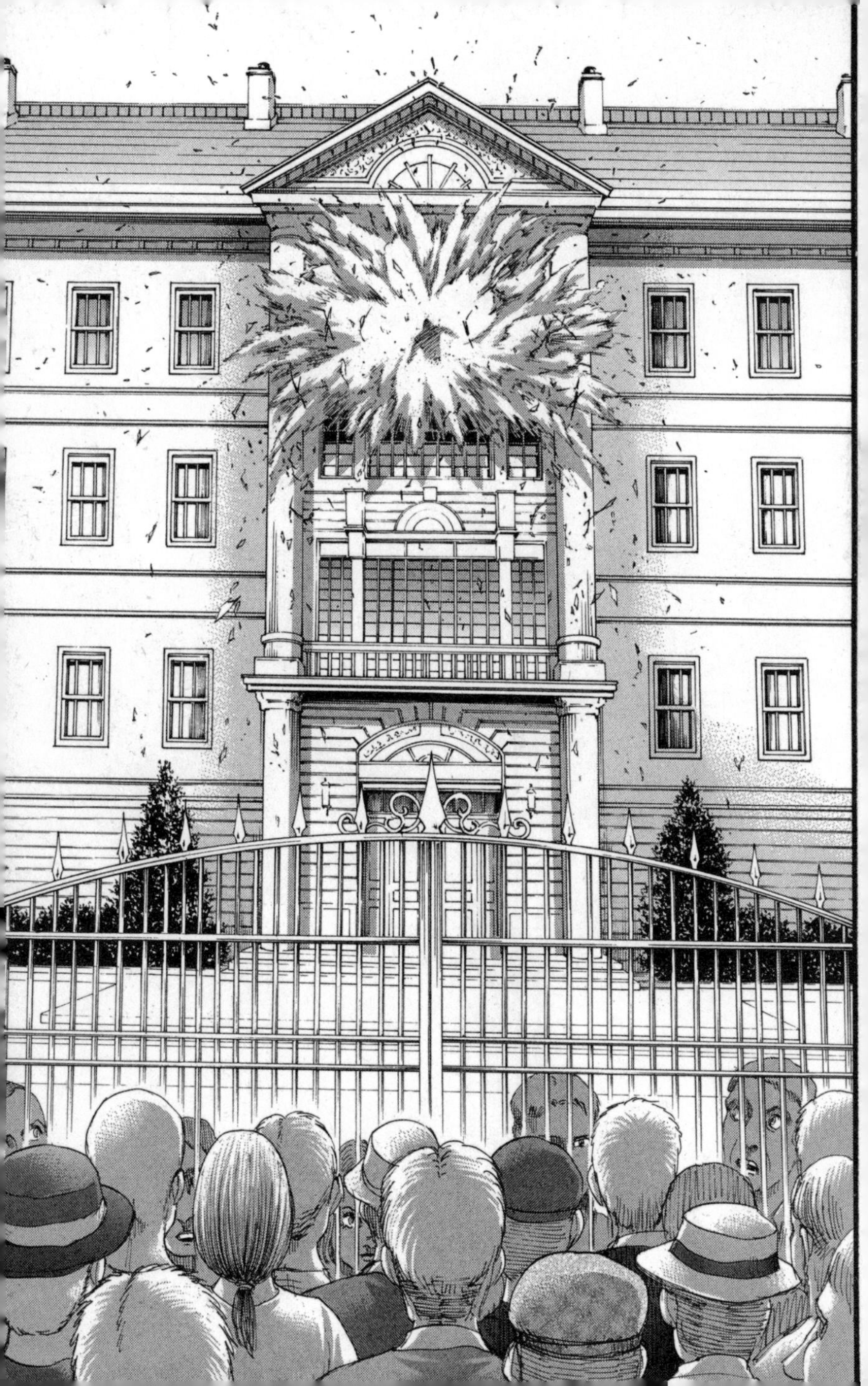

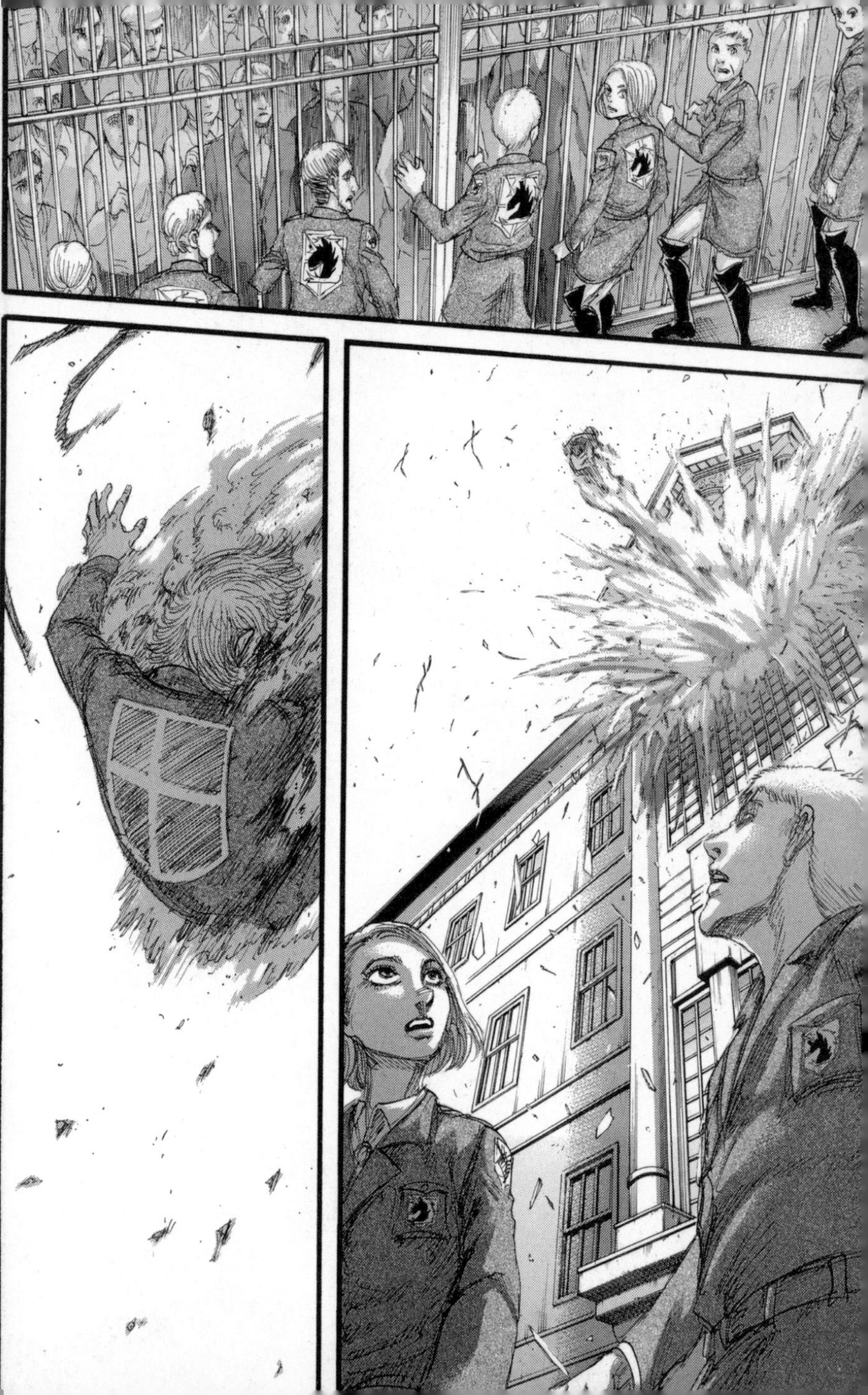

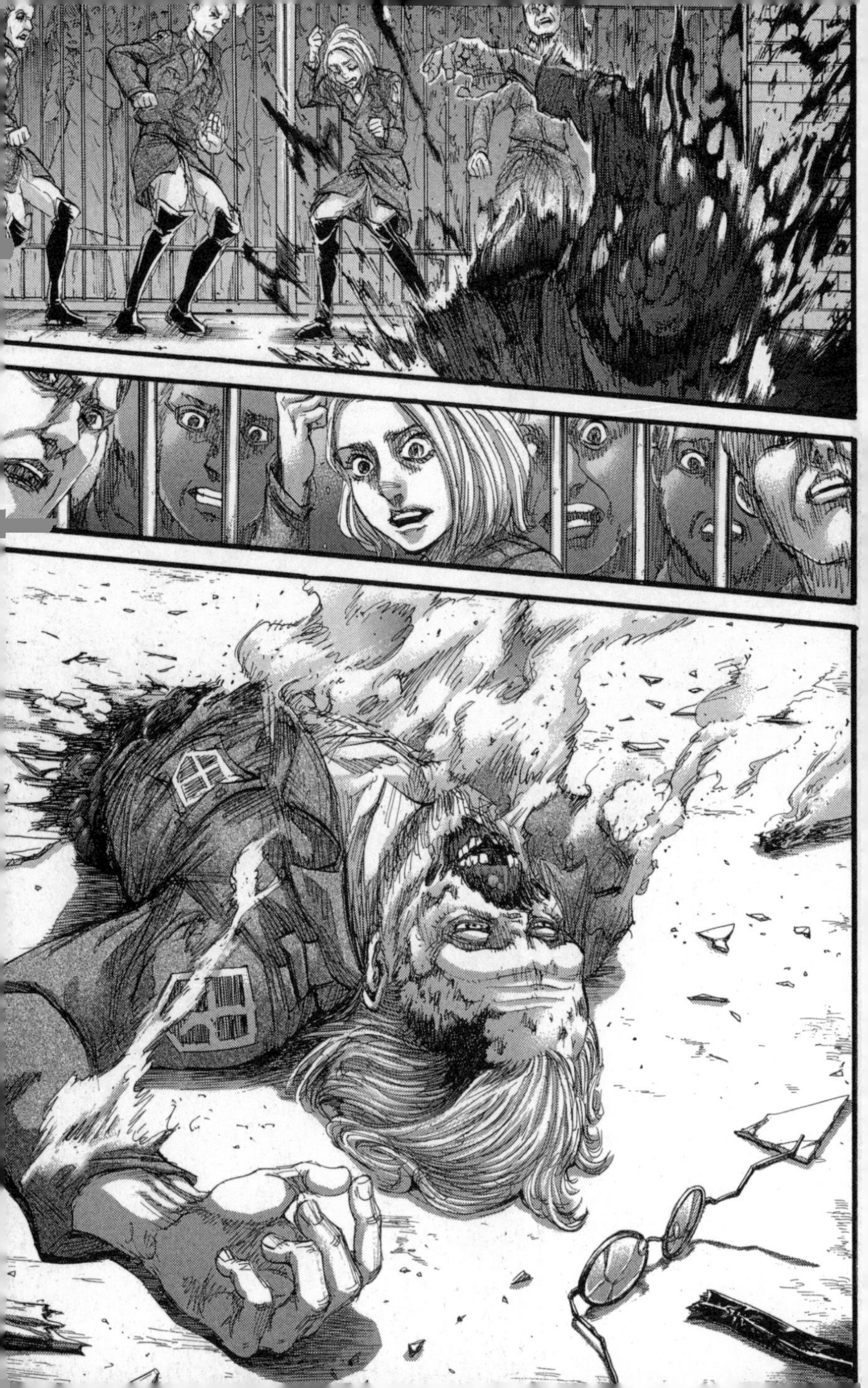

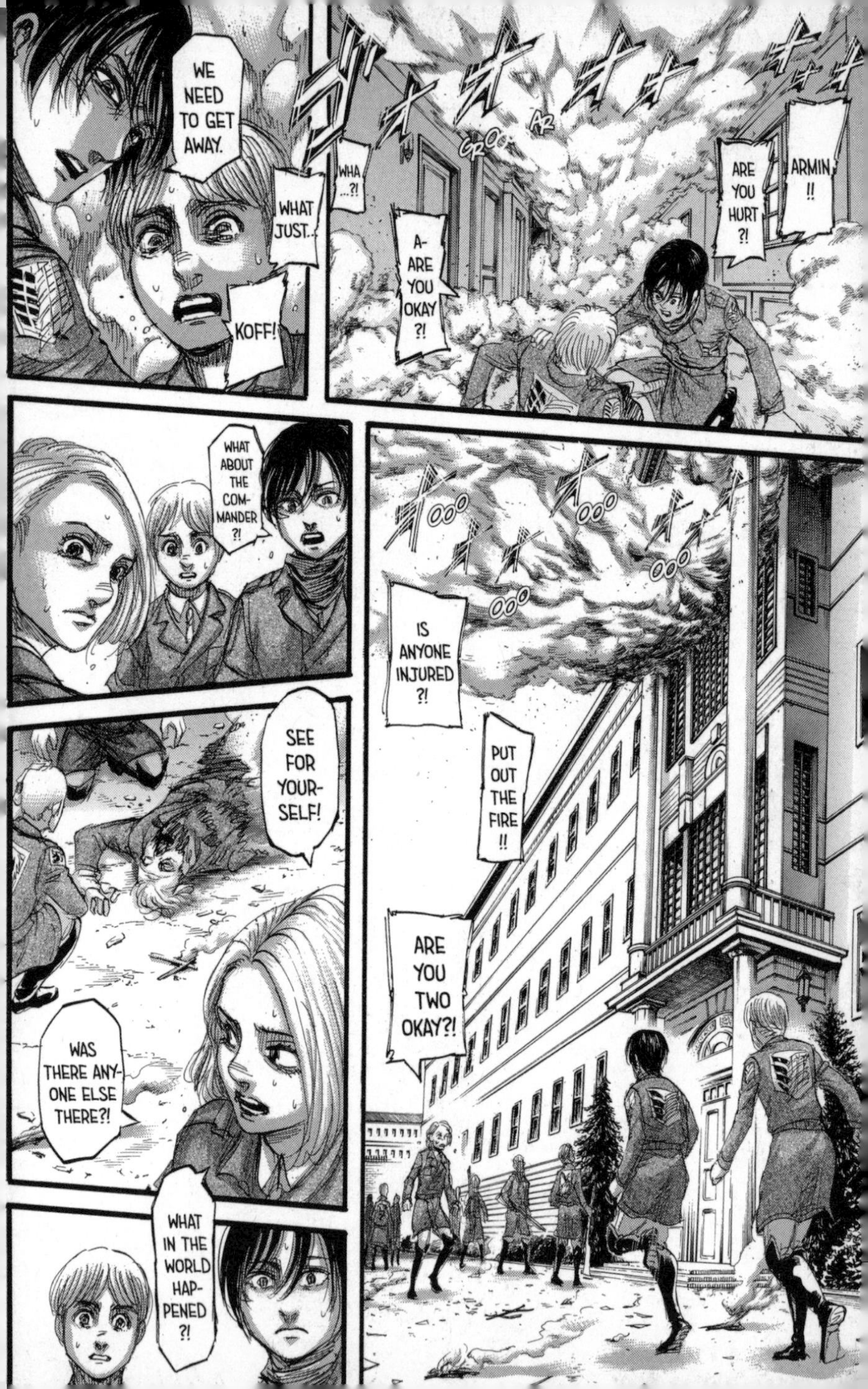

ARMIN!!
ARE YOU HURT?!
GROOOAR
A-ARE YOU OKAY?!
WHA...?!
WHAT JUST..
KOFF!
WE NEED TO GET AWAY.
IS ANYONE INJURED?!
PUT OUT THE FIRE!!
ARE YOU TWO OKAY?!
WHAT ABOUT THE COMMANDER?!
SEE FOR YOURSELF!
WAS THERE ANYONE ELSE THERE?!
WHAT IN THE WORLD HAPPENED?!

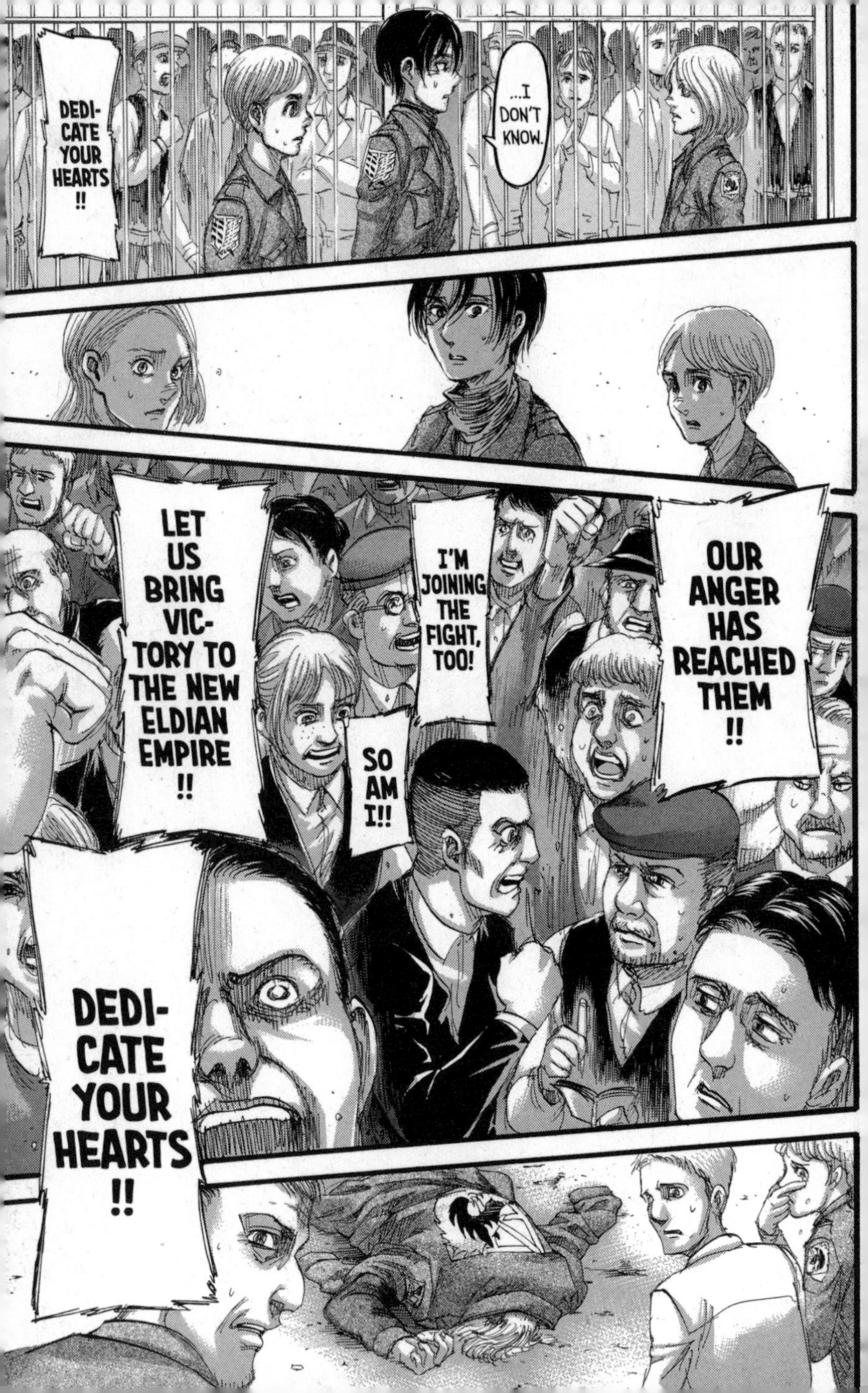

...I DON'T KNOW.
DEDI-CATE YOUR HEARTS!!
OUR ANGER HAS REACHED THEM!!
I'M JOINING THE FIGHT, TOO!
LET US BRING VIC-TORY TO THE NEW ELDIAN EMPIRE!!
SO AM I!!
DEDI-CATE YOUR HEARTS!!

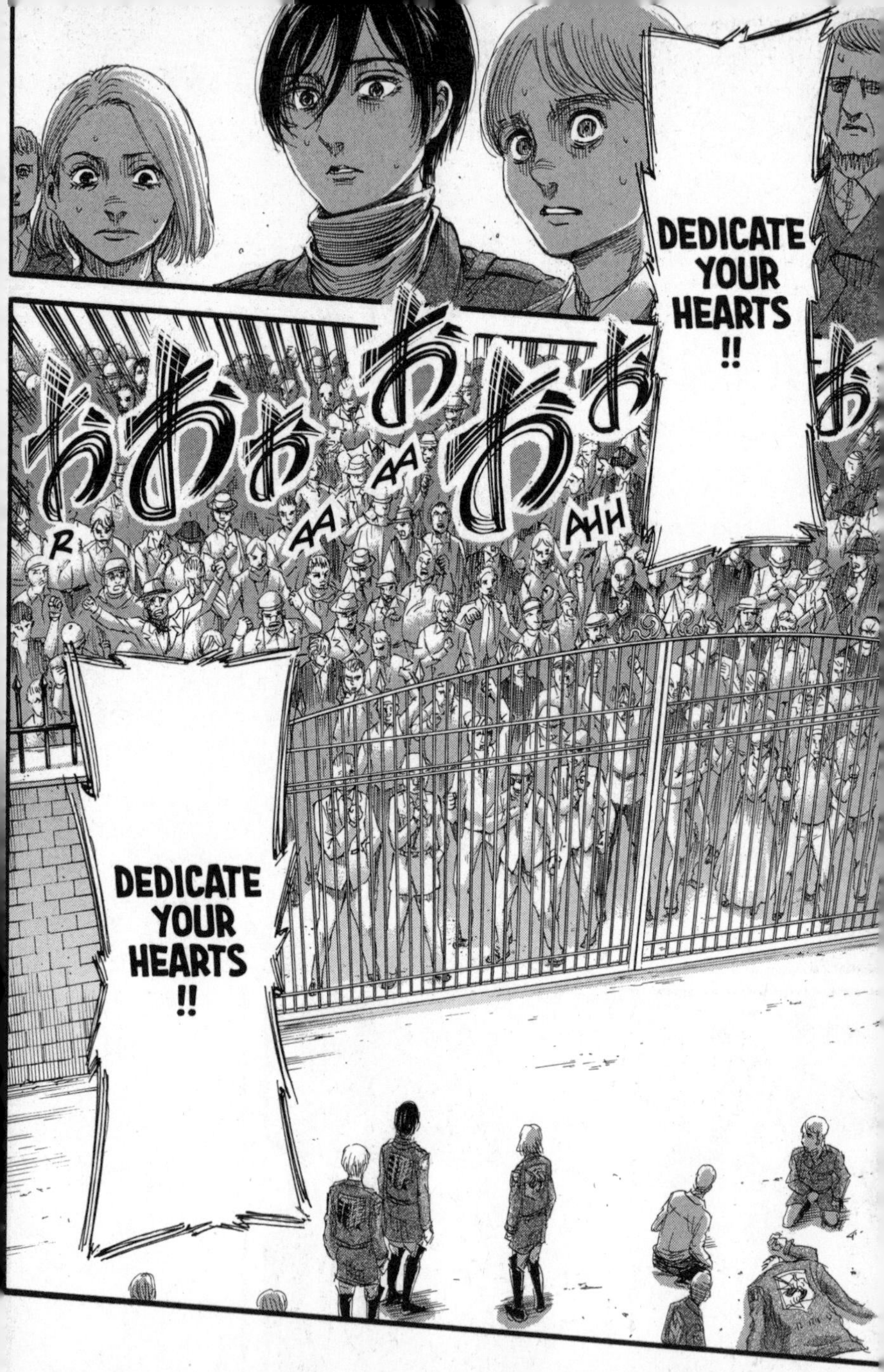
DEDICATE YOUR HEARTS !!
おおぉぉおおおぉぉぉおお
R
AA
AA
AHH
DEDICATE YOUR HEARTS !!

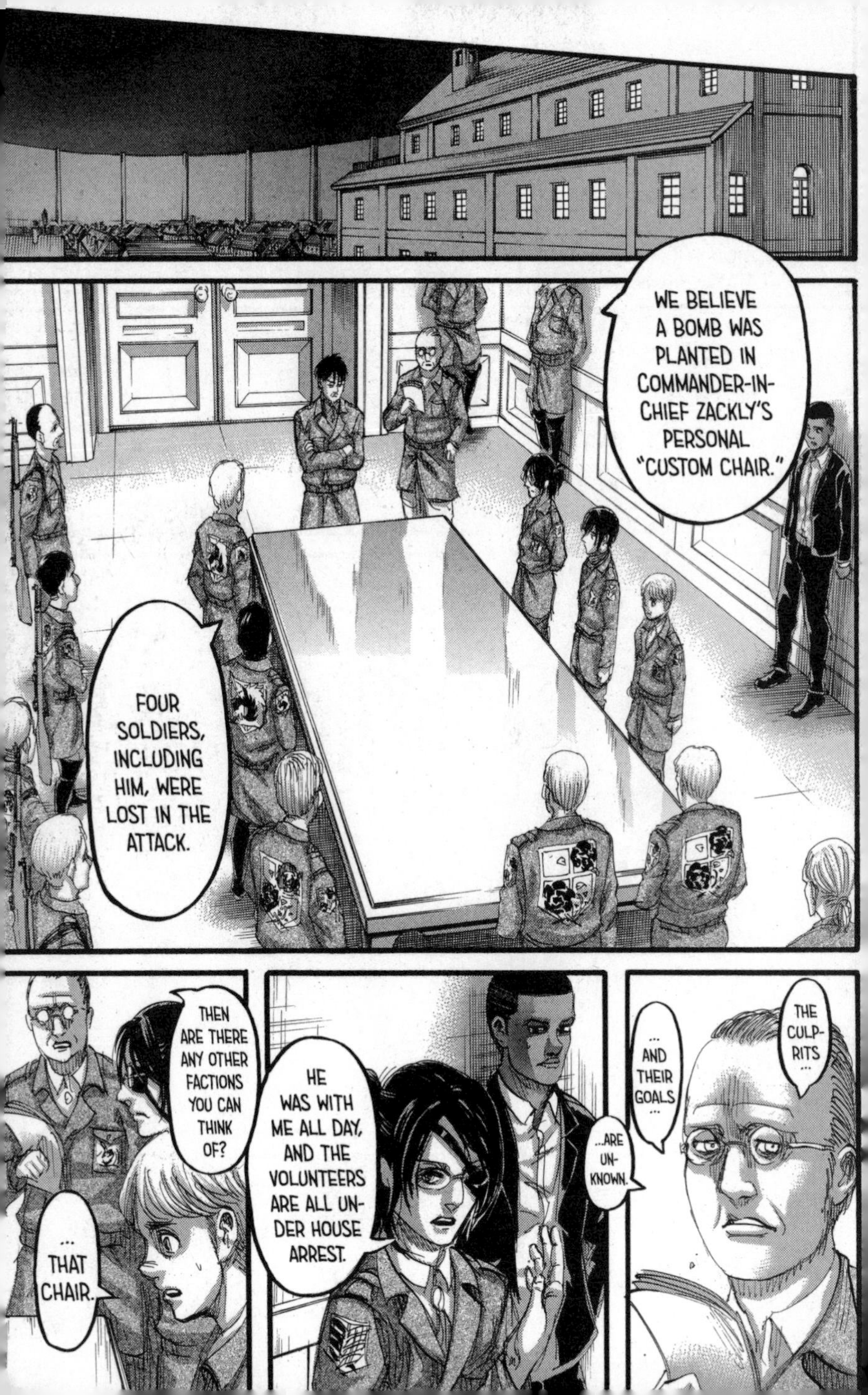
WE BELIEVE A BOMB WAS PLANTED IN COMMANDER-IN-CHIEF ZACKLY'S PERSONAL "CUSTOM CHAIR."
FOUR SOLDIERS, INCLUDING HIM, WERE LOST IN THE ATTACK.
THEN ARE THERE ANY OTHER FACTIONS YOU CAN THINK OF?
... THAT CHAIR.
HE WAS WITH ME ALL DAY, AND THE VOLUNTEERS ARE ALL UNDER HOUSE ARREST.
THE CULPRITS...
... AND THEIR GOALS...
...ARE UNKNOWN.

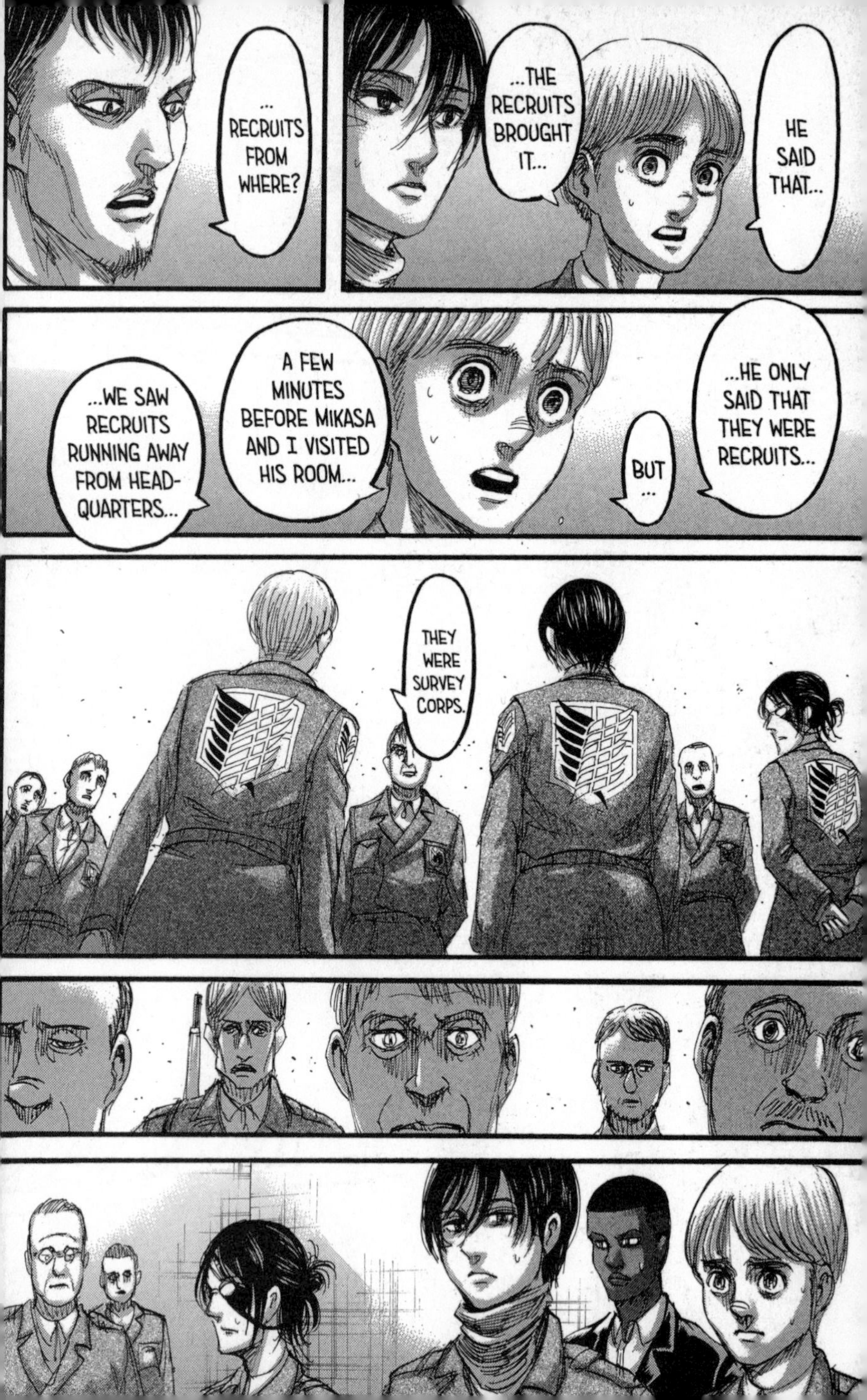
HE SAID THAT...
...THE RECRUITS BROUGHT IT...
... RECRUITS FROM WHERE?
...HE ONLY SAID THAT THEY WERE RECRUITS...
BUT ...
A FEW MINUTES BEFORE MIKASA AND I VISITED HIS ROOM...
...WE SAW RECRUITS RUNNING AWAY FROM HEAD-QUARTERS...
THEY WERE SURVEY CORPS.

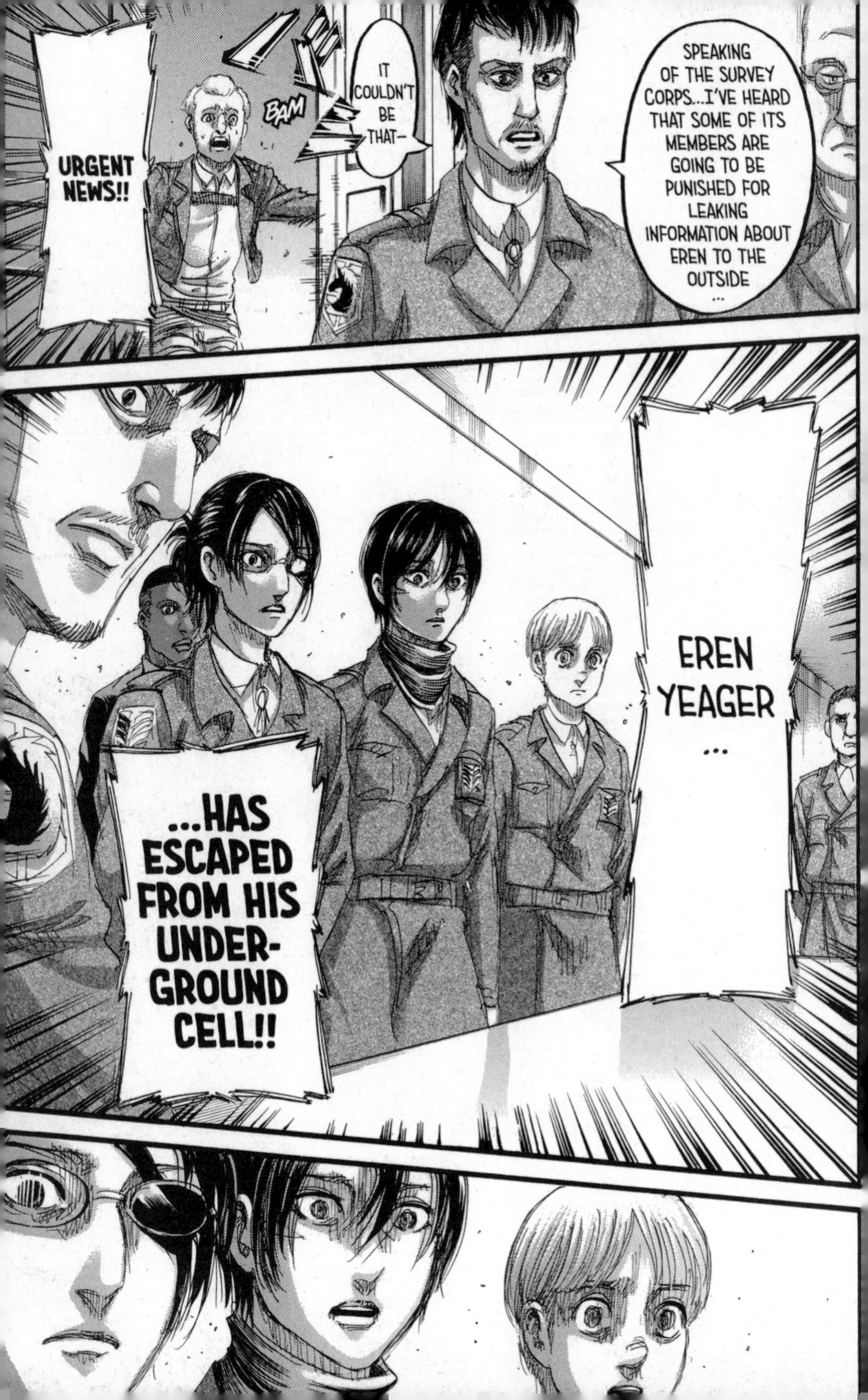
SPEAKING OF THE SURVEY CORPS...I'VE HEARD THAT SOME OF ITS MEMBERS ARE GOING TO BE PUNISHED FOR LEAKING INFORMATION ABOUT EREN TO THE OUTSIDE ...
IT COULDN'T BE THAT—
BAM
URGENT NEWS!!
EREN YEAGER ...
...HAS ESCAPED FROM HIS UNDER-GROUND CELL!!

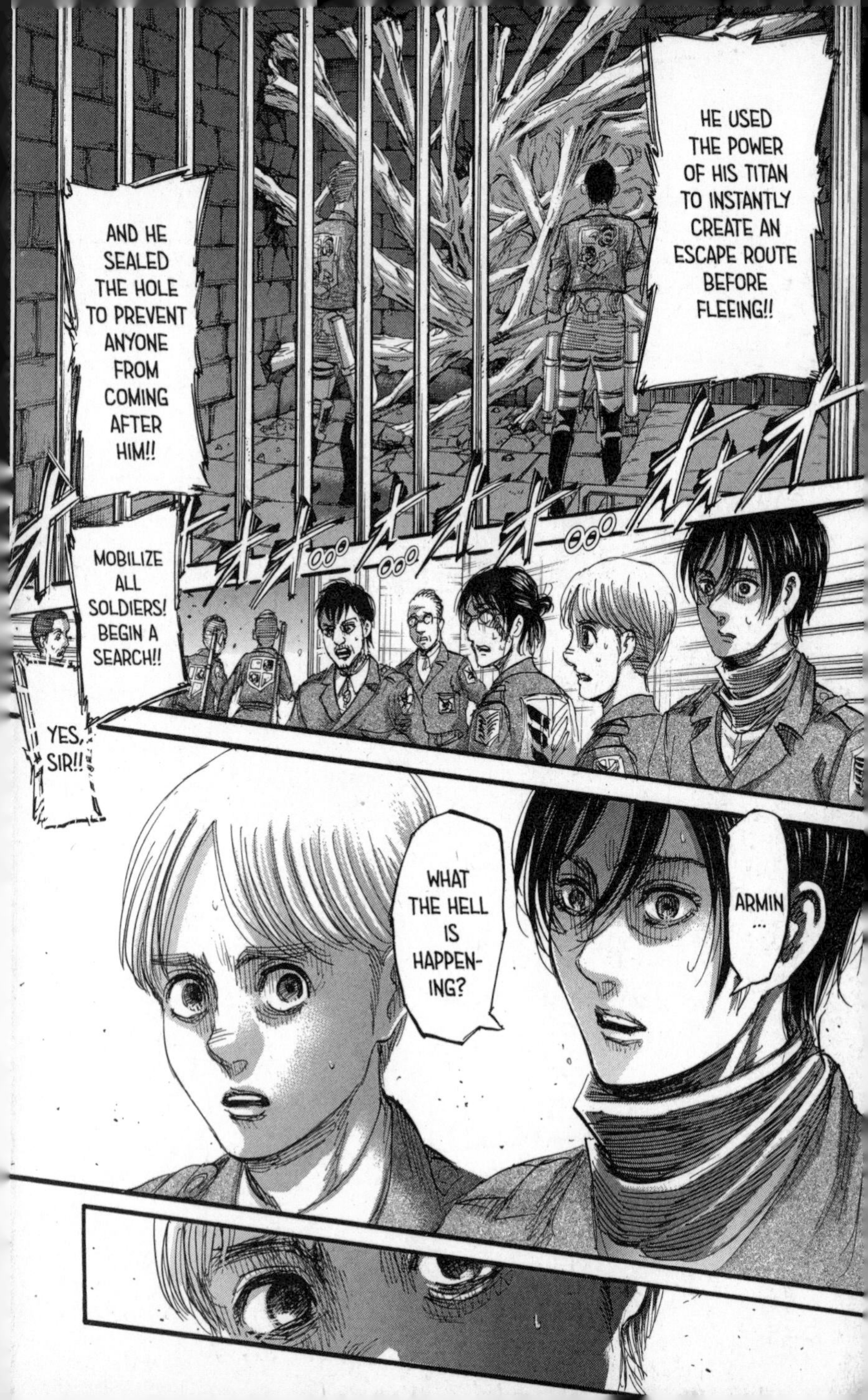
HE USED THE POWER OF HIS TITAN TO INSTANTLY CREATE AN ESCAPE ROUTE BEFORE FLEEING!!
AND HE SEALED THE HOLE TO PREVENT ANYONE FROM COMING AFTER HIM!!
MOBILIZE ALL SOLDIERS! BEGIN A SEARCH!!
YES, SIR!!
ARMIN ...
WHAT THE HELL IS HAPPEN-ING?

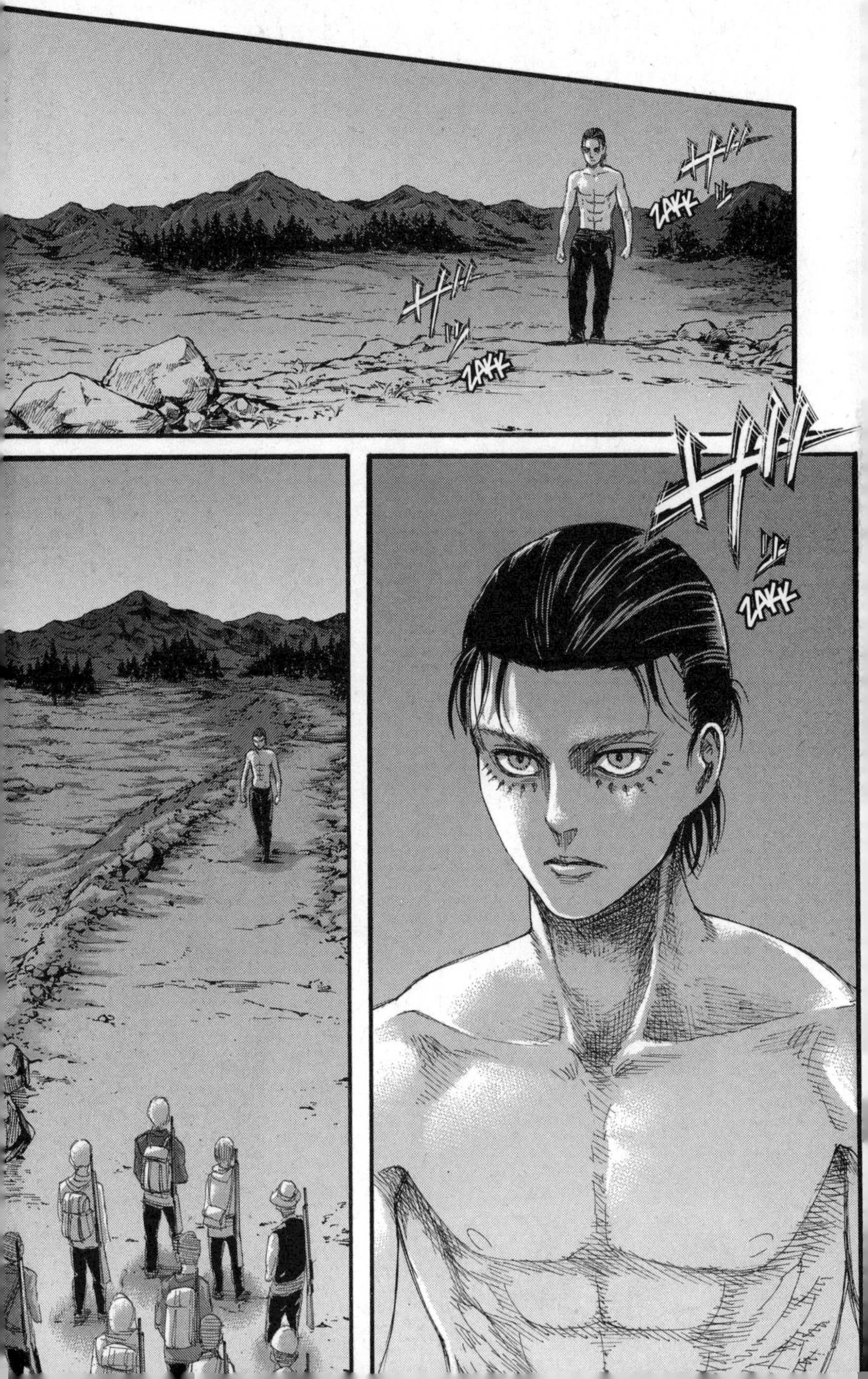
ZAKK
ZAKK
ZAKK

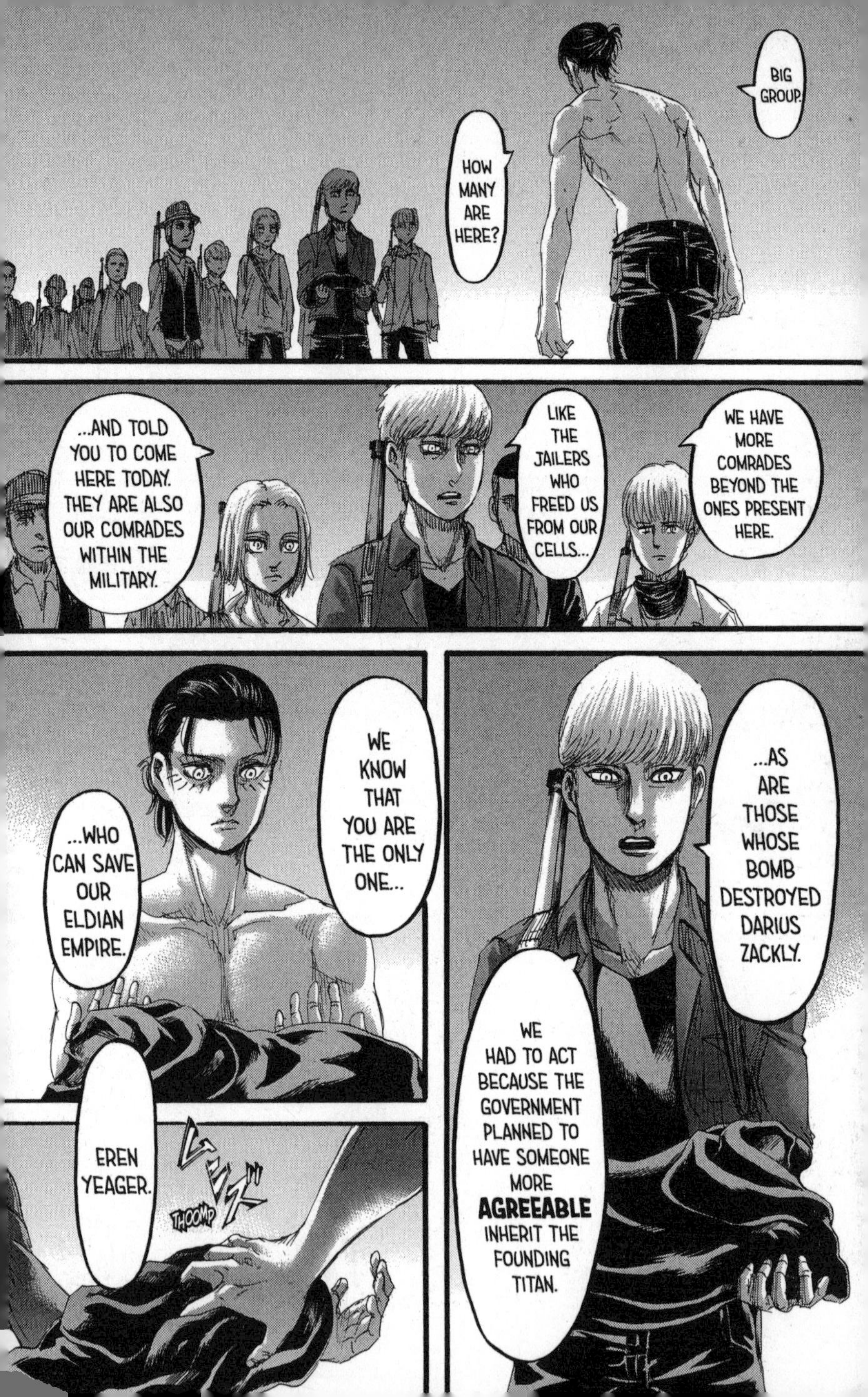
BIG GROUP.
HOW MANY ARE HERE?
WE HAVE MORE COMRADES BEYOND THE ONES PRESENT HERE.
LIKE THE JAILERS WHO FREED US FROM OUR CELLS...
...AND TOLD YOU TO COME HERE TODAY. THEY ARE ALSO OUR COMRADES WITHIN THE MILITARY.
...AS ARE THOSE WHOSE BOMB DESTROYED DARIUS ZACKLY.
WE HAD TO ACT BECAUSE THE GOVERNMENT PLANNED TO HAVE SOMEONE MORE AGREEABLE INHERIT THE FOUNDING TITAN.
WE KNOW THAT YOU ARE THE ONLY ONE...
...WHO CAN SAVE OUR ELDIAN EMPIRE.
EREN YEAGER.
THOOMP

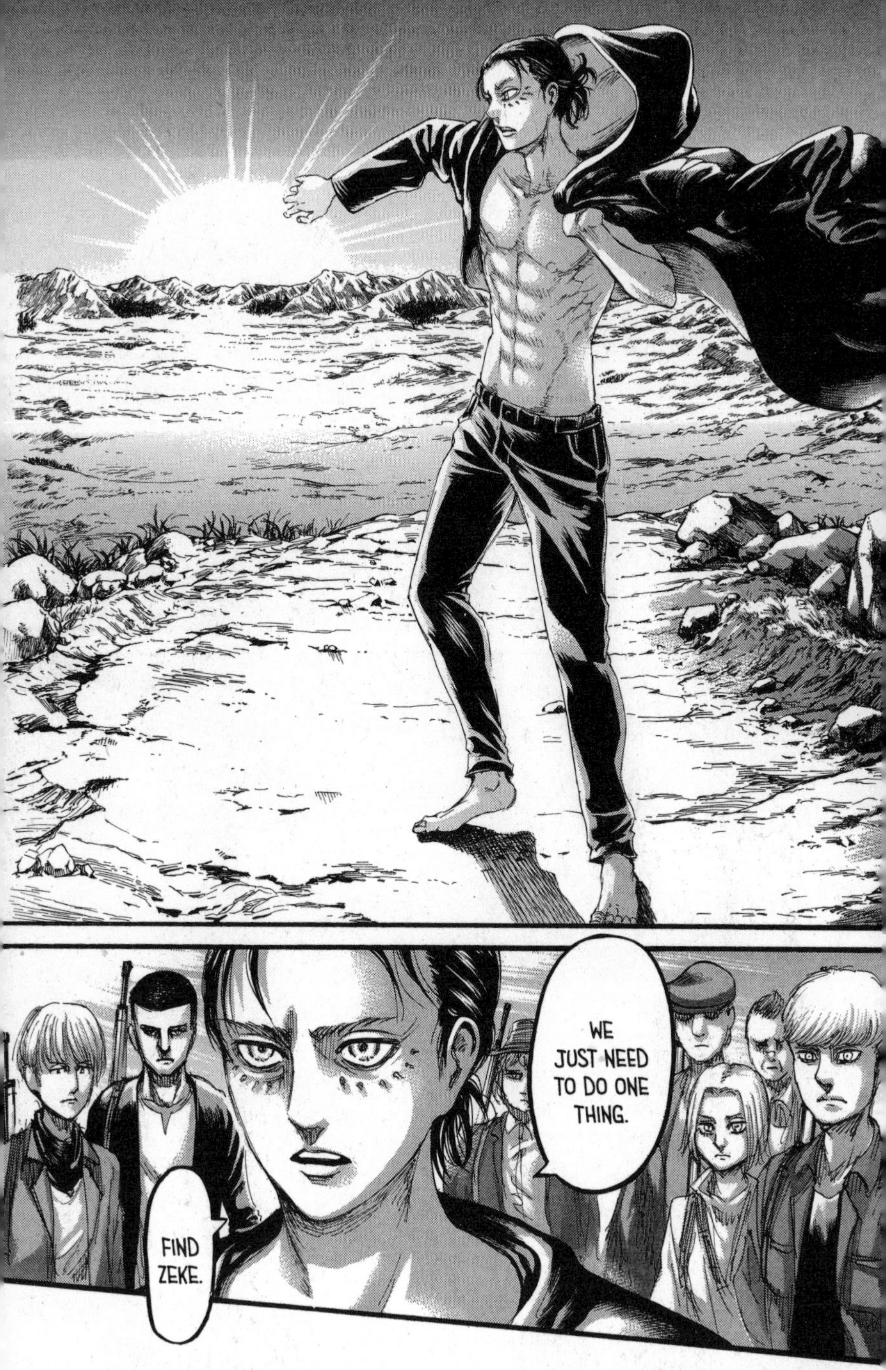
WE JUST NEED TO DO ONE THING.
FIND ZEKE.

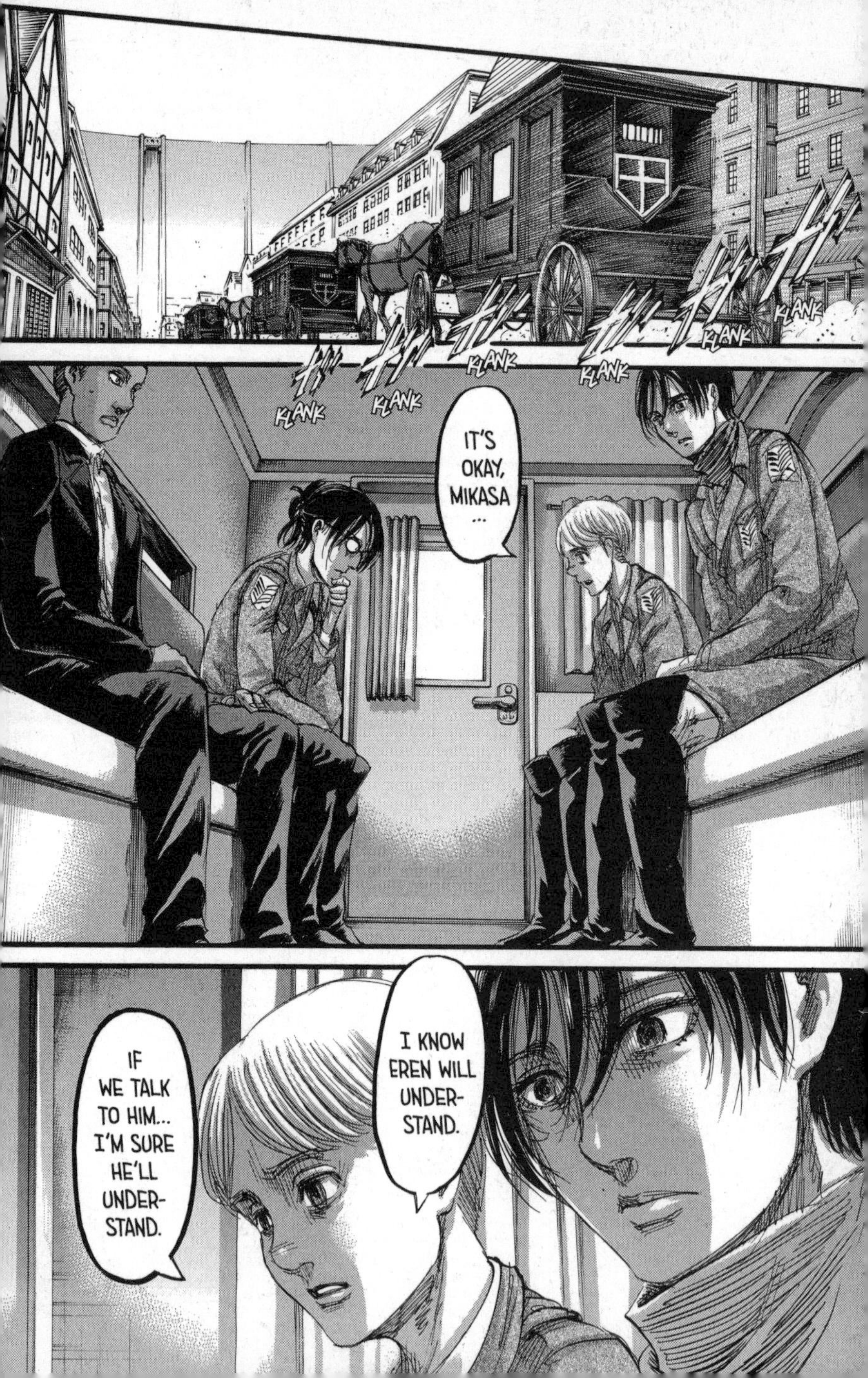
KLANK
KLANK
KLANK
KLANK
KLANK
KLANK
IT'S OKAY, MIKASA...
I KNOW EREN WILL UNDERSTAND.
IF WE TALK TO HIM... I'M SURE HE'LL UNDERSTAND.

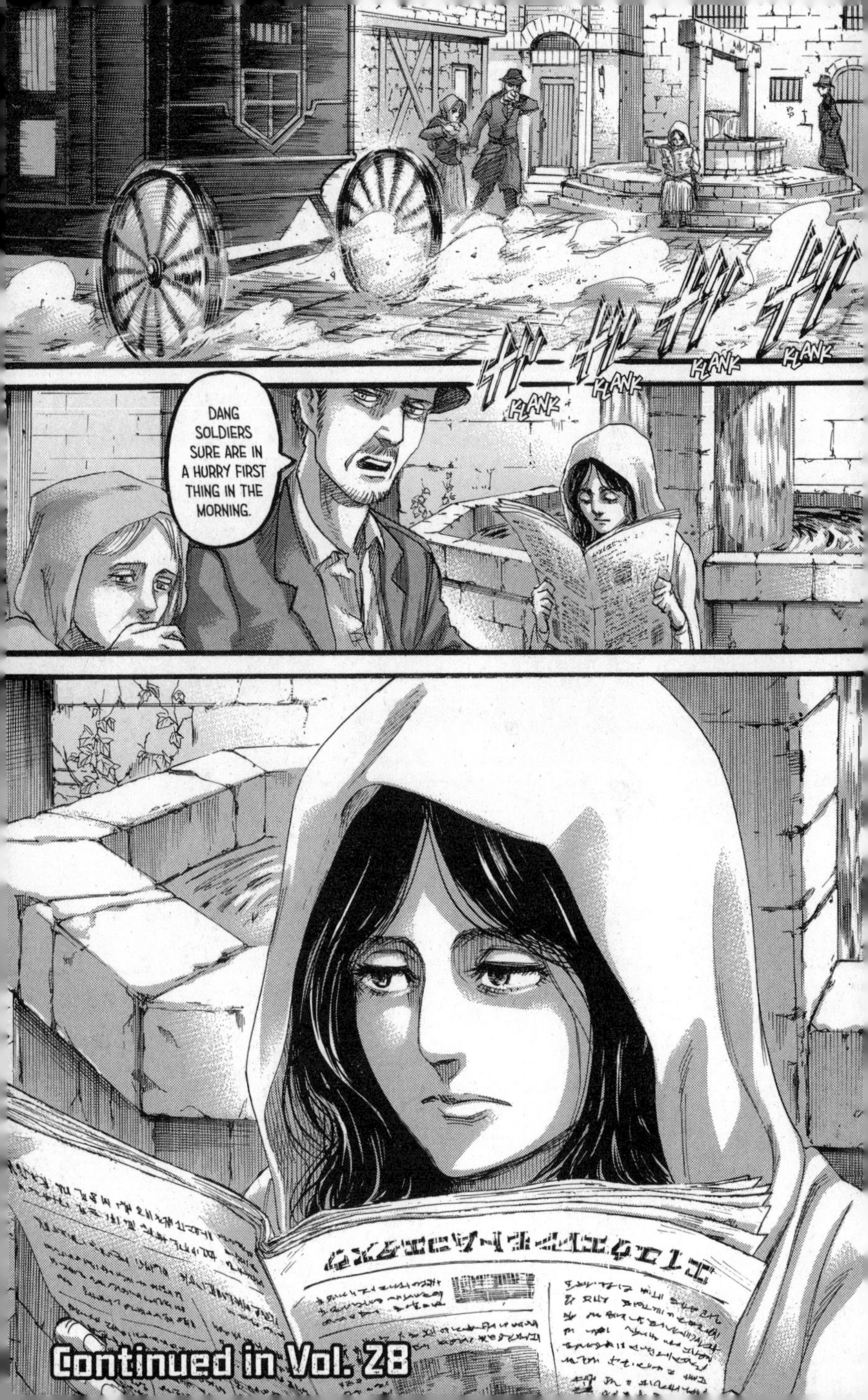
KLANK
KLANK
KLANK
KLANK
DANG SOLDIERS SURE ARE IN A HURRY FIRST THING IN THE MORNING.
Continued in Vol. 28

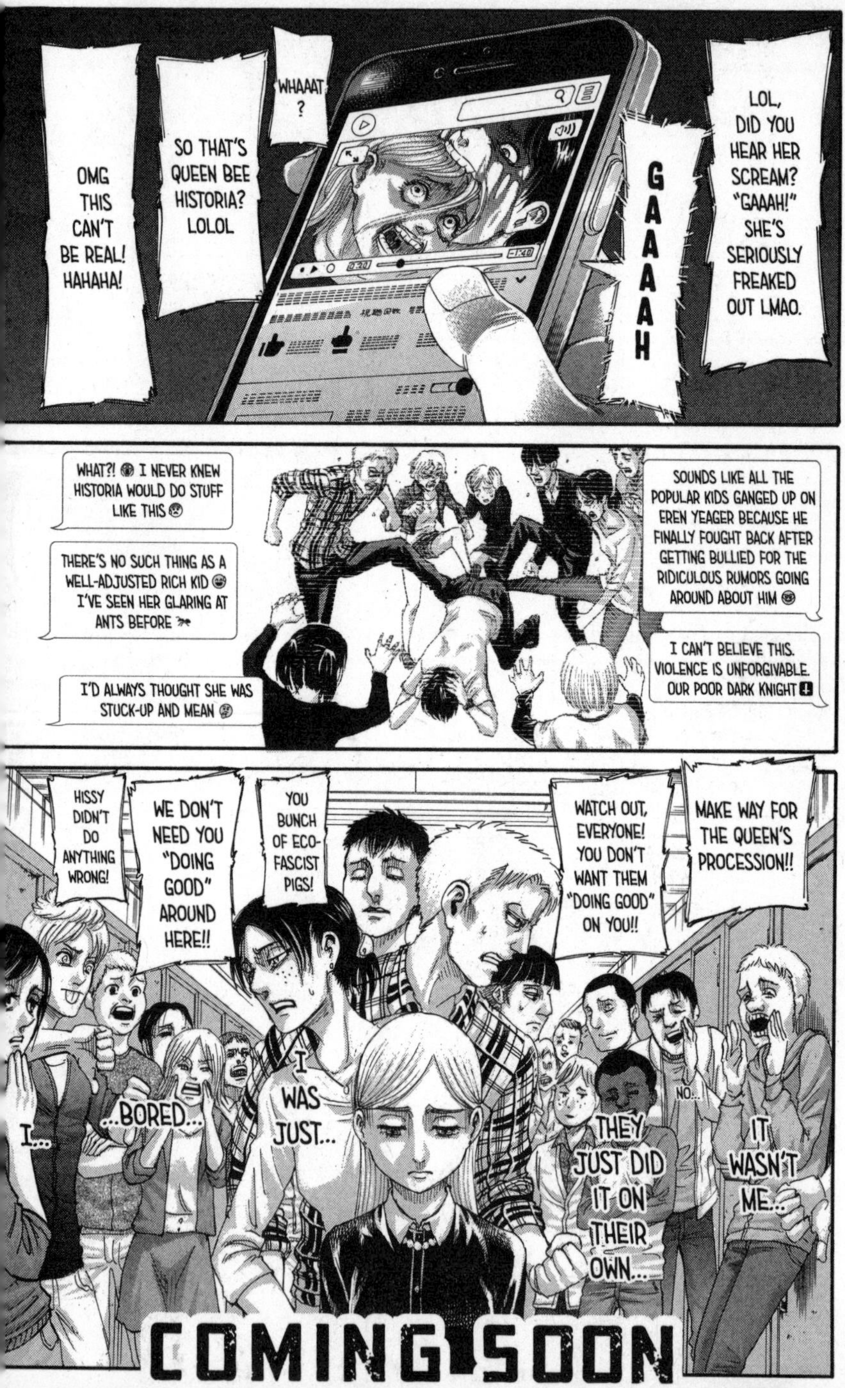
LOL, DID YOU HEAR HER SCREAM? "GAAAH!" SHE'S SERIOUSLY FREAKED OUT LMAO.
GAAAAH
WHAAAT?
SO THAT'S QUEEN BEE HISTORIA? LOLOL
OMG THIS CAN'T BE REAL! HAHAHA!
SOUNDS LIKE ALL THE POPULAR KIDS GANGED UP ON EREN YEAGER BECAUSE HE FINALLY FOUGHT BACK AFTER GETTING BULLIED FOR THE RIDICULOUS RUMORS GOING AROUND ABOUT HIM
I CAN'T BELIEVE THIS. VIOLENCE IS UNFORGIVABLE. OUR POOR DARK KNIGHT
WHAT?! I NEVER KNEW HISTORIA WOULD DO STUFF LIKE THIS
THERE'S NO SUCH THING AS A WELL-ADJUSTED RICH KID I'VE SEEN HER GLARING AT ANTS BEFORE
I'D ALWAYS THOUGHT SHE WAS STUCK-UP AND MEAN
MAKE WAY FOR THE QUEEN'S PROCESSION!!
WATCH OUT, EVERYONE! YOU DON'T WANT THEM "DOING GOOD" ON YOU!!
YOU BUNCH OF ECO-FASCIST PIGS!
WE DON'T NEED YOU "DOING GOOD" AROUND HERE!!
HISSY DIDN'T DO ANYTHING WRONG!
IT WASN'T ME...
NO...
THEY JUST DID IT ON THEIR OWN...
I WAS JUST...
...BORED...
I...
COMING SOON

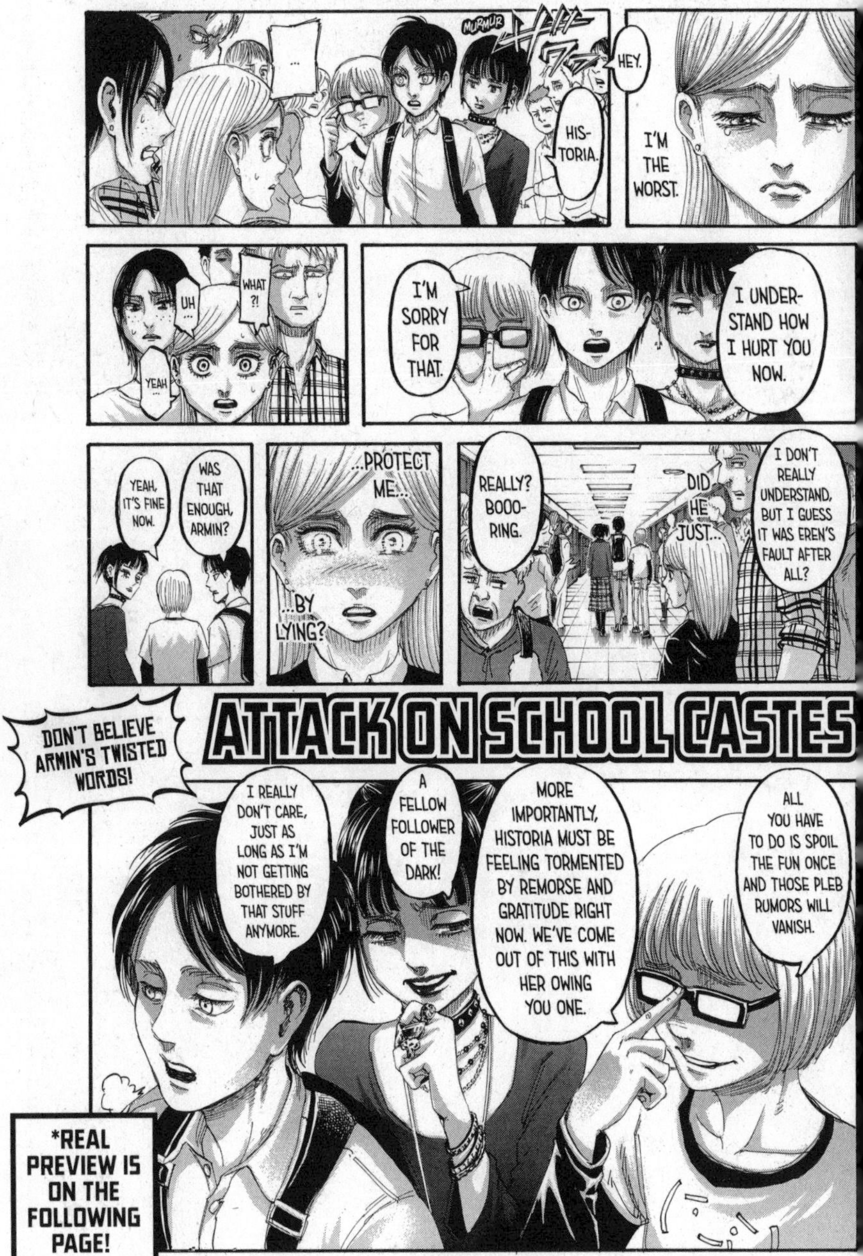
I'M THE WORST.
HEY.
HIS-TORIA.
MURMUR
...
I UNDER-STAND HOW I HURT YOU NOW.
I'M SORRY FOR THAT.
WHAT ?!
UH ...
YEAH ...
I DON'T REALLY UNDERSTAND, BUT I GUESS IT WAS EREN'S FAULT AFTER ALL?
DID HE JUST...
REALLY? BOOO-RING.
...PROTECT ME...
...BY LYING?
WAS THAT ENOUGH, ARMIN?
YEAH, IT'S FINE NOW.
ATTACK ON SCHOOL CASTES
DON'T BELIEVE ARMIN'S TWISTED WORDS!
ALL YOU HAVE TO DO IS SPOIL THE FUN ONCE AND THOSE PLEB RUMORS WILL VANISH.
MORE IMPORTANTLY, HISTORIA MUST BE FEELING TORMENTED BY REMORSE AND GRATITUDE RIGHT NOW. WE'VE COME OUT OF THIS WITH HER OWING YOU ONE.
A FELLOW FOLLOWER OF THE DARK!
I REALLY DON'T CARE, JUST AS LONG AS I'M NOT GETTING BOTHERED BY THAT STUFF ANYMORE.
*REAL PREVIEW IS ON THE FOLLOWING PAGE!

VOLUME 28

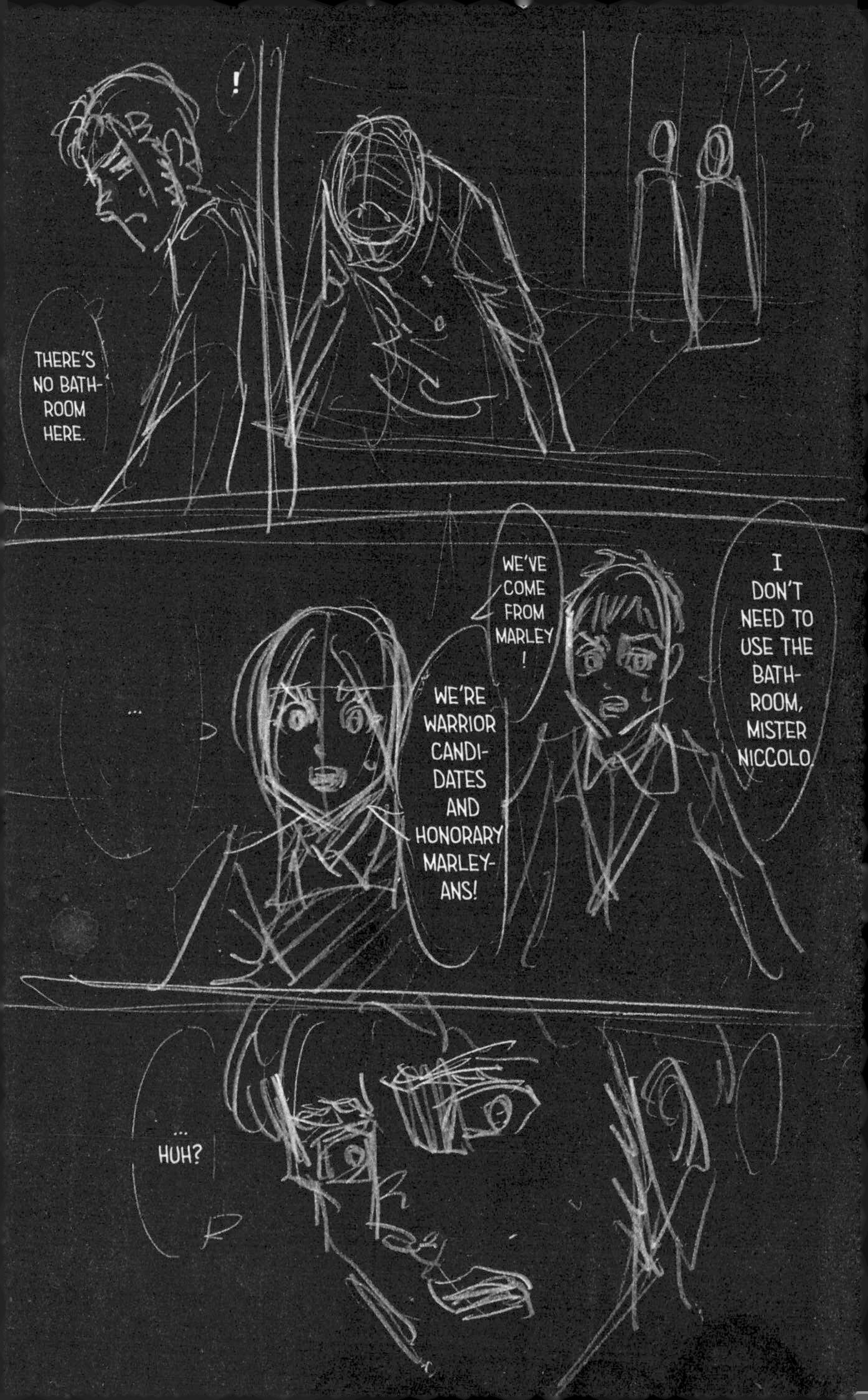
!
THERE'S NO BATH-ROOM HERE.
I DON'T NEED TO USE THE BATH-ROOM, MISTER NICCOLO.
WE'VE COME FROM MARLEY!
WE'RE WARRIOR CANDI-DATES AND HONORARY MARLEY-ANS!
...
... HUH?